Balancing the Big Stuff

Balancing the Big Stuff

Finding Happiness in Work, Family, and Life

Miriam Liss and Holly H. Schiffrin

ROWMAN & LITTLEFIELD
Lanham • Boulder • New York • Toronto • Plymouth, UK

650
.1
Li
Cop. 3

Published by Rowman & Littlefield
4501 Forbes Boulevard, Suite 200, Lanham, Maryland 20706
www.rowman.com

10 Thornbury Road, Plymouth PL6 7PP, United Kingdom

British Library Cataloguing in Publication Information Available

Library of Congress Cataloging-in-Publication Data

Liss, Miriam.
Balancing the big stuff : finding happiness in work, family, and life / Miriam Liss and Holly H.
Schiffrin.
    pages cm.
Includes bibliographical references and index.
ISBN 978-1-4422-2335-6 (cloth : alk. paper) -- ISBN 978-1-4422-2336-3 (electronic)
1. Work and family. 2. Work-life balance. 3. Quality of work life. 4. Quality of life. I. Schiffrin,
Holly H. II. Title.
HD4904.25.L57 2014
650.1--dc22
2014006805

Printed in the United States of America

Contents

Foreword

If you're alive and breathing in the early twenty-first century, you need to read this book. Authors Miriam Liss and Holly Schiffrin are not only offering an insightful and thoroughly researched portrait of the way we're living now—and why it feels so crazily out of balance—but they stretch as far back as the Greeks and as far forward as the cutting-edge science of positive psychology, human motivation, happiness and well-being, and have fashioned a comprehensive guide for how to live the Good Life.

The need for this book is clear. Survey after survey shows that many people are feeling overwhelmed by life. They work too much. They're exhausted all the time. Parents worry they don't spend enough time with their children. And no one seems to have time for fun. Americans work among the most hours of any developed country in the world. They take among the fewest vacation days, and tend to work on those days anyway. Workplace cultures are firmly entrenched in the idea that working 24/7 is the only way to get ahead. And to top it all off, the United States not only has virtually no supportive family policy, but one work-life expert has even labeled them "family hostile."

We're seeing the result: New research is finding that young, college-educated men and women don't see a way to combine work and family in a meaningful way, so they're opting not to have children. Birth rates among college-educated Americans have fallen to what some demographers describe as crisis levels, leading one to say that those who can most afford to have children have gone on "baby strike."

In the meantime, rates of depression, stress, and anxiety, even among teens and adolescents, is on the rise, the World Health Organization reports, and higher than in some countries in the midst of violent civil wars. And research is finding that this stress—which can lead to serious medical illness—acts like a virus. Studies are finding that when harried parents come home from work with elevated cortisol levels, the level of that stress hormone also spikes in their partners, spouses, and children.

And after stunning, groundbreaking moves toward gender equity in the 1970s and 1980s, we've been stuck and haven't moved much since. Even though 40 percent of married and single mothers with children under eighteen are now the sole or primary breadwinners in their families, those in relationships still do twice the housework and childcare, on average, as men. And even as standards for being a good mother ratchet up, the wage gap, glass ceiling, and maternal wall in the workplace are still firmly entrenched.

Is it any wonder, now that the American Time-Use Survey is asking people not only what they *do* with their time, but how they *feel* about it, that women report being more exhausted, sadder, and more in pain than men? And let's not forget that surveys by the Families and Work Institute and the Pew Research Center are finding that men, too, are feeling more strain from the juggle, now that many want to have meaningful work and a full, involved family life. And the two activities we tend to spend the most time doing—working and watching TV—are actually on the bottom of the scale of what makes us happy.

Clearly, the way we're living and working isn't working. For anyone.

Enter Liss and Schiffrin. Both are both professors of psychology at the University of Mary Washington in Virginia. Both are wives and mothers. And both have struggled to thread that tiny needle to secure meaningful work, full family lives, and time for themselves, which they include in their instructive and graceful book.

Some of their findings made a big media splash when they were released, simply because they were counterintuitive yet made profound common sense. We live largely in an either/or society—either you work, or you stay home with kids—that has somehow morphed from being not just child centered, but, as one UCLA researcher put it, "child dominated," where mothers who give up careers and breastfeed, not just the recommended six months to a year but three or four years, are celebrated, and guilt-soaked working mothers worry they can't keep up.

Yet Liss, Schiffrin, and colleague Kathryn Rizzo surveyed 181 women with young children and found that those who believed such self-sacrificing, intensive mothering was best, or that mothers were better, more natural parents than fathers, had higher levels of stress, decreased satisfaction with life and lower levels of social support.

"If intensive mothering is related to so many negative mental health outcomes, why do women do it?" they wrote in the *Journal of Child and Family Studies*. "They may think that it makes them better mothers, so they are willing to sacrifice their own mental health to enhance their children's cognitive, social and emotional outcomes. In reality, intensive parenting may have the opposite effect on children from what parents intend."

The key, not only for parenting but for all of work and life, Liss and Schiffrin write in this resonant book, is finding the "sweet spot." If all of work, life, money, love, happiness, and other attributes of the Good Life could be put on an inverted U scale, the sweet spot would be somewhere right in the middle. Not too much of any one thing, but just enough of everything.

As I read the book, I found myself highlighting sections and scribbling *YES*! in the margins. The authors write cogently about self-determination theory and weave the theme throughout every chapter of the book. Self-determination theory holds that we are happiest when we are "intrinsically" motivated and doing the things we most want to do, rather than being "extrinsically" motivated and doing what we think we should do or what others expect us to do.

The three factors, they write, that shape intrinsic motivation are autonomy, competence, and relatedness.

I've since spent days pondering intrinsic motivation. I had been reading the Facebook post of a friend who is a stay-at-home mother. Her daughter had just won the middle school science fair competition. And while I was, indeed, happy for her and her daughter, I had a sudden pang about my own middle school daughter who did *not* win the science fair competition. Had my decision to be a working mother disadvantaged her somehow? Was I not doing enough, paying enough attention? Was I not a good mother?

Then I took a breath. My daughter and her friend had done their science fair project completely on their own and had had a ball mucking around in streams and looking under microscopes. She learned about science, working on a big project on deadline, and about teamwork all on her own, building the skills of grit and perseverance that will serve her far better in the future than any parental hovering. My husband had taken them to the stream to muck around in, sharing in the joy and burden of parenting. I hadn't taken a ride in the intensive parenting helicopter and we were all better off for it.

Liss and Schiffrin's focus on intrinsic motivation is welcome and comes at a time when the conversation about work-life balance has exploded from obscure and tired Mommy Wars and Battle of the Sexes arguments that no one listened to, to mainstream books like *Lean In* by Facebook executive Sheryl Sandberg hitting the bestseller lists, and former State Department official Anne-Marie Slaughter writing "Why Women Still Can't Have It All"—which garnered more viewers than any story ever published by *The Atlantic* magazine.

The fresh conversation has, as the authors call for, made clear to everyone that living a Good Life is not and never has been solely a "mommy issue," but that it falls to each of us to figure out, collectively as a society and individually as we define for ourselves what intrinsically motivates us, what gives us happiness and how we define the "all" in having a Good Life.

In the end, the authors ask us to imagine a different, better world. A world where Boston would not be the only city to vow to close the pay gap between men and women. Where California, New Jersey, and Rhode Island would not be the only places where workers could take paid leave to care for their families. Where companies would recognize that those with more women on the boards perform better, and that work cultures that stress intrinsic motivation and time for life are more innovative and productive.

Where men and women share equitably in the raising of their children and the keeping of their homes. Where the values of happiness, well-being, and meaning trump money, class, and status as drivers of behavior.

If there are any recurring themes in this full and wide-ranging book, it would be this: More is not more; enough, sometimes, really is enough. And we must change the way we work and live. Our sanity, our society, and our own brief and incandescent lives depend on it.

Brigid Schulte, author of
Overwhelmed: Work, Love, and Play
When No One Has the Time

Acknowledgments

We would like to thank the following individuals. Without their contributions and support this book would not have been possible.

First, many thanks to our undergraduate research assistants who helped pull background research for the book, including Janine Crossman, Megan Champion, Lindsay Nebhut, Rachel Youmans, Joshua Garvey, Hester Godfrey, and Brittany Scites. A special thanks to Emma Leheney, who learned Chicago style and meticulously documented our references. We would like to thank our friends who gave feedback on our proposal and earlier versions of several of the chapters, including Julie Rettinger, Chris Kilmartin, Emily Epstein Loeb, Bernie Chimner, Andrea Green, Sarah Dewees, and Robyn Van Brunt. A further thanks to the many friends who answered our questions about how they balanced work and family, and those who provided stories and quotes for us to share. We would also both like to thank our editor, Suzanne Staszak-Silva, for taking a chance on first-time book writers. Finally, we would like to thank Brigid Schulte for graciously agreeing to write our foreword.

I, Holly Schiffrin, personally wish to thank my friend and coauthor, Miriam Liss, for encouraging me to write this book. I know that it's not something I would have ever done without her boundless energy and enthusiasm to get us started and keep me going. I would also like to thank my husband, Jon, and our daughters, Lauryn and Jordan, for their love and support while I worked on this book. At times, I didn't achieve perfect work-family balance, so I appreciate them putting up with me throughout.

I, Miriam Liss, would like to thank Holly for taking on this challenge with me and being a great partner. A particular thanks to my sister-in-law Deirdre Kilmartin for reading several chapters, pointing out important articles that I should review, and generally giving me support and encouragement. I would also like to thank my husband, Julian, for his love, support, encouragement, home-cooked meals, vacuumed carpets, and loads of laundry. Finally, I would like to thank my two beautiful children, Daniel and Emily, for their love, hugs, and kisses.

Chapter One

The Search for Balance

The American Dream is to "have it all." People think that if they work hard they can have the high-powered job that comes with status and a lot of money to buy a big house, a nice car, and a vacation home in the Turks and Caicos. At the same time, people want a loving marriage and two adorable children who are happy, healthy, and bright. But is that even possible? If it is possible, is that enough? It's possible to have a wildly successful career that earns fame and fortune but still be miserable. Even if you don't have to work so hard that you sacrifice other important aspects of your life, you may have had to give up your childhood dream (e.g., being a social worker who helps orphans find permanent homes) to gain status and income. Is the money and prestige fulfilling? Does it make you happy?

We all want to have fulfilling lives that bring true joy and satisfaction. But it is not entirely clear how to do that. Women in particular are given all sorts of messages about what they are supposed to do. As women, we are told, "Lean in."[1] If you do not strive for success and high levels of achievement in the workplace, you are not living up to your full potential. Be a perfect mother. Children need their mothers. Children need constant intellectual stimulation and attention or else they may fall behind. Be a perfect wife. Prepare a homemade, well-balanced meal every night and meet your husband at the door with his pipe and slippers. Be a domestic goddess. Have homes that could be on the cover of a *Martha Stewart Living* magazine. Put awesome party ideas and cupcake recipes on Pinterest and bask in the admiration of others. Be beautiful and thin. Never leave the house without lipstick and make sure to fit in a run and Pilates class as well. Men are not spared these pressuring messages. Be a real man. Don't show your feelings. Don't be "whipped"—you actually do the vacuuming? Support your family. Be a success. Make a lot of money. We don't know about you, but all of this pressure

1

wears us out. In response, we feel overwhelmed,[2] "maxed out."[3] We get depressed and anxious. We do not feel fulfilled.

But is being highly successful in all domains the path to happiness? Should we constantly be striving to have more and do more? Doesn't it frankly seem exhausting? The conversation on these topics often lacks a sense of balance. People generally assume that if something is good, more and more is better and better. Yes, it is good to give children love, care, attention, and intellectual stimulation. But does giving more and more of these necessarily lead to better and better outcomes? Yes, it is good to be meaningfully involved in work that is stimulating and exciting. But does working more and more translate to being more and more fulfilled? Yes, it is important to have some level of financial security. But does more and more money make people happier and happier?

TOO MUCH OF A GOOD THING

The fact is that for almost all things in life, there can be too much of a good thing. Even the best things in life aren't so great in excess. This concept has been discussed at least as far back as Aristotle. He argued that being virtuous means finding a balance. For example, people should be brave, but if someone is too brave they become reckless. People should be trusting, but if someone is too trusting they are considered gullible. For each of these traits, it is best to avoid both deficiency and excess. The best way is to live in moderation—at the "sweet spot" that maximizes well-being.

Aristotle's suggestion that virtue is the midpoint between of two extremes can be portrayed graphically as an inverted U-shaped curve (see Figure 1). The sweet spot is the middle (the hump on the top), where someone is neither too surly nor too obsequious, neither too generous nor too stingy, neither too afraid nor recklessly brave. Recently, Barry Schwartz from Swarthmore College and his colleagues applied the inverted U-shaped curve to psychological characteristics that are generally thought of as beneficial such as wisdom, happiness, and even love.[4] They proposed that there is no such thing as an unmitigated good—any good thing can have negative consequences when taken to an extreme.

Understanding the inverted U may be the key to achieving work-family balance. Work is good, but overinvolvement in work can have negative effects. Family is good, but overinvolvement in family life can have negative effects. When someone says that it is impossible to have it all, what they generally mean is that it is impossible to be at the extreme end of involvement in both work and family life. We think Anne-Marie Slaughter used that logic when she complained, in her controversial article in *The Atlantic*, that she could not have it all because she could not have both an extremely high-

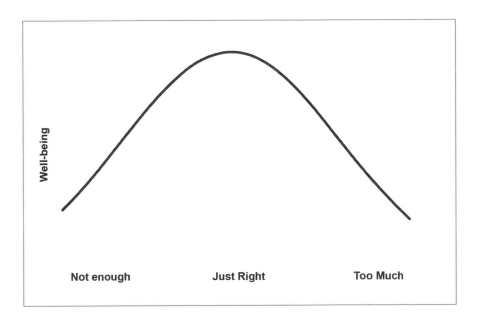

Figure 1.1.   Inverted U-shaped Curve

powered job at the State Department and be completely available for her children.[5] For her, *not* "having it all" involved going back to her job as a professor at Princeton and spending more time with her children. This arrangement actually sounds pretty good to us. One of our friends noted: "I wish I could *not* have it all like Slaughter." Understanding the inverted U-shaped relationship can help people realize that the goal is not to maximize involvement in both work and family life. The goal is to find the "sweet spot" for each, the top of the hump of the U-shaped curve where involvement maximizes well-being.

DO WHAT'S INTRINSICALLY MOTIVATING

Finding balance also does not necessarily mean that people have their work and family weighted exactly 50/50, balancing precariously on some imaginary scale. Some people may spend more time on one role versus the other. It is not a one-size-fits-all model! People need to take a careful look at whether the activities that they are involved in are truly satisfying and meaningful to them in order to find their own sweet spot. Self-determination theory holds that well-being is maximized when people are motivated intrinsically[6]—in other words when they do things because they actually want to rather than because they feel that they have to or because someone is making them.

There are three factors that determine whether people feel intrinsically motivated when doing an activity: feeling a sense of autonomy, competence, and relatedness. Autonomy is the freedom and ability to organize your own experience such that you feel comfortable. When other people are dictating when and where you have to do things, you do not have a sense of autonomy. Competence is the sense that you are good at what you are doing, that you can accomplish your goals and make meaningful contributions. Relatedness involves having meaningful relationships with other people, and includes the fundamental need to love and to be loved by others. When people's need for autonomy, competence, and relatedness are met, they experience enhanced well-being, motivation, and functioning. When they are not met, people feel unsatisfied. The thwarting of needs can be related to a host of negative psychological effects including depression, ill health, and dissatisfaction with life.[7]

You can visualize the relationship between intrinsic motivation and basic-needs satisfaction if you imagine someone at the piano playing for the sheer enjoyment of the music. The piano player would not enjoy playing if she felt coerced, nor would she enjoy it if she did not feel competent to play the music. Playing the piano may also foster relationships with others such as the piano teacher or other musicians. People who have their basic needs met are happier and have a greater sense of vitality. They even get sick less frequently.[8] When basic needs are met, people feel as though they are having a good day.[9]

Both work and family give people opportunities to meet, but also to thwart, these basic needs. Family involvement often fulfills the need for relatedness and may fulfill the need for competence if people feel confident in their abilities to parent. However, family involvement often involves meeting other people's needs and much of parenting happens on other people's schedules, interfering with personal autonomy. Furthermore, while aspects of parenting are challenging, some are mundane and boring, thwarting people's needs for competence. Conversely, doing well at a job can enhance people's feelings of competence, and being allowed to decide when and how to get work done enhances feelings of autonomy. Relationships people make at work can be valuable and rewarding. However, if people are working a job that they do not care about, do not have any control over their schedule, and have coworkers that they do not get along with, it can negatively impact autonomy, competence, and relatedness. In order to maximize the ability to meet these basic needs, people need to find balance among the various roles they hold. When people overinvest in either work or family, they lose opportunities to have their needs met in the other domain. Furthermore, overinvesting in either work or family may be a sign that people are working for some sort of extrinsic motivation (e.g., money, status, or approval of others).

FINDING BALANCE ISN'T JUST A WOMEN'S ISSUE

Autonomy, competence, and relatedness. Meaningful involvement in both work and family. A deeply satisfying life. These are things that *all* people want and need. Yet, work-family balance is generally only framed as a problem for women. How many times have you heard women say they wished their husbands "helped out" more with the housework and parenting? Similarly, it's not uncommon to hear someone say that fathers are "babysitting" their children when, in fact, fathers actually parent them. This terminology frames the responsibility of housework and childcare as the wife's, and any contribution the husband makes as a voluntary and altruistic act. Why isn't it framed as both partners working together to take care of the house that they both live in and the children that they are raising together?

As a result, when a couple has a child, it is usually the woman who seems to struggle with whether or not to continue working at the same level as before in order to manage all the additional household responsibilities. Why shouldn't men equally consider whether they should start working part-time or cut back on their hours after they have children? Why shouldn't men advocate for flex-time or the ability to telecommute so that they can spend more time with their families? When women choose to abbreviate their maternity leave, as did Marissa Mayer, the CEO of Yahoo, the media and blogosphere exploded. Is she a bad mother or a good businesswoman or both? But when men go to work the day after they have a new baby nobody questions their family loyalty. In fact, men are expected to prioritize their work over their family. They are told to be "ideal workers" with no commitments outside of the workplace.

These pressures stifle and limit men's lives as well. Men feel the pressure of providing for their families, they feel the stresses of the inflexible workplace, and they feel guilty when they cannot spend enough time with their families. A Pew Research report released in March 2013 found that 50% of working fathers (and 56% of working mothers) find it difficult to balance work and family life.[10] According to a *New York Times*/CBS poll, both men and women are working more than they would like. While 52% of men say they would prefer to work full-time, 84% are actually doing so. This survey found that 30% of men said they would prefer to work part-time, but according to the Bureau for Labor Statistics, only 5% of men work part-time.[11]

The June/July 2013 issue of *Esquire* magazine featured an article asking why men can't have it all.[12] Richard Dorment, the author, noted that men are struggling just as much as women with demanding jobs and the desire to be there for their children. He described men that are haunted by the lyrics of "The Cat's in the Cradle"[13] wanting to be fully involved in their children's lives while simultaneously attempting to maintain their position as the ideal worker. Dorment stated, "In the interviews I conducted for this article, nearly every subject admitted to missing his kids on late nights at the office or aching for home while on a business trip, yet they couch any guilt or regret in the context of sacrifice." Men, like women, are struggling and trying the best they can to make things work. The desire for balance is not just an issue for women. Both men and women want to have fulfilling, meaningful invest-ment in both work and family.

This dual desire may be especially true in younger generations, notably the millennials. In her book *The Unfinished Revolution*, Kathleen Gerson interviewed young men and women about their hopes and expectations for their lives. [14] She found that the vast majority of both men (70%) and women (80%) hoped to have balanced and egalitarian lives where both they and their partners share work and family responsibilities. Even among those raised in traditional families, seven out of ten men and women wanted egalitarian partnerships. These young men and women contrasted the lives they want to live with those of their parents. One young man noted: "It represents me hoping to be less workaholic than my father. I want to be more active in the early years." [15] Another man said: "I would like to be more like my mother and be very involved with the kids." [16]

Just because people want something does not mean they think they can have it. Gerson found a gap between what young men and women actually want to have in their lives and what they thought would happen to them after they got married and had children. These young men and women realized that achieving an egalitarian and balanced relationship is difficult and may not happen. Women were most likely to say that if they could not achieve an egalitarian partnership they would rather be self-reliant and choose their career over a family. On the other hand, men were more likely to choose a traditional relationship where they are the breadwinner and their wife is the homemaker. Hopefully the young men and women will be able to achieve their ideal: a long-lasting egalitarian partnership where both share the chal-lenges of work and family life. However, if they do not achieve this, they are both facing disappointment.

Why did these young women and men think it would be so difficult to achieve a balanced, egalitarian marriage? They probably sensed that we live in a world where men and women are not expected to focus on the same things: Men are expected to focus on work and women are expected to focus on family. Despite much evidence to the contrary, many believe that men and women are fundamentally different—that women are especially inclined to nurture while men are especially inclined to be assertive and lead. These young women and men may have also sensed that something was askew in our society. They probably know that women make less money than men, that parental-leave policies and lack of affordable childcare make balancing work and family difficult, and that many jobs require unreasonably demand-ing hours. They may also know that women generally do the lion's share of work at home and that expectations for parenting have gotten a bit out of control.

What often happens is that couples start out with egalitarian expectations, but in their efforts to have the best and be the best in everything, egalitarian expectations can be hard to maintain. Pamela Stone, a sociologist, interviewed highly educated women with high-status jobs who left the workforce after having children.[17] Most of these women had started their marriages hoping for egalitarian partnerships. These women had husbands who were extremely successful at work and many of these women were extremely successful in their careers as well. However, their husbands' jobs had become so demanding that they felt that they had become solely responsible for the childcare and household management. However, not one of them suggested that their husbands cut back. Despite the desire for egalitarianism and balance, there is often the (not always overtly articulated) assumption that women are the ones ultimately responsible for family life. Thus, although they may have entered the marriage wanting an egalitarian partnership, they ended up in an unbalanced, more traditional relationship.

Both men and women are harmed when the conditions make it impossible to combine meaningful work and family life. They both have everything to gain from reevaluating what it means to have it all and to fight for the changes in their relationships and society to make greater equality possible. We hope this book contributes to changing the conversation. The issue is not how women can balance work and family, but how *people* can.

OUR MOTIVATION

We became interested in the topic of how to integrate work and family life as a result of our own experiences. We are psychology professors and mothers who have made conscious decisions in order to achieve some sort of balance between work and family; however, it remains a work in progress for both of us. Throughout this book, we use the term "we" to describe our opinions and views as authors. Occasionally, we will share individual examples and personal experiences with you. When we do, we will use "I" followed by our initials to let you know which author is talking. In other words, I (ML) will indicate experiences shared by Miriam Liss, while I (HS) will be used when Holly Schiffrin is describing personal stories.

Miriam's Story

I (ML) remember a key decision I made after graduate school. I was offered both a chance to work at the University of Mary Washington (UMW), a small public liberal arts college in Fredericksburg, Virginia, and was encouraged to apply for a postdoctoral position at Yale. Pursuing the Yale position would have set me up for a more prestigious academic career, maybe at a top research university. The University of Mary Washington expects faculty to teach four classes a semester, does not have graduate assistants, and generally allows very little time for research. Taking this job was clearly not the path to academic fame. But professors at Mary Washington seemed more relaxed than anyone I had met at Yale. For example, they spent time with their families by the pool during the summer. I chose Mary Washington, even though it meant moving to Virginia and giving up my treasured status as a New Yorker (which was where I grew up), or at least a New Englander. Meanwhile my husband, Julian, after a period of career contemplation, made the choice to become a guidance counselor. This job is not high paying, nor is it one that will bring him status or fame. But, he is home every day at three in the afternoon and never has to bring work home or work on weekends or holidays. Because we both made conscious choices not to choose careers that would make it difficult to spend a substantial amount of time with our family, we have both managed to balance work and family pretty well.

My university has relatively generous infant-care leave—a semester off at half pay and full benefits. My son, Daniel, was born in April and I did not go back to work until the next January when I placed him in full-time childcare. When my daughter, Emily, was born two years later I combined a sabbatical with infant-care leave, and she did not need outside childcare until she was fifteen months old. For the next two years, I took advantage of the flexible work schedule afforded by my job to avoid placing my two children in full-time childcare. (This decision was financial because full-time childcare for two children is very expensive.) I watched the children in the morning and went into the office at 1:00 p.m., where I held office hours and taught at 2:00 and 3:00. My husband came home at 3:00 and we hired babysitters to cover the gap. This arrangement meant that he cooked dinner and played with the kids until around 6:00, when I would come home. When my oldest son went to kindergarten, I put my three-year-old daughter in full-time preschool. My husband got my son off the school bus at 3:20, and I generally picked up my daughter at 4:20, but if I needed to stay later he picked her up. I have started helping out with dinner more, but my husband is still a better cook than I am.

We generally share the chores around the house. We both clean up after dinner, we both try to remember to push the laundry through, he does most of the grocery shopping, and I do most of the managing and planning of the kids' activities. One day I was discussing work-family balance with my psychology of women class. I wanted to tell them not to give up on the hope that they will not have to choose between work and family and that they should strive to have it all. I found myself starting to tear up when talking about it. (I think they thought I was crazy, although some of them came to my office after class and told me they were really touched and inspired that day.) That was when I started thinking—wow, I really care about this topic, and the idea of this book started to germinate.

I feel incredibly blessed to have been able to combine a meaningful career with my family life, and I know my husband loves that he has been able to spend so much time with his children. I asked him the other day if he thought we had it all, and he said he thought we did. I pointed out that we live in Virginia and not New York, and we bought a house in the suburbs instead of right in the city because it was less expensive. We don't have the nicest cars and our children are not dressed in brand-name clothing, unless they come as gifts or hand-me-downs. But, I also realized he was right: We do have it all; our version of "all" is enough. However, I know that I am extremely lucky. Even though both my husband and I made conscious decisions to scale back the status of our careers, the flexibility of our lifestyle is unique to academia and a far cry from the choices that I have watched my friends who are not in academia have to make. I have watched many of my highly educated friends struggle with the choice of staying in an inflexible and unrewarding corporate setting or quitting their job and staying at home. Given the inflexibility of the corporate world, combined with what was usually a long commute, there was often no choice to make; they quit their job to stay at home. Other friends have kept working but struggle with feeling that they are not spending enough time with their children. Most people have demanding work schedules and inflexible jobs, and given this reality, there are rarely easy answers to the question of work-life balance.

Holly's Story

I (HS) also made a nontraditional choice when I finished graduate school. The expectation of my faculty was for graduates to take an academic position. I had several offers for postdoctoral placements that would probably have opened doors for me to have a much more prestigious academic career. However, I had met my future husband, Jon, who had recently graduated from law school. The three states where I was offered a postdoctoral position did not reciprocate his Florida bar membership. In addition, I was born and raised in Virginia, which is where the majority of my family still lived. It was very important for me to live within driving distance of my family, especially my nephew and niece, so I began applying for research positions at firms located in the Washington, D.C., area. This location met my requirements for being near my family while having ample job opportunities for attorneys and a bar that was reciprocal with Florida's. So, even before I had my own children, I was already making decisions to balance my work and family life.

I started working at a private research company straight out of graduate school. At first, it wasn't too bad. The research I was doing wasn't directly related to my degree in child development, but I was using many of the skills

I developed in graduate school. However, the longer I stayed, the more responsibility I was given, and the longer my hours became. I frequently brought work home and was expected to travel periodically for my projects. Although I was stressed at times, it was working OK until the birth of my first daughter, Lauryn, in 2003. My company did not have any official maternity leave, but I was able to stay home with Lauryn for three months using my sick leave, vacation days, and working from home. I was also able to negotiate a break from travel while I was breastfeeding, as well as a four-day work week so that I could spend more time with my infant daughter. However, even though I went into the office only four days a week, my duties at work had not been decreased. So I was really doing the same job, but only getting paid 80% of my salary for it. In addition, at this time, my husband was working at a law firm in downtown D.C., making a long commute and working long days to meet his "quota" for billable hours. Eventually, the long commute (to Maryland on the D.C. beltway) and long hours I was working, as well as the expectations for travel and bringing work home to meet contractual deadlines became too much on top of the demands of caring for an infant.

I started looking for an academic position. I believed that there might be more autonomy and flexibility working as a university professor. However, I didn't want to relocate geographically, so that I could still be near my family in Virginia, which limited my options considerably. It took me several years, but I finally got a position in the psychology department at UMW. Although I took a significant pay cut moving from the private sector to academia, I was willing and able (thanks to my husband's income) to make that trade-off to have summers home with my daughter. Although I wanted to start trying for a second child around the time Lauryn was two, I had just changed jobs, so I delayed conception for a year. This delay put my daughters four years apart in age, which is more than I wanted, but again I was trying to balance the needs of my career and family.

The experience I had after the birth of my second daughter, Jordan, was very similar to what Miriam described. I had her in May and didn't have to go back to work until January. To avoid having two children in paid care at the same time, I taught evening classes two days a week so that I could be home with her during the day. My mother came up and stayed with us half the week to cover two of the days, and my husband stayed home the fifth day. I was very fortunate that my mother had retired and was able to do that for four months until I was off again in May. I am also very fortunate that my husband decided to start his own practice, so he had a much more flexible schedule (although the trade-off was less financial stability) and was able to work from home one day a week.

My children are now six and ten years old. My husband's firm is more stable now, so he has even more flexibility in his schedule. He is the one who meets the bus in the afternoons because I often have meetings after work and am not home by 4:00 when the kids arrive. When I'm teaching, he is the one who stays home with them when they get sick and when they have one of the myriad school holidays and early dismissals during the school year. However, I primarily have the kids over the breaks when our school calendars align, and we have lots of time by the pool all summer. Although there is certainly some stress associated with both my work and my time at home with the kids, I feel like I have a pretty good work-family balance most of the time. I frequently say that by the time the semester is ending, I am ready for a break from work. However, by the time the summer is over, I am usually itching for some intellectual stimulation and interaction with adults. While there's always room for improvement, I tend to think that I have the best of both worlds.

A Comment on Our Stories

So do we have it all? Yes and no. We both have some balance between work and family, but we both have made compromises along the way. Our husbands have had to compromise as well, both pursuing jobs that allowed for greater flexibility at the expense of greater income or prestige. Neither we nor our husbands have completely "leaned in" to our careers. But, by leaning out a bit, we have achieved some balance. We both feel competent in our work and enjoy the fact that we have a significant amount of autonomy over our schedules. We cherish our relationships both with our families and with our colleagues at work. The temptation to compare ourselves to people with greater status, wealth, and fame is always there, of course. But we also know that constantly looking at people who (you perceive to) have more than you do can undermine your sense of well-being. Focusing on what others have can keep you from enjoying all you do have.

We would like to make a final comment on our stories. We realize that we are very fortunate and that our solution to the work-family balance problem is not available to everyone. We recognize that people come from a variety of different backgrounds and unique situations. Single parents only have one paycheck coming into the household, many families need both parents working as many hours as possible to survive, and others can't find work due to disability or general economic conditions. We know that there is not a one-size-fits-all answer. While the solutions are neither obvious nor simple, they are worth striving for. We hope that this book will provide some of the inspiration and tools to do so.

OUR APPROACH

These are the central messages of this book: (1) Balance involves finding the "sweet spot" for level of involvement in each role—it is best to approach everything with moderation. (2) People should strive to make each of their roles high quality and intrinsically motivating by attempting to maximize their sense of autonomy, competence, and relatedness. When people strive for these goals instead of money, success, and prestige, they are happier. (3) Both women and men need balance and want meaningful and satisfying lives. Work-family balance is not a woman's issue, it is a person issue. (4) There are many obstacles to achieving balance among roles and increasing our well-being—some are under personal control and some are not. In order to truly change things, individual action is not enough. People will need to work toward social changes for families in terms of parental leave, flexible work schedules, and high-quality affordable childcare for all.

These messages could be interpreted as an idealistic, but impractical, suggestion that everyone should just be nice and get along. But there is solid psychological and sociological research to back up our messages. We hope this book will move the discussion beyond people's opinions about "having it all" and finding balance to what the data say about it. This book will answer a number of questions about work-family balance. The answers are not always easily tied up in simple bows—sometimes they are complex. By reading this book, we hope you will have a much better grasp of what the research actually says and be able to make informed decisions about how you can balance work and family, maximize your personal well-being, and work toward a society that is more balanced and egalitarian for all.

Chapter 2 asks why people would want to achieve a balance between work and family. Does having children make people happy or miserable? What are the mental health benefits of being involved in work? Does being involved in multiple roles make us more stressed or more fulfilled? If parents work, will their children be harmed by being put in day care?

Chapter 3 focuses on parenting and how to find balance in the parenting role. This chapter takes the perspective that parenting is something best done in moderation—at the sweet spot of the inverted U. We will try to answer how much involvement children actually need. How important is breastfeeding? Should people be tying themselves up in knots and buying breast milk over the Internet if they are unable to breastfeed? How important is it to carry a child constantly? How much intellectual stimulation does a child actually need? How many extracurricular activities are optimal? How can people promote a sense of autonomy in their children and not be a controlling or helicopter parent? How does too much involvement affect children's and parents' well-being? We will also discuss why parenting has gotten out of control in the first place. What are parents so scared of? What can we do about it?

Chapter 4 focuses on finding balance at work. Although work is good, overwork is not. Why are people so driven to overwork? How do the inflexible expectations of the workplace contribute to overwork? Why don't people always take advantage of flexibility policies even when companies offer them? Is there any better model for setting up the workplace? This chapter will also address people's drive for money—which often fuels their drive to overwork. What is the relationship between wealth and well-being? Does money lead to happiness? How can we use thrift to approach our financial needs with a sense of moderation?

Unfortunately, balance is difficult to achieve because of stereotyped assumptions about men and women. Chapter 5 challenges the ingrained beliefs that men and women are fundamentally different and that women are more "naturally" inclined to be caretakers while men are more "naturally" inclined to be workers. Are men and women really so different? Can we undo assumptions about gender? What happens when women lead? What happens when men take on caretaking roles?

Chapter 6 brings the issue of work-family balance into the home—a major area where men and women are often out of balance. Why do women continue to do more household labor and childcare than men even when both are working full-time? Do men really not see those dirty socks on the floor? How can we achieve greater balance and egalitarianism in our home life?

Chapter 7 examines the barriers in society that make achieving work-family balance and egalitarian lives difficult for both men and women. Imbalance at home and at work also stems from larger social issues such as the gender pay gap, inadequate parental-leave policies, and lack of affordable childcare. Why do men continue to earn more than women? What can be done about it? How do the parental-leave policies of the United States compare with those of other countries? Is there an optimal amount of leave? How expensive is childcare, really? How can our country increase accessibility to affordable childcare?

Finally, we move beyond balance. Balance is important, but being balanced does not necessarily mean people are leading happy, fulfilling, and satisfied lives. Chapter 8 will discuss what everyone can do to maximize their personal well-being. Can people actually change their levels of happiness? How do they do that? How can lifestyle choices, mindfulness, savoring, gratitude, and forgiveness increase well-being? How does comparing yourself to others affect you? How can you increase your autonomy, competence, and relatedness in order to create truly meaningful and satisfying lives?

Finally, we will revisit the issue of what needs to change in order to create a world where men and women can both seek egalitarian and balanced lives.

The ability for men and women to have it all is about both individual choices and personal growth as well as about social change. What do men and women still need to be fighting for? Our goal is to describe these issues and stimulate discussion on how to advocate for these changes in society.

Chapter Two

Balancing Multiple Roles

Sometimes I feel like the "jack of all trades, master of none"—nothing is ever completely done, never completely right. Either the house is a wreck, we're eating chicken nuggets way more than we ought to, homework is barely getting done, or our work is happening at 3:00 a.m.! Still, personally I wouldn't trade the chaos for anything.—*Working mother of three*

Trying to juggle work and family is often fairly chaotic. But is it worth it? Does being a parent increase or decrease well-being? Parenting sometimes seems to increase stress, conflict, and time demands. Would people be happier if they just remained childless? Similar issues can be raised about work. On the one hand, it's clear that working generally has mental health benefits; on the other hand, not all work environments are equally beneficial. Although a great deal of research has focused on the conflict that occurs when people try to combine work and family, more recent attention has been given to the benefits of combining these roles, and to finding the right balance for each person. Balancing work and family has consequences for children as well. For each family, though, learning how to strike that perfect balance is often a guessing game, but it is worth striving for. We can find joy in the chaos.

DOES BEING A PARENT MAKE YOU MISERABLE?

A recent *New York* magazine article, "All Joy and No Fun: Why Parents Hate Parenting," presented a rather grim picture of the mental health effects of parenting, documenting the stresses, frustration, and anxiety that are part of the day-to-day experiences of raising children. The author noted: "Children may provide unrivaled moments of joy. But, they also provide unrivaled moments of frustration, tedium, anxiety, heartbreak." A psychologist quoted in the article summed up both the stresses and joys of having children, saying: "They're a huge source of joy, but they turn every other source of joy to shit."[1]

Indeed, research of the mental health effects of becoming a parent can certainly paint a discouraging picture. Daniel Kahneman, a professor at Princeton University, conducted a study of employed women including both mothers and non-mothers. He asked them to rank a variety of daily activities that they had completed and rate how they felt while doing each of those tasks.[2] Childcare was ranked one of the lowest among everyday activities. Eleven activities elicited more positive emotions than parenting including watching television, preparing food, and eating, while only four elicited less (being on the computer, doing housework, working, and commuting).

Other studies have identified negative mental health consequences of becoming a parent.[3] According to the results of over a hundred studies on new parents, the transition to parenthood is particularly difficult. Despite an initial boost in satisfaction immediately after the birth of the infant, over time new parents experience a decrease in both life and relationship satisfaction.[4] Other studies have found that parents exhibit a higher rate of depression compared to people who are not parents.[5] Parenting appears to have become more stressful over the past several decades, largely due to increases in women's employment and divorce rates.[6]

How Childbirth Affects Parents' Self-Determination

The impact of parenthood on well-being is partially affected by a person's sense of autonomy (which is a critical determinant according to self-determination theory) in making the decision to become a parent. Women who are unable to have children, but wanted to have them (i.e., it was not an autonomous decision) experience decreased well-being and life satisfaction.[7] In contrast, some people intentionally chose not to become parents. Research shows that people who are childless by choice have personal well-being that is similar to parents.[8] The key issue seems to be the freedom to make the choice to become a parent or not.

Autonomy, or lack thereof, is also a key factor influencing well-being among people who have children. People lose a great deal of their personal autonomy when they become parents. In other words, having a child involves doing a lot of things because you *have* to do them, not necessarily because you *want* to do them. Parents often do not decide basic things for themselves—like when to wake up or even when to use the restroom. One mother said in a CNN article on parenting: "There are just So. Many. Chores."[9] All of the time spent caring for their children leaves parents with less time for their own leisure activities.[10] Giving up a round of golf for dirty diapers and laundry does not seem like the choice most people would make if given complete freedom and autonomy. Non-mothers report more flexibility, freedom, and independence in how they spend their time as well as more personal privacy and time to relax.[11] In addition, people who feel less autonomy or sense of control during pregnancy experience more depression and anxiety as they transition into parenthood.[12]

Parenting can also interfere with people's sense of competence. At some point, almost every parent feels as if they do not know what they are doing.[13] Parents who do not feel they are effective report decreased satisfaction with their family life.[14] In addition, many parents take at least a short break from work after the birth of a child—trading in the opportunity to demonstrate their competence at work for some rather tedious aspects of infant care. A thread from the online parenting message board Urban Baby captures this sentiment:

> MOMS: Ever feel alone in how you perceive this role? I swear I feel like I'm surrounded by women who were once smart & interesting but have become zombies who only talk about soccer and coupons.[15]

Finally, parenting can interfere with an individual's sense of relatedness to others. The Urban Baby discussion thread in response to this post went on to describe how mothers felt they could no longer connect with other women on a meaningful level. However, it is the marital relationship that takes the biggest hit after the birth of a child. The results of almost a hundred studies investigating the effects of having children on relationship satisfaction paint a dire picture.[16] Raising children was related to decreased marital satisfaction, especially for mothers of young children. This pattern was particularly true for parents of higher socioeconomic status, people who became parents at younger ages, and parents born in more recent generations. One of the biggest contributors to decreased marital satisfaction after the birth of a child is that fathers may participate less in childcare than had been expected prior to childbirth. Couples that had ideals of being egalitarian before childbirth may find it difficult to maintain equality afterward.[17] This violation of expectations may lead to a cycle of resentment, a phenomena that we will discuss further in chapter 6 on division of labor in the home.

Marital satisfaction can also decrease after the birth of a child due to decreased parental intimacy and a less active sex life.[18] After childbirth women may feel as though their bodies are not fully their own and not meant for sex, especially if they are breastfeeding.[19] But men's sexual desire has generally not waned, and this disconnect between the desires of the mother and father can result in sexual dissatisfaction and martial tension. Furthermore, the exhaustion that comes from having young children can make couples too tired to have sex. One father was very open about how children negatively affected his relationship: "I already felt neglected," he says. "In my mind, anyway. And once we had the kid, it became so pronounced; it went from zero to negative 50. And I was like, *I can deal with zero. But not negative 50.*"[20]

However, research has suggested that while there may be some initial sexual dissatisfaction after the birth of a child, it is not the driving force behind decreased marital satisfaction. If it were, then husbands (who feel their sex lives are being thwarted) would be less satisfied than wives. However, women actually report more marital dissatisfaction after having children than men. Researchers have suggested that the loss of freedom women experience and the more traditional roles (i.e., doing a greater share of the childcare) they find themselves in after the birth of a child are the variables that most adversely affect marital satisfaction.[21]

If both life and relationship satisfaction decrease after the birth of a child, then perhaps the best way to balance work and family demands is to not have children at all! Studies have found that childless couples have greater martial satisfaction,[22] likely due to the additional time, money, and freedom they have. However, becoming a parent may not have as negative an impact on mental health as the research we have just reviewed suggests. In fact, being a parent may actually increase certain attributes of mental health, particularly the sense of leading a meaningful life.

The Upside of Parenting

In 2013 three studies conducted by the same researchers used different methods to provide evidence that having children may actually be associated with more joy than misery.[23] In the first study, a nationally representative sample of parents and nonparents were surveyed about their life satisfaction, thoughts about the meaning of life, and happiness. Overall, parents had greater life satisfaction and thought more about the meaning of life. However, some differences emerged when the data were examined separately for men and women. While both parents thought more about the meaning of life than nonparents, only fathers reported greater life satisfaction and happiness than non-fathers. The benefits of parenting also were not found for young parents (under age twenty-five) or for single parents.

The second study paged participants throughout the day and asked them to report on their well-being at that moment. Parents reported greater well-being, happiness, and sense that their life had meaning than did nonparents. Again, fathers seemed to benefit more than mothers from being a parent, given that they scored higher than non-fathers on every aspect of well-being measured. However, mothers appeared to benefit from parenting as well; they reported lower levels of depressive symptoms and higher levels of positive emotion than non-mothers. The third study required parents to recreate their activities from the previous day and rate how much positive emotion they experienced while doing them. Overall, parents reported more positive emotions and a greater sense that their life had meaning when they were taking care of children than when they were not.

Research has started to converge on the idea that although parenting may be a source of stress, it may also provide greater life satisfaction and meaning.[24] One study of Norwegian mothers suggested that women with children have a greater sense of life satisfaction and self-esteem than women without children.[25] Another study reported that mothers were less likely to be depressed than non-mothers.[26]

Although fathers have received less attention in research on parenting, they clearly experience both the joys and stresses of raising children. Steve Wiens, a pastor and father, posted an honest account of parenting on a blog for the *Huffington Post*:

> I am in a season of my life right now where I feel bone-tired almost all of the time. Ragged, how-am-I-going-to-make-it-to-the-end-of-the-day, eyes burning exhausted. I have three boys ages 5 and under. I'm not complaining about that. Well, maybe I am a little bit. . . . There are many moments where they are utterly delightful. . . . But there are also many moments when I have no idea how I'm going to make it until their bedtime. The constant demands, the needs and the fighting are fingernails across the chalkboard every single day.[27]

In contrast, a qualitative study interviewed fathers about their experiences and found many reports of the joys of fatherhood. For example, one father reported:

> I think the nicest bit is just spending time sitting around on the bed and just playing with him, and just talking to him and being talked back at, and changing his nappy when that happens as well, and you know, time looking at him and him looking at me really is the bit that I'm really enjoying.[28]

As mentioned above, some research has suggested that the positive mental health effects of parenting are stronger for men than they are for women.[29] Studies have found that men benefit not only from being fathers, but also from being involved caregivers. When fathers are engaged with their children, they are less likely to experience psychological distress.[30] In a sample of low-income minority men, commitment to fathering was found to have positive effects on the father's well-being and his relationship to the birth mother.[31] On the other end of the financial spectrum, men in top managerial positions reported a sense of regret over not being able to spend enough time with their families.[32]

In contrast to earlier research suggesting that having children dooms a parent to a life of misery, parenting seems to have numerous benefits, especially for fathers. Studies painting a dire picture of the effects of parenting on mental health seem to have missed the distinction between feeling happy on a moment-by-moment basis and experiencing a sense of purpose in life. Parents might not enjoy specific childcare tasks, such as changing a dirty diaper or listening to children whine and argue, but they may have an overall sense that their life has more meaning because they have children. In addition, parents may be able to offset some of the less enjoyable aspects of parenting through their involvement in other domains of life, especially doing some sort of meaningful work that supports the intrinsic needs for autonomy, competence, and relatedness.

THE BENEFITS OF WORK

The other side of the work-family balancing act is work. In many ways, the benefits of working are obvious—work provides money for the basic necessities of survival as well as opportunities to feel autonomous, competent, and related to others. The data on the negative physical and mental health effects of unemployment, particularly when unemployment is not chosen or desired, are clear.[33] In one study, interviews were conducted with over a thousand adults in low-income neighborhoods.[34] Being unemployed was associated with being more stressed and depressed as well as with eating less healthily, smoking, getting less exercise, and drinking more alcohol. Being underemployed had similar negative effects. Only people who were employed full-time enjoyed the positive mental and physical health outcomes associated with work.

What about women who have left the workplace to care for their children? Do they suffer from the same negative mental health effects of unemployment? Conventional wisdom might say "no" because these are women who have made a "choice" to stay home. However, it's questionable whether the decision to stay home is actually an autonomous choice or not. Despite the media attention given to highly educated women who have chosen to opt out of the workplace,[35] the largest group of stay-at-home mothers is lower-income women for whom the cost of childcare is prohibitive.[36] In other words, while people may think that staying home is a luxury for women who can afford not to work, it is more common for women to work if they can afford to stay in the workplace. Across seventeen countries, women with higher levels of education were more likely to be employed than those with less education.[37] Thus the ability to combine work and parenting can be seen as a privilege of the educated who are able to have jobs that are meaningful, satisfying, and pay enough to justify the costs of childcare, transportation, and clothes for work. Given the negative mental health effects of unemployment, the ability to combine work and family seems like an opportunity that everyone should be allowed to have.

On the surface, it might appear *more* stressful to combine work and family because working mothers have to complete their parenting responsibilities within the time constraints created by working outside of the home all day. However, the majority of research has found that stay-at-home mothers experience the same negative physical and mental health consequences as the unemployed. Telephone interviews conducted with nationally representative samples of women in both the United States[38] and Canada[39] found that stay-at-home mothers experienced worse mental health (e.g., sadness, anger, and depression) than women who worked at least part-time. Stay-at-home mothers from lower-income levels, as well as those with young children, seemed to fare even worse. Low-income mothers who stay at home reported being less likely to smile a lot, learn something interesting, experience enjoyment, or experience happiness than mothers of similar incomes who were working.[40] In a longitudinal study following children from birth through fifth grade, stay-at home mothers, especially mothers of infants through preschoolers, were more depressed than mothers who worked full- or part-time.[41] One mother we know reported the following experience:

> I had been a stay-at-home mom for three years when my second child was born. My husband had a job and was a college student, so he wasn't home very often. This left me alone in the house with a new baby and a very needy three-year-old. I found myself pacing around the house feeling empty and depressed. One day on a trip to the zoo, I stood in front of the tiger cage, watching the mother tiger pace the perimeter of her cage. I felt a strange connection with her and began to cry. I knew something had to change.

Another longitudinal study of approximately twenty-five hundred women has documented the positive benefits of full-time work on women's mental and physical health. Women with the highest levels of both physical and mental health were the steady workers who stayed in the workforce full-time throughout their children's lives. Women who worked part-time after childbirth were similar to full-time workers in mental health, but had lower levels of physical health. The stay-at-home mothers and mothers who had frequent interruptions in their work history had the lowest levels of both physical and mental health. This study demonstrates clear advantages for women who maintain a steady work history after the birth of their children. This sentiment maybe captured by another mother we know who expressed:

> I always wanted to be a stay-at-home mother until I was one for three months. Now I'm happy to go to work most days of the week; for me it's much easier than staying home and truthfully it probably makes me a better mother. I have so much respect for my mother who did it with much less help and much less

money! I find so much solace in knowing that other moms feel the same way
and face the same struggles.

It is possible that some women may make a truly autonomous choice to stay
home that is not based on financial or other types of constraints. If these
women are able to meet their basic needs for autonomy, competence, and
relatedness in this role, then we would predict they may not experience the
negative physical and mental health consequences associated with unemployment. However, to the extent that staying home is involuntary, even if it
appears voluntary on the surface, it is likely to be associated with reduced
well-being. The reasons why the "choice" to stay home is often less of a
choice than it appears will be discussed further in chapter 7.

Not All Work Is Created Equal: Getting the Most Benefit out of Work

Of course not all work is equally beneficial to mental health. Work can be
stressful and demoralizing.[42] It is important for people to have control over
what they do on a day-to-day basis as well as feel as though they can manage
the demands of their jobs.[43] The extent to which work provides a sense of
autonomy, competence, and relatedness affects whether work is beneficial to
mental health and satisfaction with life.[44] There are negative consequences
that occur when people have low levels of control over their job (i.e., lack of
autonomy) and highly demanding jobs (i.e., insufficient competence).[45] Conversely, employees who think they are included in decision making on the
job are more invested in their work, have greater physical and mental health,
have greater commitment to their jobs, and have higher levels of job satisfaction.[46] Similarly, feeling connected to coworkers (i.e., relatedness) has been
associated with increased well-being and reduced potential for job burnout.[47]

When basic needs are met, people feel intrinsically motivated to do their
jobs. In two studies conducted in Canada, workers on a school board and in a
college setting who felt intrinsically motivated to do their job were less
negatively affected by the demanding characteristics of their job than those
who were not. They were also more likely to see the demands of their job as
challenges rather than as stresses and were less likely to experience distress
even when their job felt particularly difficult.[48] What is good for the worker
is also good for the employer. People who felt higher levels of autonomy,
competence, and relatedness on the job also received higher performance
evaluations.[49]

People do not need to work at highly prestigious jobs to experience the
benefits of working. One study of workers at a shoe factory found that when
employees felt they had a sense of autonomy at work (e.g., they were able to
make their own decisions about when and where to get their work done), felt

connected (e.g., had good relationships with their coworkers), and felt competent on the job, they had greater job satisfaction and a sense of greater personal well-being.[50]

Another way researchers have described people's motivation for work is whether people view working as either a job, a career, or a calling.[51] A job is something that someone does purely for the money, but would stop doing if money were not an issue. People who view their work as a career are highly invested in their work and hope to advance to higher positions within their organization. People who view their work as a calling see it as inseparable from their life and one of the most important parts of who they are (i.e., autonomous motivation). Not surprisingly, people who view their work as a calling have higher job and life satisfaction as well as better health overall. Work that is more challenging and involves greater autonomy is more likely to be perceived as a calling than as a job. However, even among people who held the same job (in this particular study a group of administrative assistants), those who saw their work as a calling (about a third of the assistants) had higher work and life satisfaction than those who saw their work as simply a job.[52] Other studies have confirmed that people who are fully engaged in their jobs and work for the sheer enjoyment of working, rather than out of obligation or necessity, experience greater positive emotions in both work and family life.[53]

Thus the first step to finding work-family balance is to make sure each role is individually meaningful and contributes to personal well-being. However, even if both work and family domains are optimized for well-being, there may still be times when they are in conflict with each other (e.g., a deadline is looming requiring late hours, but the school play is that night). Does involvement in both work and family mean that one role must interfere with the other, or can involvement in both domains actually result in a mutually beneficial effect?

WHY ARE MULTIPLE ROLES GOOD?

Sometimes it feels like there just are not enough hours in the day. I (HS) remember when I finished graduate school and started working at my first "real" job. It was a huge adjustment to get used to full-time hours, a long commute in D.C. traffic, and lack of flexibility in my schedule to run errands. Fortunately, I lived with my grandmother for a few months, so I did not have to worry about cooking, washing my clothes, or keeping the house clean. A few months later, I moved into an apartment with my future husband, which was a big adjustment. I had a longer commute, had to do my own chores, and had to learn to live with another person. A few years later, my husband and I bought our first home, which added yard work and home maintenance to the mix. Then we had our first child, which really threw us for a loop! As I began down each new avenue of my life, I found that there were additional demands for my time and attention that were often difficult to meet.

This life path is fairly typical and probably sounds familiar to most people. But what are the consequences of taking on each additional responsibility (i.e., employee, partner/spouse, and parent)? An intuitive response might be that life gets more stressful at each step, so the consequences would be negative. This view is consistent with *role strain* researchers who have argued that there is a limited amount of time and energy that gets increasingly divided among these multiple roles, which leads to negative effects on health and well-being.[54] This approach is often illustrated with a metaphorical pie: The time and energy needed for one role (e.g., work) detracts from the time and energy that could be given to another role (e.g., parent).[55] According to this theory, if work and family are competing for the same time and energy, then they are inherently in conflict.

Work-family conflict occurs when role obligations interfere with each other in either direction—work can interfere with family, and family can interfere with work.[56] Research has shown that when there is conflict between work and family life, it is unequivocally related to negative mental health outcomes.[57] The results of sixty-seven studies found strong connections between work-family conflict and a host of negative outcomes including depression, stress, and physical symptoms.[58] An analysis of change in work-family conflict between 1977 and 1997 found that conflict between work and family has been increasing over time and is particularly strong for parents with young children in the home.[59] It is less clear whether men or women are more affected by work-family conflict. Some studies have found decreased well-being[60] and increased guilt[61] only among mothers when work interferes with family time, but other studies have found that men report being depressed as a result of work-family conflict.[62]

However, just because work and family *can* come into conflict does not mean that combining work and family is automatically negative for mental health. In fact the majority of research has supported the opposite view, the *role enhancement* hypothesis, which states that participating in multiple roles is beneficial.[63] In other words, when people are engaged in multiple roles, their energy expands to meet the challenges and their well-being is enhanced. While historically men have taken on a workplace role and women have been more involved with parenting, studies have shown that sharing aspects of each of these roles results in positive mental health benefits for both parents.[64]

Multiple Roles Increase Self-Determination

Multiple roles can be beneficial because they allow more opportunities for people to have their basic needs for autonomy, competence, and relatedness met. First, being involved in multiple roles can enhance autonomy by providing opportunities to exert some control over choices in life. One obvious way that working affords autonomy is through added income. Having disposable income allows choice in how time and money can be spent (e.g., people can hire a babysitter to spend alone time with their spouses or hire someone to clean so that they have more family time on the weekends). The financial benefits of working are particularly important when the added income is necessary for the financial security of the family. In such cases, working is related to increased marital satisfaction.[65] Having multiple roles also can provide alternatives to the tedious components of working or childcare.[66] One of our friends expressed this sentiment:

> When my youngest son was two, I enjoyed going to work for my four-hour class because it was a guilt-free way of having four hours away from my son and enjoying the company of other adults. One evening one of my students commented that he was always amazed by how happy I seemed to be to be at work, but that he had realized that I was getting a break from my two-year-old, so of course I was in a good mood.

Another key reason that having multiple roles is associated with greater well-being is that each role provides opportunities for experiencing a sense of mastery (i.e., competence).[67] People have opportunities to demonstrate and be recognized for their competence in multiple settings. At work, employees may learn a new programming language, feel pride in winning an important contract, or get promoted for their competence. At home, parents may master a new cooking technique, feel pride in a well-kept lawn, or bask in being told: "You're the best mommy in the world." In addition, men and women who are involved in both work and family roles develop competence in both domains. This competence enhances their ability to take each other's perspectives, which is associated with greater marital quality.[68]

Finally, being engaged in multiple roles is good for relationships.[69] When couples are in separate spheres and do not share similar experiences (e.g., the man works and the woman takes care of the children), they have less in common and become more disengaged from each other.[70] Additionally, being involved in multiple roles allows people to gain social support through their interactions with people in other domains. When men who have been primarily focused on work add the family role, they gain the social support of their wives and children. Similarly, when women add the work role, they gain a social network of coworkers. The social support provided by these relationships is essential to well-being.[71] It provides a network of people to talk to about a difficult experience, turn to for another perspective, have fun with when a distraction is needed, or provide tangible support such as child-care when stressed or chicken soup when sick.

How Multiple Roles Interact

There are many ways that being involved in both work and family can be mutually enriching. Research suggests that positive experiences in one role can act as a buffer against the negative aspects of another one. For example, when men have good relationships with their wives and children, they are less negatively affected by stress at work.[72] Similarly, rewarding experiences on the job decrease the stress experienced by difficult experiences with children.[73] I (ML) recall one morning when getting my children off to school was a disaster. My son was late for the bus and ended up running to the bus with only one shoe on, crying hysterically as I chased him down with the other shoe. My daughter awoke in a spectacularly grumpy mood and her monosyllabic conversation with me was punctured by screams as I tried to brush her hair. I started the day in a miserable mood. Fortunately, that day at work my general psychology class was particularly lively and engaged, research students were excited about analyzing their data, and I was able to tell the story to a colleague, which helped turn the experience from a stressor into an amusing story. By the time I got home from work, I was reenergized and happy again. Fortunately, and largely due to my improved attitude, the evening went considerably more smoothly!

Additionally, work roles can enhance family life and vice versa. The positive benefits from work such as income, workplace engagement, and workplace satisfaction have been linked to positive family outcomes such as marital quality, family engagement, family satisfaction, and positive parenting.[74] For example, you may learn a great filing system at work that can help you organize your home files or you may learn about a great after-school program from a work colleague. In addition, good experiences at work can lift your mood at home, creating an upward spiral associated with greater well-being.[75] Similarly, aspects of family life, such as feeling support from family, have been related to a variety of positive work-related variables such as income, positive attitudes about work, and job satisfaction.[76]

The positive effects of allowing work and family roles to enrich each other have been supported consistently in the research literature. One study interviewed female managers who felt that participation in nonwork roles helped their performance at work.[77] For example, some reported that being a mother enhanced their interpersonal skills: "I think being a mother and having patience and watching someone else grow has made me a better manager."[78] Another remarked that she learned how to better recognize the special needs and requirements of different employees from being a mother who responded to the individual needs of her children. These women also noted that their ability to handle multiple tasks was enhanced by their experiences as mothers. One noted: "My planning skills have improved tenfold since becoming a parent." Another said: "Taking on all those roles, being a mother, tending a household, working with an au pair, being a spouse, friend . . . I think all those aspects add organization into your life so that you're much more efficient and organized at work."[79] A friend of ours who is a psychologist noted that having children gave her resources and skills to help her deal with adult tantrums in the office!

Work-family enrichment is related to increased life satisfaction, job satisfaction, marital satisfaction, mental health, and physical health.[80] In one study of over two thousand people, participants reported higher levels of work-family enrichment (e.g., having a good day on your job makes you a better companion when you get home) than work-family conflict (e.g., responsibilities at home reduce the effort you can devote to the job).[81] People did not experience the decline in mental health that they normally would due to work-family conflict *if* they felt that their family enriched their work life. The authors hypothesized that when people are given positive support from their families, such as love and respect, they are better able to withstand the stresses associated with work that might interfere with family life.

The positive interaction between work and family is enhanced when people's need for self-determination, especially relatedness, are being met in each domain. People who are highly engaged at work (e.g., felt absorbed in, dedicated to, and energized by a sense of challenge), and have a lot of social support feel more positive after work when they get home.[82] These positive effects were more likely to occur if people talked with their spouse or partner about the good things that had happened at work that day. Another study found that when people felt social support at work, they felt better at home. Similarly, when they experienced social support at home, they felt better at work.[83]

Interestingly, the benefits of combining work and family are not restricted to the individual experiencing them. When wives felt as though being at work enhanced their family life and when husbands felt that their home life enhanced their work, their spouses reported less depression a year later.[84] Thus, the positive interaction between work and family benefit the well-being of both people in a relationship.

In sum, engagement in both parenting and work has been shown to enhance well-being, especially if the roles are meeting people's needs for autonomy, competence, and relatedness. Having more social roles (which is not restricted to being a parent and employee, but also includes being a volunteer, student, friend, neighbor, etc.) tends to be associated with better physical and mental health. But why does personal experience sometimes seem that doing more makes life more stressful? Sometimes having multiple roles feels stressful because they are not appropriately balanced. One role may be taking up too much time and energy, which creates role conflict. Research has shown that people who are focused on both career and family are more satisfied with their careers, families, personal development, and life in general than people who were either career focused or family focused.[85] It is important to find the "sweet spot" in the inverted U-shaped curve for both the parenting and employee roles, which we will discuss further in chapters 3 and 4.

WHAT ABOUT THE CHILDREN?

However, the question remains: Is what's good for the parents also good for their children? The general sentiment seems to be that there are negative consequences of non-maternal childcare on children's development. Twice as many mothers say they would prefer to work full-time (32%) than think working full-time is what is best for their children (16%).[86] As a result of this disconnect, women have been opting out of the workforce to stay home and raise their children in increasing numbers.[87] Many described their rationale in terms of the needs of their child. One woman noted: "A child minder does not raise a family the way a mother does." Another woman succinctly put it: "There isn't a substitute, no matter how good the childcare."[88] But, what are the data on the effects of childcare on children's well-being? Is there evidence to support the idea that children would be better off having a parent stay home with them throughout their childhood?

Two Things to Keep in Mind

Before reviewing the research, we wanted to mention two important things. First, all of the research we are familiar with focuses solely on whether maternal employment is good or bad for children. No one seems to question the effects of paternal employment on children—it just seems to be a given that children benefit when their fathers work. Furthermore, although the definition of childcare varies from study to study, many studies, including the largest longitudinal study on childcare, conducted by the National Institute of Child Health and Human Development (NICHD), define childcare broadly to include all non-maternal care—including care by fathers![89]

Second, we wanted to note a limitation in the conclusions that can be drawn about the effects of non-maternal childcare on children. Although researchers can compare how children with employed mothers differ from those whose mothers are not employed, they cannot conclude that the differences are caused by maternal employment. This is a classic psychology research conundrum—correlation does not imply causation. For example, just because umbrella sales increase when grass is taller does not mean that lawns should be left to grow in order to increase umbrella sales. Rather, both the taller grass and the umbrella sales may be caused by a third factor (e.g., rain).[90] Working and stay-at-home mothers may differ on many variables other than work (e.g., income or number of children in the family) that could explain differences observed among their children. Researchers attempt to control for as many of these other explanations as possible during the statistical analysis, but causal conclusions still cannot be made. The only way to make causal conclusions about the effects of maternal employment would be to conduct a true experiment in which mothers are randomly assigned to either go to work or stay home with their children. Obviously, researchers cannot dictate these decisions for families, so they are left drawing the best conclusions they can from the data they have.

What Does the Research Say?

Despite these limitations, many studies have examined the effects of maternal employment and childcare on children's well-being. The biggest conclusion from these studies is that the effects are fairly minimal. Although the results of individual studies vary, the majority of studies generally have found either very small or no effects.[91] The authors of one study reviewing forty years of research on maternal employment concluded that: "Early maternal employment per se is rarely associated with children's later outcomes."[92] Similarly, research has shown consistently that the quality of mother-child interactions is a more important predictor of child outcomes than the effects of childcare.[93] Once again, fathers are generally ignored in this research so the effects of father-child interactions cannot be clearly determined.

The results of sixty-nine studies have yielded the conclusion that maternal employment generally has small, positive advantages for children's academic achievement.[94] The academic achievement of girls[95] and children from working class and lower-middle-class families[96] particularly benefited from maternal employment. Children whose mothers worked part-time experienced advantages over those whose mothers stayed at home or worked full-time.[97] However, it is unclear whether part-time employment benefits achievement by allowing more time for maternal involvement with children or whether mothers who work part-time come from families with more financial resources (i.e., they do not need full-time incomes), which also are associated with higher achievement. There were, however, small negative effects when women worked before their children were a year old, especially for white, non-Hispanic children, suggesting that better maternal-leave policies might benefit children.[98] Finally, the positive effects of maternal employment on academic achievement were somewhat larger in more recently

published studies, indicating that as maternal employment has become more
common there are increasingly more benefits associated with it. [99]

The beneficial effect that maternal employment has on academic achievement is enhanced when childcare quality is high. The NICHD childcare study
has followed 1,364 children from their birth in 1991 to the present. This
study distinguished among low-, medium-, and high-quality childcare sites.
High-quality childcare includes characteristics such as a high ratio of caregivers to children as well as caregivers who are educated about child development, respond sensitively to children's needs, and maintain employment at
the same location long term. The NICHD childcare study consistently found
that higher-quality childcare was related to better academic skills from kindergarten through the freshman year of high school. [100] Additional intellectual advantages at various ages, such as better memory in third grade as well as
increased language skills in fifth grade, have also been identified. [101] Participation in high-quality, early childcare seems especially beneficial to the academic achievement of children whose parents are less educated and have
lower incomes. [102]

There is some evidence suggesting that there may be some negative effects of early childcare on children's behavior (e.g., increased aggression).
The overall amount of time children spent in nonparental care was associated
with behavioral problems at age two and in kindergarten, and reemerged as a
predictor of risk taking and impulsivity among adolescents. [103] However,
children in higher-quality childcare were less likely to have behavioral problems than those in lower-quality childcare [104] In Norway, where high-quality
childcare is the norm due to government subsidies, there was no relationship
between behavior problems and childcare up to forty hours per week. [105]

Despite some studies showing potential behavioral effects of childcare,
other research suggests that there may be social benefits of childcare due to
children's increased opportunity for social interaction. Children who attend
high-quality childcare seem to have a better understanding of how to interact
appropriately with others [106] and are more helpful and cooperative than children who stay at home full-time. [107] A longitudinal study of British children
found that both boys and girls had the best social-emotional outcomes in
dual-earner families, with girls particularly benefiting when mothers
work. [108] In addition, high-quality early childcare for children from low-income families has long-term social benefits such as higher employment rates
and lower levels of criminal activity. [109] However, similar to the research on
behavior problems, the amount of time spent in childcare may adversely
affect social development: Children who began childcare during the first year
of life with extensive usage throughout childhood were found to demonstrate
less social competence and cooperation than peers who did not. [110] One important factor that might explain the mixed findings on social outcomes is a
mother's sense of autonomy about her decision to work or not work. Mothers

who are happy with their role choice (i.e., working or staying at home) tend to have children with better social competence.[111]

Does being in childcare negatively affect children's relationship with or attachment to their parents? Despite earlier studies that found that over twenty hours a week of childcare in the first year of life was related to insecure attachment,[112] subsequent research has failed to support a link between any aspect of childcare (i.e., age of entry into childcare, quality of care, or type of care) and attachment security (i.e., the ability to form a warm and loving bond with the primary caregiver).[113] Interestingly, children in childcare do not spend that much less time with their mothers than children who stay at home with their mothers.[114] When mothers of fifteen-month-olds were asked to record all of their activities over a twenty-four-hour period, researchers found that women who stayed at home full-time spent only twelve hours more per week caring for their children than women whose children attended thirty hours of childcare outside of the home. Furthermore, the fathers of the children who attended childcare were more involved in caregiving than fathers of children who did not.[115]

Other research that has put fear in the heart of parents has suggested that children in childcare settings may experience more daily stress. They experience increased production of the stress hormone cortisol in the mornings, indicating that they may be more stressed than children in home settings. The cause of this stress may be due to difficulties associated with negotiating relationships with others and having to share. However, rises in cortisol are less pronounced when quality of care is higher and when children have better social skills.[116] Despite the elevated cortisol levels, it is not clear that children attending childcare actually experience more anxiety as a result. In fact research suggests that children who have been in childcare actually may have less anxiety.[117] A review of sixty-nine studies on the effects of early maternal employment on children found that children whose mothers worked early in their lives were less likely to experience depression and anxiety than those whose mothers did not work.[118]

Thus, the perception that children benefit when mothers stay home to take care of them is not really supported by the evidence. Most of the research has suggested that there are few effects of maternal employment and possibly some small, positive benefits. Children, especially girls, seem to have higher academic achievement when their mothers are working. High-quality childcare is also associated with better academic outcomes, especially among children from lower socioeconomic status families. Although there are some mixed findings about the impact of childcare on the development of social skills, it does not seem to compromise infants' attachments to their caregivers, as originally feared. There may be some increased behavior problems associated with being in childcare, especially when children start young and attend long hours. However, attending a high-quality childcare facility seemed to buffer the negative consequences observed. Ultimately, across these studies on maternal employment and childcare, the biggest predictor of all child outcomes was the sensitivity of maternal-child interactions. Whether mothers work outside of the home or not, having warm, loving, and supportive interactions is associated with the best child outcomes. Of course, being warm, loving, and supportive is considerably easier if a mother is engaged in activities that she finds satisfying and that meet her basic needs—whether that be predominately working or staying at home.

CONCLUSION

Attempting to balance work and family life is a worthy goal for both men and women. Being a parent may be stressful at times but, ultimately, increases the sense that life has meaning. Working provides a number of benefits, especially if the workplace environment fosters a sense of autonomy, competence, and relatedness. When work and family roles are combined and mutually enhancing, positive benefits can occur in each domain. Of course balance means not overinvesting in either domain—how to find the "sweet spot" for both parenting and work will be discussed more fully in chapters 3 and 4. Finally, when parents combine work and family roles, children are not adversely affected, and can even benefit.

Although it is apparent from the research that finding work-family balance benefits individuals, families, and businesses, there are a number of obstacles to achieving it. One of the fundamental barriers stems from assumptions about men's (i.e., providers) and women's (i.e., caregivers) natural roles. This mentality is pervasive and contributes to additional barriers both at work and at home. In the realm of work, there are barriers to work-family balance due to unequal treatment of men and women, parental-leave policies, and the availability of childcare. At home, unequal division of household labor and childcare impede work-family balance. The remainder of the book will discuss these issues and how both attitudes and social policy need to change to maximize both men's and women's ability to enjoy the benefits of combining work and family life.

Chapter Three

Balance as a Parent

> With the exception of the imperial offspring of the Ming dynasty and the dauphins of pre-Revolutionary France, contemporary American kids may represent the most indulged young people in the history of the world. It's not just that they've been given unprecedented amounts of stuff—clothes, toys, cameras, skis, computers, televisions, cell phones, PlayStations, iPods. . . . They've also been granted unprecedented authority. . . . In many middle-class families, children have one, two, sometimes three adults at their beck and call. [1]

How did things get this way? How did the balance of power switch from children "being seen, but not heard" to parents serving at their children's "beck and call"? In the not-too-distant past, the word parent referred to something people *were* (a noun) and not something people *did* (a verb). [2] However, things seem to have gotten out of control. Since the mid-1990s, parents have significantly increased the amount of time they spend caring for their children. [3] Indeed, according to time diary studies, employed mothers spent as much time in direct care of their children as unemployed mothers did in 1970. [4] While being a parent has been associated with greater well-being, [5] if it takes up too much time and energy, it reduces the amount of time available for other social roles, such as work. As seen in chapter 2, participating in multiple roles is beneficial for well-being when the quality of each role is high and people are able to find balance among their various roles. However, the intensive involvement expected of parents can compromise the quality of this role and make it difficult to achieve work-family balance.

Of course these expectations of parenthood are not gender neutral; the pressures are generally focused on mothers. One blogger for the *Huffington Post* described the tiredness that women feel trying to balance work and family by saying: "Motherhood is so often this giving of self in our homes that no one sees. . . . We go to work, come home from work, we work at home, we mother all day . . . and then we go to bed."[6] In addition, highly educated women who opt out of the workforce often identify the intense demands of parenting as one of the reasons that they do so.[7] Women clearly feel pressures to parent intensively, but it is not always clear why there is so much pressure and where it is coming from.

The dominant view of parenting for the past few decades has been that it is demanding and time consuming.[8] Sociologist Sharon Hays coined the term "intensive mothering" to describe the pervasive set of beliefs about parenting in the United States. These beliefs advise that mothers should spend a great deal of time, energy, and money raising their children. Based on interviews with mothers of preschool-age children, Hays outlined three tenets of intensive mothering ideology. First, women described the pressure they felt because *mothers* are the ones responsible for every aspect of this intensive style of parenting—no one else, not even the father, can be trusted to provide sufficient care. Second, women described the intensive methods required to constantly engage their children in intellectually stimulating activities to promote positive emotional, intellectual, and social development. Mothers interviewed by Hays described sacrificing their own needs and orienting their lives around their children. Finally, the women interviewed saw themselves as being in charge of the care and protection of the most cherished of all beings—their sacred children. Hays also noted that both stay-at-home mothers and working mothers felt these pressures to parent intensively. In fact, research has suggested that employed mothers spend a similar amount of time (approximately 86% as much) with their children as nonemployed mothers.[9]

Given the high expectations for parents, combined with the belief that only mothers can perform these duties, it is a wonder that any woman can find a balance between work and family. Judith Warner identified the pressures that mothers put on themselves as a kind of "perfect madness" and a general sense of "too muchness."[10] Mothers feel a pervasive anxiety about whether or not they are doing it "right" and whether something they do or fail to do may harm their children. It begins *prior* to conception by taking prenatal vitamins, making dietary changes, (e.g., cutting out caffeine, alcohol, artificial sweeteners, etc.), and getting on waiting lists for the best preschools. During pregnancy, mothers read numerous books providing expert advice about what women should and should not do.[11] The "madness" continues after the baby is born when women are given numerous messages about the "correct" ways to feed, carry, and help their children sleep. The majority of the pressure is aimed at mothers and makes women feel as though they are never doing enough, never getting it right. Warner cautions: "The more women bought into the crazy competitiveness of our time, the more they tended to suffer as mothers."[12]

But what is the effect of this intensive approach to parenting? Does it help children become more successful? How does it impact women's mental health? We argue that parenting, like most things, is best done in moderation. In other words, the inverted U-shaped curve introduced in chapter 1 applies to parenting. Parental involvement and engagement with children is essential. Children need love, attention, intellectual stimulation, and activities. However, at a certain point, the benefits of parental involvement level off. Past this point of optimal involvement, there can be negative effects of too much involvement. There are also certain types of intrusive and controlling involvement that have been found to be particularly detrimental. When parental involvement violates children's sense of autonomy, competence, and relatedness, it adversely affects their well-being. Overinvolvement creates feelings of guilt and stress for parents that reduce their satisfaction with life as well.

THE RIGHT AMOUNT OF INVOLVEMENT: IS MORE ALWAYS BETTER?

One of the most well-known and well-established findings in the research on child development is that parental involvement is associated with positive child outcomes.[13] Parental involvement includes a variety of behaviors such as cuddling with, talking to, reading to, playing with, and providing children with activities that help them develop and learn. There is evidence that children who are neglected or deprived of parental interaction in early years experience intellectual and social delays.[14] In fact, early intervention with at-risk children attempts both to teach parents how to be more involved as well as to have teachers provide this type of stimulation in the intervention environment. Children who have parents who are actively involved and provide developmentally appropriate structure have better academic performance,[15] fewer behavior problems,[16] and greater well-being.[17] Parental involvement also has been associated with better social outcomes such as more positive relationships with peers[18] and a greater willingness to help others.[19] The data are clear: Parental involvement is good. So, it would be natural to conclude that the more involvement, the better.

However, these benefits of parental involvement are found when researchers compare parents who are generally uninvolved to parents who already play an active role in their children's lives. When going from low involvement to moderate involvement, the benefits are numerous. But just because some involvement is good does not mean that more and more involvement leads to better and better outcomes. A fundamental problem with modern beliefs about parenting is the assumption that if it is beneficial to spend time holding, breastfeeding, intellectually stimulating, and engaging in enrichment activities with children, then spending more time participating in these activities will yield increasing benefits.

Attachment Parenting: The Belief That More Is Always Better

There is ample research evidence that close physical contact between parent and child is beneficial. In Harlow's classic study, baby monkeys were put in a cage with a soft terrycloth mother and a hard wire mother. Despite the fact that the wire mother had the food, the baby monkeys clung to the soft mother and only left for brief periods to eat.[20] More recently research has revealed that close physical contact releases the hormone oxytocin, which has been called "the great facilitator of life" because of its role in social behaviors such as human bonding, attachment, and trust.[21] Research on the importance of parent-child contact has revolutionized the treatment of infants in the neonatal intensive care unit (NICU). Rather than isolate babies in sterile incubators, the current standard of care is to encourage periods of skin-to-skin contact known as Kangaroo Care, which has increased survival rates and reduced time in the NICU.[22] In addition, research on children raised in orphanages who are deprived of close physical contact has shown differences in their brain functioning that are associated with intellectual deficits and behavioral problems.[23]

Based on research about the benefits of physical contact and detriments of deprivation of this type of contact (e.g., in Romanian orphanages), William and Martha Sears have advocated for a style of parenting they call attachment parenting.[24] Attachment parenting involves utilizing parenting techniques that are popular in non-Western cultures, which are viewed as a more "natural" form of parenting.[25] It involves a variety of behaviors designed to enhance the connection between mother and child. Attachment parenting involves baby wearing (i.e., carrying in a sling or wrap), co-sleeping, and breastfeeding at the initiation of the infant (i.e., on demand) and for an extended period of time to maximize physical closeness between mother and child.

Attachment parenting is a time-intensive style of parenting that can be difficult to implement due to the demands it places on the mother's time. Although fathers could co-sleep and carry children as much as mothers, only women can breastfeed. In fact the 2012 cover of *Time* magazine, containing a feature article on attachment parenting, asked the question, "Are you mom enough?"[26] It portrayed a picture of a woman breastfeeding her almost four-year-old son, which garnered significant attention as well as sparked controversy over the extreme lengths women go through to meet the recommendations of attachment parenting.

Adopting this parenting style can make it challenging for women to work outside of the home given the need for their physical proximity to the baby.

In a sample of women who identified themselves as attachment parents, none of the mothers were working outside of the home despite generally high levels of education. Approximately 30% of mothers practicing attachment parenting reported that they had never left their infant with anyone during the child's first year, including the father. An additional 28% reported that they left the infant with the father or another close relative for only up to two hours a week.[27] In an article in *The Atlantic*, Hanna Rosin suggested that breastfeeding was a primary reason that couples are unable to maintain equality after the birth of a child. She noted that spending a half an hour every three hours breastfeeding is extremely difficult while attempting to work. Rosin quipped: "When people say that breast-feeding is 'free,' I want to hit them with a two-by-four. It's only free if a woman's time is worth nothing."[28]

If this level of maternal involvement is presented as the ideal for women, then it would be extremely difficult to achieve balance between work and family. Nevertheless, attachment parenting is promoted as the most natural form of parenting, so it is seen by many women as the "best" way to parent. But what evidence is there that it actually is a better way of parenting? Noticeably, attachment parenting advocates have conducted very little research about the benefits of practicing its tenets. Other researchers have demonstrated that there are benefits of each major aspect of attachment parenting—baby wearing, co-sleeping, and breastfeeding. However, the evidence for the benefits of these techniques tends to indicate an inverted U-shaped curve. In other words, doing the activity more and more does not translate to better and better outcomes.

Benefits of Baby Wearing

Attachment parenting promotes caregiver and child proximity as the best way to increase the caregivers' sensitivity and responsiveness to the child. They argue that parents (although they are generally referring to mothers) who spend more time with their children learn to read their cues more effectively and are able to respond to them immediately, which promotes a close emotional bond between parent and child. Thus they advise women to use a baby sling or similar device to "wear" their baby the majority of the time.[29]

There is some experimental evidence to support the benefits of holding infants. For example, children who were randomly assigned to be carried more by their mothers cried significantly less than infants who weren't.[30] In another study, low-income mothers were given either a baby sling or a car seat by the researchers. Children of mothers who had received the sling were carried more and were more securely attached than those who received the car seat. Furthermore, the mothers who received the sling were more responsive and sensitive to their infants than those who received the infant seat.[31]

Prior research has found that sensitive caregiving is a key precursor to children feeling securely attached to their caregivers.[32]

Thus these studies clearly show benefits of mothers spending time in close physical contact with their children. While the results appear to support the attachment parenting recommendation for baby wearing at first glance, we would like to provide a note of caution in interpreting the results. In the crying experiment, the positive effects of increased carrying were only measured until the infants were three months old. No evidence was provided as to whether carrying the infants enhanced their adjustment after that point, which is when crying naturally tends to decline.[33] Among the mothers who found benefits of using a baby sling, 48% reported that they used it every day at the two-month follow-up, and 48% reported using it two or three times a week.[34] Carrying a baby in a sling two or three times a week is a far cry from carrying a baby all day, every day!

Carrying an infant is a good idea, especially in the early months, if it feels comfortable and fits well within the parents' lifestyle. It is something that both a mother and father can do that may decrease crying and increase the bond between caregiver and child. I (ML) personally remember wanting to hold my babies as much as possible, but sometimes being tired or simply needing to feel my own body without a baby attached to it. Carrying and holding children is definitely beneficial, but this does not mean that more and more carrying is better and better. Taken to an extreme, mothers may feel guilty if they *ever* put their children down. Proponents of attachment parenting have inflamed this guilt by, for example, calling bouncers or strollers "neglectomatics"[35]

Benefits of Co-sleeping

Advocates of attachment parenting see co-sleeping as a natural extension of the increased physical contact promoted by baby wearing during the day, which increases the bond between parent and child. They argue that co-sleeping is the norm in other cultures where the sleep difficulties experienced in the United States are almost nonexistent.[36] However, co-sleeping is a rather controversial practice. There tend to be two major issues that people raise when it comes to co-sleeping—safety issues and children's level of independence.

One issue that has received a lot of attention pertains to potential safety risks. Data from the U.S. Consumer Product Safety Commission have been used to argue that bed sharing increases the risk of children suffocating due to parents rolling on top of their children or children being wedged into the bedding or bed structure.[37] Other research has found that there is a decrease in the risk of Sudden Infant Death Syndrome (SIDS) among infants who co-sleep with a parent.[38] However, in some SIDS studies these children are "co-sleeping" on a separate surface within close proximity of the parent. So it may be possible to get the benefits associated with co-sleeping without the risks associated with bed sharing.

Parents also worry that children who co-sleep will never sleep through the night in their own beds. Parents who co-sleep with their children do report more frequent night wakings that interfere with sleep.[39] In one study, children who slept by themselves showed more independent sleep behaviors. They were able to fall asleep on their own and slept through the night earlier than those who co-slept with their parents. However, children who co-slept demonstrated a different type of independence. They were earlier to develop self-reliance (e.g., getting dressed on their own) and social independence (e.g., making friends). However, these benefits were only observed for children who co-slept with their parents from an early age as part of their parents' general philosophy of child rearing as opposed to those who started co-sleeping later in life in response to sleep difficulties. The research does consistently point to the fact that when babies come into the parents' bed in reaction to sleep difficulties there is a relationship to negative outcomes. These reactive co-sleepers tend to wake up the most often during the night as well as have parents who find their night wakings to be most disruptive.[40]

However, none of the studies mentioned above were experimental. Rather, they simply describe the sleep patterns naturally selected by families. There may be differences between families that choose to co-sleep versus those who do not. Parents whose children sleep in a separate room have been found to be slightly older, married, white, and college educated.[41] These or other differences (e.g., better access to health care or a more regular routine during the day) could also account for differences in sleep outcomes. Therefore, we cannot conclude that sleeping arrangements *cause* differences in children's sleep safety or independence.

It appears that there are both advantages and disadvantages to co-sleeping. Thus parents need to weigh the evidence available and come to an informed decision about their sleeping choices. Sleep independence may be preferable for the two-working-parent lifestyle typical in the United States because sleep deprivation can have a significant impact on people's intellectual functioning as well as their mental and physical health.[42] On the other hand, some have argued that co-sleeping can enhance mother-child bonding for women who work outside the home and need not interfere with their ability to work.[43] We don't think there is a right or wrong answer here—the key is for parents to make choices that are consistent with their values and work best for their particular situations.

The benefits of choosing to co-sleep may have a lot to do with how well both parents and children are able to sleep when they share a bed. I (ML) am a light sleeper and immediately wake up if someone touches me while I sleep. Co-sleeping would not work for me because I simply could not sleep if my children were in my bed. On the other hand, we both have several friends who happily and successfully co-sleep. Thus, the decision to co-sleep is a personal one for a family and there is no "right" choice to make. As researchers of co-sleeping have noted: "The traditional habit of labelling one sleeping arrangement as being superior to another without an awareness of family, social and ethnic context is not only wrong but possibly harmful."[44]

Benefits of Breastfeeding

Attachment parenting promotes breastfeeding on demand until the child initiates the weaning process, which averages between two to four years old in other cultures. They argue that breastfeeding encourages frequent contact between the mother and child, extending the contact promoted by baby wearing and co-sleeping. Advocates for attachment parenting cite research on the benefits of breastfeeding, including better health, emotional attachment, and intellectual development.[45] In fact there is a good deal of research on the nutritional and health benefits of breastfeeding (although it may not be quite as strong as attachment-parenting advocates have suggested).

The American Academy of Pediatrics recommends that babies should be exclusively breastfed for six months, and for breastfeeding to continue up to a year and as long afterward as mutually desired by parent and infant.[46] They point to research indicating that the risk for a variety of illnesses is decreased when children are breastfed. The health benefits generally apply to being breastfed for the first six months. For example, babies who are breastfed during the first month of their life are at lower risk for SIDS. Those who are exclusively breastfed for three months have lower risks of asthma, allergies, and type 1 diabetes. Furthermore, any breastfeeding at all is related to decreased child obesity. Breastfeeding also has benefits for the mother, including decreased blood pressure[47] and stress response[48] as well as increased levels of confidence,[49] responsiveness to infant cues, and maternal role adjustment.[50]

Based on this research, many women experience an intense pressure to breastfeed.[51] Women who are unable to breastfeed or choose not to describe the pressure and guilt they feel from a variety of sources. One mother expressed these sentiments, saying: "I suppose it's the culture. Even some women think that the others are doing wrong if they don't breastfeed their babies."[52] The cultural expectations come through the media as well: "When you read magazines, you read books it's 'breast is best,' you must breast-feed . . . it was baby magazines, they used to freak me out. . . . It's that kind of pressure that just sticks in [your] head. . . . You've just had a baby, it's your first one, you've no idea what you're doing. . . . Baby magazines are horrendous. They made me so paranoid."[53] Women also feel pressure from health-care professionals to breastfeed and view themselves as bad mothers who have failed at their earliest childcare responsibility if they do not.[54] Women across all income levels complain that the information on breastfeeding is presented as if it is natural and easy and that they are not given enough support to help them successfully breastfeed.[55]

National correspondent for *The Atlantic* Hanna Rosin described the disdain and ostracism she encountered when she mentioned to mothers she had met at the playground that she might stop breastfeeding her child, saying: "The air of insta-friendship we had established cooled into an icy politeness."[56] Writer Jessica Valenti described the pressure she put on herself to breastfeed exclusively. She consulted with lactation advisors, drank oatmeal shakes, and tried to pump—every hour, even through the night—to increase her milk supply. She finally gave up pumping when she realized that what her daughter needed "more than breast milk was a mother who wasn't exhausted and stewing in shame."[57] Some women have even begun purchasing breast milk online in response to these feelings of pressure and guilt.[58] However, this approach likely misses many of the supposed benefits of breastfeeding, such as convenience, low cost, immune-system benefits, and mother-infant bonding, as well as increases some health risks if sanitary conditions for collecting, storing, and shipping the breast milk are not followed.[59]

Despite the benefits associated with breastfeeding described above, the data do not justify the intense pressure that many women feel to breastfeed. The studies on breastfeeding do not use the experimental designs necessary to draw causal conclusions. The only way to determine whether it is breastfeeding, per se, that causes the positive outcomes would be to do an experiment that randomly assigns some women to breastfeed and not others. It would be impossible to require some mothers to breastfeed (e.g., some women do not produce enough milk to breastfeed) and prohibit others from breastfeeding. However, data from an experimental study of an early-intervention program designed to increase breastfeeding found disappointing re sults. Approximately seventeen thousand mothers in a small, Eastern European country were randomly assigned to either a breastfeeding intervention that encouraged and supported breastfeeding or the "usual care" control group. Although women who received the intervention did breastfeed longer than those in the control group, there were no differences in health or emotional outcomes for either the mothers or their children.[60] Thus when random assignment was used to ensure that two groups were similar in all ways (e.g., education, income, and health problems) except the intervention training, breastfeeding did not have much of an effect on mother and child outcomes.

Despite this one experimental study, the vast majority of research on breastfeeding has compared women who choose to breastfeed with those who do not. In these studies, children who are breastfed may have better outcomes than those who are not, but that does not necessarily mean that breastfeeding is *causing* these outcomes. In other words, women who want to breastfeed may be different in other ways from those who do not. In fact breastfeeding is more common among mothers who are older, more highly educated, and from higher socioeconomic status (SES) backgrounds. [61] It is possible that many of the positive effects of breastfeeding may actually be due to these demographic differences. For example, there is substantial research that children raised in poverty are at risk for poor health, emotional, social, and academic outcomes. [62] This muddies the findings: Are the positive outcomes associated with breastfeeding actually caused by breastfeeding or are they due to the fact that, on average, women who breastfeed tend to have higher incomes and be better educated than those who do not?

One study attempted to account for the demographic differences (e.g., different education and income levels), between families who breastfed and those who did not. [63] This study had two components—comparing the outcomes of children from different families that did and did not breastfeed, like most studies do, and comparing siblings within the same family who were breastfed for different lengths of time. When comparing different families, breastfeeding was related to many positive outcomes in adolescents, including lower body mass index, higher grade-point average, lower rates of depression, and a closer mother-child relationship. No surprise there—these findings were similar to other studies demonstrating advantages of breastfeeding. But when looking at the sibling data, most of the benefits of breastfeeding disappeared. The only advantage found for children who were breastfed longer is that they understood slightly more words than their siblings. Thus many of the positive outcomes traditionally attributed to breastfeeding may not be caused by breastfeeding at all. They may be due to the fact that families who breastfeed are different than those who do not for many reasons. Furthermore, the results of *this* study cannot even be interpreted to mean that breastfeeding caused siblings who were breastfed longer to understand more words. There still could be some other issue (e.g., being born low birth weight) that interfered with both breastfeeding length and intellectual ability.

Understanding the bigger picture and the existing research helps put advice on breastfeeding in perspective. Based on the research, it appears that a more relaxed approach to breastfeeding is appropriate. While some research has suggested that there are certain health benefits for the infant and mother, it is likely that many of the benefits come from other aspects of parenting that are more common among people who breastfeed (e.g., higher income, close physical contact, etc.). [64] So children who are bottle fed, which can be done by both mothers *and* fathers, may receive many of the benefits associated with breastfeeding as long as they are held and cuddled during feedings. Furthermore, there is no research-based evidence that there are benefits of breastfeeding children beyond the first six months of life. Given the potential benefits, women are encouraged to breastfeed if it is possible given their life situation. However, the stress and strain that some women experience attempting to breastfeed might outweigh the benefits.

Attachment parenting demands significant time and resources. In addition, it involves an inherent assumption that mothers are the best people to carry out the majority of the attachment-parenting tasks and prioritizes a child's needs over the mother's. Indeed, mothers are the only ones who can breastfeed. Because of this, women who try to implement the attachment-parenting style may have difficulty finding work-family balance given the intensive demands it places on women's time and energy. Therefore, we think it is somewhat ironic that some feminists seem to be supporting this style of parenting. In a study that I (ML) conducted with colleagues, we found that women who identified themselves as feminists were actually *more* supportive of attachment-parenting practices than women who did not.[65] In contrast, some feminists have critiqued the notion of attachment parenting as being oppressive for women, saying: "It's a prison for mothers, and it represents as much of a backlash against women's freedom as the right-to-life movement."[66] The reality is that this "return to a supposedly simpler, more 'maternal' kind of parenting is being touted as the new feminist and feminine ideal."[67] Given the disproportionate burden that attachment parenting places specifically on mothers, it is difficult to argue that it is consistent with feminist ideals to help women become fully engaged in the workforce.

In conclusion, women put a great deal of pressure on themselves to feel as though they are parenting "right." The pressures to breastfeed are especially intense. However, the data do not justify the level of pressure that women feel from society, health-care providers, other women, and themselves. We think that women should approach breastfeeding and the other aspects of attachment parenting with a sense of moderation that allows them to maintain their sense of autonomy in choosing what is best for their family and situation. If these practices work for you and your lifestyle, that is great. Spending time holding your child and breastfeeding are both beneficial. But feeling pressure to do so and guilt if you cannot benefits no one.

Intellectual Stimulation in Moderation

Another domain in which parents fall prey to the "more must be better" mentality is in the realm of providing intellectual stimulation for their children. Much of the focus on how the environment impacts brain development stemmed from research conducted in the 1970s indicating that rats raised in impoverished environments (i.e., an empty cage) had smaller brains than those raised in enriched environments (i.e., with other rats and toys).[68] Given that children's brains are only about a quarter of their adult weight at birth and develop rapidly over the first five years of life,[69] discussion exploded over how to provide early intellectual stimulation that would promote optimal brain development.[70] Furthermore, if highly educated women opt out of the workforce to care for their children, the energy they once put into their work may become invested into their children's outcomes. Their full-time jobs become how to provide this type of enriched environment that will give their kids a "leg up" in the world. As one mother explains: "For nothing wrong that you did, your kids could wind up a mess, and there's your life's work."[71] So every moment of every day becomes a "teachable moment," from narrating what is outside of the car window while running errands to learning colors and letters using items in the grocery cart. Brigid Schulte describes the sense of pressure she felt to intellectually stimulate her child in her book *Overwhelmed*:

> All those tiny little neurons, we mothers were warned, needed to be properly "stimulated" or they would *disappear forever* before our babies could drink without a sippy cup. You could so easily be a bad mother, dulling your child's potential forever, if you didn't spend hours twirling those expensive black, white, and red mobiles over their heads, playing Mozart, or plopping them in front of those weird Baby Einstein videos that looked like something out of an acid-tripping Grateful Dead concert.[72]

This mentality has sparked parents to provide intellectual stimulation in utero by reading books and playing Mozart during pregnancy. After birth, parents continue to read to their infants and play classical music, but also take trips to the museum and give a blow-by-blow description of every aspect of daily life to ensure language development is on target, if not ahead of the curve. As technology has advanced, parents have begun purchasing videos geared toward promoting the intellectual development of infants (e.g., Baby Einstein) as well as playing computer games with infants on their laps. For example, Sesame Street has a game where an infant can randomly hit any key on the keyboard and make the letter appear on the screen along with a picture of something starting with that letter while an automated voice narrates (e.g., B is for ball). More recently, videos that claim to "Teach Your Baby to Read" have entered the market.[73] Companies are making a lot of money preying on the fears of parents that their children will fall behind and not be successful. But what is the evidence that any of this early stimulation works?

Similar to attachment parenting, there is research evidence supporting the benefits of many of the activities. However, the majority of this evidence is correlational, not causal, as well. Parents who have more education and higher incomes are also more likely to talk and read to their children as well as provide other forms of intellectual stimulation.[74] In addition to these environmental advantages, parents with more education may also provide a biological advantage. If people who are more intelligent are also more likely to earn advanced degrees and earn more money as a result, then their children also inherit a propensity for higher intelligence.[75] The best way to untangle these relationships is to conduct experiments where some children are randomly assigned to be intellectually stimulated and others are not. Of course, this type of experiment would not be practical (if you told people they could not read to their children, many would do it anyway) or ethical.

Enriched Environments

However, there has been a fairly extensive amount of experimental research on the impact of early intervention with children from low-income backgrounds, which can shed some light on the issue. A review of every randomized, controlled intervention intended to increase intelligence found that children from low-income families who attend early-intervention programs benefit considerably.[76] At the end of the intervention, children who participated in interventions scored an average of four to seven points higher on tests of intelligence than those who did not. Some of the effective interventions included training parents to model and encourage rich communication (e.g., asking children to describe events and speak in complete sentences) as well as to read in an interactive manner (e.g., ask open-ended questions about the book and elaborate on questions their children ask them). Thus early interventions targeting children from low-income backgrounds do seem to positively impact intelligence. When these children receive care in an environment rich with toys, books, and other people to interact with, they do better. When interventions encourage parents who would not normally talk or read to their children regularly to do so, it changes the home environment into a more enriching one and encourages language development. However, these results do not suggest that there is no upper limit to the benefits of reading, talking, and interacting with children.

The Mozart Effect

In addition to talking and reading, there has been a lot of discussion on the benefits of music on intelligence—the Mozart effect. Don Campbell's book *The Mozart Effect for Children* reviews research on the positive impact that music has on children's development.[77] He cites research that playing music in utero impacts brain development (i.e., more complex neuronal connections, especially in the part of the brain associated with hearing), and babies show a preference for music that they hear in the womb after they are born. But does music really make people smarter?

There actually has been little research to support that simply listening to music increases intelligence.[78] However, there is experimental evidence that musical training has a small, positive impact on children's scores on intelligence tests.[79] Positive effects of up to six IQ points have been found even when children had relatively brief training (e.g., an hour or less per week for several months).[80] So while taking music lessons may be beneficial, the evidence hardly suggests that intense music practice is necessary.

Technology

There are numerous electronic products being marketed to parents of infants and toddlers, despite the recommendation by the American Academy of Pediatrics that children under the age of two should not have any "screen time" (e.g., television, computer, and video games).[81] The Baby Einstein videos are probably the most well-known videos for children, with approximately 90% of the market share.[82] In 2007 a research study found that parents were introducing these videos to children (40% by age three months) largely because they thought the videos were educational.[83] However, for every hour per day children spent watching baby videos, infants understood approximately six to eight fewer words on average.[84] These data provided the advocacy group Campaign for a Commercial-Free Childhood with the ammunition they needed to get Disney (the company that owns Baby Einstein) to drop the word "educational" from their marketing materials as well as to offer a refund to parents who purchased the videos under the impression that they would make their children smarter. While there is probably not much harm in having children watch some television on occasion to keep them entertained while a parent needs to prepare a meal or take a break, the evidence suggests that watching these videos is not going to make them any smarter.[85]

The research on intellectual stimulation through talking, reading, music, and technology definitely does not suggest that parents need to intellectually stimulate their children every waking moment of the day. Providing intellectual stimulation is something parents could benefit from implementing in moderation. Children are intrinsically interested in learning. Any parent of a preschool-age child knows that one of the most common words they use is "why." So, if learning starts to feel like a job and is no longer enjoyable for the parent or the child, there is a problem. Reading books, talking with children, and listening to music should all be fun! If it stops being fun, then it is probably a sign that parents are past the optimal point in the inverted U-shaped curve.

In addition, it is also important to keep in perspective the practical importance of the gains in intelligence that can be made using these techniques. Even the best interventions only demonstrated an increase of six to seven IQ points for children from a low-income background. First of all, what is considered the normal range of intelligence varies from an IQ of 85 to 115. In addition, people are not classified as having impaired intelligence until their IQ is below 70 and they do not qualify as gifted unless their IQ is 130 or above. Given that there is a sixty-point IQ range between a diagnosis of intellectual disability and being gifted, a gain of six IQ points is really just a drop in the bucket. Second, there is no guarantee that the same benefit in intelligence found for children from low-income backgrounds would even be experienced by children from middle- to upper-middle-class homes. In other words, going from no reading to some reading benefits IQ, but reading more and more does not necessarily translate into higher and higher intelligence.

Extracurricular Activities in Moderation

The extent to which children engage in extracurricular activities is another area where moderation is best. This is especially the case for college-educated parents of older children who spend a significant amount of time bringing their children to one set of enrichment activities after another.[86] Annette Lareau, a sociologist, interviewed families across the income spectrum and found that middle- and upper-middle-class families had a particular philosophy of child rearing she termed "concerted cultivation." This philosophy involves parents actively fostering children's talents and involving children in adult-directed leisure activities (e.g., soccer practice) to promote these talents.

Being involved in extracurricular activities can have many positive benefits. It can increase children's social networks, psychological well-being, motivation, and grades.[87] One study found that involvement in academic/leadership activities and school clubs was particularly related to positive academic outcomes and GPA. Involvement in sports was not related to better grades but was associated with decreased high school dropout rates. This does not necessarily imply that involvement in activities causes these positive outcomes. It may simply be that children who are engaged in extracurricular activities are also more likely to be academically inclined.[88]

When Does It Become Too Much?

Some have argued that overscheduling can lead to stress and less time available to relax with friends and family as well as less time dedicated to academics.[89] There may be an upper limit beyond which participation in extracurricular activities does have detrimental effects. A study of tenth-grade students found that being involved in up to five extracurricular activities for up to fourteen hours a week had a positive effect on academic performance. However, involvement beyond this point was related to lower levels of academic achievement.[90] A study of urban, ethnically diverse eleventh-grade students found a similar inverted U-shaped relationship. Academic achievement, academic engagement, and a sense of belonging in school peaked when students were involved in two school-based extracurricular activity domains (e.g., leadership, arts, sports, or clubs).[91] However, when students reported being involved in more than two domains of activity, their achievement, belongingness, and engagement declined. Finally, the number of hours spent on activities (thirty per week on average) was related to higher levels of anxiety in upper-middle-class high school students in the suburbs of New York.[92]

In the documentary *Race to Nowhere*, these "cultivated" children described the pressure they felt to achieve: "You have to have all As. You have to have these extracurriculars."[93] When they got home from school after sports practice, they spent hours doing homework to ensure the requisite grades to get into a good college. Students described responding to these pressures through increased cheating, because they were unable to meet all of the demands placed on them, as well as mental health problems such as depression, anxiety, and self-injury. One student noted that there had been six suicides in her school district. Ironically, the very activities they were participating in to prepare them for life beyond high school seemed to be undermining their ability to function independently. One female student commented, "I wasn't eating. I wasn't taking care of myself." A male student said, "I couldn't cope." The excessive pressure in affluent families to achieve has been associated with increased depression—twice the national average— among seventh-grade girls.[94] Substance use (e.g., alcohol and drugs) was high for both males and females, which may be a sign of self-medication for the emotional distress they were experiencing. Children who had these negative outcomes tended to internalize the pressure for high achievement they felt from their parents, resulting in perfectionistic tendencies and fear of failure.

There appear to be two simultaneous pressures on parents. On the one hand, parents are under pressure to provide stimulation and engagement for their children. On the other hand, they are under pressure to avoid overscheduling their children. There have been several books railing against overscheduling, including *The Over-Scheduled Child*[95] and *The Pressured Child.*[96] One parent whose child had an active schedule complained: "To absorb the conventional wisdom in parenting circles these days, what we're doing to our children is cruel, overbearing and destructive to their long-term well-being."[97] Parents feel as though they are neglecting their children if they underschedule them and are tyrants if they overschedule them. How can parents find their way out of this conflict?

One way to figure out how many activities a child should be involved in is to conceptualize participation in extracurricular activities as the inverted U-shaped curve. The trick is to figure out how many activities are right for your child—there is no one-size-fits-all answer. However, quantity of activities is only one element in determining whether extracurricular activities are beneficial or harmful to children's well-being. The extent to which the activities enhance or interfere with the basic needs identified by self-determination theory may even be a better marker. Extracurricular activities have the potential to enhance children's autonomy, competence, and relatedness. Children can choose their own activities, develop competence in their areas of interest (e.g., soccer, piano, leadership, etc.) and form relationships with peers in those activities. The problem occurs when children are overscheduled to the point that it diminishes their sense of autonomy (i.e., they no longer have choices about how to spend their time), competence (i.e., they are unable to keep up with school work), and relatedness (e.g., they have less time with family and friends who are not involved in the extracurriculars). In other words, if children enjoy and are motivated by their activities, make friends doing them, and feel a sense of competence, then they are going to benefit from being engaged in them.

One mother of a child heavily engaged in travel soccer noted that friends wondered why they spent so much time and money on this sport. For this child, the soccer was motivating and provided a sense of competence: "Every season she is stronger, faster, more skilled—and she knows it."[98] Intense involvement in soccer increased the child's sense of autonomy, competence, and relatedness—there was a sense of connection with teammates and family support for her involvement. When my (ML) son tried soccer he commented to me: "I am the worst person on the team." For him, soccer did not increase a sense of competence, and he didn't continue playing. Keeping the principles of self-determination theory in mind may help parents determine whether the amount and type of activities their children are participating in works for their children and their situation.

THE RIGHT TYPE OF INVOLVEMENT

We have suggested that a sense of moderation in the *amount* of involvement is critical in a wide variety of parenting domains including attachment parenting, providing intellectual stimulation, and extracurricular activities. However, parents also need to be careful about the *type* of involvement they have when they interact with their children. Therefore, we think another area where moderation is important is in how much control parents exert over their children's behavior. While some control is necessary, and even beneficial, too much is not. So, what is the optimal amount?

Parental Control in Moderation

There are three well-known parenting styles that vary on the amount of control they use to elicit appropriate behavior from their children: permissive, authoritarian, and authoritative.[99] The description of these styles has a bit of a Goldilocks flair: Permissive parents are too lenient and allow their children to do anything they want. Although it might seem that these children would enjoy getting their way, this style of parenting is actually associated with reduced well-being. Authoritarian parents are too strict. They expect children to behave and their explanations are generally more along the lines of "because I said so." These parents have children who tend to be obedient, but not well-adjusted.[100]

Psychologists generally encourage parents to aim toward a level of control that is "just right" – neither too strict nor too lenient. Authoritative parents exhibit a moderate amount of control by setting age-appropriate behavioral limits and tend to have the most successful and happy children.[101] These parents have found the "sweet spot" on the inverted U-shaped curve. Children are given structure but are not overly controlled. This style of parenting ideally enhances a child's sense of autonomy and independent decision making. The tricky thing about attempting to be an authoritative parent is that the optimal amount of control is a constantly moving target. For example, it is appropriate for parents to provide almost constant supervision of their two-year-old child, do the majority of things for him, rush to the rescue when he needs help, and scoop him up in their arms during times of trouble. However, that same level of parental involvement would not be appropriate for a teenager. Parents who start out as authoritative may find themselves slipping away from the optimal amount of control if they do not adjust their level of involvement as their children get older. When parents move in to wipe their teenager's nose, they may have missed the target!

There are different ways parents can exhibit control over their children's behavior. Having clear expectations about appropriate behavior and consistently enforcing consequences for inappropriate behavior has been related to positive child outcomes.[102] Another way of controlling behavior is through the use of psychological methods that are manipulative of children's thoughts and emotions, such as guilt trips (e.g., "I carried you for nine months in my womb and this is the gratitude that I get?"). As tempting as it may be to use guilt, this method is associated with negative outcomes.[103] Research consistently has shown that psychological control is associated with higher rates of anxiety and depression across a variety of age ranges and cultures[104] as well as increased behavior problems and risk-taking behaviors.[105] Using guilt and coercive techniques are particularly damaging to children because they intrude on the child's psychological development and sense of autonomy,[106] which are essential to well-being.

Autonomy Support

Parents generally want their children to do what they want them to do—this is known as "behaving." However, a parenting style that explicitly supports a child's sense of autonomy and independent decision making, rather than a style that focuses on getting the child to do what the parent wants, is related to numerous positive benefits.[107] Parents who provide autonomy support are able to take their children's point of view, provide them with choices (within reason), and assist their children in developing personal values and interests.[108] The benefits of autonomy-supportive parenting have been demonstrated in children from infancy through college.[109] Mothers who provided autonomy support by encouraging their one-year-old children to continue playing with the toy they selected had children who were more engaged and competent when playing alone eight months later compared to mothers who were more controlling of their children's play.[110] Children with mothers who provided autonomy support at age five had better social and academic adjustment as rated by their third-grade teachers as well as higher reading achievement scores.[111] In adolescence, autonomy support was associated with better social and academic competence, a higher GPA, and greater intention to search for a job after graduation.[112] In addition, university students who perceived higher levels of parental autonomy support reported higher GPAs.[113] Autonomy support has also been associated with higher levels of self-determination[114] and greater well-being.[115]

It is important to note that supporting a child's autonomy is not the same thing as encouraging the child's independence—even though these terms are often used interchangeably in day-to-day conversation. Autonomy support refers to assisting children in making choices that are consistent with their values; whereas independence refers to children being able to function separately from their parents. Research has found that autonomy-supportive parenting was related to well-being (e.g., lower depression, higher self-esteem, and higher social well-being), while parenting that promoted independence was not.[116] It is possible that some parents may push children to be independent before they are ready (e.g., "You're eighteen now, so it's time to move out."). If parents do not take their children's feelings and perspectives into account and allow them to make their own choices, then they are actually being controlling rather than autonomy supportive.

Helicopter Parenting

There has been a lot of media coverage of helicopter parents who "hover" over their children and swoop down to rescue them in times of need. This exemplifies the problems associated with parenting that is too involved and controlling rather than autonomy supportive. Interestingly, the research on the effects of helicopter parenting has been somewhat mixed depending on how it is defined. A closer examination of the research reveals that it is not involvement, per say, that is problematic, but a controlling type of involvement that violates the child's sense of autonomy.

Studies that focus on the amount rather than type of support that children receive from their parents find results consistent with the idea that involvement can have positive effects. One study found that students with higher levels of parental contact were more engaged in learning, had higher personal competence, and had better social development.[117] Another study looked at the effect of intense support on grown children's (aged eighteen to forty-one) level of psychological adjustment and life satisfaction.[118] In this study, about 20% of adult children reported receiving various types of support (e.g., emotional support, practical support, socializing, advice, financial support, and listening to talk about daily events) from their parents several times a week. Adult children who received this amount of intense support were more likely to have a clear sense of their goals and higher life satisfaction. Thus when helicopter parenting is defined as being very involved and giving a great deal of support to children, it appears to be related to positive outcomes.

However, when studies define helicopter parenting as a controlling kind of involvement, negative outcomes tend to be observed. Even studies that found the overall amount of involvement benefited student outcomes, showed that controlling involvement did not. For example, when parents intervened on their college students' behalf, students earned lower grades.[119] When helicopter parenting was measured by items such as "My parents supervised my every move growing up" and "I sometimes felt that my parents didn't feel I could make my own decisions," college students reported decreased psychological well-being and increased use of medications for depression and anxiety.[120] Another study found that overparenting was related to higher levels of narcissism and less effective coping abilities, which were associated with higher levels of anxiety and stress among college-age children.[121]

Helicopter parenting, defined as the extent to which parents make decisions and solve problems for their children, has been found to be related to less autonomy and school engagement.[122] However, helicopter parenting was also related to some positive aspects of parenting, including feeling more guidance, disclosure, and emotional support. It may be that sometimes adult children would like parents to help them solve problems, and when parents do so, the child feels closer to them. If a child is having trouble in a class, they may ask a parent for help. The parent might serve as a sounding board for how to approach the professor and even role-play the conversation. This interaction would provide the support the student needs to approach the professor. However, it's a far cry from parents who call the president of the university to complain about how the professor is mistreating their child. Thus when parents provide help at their children's request, it does not necessarily interfere with their children's sense of autonomy. On the other hand, if a child is having a problem in class and is not seeking parental advice, continual reminders to talk to the teacher may be perceived as controlling. When involvement is not initiated by the child, it can have a sense of "too muchness," which can be related to negative outcomes.

We conducted a study to determine whether helicopter parenting led to negative mental health outcomes specifically because this style of parenting interferes with children's autonomy, competence, and relatedness. We defined helicopter parenting as behaviors such as monitoring who their college-age child spends time with, having a say in choosing a major, intervening in a fight with a roommate, and calling a professor. These behaviors are not simply about being involved and close, but reflect a level of parental monitoring of adult children that is intrusive and controlling.

College-age children who reported that their mothers engaged in helicopter parenting felt lower levels of autonomy, competence, and relatedness. Feelings of decreased autonomy and competence were related to increased depressive symptoms and decreased satisfaction with life. The sense of decreased competence associated with helicopter parenting had the strongest relationship with decreased well-being. We think that when parents intervene on behalf of their adult children, they send the likely unintentional message that they do not think their children are competent enough to complete the task. Furthermore, they are not giving their children the opportunity to practice handling difficult situations and solving problems, so their kids do not develop competence in these areas. We also think it is interesting that even though these parents were highly involved in their children's lives, their children reported feeling a lower sense of relatedness. The intensity of involvement may have had the opposite effect of what was intended by the parent (i.e., damaging rather than bolstering the parent-child relationship).

This type of controlling parenting style was taken to a new level when Amy Chua, author of *The Battle Hymn of the Tiger Mother*, described how she believed Chinese mothers raise successful children.[123] Chua lists the things that she never allowed her daughters to do, in order to focus on academic excellence and sanctioned extracurricular activities, including: "attend a sleepover, have a playdate, be in a school play, complain about not being in a school play, watch TV or play computer games, choose their own extracurricular activities, get any grade less than an A, not be the No. 1 student in every subject except gym and drama, play any instrument other than the piano or violin." However, research suggests that "tiger mothering" does not lead to well-adjusted, successful children as Chua argues.[124] Instead, children of "tiger mothers" actually have lower academic achievement and report feeling more academic pressure. They also feel a lower sense of family obligation, more depressive symptoms, and a greater sense of alienation compared to children of more supportive Asian-American parents.

Although parents likely have the best of intentions when they hover over their children to help them with every possible need, it may actually be undermining children's motivation to complete tasks on their own. Research has shown that even just thinking about how supportive or helpful someone has been in the past can decrease the effort people spend doing a task.[125]

When parents provide a lot of assistance with their children's school work they may be creating a cycle of more and more dependence on parental help in the future.

In addition, parental "help" may undermine children's competence in completing tasks independently. In cultures where children are given more responsibility, their children make themselves useful and are more independent. Among the Matsigenka people of Peru, toddlers cook their own food over the fire. By contrast, in a family living in Los Angeles, "an eight-year-old girl sat down at the dining table. Finding that no silverware had been laid out for her, she demanded, 'How am I supposed to eat?' Although the girl clearly knew where the silverware was kept, her father got up to get it for her."[126] When parents do everything for their children, they may never become competent enough to do these tasks for themselves. So, it is just easier for parents to do it, which perpetuates the cycle of dependence. It seems as if everyone would benefit from giving children more responsibility and less "enrichment"—parents would have help around the house and children would develop competence in skills that are vital to being successful adults.

Parent Outcomes

This level of overinvolvement is not good for parents either. When parents think that they are providing more assistance to their children than other parents do, they are less satisfied with their lives.[127] All of the pressure to parent "correctly" leads parents, especially mothers, to report feeling an enormous amount of guilt. Maternal guilt is such a pervasive feeling that some have argued it has an evolutionary basis—guilt ensures that mothers will provide adequate care that ensures the survival of their offspring.[128] Although it is unclear why mothers feel so much guilt, it *is* clear from the research that it is an extremely common experience. Mothers who work often feel guilty because they pay someone else to be with their children and may think they are not spending enough time with them.[129] Fighting back tears, one mother said:

> He'll say things like, 'No Mommy, stay now.' And that really tugs at my feelings of guilt. And then he gets settled. I know what he does all day because they write it down for us, but there's a lot of things that I really miss [crying] . . . like his first experience going to a zoo or riding the train in the park. To be able to see his responses to these things . . . I'm always the second one to see them. We try to repeat the activities but I don't think it's ever the same [crying]. . . . It's like somebody else is raising my child![130]

Mothers who stay home with their children may feel guilty about not earning additional income that would allow more opportunities for their children and about not fulfilling their own career goals.[131] One mother realized: "Once I made the decision, I felt a lot of relief and I went through kinda a depression, mourning, kinda, 'Oh my God.' Because I had given up my dream or my identity and it's still hard."[132] Women feel guilty because they cannot live up to the "motherhood myth,"[133] that mothers must completely devote themselves to their children because they are fully responsible for their outcomes.[134] When women are unable to meet this expectation, they may perceive themselves as "bad" mothers.[135]

We conducted a study explicitly testing the hypothesis that mothers feel guilty because they fail to live up to societal standards for being an ideal mother.[136] We also wondered whether people who were concerned about what others thought of them might be more likely to feel guilty because they not only fall short of the ideal standard in their own minds, but also fear what others think of them. We asked mothers with children under the age of five how much they thought that the ideal mother had various qualities (e.g., loving, patient, responsible, etc.) as well as to what extent they exhibited those qualities. Women who reported a discrepancy between their qualities as a mother and those of the ideal mother experienced higher levels of guilt and shame. However, it was really only women who worried a lot about what others thought of them who reported these negative outcomes. Women who have unrealistic expectations for what it means to be a mother, and experience guilt and shame as a result, may be at increased risk for negative outcomes such as depression.[137]

If people constantly strive to meet the incredibly high standards of being an ideal parent, they may begin to feel that parenting is very difficult. While approximately three-fourths of the mothers interviewed in one study felt this way, one mother summed up the sentiment well, saying:

> I think the hardest job in the world is being a mom. I really do. I will argue the matter with any corporate lawyer. See if they can do that twenty-four hours a day. This is a job that, if it were any other job, you would have to wear a beeper around your neck. You're on call constantly. Your life is not your own anymore after you have a child, because it's theirs."[138]

What are the consequences for parents of holding this belief? We did a study and found that when mothers believed that parenting was the hardest job in the world, they had higher levels of stress and depressive symptoms and less satisfaction with life.[139]

Based on our study, we cannot rule out the possibility that people who are more stressed and depressed view being a mother as harder, but we think that when people view their role as a parent as the hardest job in the world it is a sign that something is out of balance. People who solely focus on parenting may be missing the benefits of participating in multiple roles and having a sense of balance in their lives (see chapter 2). There can certainly be benefits to focusing on children. One study found that parents who were more child centered and spent more time with their children received a greater sense of joy from them than parents who were less child centered. [140] However, in our study, we found that parents who indicated that they made their children the center of their lives actually reported lower levels of satisfaction with their lives in general. [141] It is possible that parents who are child centered may obtain a great deal of joy from their children, but may gain less joy from their nonparenting roles. If so, the answer seems to be finding a sense of balance and moderation.

WHAT MOTIVATES OVERINVOLVED PARENTING?

In her book *Parenting out of Control: Anxious Parents in Uncertain Times*, Margaret Nelson describes the anxiety underlying intensive parenting. [142] She identifies multiple factors associated with the movement toward highly involved, controlling parents. As might be expected, parents who are anxious in the first place are more likely to be overinvolved and overcontrolling. [143] They try to reduce their own worries by controlling their environment, including their children. In addition, there is a general sense that the world is a less safe place to raise children than it used to be. [144] As a result, families have shifted from allowing their children to have unstructured free play to enrolling them in more structured, adult-supervised activities. [145] This pattern has resulted in parents having considerably more control over where their children are and who they are with than the days when I (HS) was a kid. We had a several-block area where we were allowed to play and the rule was that we came home when the street lights came on. Other than that, my parents had little knowledge of how or with whom I spent my time.

It has been hypothesized that much of the stress about raising children revolves around anxiety about college admissions. [146] Parents' sense of economic uncertainty and competitiveness in the marketplace leads them to want to prepare their children to get into the best college. They hope a good education will allow their children to get a good job and, ultimately, be successful. One mother interviewed by Brigid Schulte in the book *Overwhelmed* stated: "I worry about them getting into college. And it feels like people are panicked because they can't identify the formula for success anymore." [147]

Parents who view their children's success as a personal reflection upon themselves may be particularly motivated to overparent. One study examined whether mothers are more likely to act in a controlling manner when they feel pressure for their children to succeed. [148] Half of the parents were told to make sure their children performed "well enough" (the high-pressure group), and the other half of parents were told that there was no particular way that the child had to perform (the low-pressure group) on the study tasks. Mothers who were in the high-pressure condition were more likely to use controlling techniques such as solving the problem for their child or giving unsolicited help or directions. Children of controlling mothers performed worse on the study tasks than those whose mothers were autonomy supportive. So if parents are acting in a controlling manner to try to help their children be more successful (e.g., doing their school projects for them so they'll get better grades), it may actually backfire.

A controlling parenting style may also stem from anxiety that the world is a threatening and unstable place in which children are not guaranteed success. Parents from the study described above were mailed follow-up questions about their perception of the world and the extent to which they saw the world as threatening and unstable (e.g., it makes me nervous to think about all the dangers kids are exposed to these days; there are not enough opportunities out there for everyone; it's getting harder and harder all the time to make a decent living).[149] Parents who saw the world as more threatening were more likely to use a controlling parenting style. They and their children were also more likely to focus on grades than whether children learned school material. Thus a sense of anxiety or insecurity about the future may drive parents to be more controlling and children to work only for the sake of getting ahead, rather than for an intrinsically motivated love of learning.

A final factor that contributes to parents' level of involvement is the recent advances in technology.[150] When we were in college, there was one pay phone for an entire hall. Both of us had conversations with our mothers once a week at a specified time. We could call more frequently if there was an emergency, but things like being upset with a roommate over her cleanliness (or lack thereof) or getting a lower grade on a paper than we thought we deserved did not constitute an emergency. We had to solve these problems ourselves or seek support from friends on campus. However, many college freshmen today communicate with their parents almost twice a day, largely by cell phone or e-mail.[151] This level of communication represents a significant amount of time investment for parents that may interfere with work-family balance.

Many parents have anxiety that the world isn't safe, so they feel they have to monitor their children more carefully. They have anxiety that the economy is not as good as it used to be, so they have to ensure their children have the right grades and activities to get into a good college and, subsequently, get a good job. The high parental investment in children has blurred the lines between children's needs and the needs of their parents. So parents view their children's accomplishments as an extension of themselves and fear being judged by others if their children are not successful.[152] The advances in modern technology have given parents the mechanism for keeping in constant contact with their children so that they can monitor their progress in every domain if they wish to do so. In general, when the world is seen as an insecure and threatening place and children are seen as projects that must be perfected in order to ensure their success in life, parenting can become an all-consuming and daunting project.

STOP THE MADNESS

While middle- to upper-middle-class parents are busy "cultivating" their children with numerous activities and extensive explanations, working-class parents often opt for an emphasis on "natural growth."[153] While it is clear from the research that children from higher-income backgrounds have many advantages over children from lower-income families,[154] there are benefits associated with a parenting style that allows children to develop more naturally, without aś much parental intervention. Working-class parents tend to provide for children's food, love, and safety, but otherwise allow children to develop naturally. They do not typically center their lives on their children's preferences but set limits that they expect their children to follow without question. However, within those limits, children are given a great deal of freedom. These children tend to participate in fewer extracurricular activities, so they have more time for unstructured, child-led play, which allows them to negotiate social rules (e.g., who will be "it") and solve their own problems (e.g., what happens if someone breaks the rules of the game). Children from working-class and poor families also tend to have close relationships with their extended family—often having birthday parties at home with relatives as opposed to their friends.

A similar dynamic was found in parents from Canada who demonstrated "organismic trust," or the belief that they did not have to intervene in order for their children to grow and develop.[155] Mothers who had higher levels of "organismic trust" were less likely to compare their children to others and more likely to provide autonomy support for their one-year-olds while they completed a puzzle. One year later, these same mothers were better adjusted to their role as a parent, and their children had fewer behavior problems. In other words, trusting that a child will develop naturally without excessive intervention is related to supporting the child's autonomy, which is associated with healthy development in children and feeling satisfied as a parent. Furthermore, the differences could not be explained just by looking at parents' general level of anxiety or how easy the children were to parent.

Parenting in a more relaxed manner seems to have benefits for the development of children's self-determination. Children with parents who believe that they will naturally grow have more autonomy in selecting their activities within the limits set by their parents.[156] They also have additional opportunities to develop social competence by playing with their peers without adult supervision. Finally, research suggests that children from lower-income families spend more time developing deep relationships with their extended family than their higher-income peers.[157] Recent initiatives to examine the strengths of children from lower-income families support the notion that they have better social competence and stronger family ties.[158] Thus a more relaxed approach to parenting that supports children's natural inclinations and autonomy can enhance children's intrinsic motivation to engage with the environment, learn, and ultimately succeed.[159]

CONCLUSION

Research has clearly established that it is beneficial for children when their parents are involved in their education and activities. Many studies have pointed to the benefits of parents holding, talking to, reading to, and providing their children with activities that help them develop and learn. Children with more involved parents tend to perform better academically, have more friends, and exhibit fewer behavior problems. However, these benefits are found when researchers compare parents who are generally uninvolved to parents who already play an active role in their children's lives. When going from low involvement to moderate involvement, the benefits are numerous. However, just because some involvement is good does not mean that more and more involvement is better and better. We think the relationship of parental involvement to child outcomes can be understood as an inverted U-shaped curve. Too little involvement is associated with less than optimal child outcomes. As parental involvement increases child outcomes improve; but at some point, the benefits of involvement reach their peak. Parental involvement in excess of this point may actually have a negative impact on children and parents. When parents are constantly feeling guilty and thinking that parenting is the hardest job in the world, it is probably a sign that they have passed the optimal level of involvement and are sliding down the other side of the inverted U-shaped curve. There is more than one "right way" to parent—children will develop naturally under a wide range of healthy circumstances. Parents need to focus on being "good enough" rather than perfect.[160] We suggest that one way to increase work-family balance is to decrease the stress associated with parenting by viewing it as something best done in moderation.

Chapter Four

Balance at Work

As we discussed in chapter 2, being involved in work is good for people's well-being. But just because something is good does not mean that more and more of it is better and better. Work can also be stressful and detract from physical and mental health. Men in particular may feel pressure to overwork because being a provider is a central component of masculinity.[1] However, women are under increasing pressure to prioritize work, to "lean in."[2] The problem with this advice is that it does not represent a very balanced approach. An alternative would be to encourage people who are letting work dominate their lives to "lean out." Expectations that ideal workers should dedicate themselves entirely to their work are harmful for both men and women. Robin Ely, a professor at Harvard Business School, noted:

> There is a culture of overwork in many organizations. There is a certain number of hours we're expected to work and an amount we are expected to travel, and we know that these are some of the things that push women out. This culture affects men as well. The most often-cited barrier to women's advancement was that they prioritize family over work. However, it's not clear that men don't prioritize family over work or that they don't find personal relationships important. . . . My male students have gotten most engaged in this topic when we start talking about it from this perspective. Some of them have young families, most of them want to have families, and they worry a lot about what kind of parents they are going to be while maximizing success in their careers.[3]

Both men and women would benefit from examining how their attitude toward work affects their health and well-being. Balance between work and family cannot be achieved without a careful examination of work.

THE EFFECTS OF OVERWORKING

Being employed has clear benefits in terms of people's physical and mental health compared to being unemployed (see chapter 2).[4] Working provides an opportunity for people to feel self-determined by having their need for autonomy, competence, and relatedness met, which increases overall well-being.[5] However, working an excessive amount may actually decrease well-being because it demands so much time and energy that it interferes with the ability to function in other social roles. In order to achieve work-family balance, it is important to find the "sweet spot" in the inverted U-shaped curve as an employee to avoid the negative impacts associated with being either unemployed or a workaholic. Although being involved in multiple roles benefits well-being, it is important to find balance among these roles so that they provide a sense of enrichment rather than feelings of being overwhelmed.

People who are more engaged at work tend to experience more individual well-being and are more likely to have the positive emotions of work benefit their family lives.[6] However, negative physical and mental health consequences occur when work involvement becomes too extensive. People who report work overload experience higher rates of injury, illness, and disease.[7] In a review of twelve studies looking at the relationship between work hours and heart disease, it was concluded that overwork was related to a 40% increase in the chance of having a heart attack.[8] Working overtime also has adverse effects on mental health. In a review of twenty studies, the majority found a link between working long hours and experiencing poor mental health such as depression and anxiety.[9] In addition, the negative mental health effects of working overtime appear to be more severe for women than men. One longitudinal study of British civil servants found that working over fifty-five hours a week was related to doubling the risk of depression and anxiety for women with no previous history of these problems. However, the increased risk was not found for men.[10]

Why Does Overworking Decrease Well-Being?

Lack of sleep and chronic stress are two of the biggest reasons overworking adversely affects well-being. Both have detrimental effects for physical health, intellectual abilities (e.g., memory), and mental health.[11] People in Japan who had less than six hours of sleep per day due to long work hours (i.e., over ten hours per day) were more likely to experience depression than those who worked a similar number of hours but slept more.[12] Since the mid-1990s, Japan has experienced a sharp increase in *karo-jisatsu*, a term used when workers commit suicide due to depression associated with work overload.[13] The wear and tear on the body due to chronic stress associated with such adverse working conditions has serious health consequences.[14] In fact,

Japan even uses the word *karoshi* to describe the phenomenon of people working themselves to death.[15]

People's perception of their workload seems to be particularly critical for well-being. In a study of Canadian mothers, the *perception* of being over-loaded by role obligations was strongly related to negative mental health.[16] However, it was not having multiple roles (e.g., mother and employee) per se that impacted well-being because mothers who worked (either part time or full time) had better mental health than those who were not employed. It was only women who felt overloaded by their role commitments who experienced negative mental health consequences. In other words, it may be less about how much people work than how they feel about their work. When work feels overwhelming or out of balance, there are negative health and mental health consequences. But when work feels challenging and invigorating—even if someone is working a lot—there are fewer negative consequences.

Finally, a key to determining whether work feels overwhelming versus challenging and invigorating may be the extent to which work meets people's needs for autonomy, competence, and relatedness.[17] As we reviewed in chapter 2, work is intrinsically motivating when people have control over their day-to-day activities, are able to demonstrate competence through meeting the challenges of their jobs, and have good relationships at work.[18] The extent to which work allows people to meet these basic needs for well-being may also increase employees' intrinsic motivation to work long hours. Furthermore, if working long hours is seen as an autonomous, intrinsically motivated decision, it likely offsets the potential negative effects of long work hours.[19]

Conversely, when people work long hours for external reasons, it can impede their ability to meet their intrinsic psychological needs of autonomy, competence, and relatedness. Being compelled to overwork decreases people's sense of autonomy—feeling that others control how they spend their time decreases well-being. Furthermore, overwork can detract from competence both at work (when fatigue interferes with performance) and at home (where overwork can result in being less available at home). Finally, overwork can detract from relatedness both at work, if resentment about work hours builds up, and outside of work, as interpersonal relationships suffer due to overwork. There are two main external reasons why people may focus on work other than the intrinsic rewards of working. These are the demanding and inflexible expectations of work environments and the belief that making more money is the path to greater happiness.

CORPORATE EXPECTATIONS: LONG, INFLEXIBLE HOURS

One reason that people work long hours is that they don't have a choice—corporate America requires it. The number of hours spent working is considerably higher in the United States than in other industrialized nations. Although full-time work is generally considered to be forty hours per week, many companies expect substantially more. For example, in highly paid professional contexts there is often an expectation that employees should work over fifty hours per week.[20] One study found that the percentage of salaried men who worked more than fifty hours per week rose from 22.7% in 1980 to 32.2% in 2001.[21] In contrast, the European Union has put forth a policy limiting working hours to forty-eight per week, and some countries limit hours even more (e.g., France has a thirty-five-hour workweek).[22] In addition, in the European Union, workers are given a minimum of four weeks paid vacation per year, which many countries exceed. In the United States, the number of vacation days is left to the discretion of employers.[23] The United States is twenty-fifth out of thirty-two countries on work-family balance based on the number of men and woman that work more than fifty hours a week.[24]

One reason that work environments are so demanding and inflexible is that expectations for work were developed at a time when the vast majority of earners were single-income earners with stay-at-home wives.[25] In a study of male managers who worked more than sixty hours per week, 99% had stay-at-home wives.[26] However, most families are not living with these traditional arrangements anymore. According to the Bureau of Labor and Statistics, in 2012 both parents were employed in two-thirds of couples (65.4%) with children under the age of eighteen.[27] Furthermore, about a fourth of all children lived in a single-parent household with their mother.[28] Thus employer expectations for long work hours that can only be met if workers have a full-time, at-home spouse are based on outdated assumptions about families.

The expectations for long work hours affect men and women across all income levels. In lower-income jobs, managers often hire workers who have maximum flexibility in their schedules and require employees to work mandatory overtime. For example, a divorced mother was working sixty hours per week as a janitor—ten-hour days, six days a week including Saturdays.[29] Also many low-paying jobs often have inconsistent or unstable work schedules as well as nontraditional work hours on nights and weekends. For example, many retail establishments use "just in time" scheduling where the company bases the next week's schedule on how many people were in the store at the same time during the prior week. Starbucks utilizes a program called "optimal scheduling" where workers must make themselves available for 70% of the store's operating hours (approximately eighty hours per week) in order to get a full-time schedule.[30] Employees may not know their schedules until the last minute or may have to work when traditional childcare facilities are closed, which makes it extremely difficult to plan for childcare.

On the upper end of the income spectrum, highly paid professionals are working longer hours than ever with no overtime pay for salaried employees. In the past, members of the upper class would distinguish themselves by the amount of time spent in leisure rather than the amount of time spent in work. However, working long hours is currently a sign of workplace commitment and is seen as a badge of honor.[31] One Silicon Valley worker noted: "Guys try to out-macho each other. . . . There's a lot of see how many hours I can work, whether or not you have a kid. He's a real man; he works 90-hour weeks. He's a slacker; he works 50 hours a week."[32] Sheryl Sandberg, the chief operating officer (COO) of Facebook, described how she had wanted to arrive at 9:00 a.m. and leave the office at 5:30 p.m. when she had her first child. She would try to hide her "reduced" work hours by scheduling the first and last meetings of the day in other buildings and bolting to her car in the evening so that no one would see her.[33]

Ironically, a review of the research concluded that working longer hours at the office is actually associated with decreased productivity.[34] It is possible that if workers know that they have to work long hours, they are not motivated to work at maximum capacity for every hour they are at work. I know for a few years when I (ML) was limiting hours at the office before my children started school, I approached each hour of my job with laser-focused intensity and, despite reduced hours, my productivity stayed relatively stable. Working long hours also has been associated with decreased productivity due to increased fatigue and mistakes on the job. One study found that white-collar employees who worked sixty or more hours a week experienced a 20% drop in productivity.[35]

In a world where sixty hours a week is expected and a forty-hour work-week would be considered career suicide, it would be impossible for both parents to work on such a fast-paced track. Generally, this results in one parent cutting back or leaving the workforce. In almost all cases, it is the woman who reduces her hours due to beliefs that women should be the primary caregivers and the resulting gap in pay between men and women (see chapter 5 and 7 for a full discussion of these issues). The more hours their husbands work, the more likely women are to stop working. Women whose husbands worked more than forty-five hours per week were more likely to leave the workplace than those who had husbands who worked forty hours a week.[36] This pattern holds even when women have a level of education similar to their husband's. For example, a study of men working at four major companies found that although almost no fathers were working part-time (0.2%), over a fourth of their wives were, despite having similar levels of education.[37]

In addition to requiring long hours, the work environment tends to be very inflexible in terms of when and where the hours must be completed—primarily during business hours at the office. In her analysis of work-family conflict, Joan Williams describes numerous parents who have been fired for being late or having to take care of their children, especially children with illness. [38] For example, the janitor described above working sixty-hour weeks had to miss a Saturday to take care of her son who required chronic care due to a disability. She called her workplace several times to explain the situation but was fired for missing work. Other examples include a bus driver who was fired because she was three minutes late when her son had an asthma attack and a teacher who was fired because she took a personal day to care for her child when her childcare provider was sick. Fathers who lose work time to care for children are also penalized. Union arbitration records show fathers have been disciplined or fired when caring for diabetic children, a son with a gunshot wound, and children who have attempted suicide. Of course, most employees are not members of unions that advocate for them; therefore, the majority of workers who are disciplined or fired for missing work to care for their children have no advocates, no record of what has happened, and no appeal of the final decision.

A Solution: Increased Workplace Flexibility

Policies promoting flexibility in the workplace (e.g., flextime and telecommuting) that allow people to balance work and family life are considered one of the key signs of a healthy work environment. [39] Research has consistently shown that initiatives reducing work-family conflict have positive effects by increasing worker satisfaction which, in turn, increases productivity as well as decreases absenteeism and turnover. Thus workplace flexibility has advantages for both the worker and the company. Workers who perceive flexibility in how and when their job gets done benefit from greater work-family balance. [40] Companies benefit from workplace flexibility through increased employee productivity. Productivity may increase because workers are grateful to their employers and, thus, work harder for the company. Additionally, flexibility is related to increased worker well-being, which allows the worker to maximize performance. A comprehensive review of the literature did not identify a single study linking flexibility policies to decreased performance. [41]

Workplace flexibility policies may promote employees' well-being and productivity by enhancing their needs for autonomy, competence, and relatedness. [42] Workplace policies promoting flexibility are intended to provide employees with autonomy in determining when, where, and how they complete their work. A review of forty-six studies involving 12,883 employees found that telecommuting benefits employees by providing them with a sense of autonomy, job satisfaction, and decreased stress. [43] In turn, telecommuting benefits the company because increased autonomy was associated with increased productivity and decreased intention to leave the company—employee turnover is extraordinarily expensive for an organization. Similarly, workers who were given autonomy to set their own daily schedules (i.e., work hours could vary on a daily basis) had increased productivity, quality of work, job satisfaction, and plans to stay with the company than those with more traditional work schedules.[44]

The increased worker productivity observed in the review of telecommuting studies[45] seems to suggest that it is generally beneficial for employees' sense of competence as well, because they are still able to meet and exceed the demands of the job. However, there is some evidence that the impact of telecommuting on competence may vary based on the type of job being performed. Organizations that primarily focus on knowledge creation and other creative endeavors may be negatively impacted when employees telecommute. These managers rated people who telecommuted as less adept at problem solving because they could not bounce ideas off of their coworkers.[46] Thus the effects of telecommuting on perceived competence may vary by occupation.

Finally, telecommuting decreases "face time" at the office, so it is possible that it might decrease the quality of relationships (i.e., relatedness) among coworkers. One study found that when people telecommute less than 2.5 days a week, their relationships with coworkers did not suffer. In fact, telecommuting was actually related to a more positive relationship between supervisor and employee![47] When telecommuting exceeded 2.5 days a week, coworker relationships were negatively affected, although supervisor-employee relationships still did not suffer. However, people who telecommuted more than 2.5 days per week experienced a reduction in work-family conflict, which suggests that relationships at home may benefit from telecommuting.[48] It appears that there may be an optimal amount (i.e., approximately 50% of the workweek) of time for people to telecommute—the classic inverted U-shaped relationship. Too much or too little time at the office may adversely affect relationships at home or at work, respectively.

Employers may be skeptical of workplace flexibility policies, such as telecommuting, because they fear that the increased autonomy they give workers may come at the cost of productivity (i.e., competence) and work relationships (i.e., relatedness). However, these fears appear to be unfounded. The majority of research has suggested that workplace flexibility has unequivocally positive effects on both employees and employers.

A Caveat: Just Because There's Flexibility Doesn't Mean You Can Use It

Despite the potential benefits of flexible workplace policies, there is often a stigma associated with using them. This "flexibility stigma" can have a negative impact on both the company and its employees. Even if companies have formal workplace flexibility policies, they will not experience the benefits of increased employee productivity and commitment to the company unless the employees think they can actually use the policy without penalty.[49] Unfortunately, there is often a penalty for employees who use these policies in terms of eligibility for raises and promotions, especially when usage decreases face time (e.g., telecommuting or working part time).[50] Managers are particularly opposed to the usage of workplace flexibility policies when they view the use to be for personal reasons (e.g., caring for a child) rather than to enhance productivity.[51] I (HS) personally experienced this penalty at a job. When my first child was an infant, I reduced my work schedule to four days a week. My immediate supervisor recommended me for a promotion during the annual review process; however, my vice president did not approve it because she thought I would leave the company as soon as I had another child. This discriminatory action prompted me to leave the company long before the birth of my second child.

Professional women in a variety of fields have noted similar examples of how job flexibility and reduced hours have made them invisible within their organization. One manager said: "I lost the vast majority of my interesting responsibilities and was really left with the more mundane responsibilities that I wasn't nearly as interested in."[52] A lawyer described: "[Going part time] has destroyed [my career] for all intents and purposes. It has completely, utterly, and irreversibly altered my future, my practice, my finances, my reputation, my relationships, and my friendships."[53] Some of these women also described the flexibility stigma as being important in their decisions to opt out of the workplace altogether after having children.[54] Other professional women who have opted out of the workplace described long, inflexible work hours and the expectation that they hide the fact that they have children. One woman noted: "You definitely would have to say you were sick, not the kid was sick."[55] At the other end of the financial spectrum, women working in low-income jobs also face significant stigma when they need time off to care for their children, such as being stereotyped as a "welfare mother" or an "irresponsible reproducer."[56]

Men who want to utilize workplace flexibility policies to take care of family responsibilities face similar, if not worse, stigma on the job. Although fathers have been found to earn more than non-fathers, this wage benefit may only apply if men appear not to have any childcare responsibilities.[57] Men who have had to take a break from working to care for a family member have significantly lower earnings than men who have not.[58] Men who ask for even a brief amount of time off for family reasons receive lower performance evaluations[59] and are viewed more negatively than women who ask for the same type of leave.[60] An additional aspect of the flexibility stigma for men comes from the stereotype that taking time off to care for family is viewed as the female's responsibility.[61] Being viewed as feminine is associated with weakness and uncertainty, which results in men being rated as less conscientious employees who are penalized (e.g., downsized) and less likely to obtain workplace rewards.[62] Therefore, it is not surprising that men are less likely than women to request the use of formal workplace flexibility policies.[63] A study of fathers found that over 80% of men who used flex-time or worked from home and 40% of those who used compressed workweeks did so informally.[64]

Another potentially negative effect of utilizing flexible workplace policies is the perception that people who work from home may "slack off" because they lack accountability. There is some evidence that family responsibilities interfere with work among people who telecommute, especially as family size increases.[65] However, the bigger problem seems to be that working from home creates an environment where the expectations for work never end. The job continually interferes with family life because the lines between work and home are blurred.[66] For example, urgent e-mails interrupt family time in the evenings or on weekends. Rather than waiting until Monday morning, people who telecommute may work after their kids go to bed because their office is at home. In fact, workers who telecommute report working more hours than office workers before experiencing a negative impact on family life, which can be good (i.e., less negative impact) or bad (i.e., work more hours) depending on how you look at it.[67] A final concern is that working from home may increase gender inequality in division of the household labor. Women are expected to perform more of the household chores when they work from home.[68] We will explore how unequal division of labor serves as a barrier to work-life balance in chapter 6.

Overcoming the Flexibility Stigma: A Model Program

There has been a movement to make workplace flexibility the norm within organizations (rather than an exception that employees obtain through special request) to help employees gain the benefits and avoid the stigma associated with it. In 2006, Best Buy began an initiative called ROWE (Results Only Work Environment) that took emphasis away from the time clock and placed it on the results produced. Benefits of employees engaged in the ROWE program included increased commitment to the organization, greater job satisfaction, lower intention to leave the job, and less unnecessary work done.[69] Employees participating in ROWE also engaged in more positive health-related behaviors including getting enough sleep, exercising, and going to the doctor when sick. These behaviors, in turn, reduced health-care costs for the organization.[70] The advantages of the ROWE program appeared to be tied to workers' increased sense of schedule control—or the perception that they had more autonomy. Furthermore, it was not only mothers who benefited from increased flexibility. The ROWE program benefited mothers, fathers, and people without children.[71]

Although the ROWE program has been discontinued at Best Buy, the concept expanded to other organizations, including a pilot program begun in 2008 at the outlet headquarters of the Gap. The results of this pilot study were extremely successful and employee turnover decreased by 50%, resulting in hundreds of thousands of dollars of savings. One employee noted: "ROWE really lets me prioritize my time, I feel empowered and actually more responsible at my job. It makes me feel more in control and in charge of my work."[72] Another employee noted: "I was recruited very strongly for another position outside the company with slightly better pay but much closer to my home, I can honestly say that if it wasn't for [ROWE] I would have taken that job." It is clear that the ability of workers to feel a greater sense of autonomy about their jobs is critical to their well-being as well as their desire to work hard for their organizations. Furthermore, the negative repercussions for taking advantage of flexibility policies seen in other organizations do not occur because the flexibility in a ROWE environment is the norm and not considered a special benefit for people with families.

In sum, overly demanding and inflexible work environments make it difficult to balance work and family. Workplace flexibility may be one of the key mechanisms that allows both men and women to balance work and family lives. The data on the advantages of workplace flexibility policies that allow workers to have autonomy and control over their schedules are consistently positive. However, the norms of the workplace continue to make it difficult for men and women to take advantages of these policies because many corporations still view the ideal worker as a person who has few responsibilities for the home and family. Given that this no longer accurately reflects reality for the majority of workers, companies need to adapt to the changing world.[73] Companies are unlikely to change unless both men and women demand reasonable schedules that allow for some autonomy or at least predictability. Until workplace flexibility, which ultimately increases the productivity of the company, is seen as an issue important for all workers, taking advantage of workplace flexibility policies will continue to be stigmatized and seen as a sign of decreased commitment to the organization.

SHOW ME THE MONEY

Another reason people sacrifice work-family balance by working long hours is that people want to maximize their financial gain and status.[74] In an article in *The Atlantic*, one husband and father put it this way: "The central conflict of domestic life right now isn't men versus women or mothers versus fathers; it's the family against money."[75] For many, the question of work-family balance is a basic financial question of whether work will provide enough money to pay for the needs of the family. At the lower end of the income spectrum balancing work and family is stressful because people need to work to afford the basic necessities of food, shelter, and clothing. Yet, there are expenses associated with working such as purchasing appropriate work clothes, securing reliable transportation, and obtaining adequate childcare. One family of six living below the poverty line in San Diego described the struggles of trying to work without adequate childcare and transportation. The mother's hours were cut at work because she had to take the bus, and she was frequently late, which reduced her income from $1200 to $500 per month. Her husband stayed at home with their children because he could not get a job that would pay enough to cover the costs of childcare. They had tried to enroll their twins in Head Start twice, but had missed the deadline because they had to rely on public transportation and were late to the sign-up fair. They planned to try again because free preschool is the only thing that would allow both parents to work so that they could do more than just scrape by in the future.[76]

However, financial considerations also contribute to imbalance at the upper end of the financial spectrum. For example, in interviews with well-educated, high-achieving women, the vast earning potential of their husbands played a big role in their decision to quit working. The husband's large salary justified his inability to equitably help with the home and childcare because of his extremely long work hours.[77] From a certain perspective these decisions make sense. If earning the highest possible salary is the goal of a family, then the sacrifices in work-family balance may indeed be worth it. But is earning the highest possible salary really the best goal to have? Is maximizing income the best way to lead a fulfilling and satisfying life? If people really want to balance work and family, they may need to reevaluate their financial goals.

Although earning an adequate income is an important life goal, the relationship between money and well-being tends to take the shape of the inverted U-shaped curve. A certain amount of money is necessary and enhances well-being up to a point. However, earning more and more money does not result in greater and greater happiness.

The Upside of Money

The negative impact of poverty is well documented. Poverty is a risk factor for almost all physical health problems (e.g., high blood pressure, heart disease, and osteoarthritis) and death.[78] In addition, people who do not earn enough to meet their basic needs for food, shelter, and clothing experience a great deal of stress and reduced well-being.[79] In addition, feeling financially helpless can decrease people's ability to cope with the stressful life events they experience.[80] Unfortunately, when money for basic needs is the primary consideration, focusing on needs for autonomy, competence, and relatedness often have to take a backseat. A study of seventy-seven thousand people living in fifty-one impoverished countries found that feeling autonomous and related to others were not even associated with increased well-being unless people were able to meet their basic life necessities.[81] The authors suggested this represents the sense of hopelessness experienced by people who live in extreme poverty.

As income increases enough for people to meet their basic needs and feel comfortable, happiness also increases. However, there appears to be a ceiling above which increased income has no positive benefits for emotional well-being.[82] In a nationally representative sample, people with a lower level of income reported more stress and lower levels of emotional well-being. However, once people had an annual household income of $75,000, additional income did not relate to any improvement in daily emotional experience. Below incomes of $75,000, lack of money is related to emotional pain and stress. However, after this level, the benefits of having more money may be balanced by the negative effects of earning a high income (e.g., longer work hours and work-related stress). Thus, even at very high incomes people may not necessarily experience higher levels of contentment and joy on a day-to-day basis.

If money really doesn't contribute much to happiness, why do people think it does? If you ask the average person what would make them happier, a lot of people might answer something like "winning the lottery." Yet one famous study compared people who had recently won the lottery to a group from the same geographic areas who had not.[83] People who won were not significantly happier, partially because they got less pleasure from ordinary life events (e.g., a beautiful sunset) after winning the lottery.

In addition, people tend to overestimate the importance of how much money matters for people's well-being. One study asked participants to estimate how happy people were at various levels of income and compared estimations to people's actual levels of happiness.[84] The authors found that wealthier people were indeed happier than poorer people, but not by as much as most thought. At the highest level of income, people rated their happiness as a seven on a ten-point scale, while people at the lowest level of income rated their happiness as just below the midpoint of five. However, people thought that those at the lowest level of income would report a happiness level around two. In general, people greatly underestimated the happiness levels of those making $55,000 and below. The strong belief that having less money makes people considerably less happy may interfere with making decisions that could actually enhance work-family balance, for example, accepting a pay cut for greater flexibility or an extra day off each week.

In general, there is very little research to suggest that earning more and more money will make people feel happier even though people think it will. However, research does suggest that there is a small, but consistent correlation between income and life satisfaction.[85] Although the correlation is small, there are meaningful differences in how satisfied people are with their lives based on their incomes. For example, the wealthiest individuals (earning over $200,000 per year) in one study were a great deal more satisfied with their lives than the poorest individuals (earning less than $10,000 per year).[86]

For people with low to average income, there is a clear, positive relationship between their income and day-to-day well-being as well as life satisfaction.[87] However, for people with higher incomes, there is little relationship between income and daily well-being and a small relationship between income and life satisfaction. Additionally, for high-income earners, the positive effects of income have more to do with how much they earn compared to people around them than their income per se.[88] In other words, for people whose basic needs are met, earning a great deal of money is less important than feeling as though they are earning more than others.[89] For example, people who think they are better off financially than a close relative experienced greater satisfaction with life.[90]

Furthermore, the income of the surrounding community affects happiness—people living in communities where others earned a very high income were less happy.[91] In other words, people feel particularly unsatisfied with their earnings when surrounded by others who are earning more. When everyone has a similar income, having a low income does not have as much of an impact on well-being. For example, despite the low income and limited material possessions of the Amish community living in America, they are quite satisfied with their lives.[92] In contrast, when people around you have a higher income, having a lower income can be particularly damaging. For example, in 1996 African American men in the United States had a median income of $26,522 and their average life expectancy was just over sixty-six years. In contrast, men in Costa Rica had an average income of $6,410, yet they had a life expectancy of seventy-five years.[93] The men in the United States compared their income to those more wealthy people around them and this may have contributed to their ill health and lower life expectancy.

The idea that people feel bad when they earn less than those around them points to the particularly negative effects of income inequality. Research has suggested that income inequality is bad for entire communities. One paper reviewed the results of 155 studies and concluded that when there is greater income inequality, the overall health of a community or country declines.[94] The negative outcomes associated with income inequality include "morbidity and mortality, obesity, teenage birth rates, mental illness, homicide, low trust, low social capital, hostility, and racism."[95] This is particularly concerning for the United States, which ranks forty-fourth out of eighty-six countries—just below Nigeria—in income inequality. It is the most inequitable country in the developed world.[96]

In sum, research has found that earning more money is associated with a greater sense of satisfaction with life. However, the impact of money on satisfaction with life may largely be due to satisfaction with how people's income compares with others. Regardless, the path to greater happiness is not to earn more and more money. Earning a higher income does not seem to have much of an effect on how much positive emotion people experience on a day-to-day basis after they earn enough to "feel comfortable."

The Downside of Money: Materialism

People often say that "money is the root of all evil." However, this is inaccurate. The actual quotation is: "For the *love* of money is the root of all kinds of evil."[97] There is a fair amount of research that suggests this might actually be true. Research has consistently found that when people desire more money than they have, it is related to lower levels of well-being.[98] There are negative consequences of putting a high value on money and material possessions. In other words, while having more money may be related to small increases in life satisfaction, focusing on money actually decreases well-being.

Focusing on Money

Viewing financial gain as the number-one priority in life is associated with decreased well-being. People who pursue financial goals as their highest priority over all other life goals tend to experience more anxiety and depression as well as lower self-esteem and vitality.[99] The negative impact of valuing money was also seen in a study of college students in forty-one different countries. Students who put more importance on money reported decreased satisfaction with life.[100] In another study, the more participants valued financial success as college freshmen the lower their satisfaction with life, especially family life, when they were in their thirties.[101]

In addition, people who overly value financial gain are more likely to overwork. As a result of working more than they need to, these "over-earners" have less leisure time and decreased happiness.[102] I (HS) remember my supervisor at a previous job who worked constantly even while on cruises with his family. When I took two weeks off work for my honeymoon, he was shocked that I had not checked my e-mail the entire time I was gone. In fact, he had actually wanted me to conduct an all-day site visit at an organization that happened to be located in Hawaii while I was there. Given that it was practically the only vacation I took during the seven years I worked there, I was determined to focus on leisure while I was on my honeymoon and declined.

People who are paid by the hour often think in terms of how much money their time is worth (i.e., If I take an hour off work to go to my child's school performance, I lose $7.25). As earnings increase, the costs of attending family activities or spending time on leisure activities also increase (attend the school play or earn one hundred dollars?). People who think that "time is money" derive less happiness from their leisure activities.[103] So they have to evaluate whether it is worth taking time for their own leisure to play a round of golf or read a good book. They may weigh the money they are losing against spending time investing in their relationships with significant others—going on a date with their spouse or getting away for the weekend as a family. When people's desire to earn money starts to take priority over all other social roles (e.g., spouse, parent, and self), well-being declines.

Focusing on Material Purchases

In addition to making money a top priority for its own sake, some people place a great value on earning money to acquire as many material possessions as possible. Numerous studies have found a relationship between materialism and decreased well-being, lower satisfaction with life, poor relationships, antisocial behavior in youth, and a sense that life has no meaning.[104] High school students who are more materialistic have decreased well-being. Materialism is associated with having lower grades, feeling more envious of others, having less satisfaction with life, being less engaged in daily activities, and feeling less socially engaged.[105] People who determine success by the amount and quality of possessions as well as those who indicate that these possessions are central to their own well-being tend to be less satisfied with their lives.[106]

It may seem as though buying new products and gadgets would be enjoyable—people certainly seem to get joy out of their material possessions. But the joy that comes from material possessions is fleeting.[107] When you first buy a new gadget such as an iPad or even a car, it does immediately boost well-being. However, people adapt very quickly to life with their new "toys" and daily levels of joy settle back to where they were before the purchase. Another problem is that new purchases often result in the desire for more. You might realize your current cell phone pales in comparison to the functionality of the iPad, so now you want an iPhone as well. And let's not forget that as soon as you buy something, they will come out with a new and better version. In some ways, materialism is comparable to a drug addiction; it takes more and more of the "drug" to get the same benefits from it. If people's aspirations for material goods rise faster than they can afford to keep up with, then they won't be happy despite having objectively good material circumstances.

How Focusing on Money Harms: The Importance of Intrinsic Motivation

People who are more materialistic have been found to have lower levels of intrinsic motivation and are less likely to meet their basic needs of autonomy, competence, and relatedness.[108] One study found that business students who were motivated by the extrinsic goal of financial success felt less energetic, had decreased well-being, and had greater levels of substance abuse compared to education students who were motivated by the intrinsic goal of feeling a sense of relationship to their community.[109]

Materialism is particularly damaging to social relationships.[110] People who put their personal relationships after their goals for financial success experience increased anxiety and depression.[111] Simply showing people luxury goods or words that enhanced thoughts of materialism (e.g., buy, money, status) made people more competitive, less trusting, and less socially engaged.[112] One study looking at more than twenty-five hundred consumers over the course of six years found a vicious cycle of materialism—people who tried to use possessions to increase happiness or saw money as a sign of success became lonelier over time. Furthermore, being lonely encouraged people to become more materialistic.[113] Thus when earning money is a person's primary goal the result is feeling dissatisfied, alienated from others, and unable to enjoy the things that could truly bring joy in life.

People who put work and financial gain before their families and personal well-being describe this feeling of dissatisfaction and alienation. One woman said: "I've cried on my way to work, I've cried on my way home from work . . . and still worked 50–60 hours in slavish devotion (or so it seemed to me) to my employer. I've lost friends over my workaholism, become distant from my family." People also acknowledge the lack of joy in their lives. She went on to say: "My dad used to tell me that he worried about me because I never seemed to have any fun. He was right—even when I thought I was having fun, I wasn't."[114]

Fortunately, people can decrease their levels of materialism, which can lead to increased well-being. Recently, four studies were conducted looking at changes in materialism. The researchers found that when people became less materialistic over time—whether it was six months or twelve years—they became happier in that time frame. Furthermore, the joy that came from decreased materialism was directly linked to participants feeling a greater sense of autonomy, competence, and relatedness. On the other hand, when people had increased materialism over time they felt less autonomous, competent, and related to others, which decreased their well-being. Additionally, the researchers were able to reduce materialism in a group of adolescents after three discussion sessions about the perils of consumer culture and how to make value-based purchasing decisions.[115] So it may be possible to reverse the trend of increased materialism and decreased well-being so prevalent in the United States today.

How Money Can Compromise Integrity

A final downside of money is that people who have a lot of material possessions and higher incomes seem to be more self-focused and feel less compassion for others. As a result, they are less likely to help other people in need and more likely to act in an unethical manner.[116] Ironically, people from high-income backgrounds are less generous in donating to charities and helping others than people from lower-income backgrounds. People with high incomes were also more likely to break the law while driving (e.g., cut off a pedestrian at a crosswalk), make unethical decisions (e.g., taking credit for something they didn't do), take candy that was meant for children, lie during a job negotiation, and cheat to win a prize.[117] These unfavorable differences remained even after the researchers controlled for a variety of factors that could be related to how generous or ethical people behave, including their age and how religious they are. Additionally, people who had more favorable attitudes about greed were more likely to lie and cheat. When study participants were told about the benefits of greed before an experiment, people from low-income backgrounds were as likely to say they would act unethically as those from higher-income backgrounds. So greed seems to be one of the primary motivators for the unethical behavior of people with more money and material possessions. Contrary to Michael Douglas's infamous speech in the movie *Wall Street*,[118] greed is *not* good.

In sum, income appears to be related to increased satisfaction with life, while poverty, especially when there is a great deal of income inequality, is associated with negative outcomes. However, when people become fixated on material purchases there are negative results both for mental health and for their sense of ethics and integrity. Furthermore, in most studies, income has not been found to increase day-to-day feelings of happiness. So what does increase happiness? We will be talking a lot more about this in chapter 8. However, one study using data from the Gallup World Poll, which represented 96% of the world population, shed light on the importance of valuing intrinsic goals.[119] People who perceived that they were respected by others, had friends they could count on, learned something new, did their best, and were able to choose how to spend their time had greater daily feelings of joy and well-being. In other words, daily experience of well-being was related, not to income, but to meeting the basic psychological needs of autonomy, competence, and relatedness.

MAYBE HAPPIER PEOPLE EARN MORE

Although earning more money has been associated with greater life satisfaction, it does not seem to have the same impact on daily feelings of happiness. So why do people seem to intuitively think that money will make them happier? Maybe it's because happiness and income do go together, but people have it backwards. Maybe it's that happier people earn more rather than earning more makes people happier. The majority of the research on income and well-being is correlational,[120] which means the relationship could go either way. In fact, there is some research that suggests that happier people may actually earn more money than less happy people.[121]

An exhaustive review of the research was conducted to untangle the causal direction of positive emotions and a variety of outcomes, including work and income.[122] The authors identified twenty-two longitudinal studies that examined the relationship between positive emotions and later work outcomes. They concluded that positive emotions predict better job outcomes such as higher evaluations, productivity, and incomes. For example, people who were happier to begin with were more likely to be hired and earn more. One study found that people rated as cheerful in college earned $25,000 more than their less cheerful peers almost twenty years after graduation.[123]

For ethical and practical reasons, no experimental studies can be conducted to determine if manipulating people's emotions actually causes them to earn more money. However, numerous experimental studies have found that when people are induced to feel positive emotions, they are perceived as being more likable by others, better negotiators, more creative, as well as better problem solvers. Given that having these types of skills are often associated with increased income,[124] it is plausible that positive emotions are causally related to earning more money.

The fact that being happier may be related to increased income makes sense within the context of self-determination theory. People who are happier are more likely to be engaged in tasks they find intrinsically motivating.[125] Thus, they may be more likely to have jobs that meet their intrinsic needs for autonomy, competence, and relatedness. As a result, they may work harder at their jobs, which could lead to more income. Furthermore, people who achieve a sense of balance between their work, family, and leisure time experience less stress and more positive emotions.[126] Being happier may result in doing better at work, given that research has shown that positive emotions are associated with greater creativity, better problem solving, and better task execution.[127] So happier people might actually earn more! Thus overworking in order to earn more money because people think that money will lead to happiness is backwards. Instead, people should focus on finding the intrinsic joy of work, avoiding the miseries of overwork, and practicing other techniques to increase personal well-being (see chapter 8). Earning more money may end up being a happy side effect!

DOING MORE WITH LESS

In order to avoid overworking, people can also learn to do more with less—in other words, be thrifty.[128] Thrift means making the most efficient use of the resources available. When people live within their means and stay out of debt, it can increase their sense of autonomy. Psychologists have identified several techniques for people to increase their happiness with less money, allowing people to live on lower incomes, and stay out of debt. One option to reduce spending is to rent rather than buy. Expensive purchases like a vacation home do not make people as happy as they think. People quickly get used to their lives with their new homes. People can choose the less expensive option of simply renting a vacation home rather than owning one, which allows them to enjoy new places and have new adventures. People can also learn how to reuse things they have in new ways—for example, by taking a car on a new adventure or putting a new app on an old iPad. In addition, people can reexperience past memories through photos and reminiscing to increase the happiness from previously paid-for experiences. Finally, research has shown that people's happiness benefits more from making frequent, small purchases (e.g., such as a great cup of coffee, a book, and a new scarf) than making one large purchase (which they adapt to fairly quickly). It really doesn't take as much money as you think to be happy.

From a personal perspective, neither I (ML) nor my husband make a great deal of money because we are both educators. We have made choices to scale back our material purchases so that we do not live beyond our income. We rarely buy new stuff—we are blessed with wonderful friends who give us hand-me-down clothing which we "pay forward" to families with smaller children. In fact, a big chunk of my daughter's wardrobe comes from my coauthor Holly—her daughters are older and have wonderful taste! We often purchase toys at thrift stores, and we tend to drive our cars until they completely run down. I am acutely aware of how quickly the joy of a new purchase wears off and tend to procrastinate buying new, expensive gadgets. I still do not have a smart phone, but have been thinking about buying one for a long time. We do spend money on date nights and vacations (see chapter 8) because those bring us lasting joy. I think if we made more money, we would probably lead a more extravagant lifestyle—we certainly lead a more extravagant lifestyle than we did when we were in graduate school! But I do not think we would be any happier.

CONCLUSION

As seen in chapter 2, people are happier and healthier when they serve in multiple roles such as employee, spouse, and parent that allow them to have their needs for autonomy, competence, and relatedness met through a variety of outlets. However, it is important to find balance among the roles. Being unemployed as well as working too much are associated with decreased physical and mental health—the inverted U-shaped curve. Working long hours also can undermine people's ability to meet their intrinsic needs for autonomy, competence, and relatedness, which are essential for well-being, especially when it's done for external reasons such as unreasonable employer expectations or a focus on material goals. Companies should try to be more flexible in their policies to allow people to find work-family balance.

In addition, people may need to reevaluate their priorities related to financial success. Working long hours to make money can become a catch-22. People may earn enough money to buy their dream life but have to work so much that they never have time to enjoy it. While having enough money to meet basic needs increases happiness, the benefits of money level off once people have enough to feel comfortable. In addition, well-being is decreased when people put financial and material goals above their other life goals, suggesting that there is also an inverted U-shaped relationship between money and well-being. One key to work-family balance is focusing on working for intrinsic reasons (i.e., to increase autonomy, competence, and relatedness) rather than making more money.

Chapter Five

Balance Is for Both Men and Women

Challenging Gender Stereotypes

Much of the debate about work-family balance is conducted with an assumption that balancing work and family is a *woman's* problem. If somebody is going to have to choose between their career and their children, it is generally assumed that it will be the mother. For example, articles on whether it is best to work or stay at home are often framed as choices only for women (e.g., "A Mother's Dilemma: Children or Jobs").[1] These articles debate whether mothers who are employed can be as good caregivers as mothers who stay at home, as well as what a family gains and loses when mothers work. Comparable questions are not asked about fathers. Why is it that choices about how to balance work and family are always framed as issues only for women? As one father noted in an article he wrote for *The Atlantic*: "When men aren't part of the discussion about balancing work and life, outdated assumptions about fatherhood are allowed to go unchallenged and, far more important, key realities about the relationship between work and family are elided."[2] Another commented on the difficulty men have even trying to enter the discussion: "Trying to talk work-life issues with other males was like showing up in the soccer try outs wearing a tutu! You just don't do that. Work-life discussion is for women."[3]

WOMEN AS THE ESSENTIAL PARENT

We think part of the answer is that people have a fundamental belief that mothers are the primary childcare providers. This belief is reflected in the popular press coverage on work-family balance. In her article on why women cannot have it all, Anne-Marie Slaughter observed:

> From years of conversations and observations, however, I've come to believe that men and women respond quite differently when problems at home force them to recognize that their absence is hurting a child, or at least that their presence would likely help. I do not believe fathers love their children any less than mothers do, but men do seem more likely to choose their job at a cost to their family, while women seem more likely to choose their family at a cost to their job.[4]

Slaughter goes on to discuss the sense that children need their mothers. She quotes Mary Matalin, former advisor to George Bush: "I'm indispensable to my kids, but I'm not close to indispensable to the White House."[5]

Conservative commentators have suggested that the natural order of things is for a woman's place to be in the home, while men serve as the primary breadwinners. When the Pew Research Center released a report stating that women are the primary breadwinners in four out of ten households,[6] pundits on Fox News network's Lou Dobb's show saw this as a national tragedy. Juan Williams said this trend represented "something going terribly wrong in American society, and it's hurting our children, and it's going to have impact for generations to come."[7] Another pundit, Erick Erickson, said: "When you look at biology, look at the natural world, the roles of a male and a female in society, and other animals, the male typically is the dominant role. . . . We as people in a smart society have lost the ability to have complementary relationships in nuclear families, and it's tearing us apart."[8] Others have linked women's traditional roles to the Bible. On his conservative radio show, Bryan Fischer expressed concern over women being breadwinners, noting that: "The biblical pattern is for a wife and a mother to focus her energies, devote her energies on making a home for her children and for her husband."[9]

The view that women are naturally better parents is also held by people who would typically oppose such conservative views. In March 2013, the *New York* magazine cover story featured a new breed of self-identified feminists described as women who embraced their role as mothers and claimed women's superiority in the domain of parenting and household management. The article featured Kelly Makino, a thirty-three-year-old woman with a master's degree in social work from the University of Pennsylvania who has won honors and awards for her negotiating skills. Kelly chose to be a stay-at-home mother and is a firm believer in women's superiority at childcare and domestic tasks. She said: "The maternal instinct is a real thing. . . . Women are raised from the get-go to raise children successfully. When we are moms we have a better toolbox."[10]

Content analyses of parenting-advice books and magazines confirm the pervasive notion that mothers are viewed as the primary parent.[11] These books typically depict fathers as "helpers" and emphasize that parenting can be fun[12]—the implication being that fathers need encouragement to be involved as parents while mothers are automatically involved. In parenting magazines, even though articles use the word "parent," pictures often portray fathers in the background playing a supporting role.[13] Mothers were the ones quoted and were the primary focus of articles about the guilt, stress, and worries of parenting.[14] When fathers were discussed, they were represented as part-time or secondary parents. Although their involvement was praised, it was not expected.

The general public tends to agree. Pew Research's 2012 American Values Survey found that 54% of both men and women agreed that women were more natural parents.[15] Parents particularly held this belief (57% versus 51% of nonparents), as did Hispanics (67% versus 59% of blacks and 49% of whites), people over sixty-five years old (65%), and Republicans (60% versus 50% of Democrats). But are women really better equipped to be parents than men? Do they have a secret ingredient (above and beyond breast milk) that makes them more competent at child rearing or more efficient at household management? Are men and women really that different?

ONE HYPOTHESIS: EVOLUTION

The basic rationale for why women are caregivers and men are providers is evolutionary in nature. The evolutionary argument goes something like this.[16] Once upon a time during the late Pleistocene era, men and women were evolving into their final human forms. During this time, human beings lived in hunter-gatherer groups. Men and women faced different challenges to survival and reproductive success. For example, women dedicated greater investment than men in their offspring because they were responsible for bearing and nursing their children, while men's contribution ended at conception. Women increased their reproductive success by being highly selective in choosing a mate who could increase survival of his offspring by providing food and shelter. Men, on the other hand, were more likely to pass on their genes by participating in short-term mating strategies (i.e., spreading their seed) and selecting mates that were young and fertile. Furthermore, given that (unlike women) a man can never be 100% sure that the child he cares for is his own, he would maximize his reproductive success by exhibiting sexual jealousy over women.

The argument goes that people who used these reproductive strategies were more likely to survive and have offspring. Therefore, the differences between men and women, which can be seen to this day, are a result of evolution. For example, men's need to compete for mates increased their tendency for violence, while their cognitive and spatial skills were enhanced through hunting. On the other hand, women evolved to focus on child rearing and seek mates that could support their families. According to evolutionary theory, these gender differences have become encoded into the human DNA and represent inherited and stable traits.

Evolutionary arguments seem to be inherently appealing, especially to those who are looking to justify sex-stereotyped behavior. In her *New York* magazine article on feminists who choose to stay home, Lisa Miller noticed that evolutionary arguments are often used to explain not only why women are more equipped to be parents, but also why they are better at other household administrative tasks. She noted that the women she talked to used evolutionary arguments to support the idea that only women are equipped to plan birthday parties, remember doctor's appointments, communicate with teachers, and buy school shoes.[17] These are not exactly skills that had survival value in the late Pleistocene era!

Evolutionary explanations have been widely criticized because it is impossible to know what life was actually like during this era. Therefore, evolutionary theorists can only make guesses by extrapolating backwards from current gender stereotypes. They assume that current behavior must have had an adaptive value in earlier evolutionary history or else it would not exist today. In some ways, these explanations are similar to Rudyard Kipling's *Just So Stories*—fictional stories that pretend to explain the origin of some characteristic (e.g., How did the camel get his hump?).[18] Similarly, evolutionary theory tries to retrospectively explain "How did the man get his proclivity to cheat?" or "How did the woman get her natural desire to stay at home with children?" In fact, it is likely that many assumptions about life in the Pleistocene era may be incorrect. For example, although it is widely assumed that men had to "spread their seed" to achieve maximal reproductive success, this strategy would not be adaptive if men and women traveled in small groups where many of the people were blood relatives. If that were the case, a man would do best having a monogamous relationship with the one woman in the tribe who was not his sister! Thus evolutionary theory seems to provide post hoc explanations based on potentially inaccurate assumptions about the past.

Fundamental Flaws

In addition to these critiques of evolutionary theory in general, there are some fundamental problems with the evolutionary rationale. First, if men and women are different due to genetic differences stemming from our ancient evolutionary past, the differences between them must be inborn, which means they would be present at birth and remain consistent across time and context. In addition, this view implies that men and women are so fundamentally different that knowing whether individuals are men or women can predict other aspects of their behavior or their personality in the same way that knowing whether an animal is a dog or a cat indicates whether it will bark or meow. This categorical view of men and women as completely different is illustrated in the book *Men Are from Mars, Women Are from Venus*[19]— which implies that men and women are so different they do not even come from the same planet! However, research suggests that there are almost no gender differences present at birth, but that differences emerge over time. Even as adults, the differences between men and women are small and vary in degree rather than kind. In fact, there is more variation within people of the same sex than between people of the opposite sex.[20]

Not That Different at Birth

First of all, virtually none of the gender differences observed later in life are evident when children are young. In an extensive review of the research on males and females at birth, very few differences of any kind were identified.[21] Males do release testosterone at around six weeks of gestation causing the male sex organs to develop, which may have some minor impact on brain development (e.g., boys are born with a slightly larger area of the brain that regulates body temperature). In addition to that, males grow faster than girls and are born bigger, heavier, and with respectively larger brains as a result. However, girls mature faster physiologically (e.g., organs, tissues, and cells) in utero as evidenced by earlier mouth movements, response to external stimuli (e.g., noises outside the womb), and development of the respiratory system. As a result of their slightly less mature neurological system, boys tend to be slightly fussier than girls in infancy. Boys are also born with a slight preference for using their right ear and demonstrate more asymmetrical reflexes than girls. Meanwhile, girls have a slightly better sense of smell and vocalize about a month earlier and more often than boys.[22] Overall, there are very few other gender differences at birth. The ones that do exist are small and have not been linked to lifelong differences in gender-related roles. However, if people really wanted to make prescriptions for gender roles based on brain differences at birth, then women's earlier vocalizations should make them better in the boardroom, and their better sense of smell should give them diaper-changing immunity!

Not That Different as Adults

Another flaw in the logic of innate gender differences is that there are actually not even very many differences between men and women as adults. There has been a great deal of research investigating gender differences between men and women. One article reviewed the results of thousands of studies looking at gender differences on a variety of outcomes including cognitive variables (e.g., abstract reasoning), communication variables, personality differences, psychological well-being, and motor differences.[23] For over three-fourths of the outcomes, there was either no difference or fairly small differences between men and women.

In addition, some gender differences changed over time. For example, in math, there was a small gender difference favoring girls in elementary school, no difference in middle school, and a small gender difference in math problem solving that favored boys in high school.[24] The fact that gender differences in math changed as children got older suggests that something more than evolved differences in math ability are at work (e.g., cultural beliefs that boys are good at math and girls are not).[25]

Other gender differences have a certain "now you see them, now you don't" quality. For example, there is a widely held belief that men are more likely than women to help others in a heroic or chivalrous manner. In a review of almost two hundred studies on helping behavior, a small difference favoring men was found—however, only in certain contexts.[26] Men were much more likely than women to behave in a chivalrous manner if there were observers; however, gender had no effect on chivalry when there were not any witnesses. In other words, men were more likely than women to behave in a chivalrous manner *only* when they believed someone was watching. A similar result is found when looking at gender differences in smiling. On average women did smile more than men; however, the difference was much larger when someone was watching.[27] The fact that these behaviors change when there are onlookers suggests that people are conforming to societal stereotypes about their sex (i.e., men are chivalrous and women are friendly) rather than that there is an inherent difference between men and women in these behaviors.

The majority of research has found that when there are differences between men and women, they tend to be small.[28] *If* men and women differed, it was simply a matter of degree—even differences in masculinity and femininity. In other words, both men and women demonstrate characteristics associated with being masculine and feminine to varying degrees. There were more differences within sexes than between sexes; the difference between the most masculine woman and the least masculine woman was far greater than the difference between men and women in general.

There were some exceptions in this general tendency for men and women to be similar. For example, men do tend to think about masturbation a lot more often than women.[29] They also tend to be bigger, stronger, and throw harder than women—although there are obviously exceptions. There were also some differences in their preferences in leisure activities.[30] Thus, if you know someone is a man or a woman you can make pretty good estimations about their body size, physical strength, tendency to masturbate, and whether or not they would rather scrapbook or watch a boxing match. However, you would not be able to make any solid predictions about whether they were more or less warm, nurturing, caring, or achievement/success oriented. On all of those dimensions—the ones essential to balancing work and family—men and women are more similar than they are different.

AN ALTERNATE EXPLANATION: SOCIALIZATION

Research *has* shown that there are some differences between men and women. However, when differences do exist, they are small and there is a great deal of overlap, which suggests that men and women do not fall into two entirely separate categories and certainly do not live on separate planets. So if the differences are not inherited, where do they come from? A lot of it has to do with the fact that boys and girls are treated differently from birth.

People have different expectations about male and female infants. A series of studies using a paradigm called "Baby X" found that adults come to different conclusions when they interact with an infant dressed in blue versus pink. In one classic study, participants viewed the same video of a baby crying in reaction to a jack-in-the box. Participants who were told they were watching a boy thought the baby was angry. People who thought they were watching a girl described the baby as afraid.[31] Imagine how this different interpretation might affect how parents respond to their children (e.g., comforting their fearful daughters but not their angry sons). Thus stereotyped expectations result in people treating children in different ways that actually create the gender differences.

Research has shown that parents encourage different activities for boys and girls throughout childhood. A study summarizing the results of 172 studies on gender socialization found that parents do not generally treat boys and girls differently in the amount of warmth they display or the amount of time they spend with their children. However, they do encourage boys and girls to play in ways that are consistent with sex stereotypes.[32] Girls are encouraged to engage in nurturing activities, play with dolls, and assist in household chores. Boys are encouraged to play actively with trucks and building toys, activities that may be related to more inventiveness and visual-spatial ability. Other research has suggested that parents expect more physical risk taking and autonomous, adventurous behavior from boys and are more cautious with girls, regularly warning them of potential dangers and reminding them to be careful.[33]

As children age, they begin to internalize the gender differences learned through interactions with their parents and other adults. Although biological sex may be present at birth, people learn gender roles through experience. At birth there are no gender differences in toy preference. However, around age one, boys and girls begin to play with gender-specific toys.[34] Thus, gender roles are not inevitable or universal but are responses to social interactions.[35] In these interactions, both males and females realize that there are very real rewards and punishments associated with conforming to or violating gender roles. Men and women may be punished if they fail to show a trait that is associated with their gender. Women may be socially sanctioned if they fail to be warm, kind, friendly, and show interest in children. Men may be ridiculed if they fail to be athletic, assertive, or show good business sense.[36] Girls who are tomboys may be ostracized by their peers, while boys who take dance may be teased or bullied to the point of having to be homeschooled. To avoid this social punishment, males act to maintain their masculinity and females act to maintain their femininity.

The idea that gender differences are learned behaviors is advocated by social-role theory.[37] According to this theory, men and women differ because of the different roles that they have traditionally inhabited. In other words, men and women develop personalities that match the different roles they occupy. Specifically, when women are in caretaking roles, they develop caring personalities. Men develop dominant personality traits as a result of serving in leadership positions with power and status. This argument holds that women may be more skilled in domestic and parenting tasks because they have more *practice* doing those activities. So if women have "a better toolbox" to be mothers, it has a lot more to do with practicing those skills than evolution.

The important implication of social-role theory is that as roles change, people can change as well. When men and women have similar roles (e.g., both are combining work and caretaking), their personality traits converge. Alice Eagly and her colleagues examined the data on mate selection and found evidence for social-role theory rather than evolutionary theory (despite the fact that evolutionary theory often has been used to explain differences in mate selection).[38] In countries with traditional gender roles, men were more interested in finding women who were good caretakers, while women were interested in finding men who were good providers. However, the pattern was different in more egalitarian countries. As gender equality in a country increased, women became more interested in marrying someone who could care for the house, while men grew more interested in marrying someone with greater earning capacity. If people's mate preferences were encoded in their genes from the late Pleistocene era, these differences would not be found across cultures.

Additional evidence for social-role theory can be seen when examining the change over time in masculine and feminine traits. As women have entered the workforce, their scores on measures of masculinity and assertiveness have increased.[39] Similarly, as men have started to engage in caretaking roles, their scores on femininity measures have increased as well.[40] These shifts in masculine and feminine traits have happened too quickly to be explained through genetic changes associated with evolution. Instead of thinking of gender differences as permanently lodged in the DNA, it may be more useful to think about them as created through the roles people take on and through the expectations of others in society.

GENDER DIFFERENCES AND THE BRAIN

People who believe that men and women are fundamentally different also assert that their brains must be different. The notion that men and women have different brains is rampant in popular press literature on gender differences. However, as Cordelia Fine points out in *Delusions of Gender*, these reports are generally misleading and inaccurate.[41] For example, the idea that women are better at multitasking, and thus are better equipped to simultaneously care for children and cook a meal, is often used to justify inequity in the home. Cordelia Fine describes a *Los Angeles Times* article in which Ruben Gur, a professor of psychiatry at the University of Pennsylvania, states that his poor ability to multitask means that his wife needs to take on the task of cooking for the family. He may be able to make a salad, but he claims: "I can't at the same time worry about whether this is in the microwave and that is in the skillet. When I do, something will burn."[42]

Despite the widespread belief that men and women have completely different brains, the actual research on the topic paints a very different picture. The idea that women are better at multitasking comes from studies that have suggested that women have a larger corpus callosum—the part of the brain that allows the left and the right hemispheres to communicate. The reasoning goes that because women have better communication between the two sides of their brains, they process information in a more global and holistic manner and are better able to go back and forth between seeing the details and seeing the big picture, allowing them to concentrate on many things at once.

Before we discuss the actual evidence for this claim, we wanted to note a point of confusion we have about this rationale. If women's brains make them better able to multitask, wouldn't that be advantageous in the business world as well? Shouldn't leaders be able to look at both the big picture and the details so that they can articulate visionary global goals as well as attend to the details of implementation? It would be concerning if world leaders were unable to remember that something was in the microwave at the same time that they were paying attention to food on the stove. Imagine if the president did not have the ability to think about both domestic and national policy at the same time: "I can't at the same time worry about deficit reduction and international crises. When I do, something will burn." If the data showed that men had bigger corpora callosa and were better at multitasking than women, then we speculate that the data would be used to justify men's dominance in the public sector. Multitasking would suddenly become a prerequisite for leadership, not a prerequisite for managing family life.

The irony here is that the data do not even support that there are gender differences in the size of the corpus callosum. Although a few early studies did find some differences between men and women, an analysis that combined the results of forty-nine different studies found that there was *no* difference.[43] The idea that women have larger corpora callosa has been deemed a "myth" by the scientific community.[44] The data demonstrate differences that vary from person to person, rather than fundamental differences between men and women.

Even when there is a legitimate difference in male and female brains, it does not mean that the brain differences are causing gender differences. People fail to take into account that the brain changes in response to experience—a characteristic known as brain plasticity.[45] Some powerful examples of plasticity include changes in the auditory cortex in response to musical training[46] and increases in areas of the brain devoted to visual memory in taxi drivers.[47] If an area of the brain differs in men and women, people jump to the conclusion that the difference is evidence of an innate gender difference. However, would they jump to the same conclusion about a taxi driver? Research has shown that women actually spend more time multitasking than men, an average of ten hours more per week in one study.[48] So any female advantage observed in multitasking is likely due to additional practice. Thus social roles can change brain functioning just as they can change personality characteristics. When men and women have different experiences, their brains change accordingly.

Why All the Hype?

Although the idea that men and women are different seems extremely appealing, we just presented research demonstrating that there are actually very few differences between male and female brains. So why does the idea that gender differences are hardwired in the brain remain so pervasive? The culprit may lie in the way research data are collected and reported. First of all, it is almost impossible to identify an absolute truth. Much of science is based on the probability of a hypothesis being true or false. In other words, there is a small chance (around 5%) that a gender difference will be identified in a study even when there isn't one in the real world. The problem is that thousands of data points are examined in brain-imaging studies, which means that on average about one in twenty comparisons may appear different due to chance alone. To illustrate this point, in 2009 researchers scanned the brain of a dead salmon while showing it emotionally laden material.[49] Lo and behold, several areas of the salmon's brain were "significantly" activated despite being dead. The point of this study was not to marvel at the empathic capacity of dead salmon or to raise national anxiety about an impending zombie salmon invasion. The salmon was dead, but areas of its brain still appeared activated using traditional brain-imaging methods. Brain-imaging techniques involve such multiple and complex measurements that, even in a dead salmon, some analyses may erroneously yield significant findings due to chance error.

To compound the problem, there is no way for scientists to know which findings are significant just by chance versus which ones reflect true differences, so they write up the results and submit them for publication. Studies that find significant differences (e.g., between men and women) are more likely to get published than those that do not find differences—a phenomenon known as the publication bias.[50] In addition, the media seems to be more interested in reporting gender differences than gender similarities. Even if a study was published indicating that there was not a difference between men and women on some stereotypical behavior, it would be unusual to see a headline proclaiming: "Men and Women Are Similar." So gender differences are more likely to get published in an academic journal and they are more likely to get media attention from the popular press—apparently gender differences sell.

Thus while people may try to link claims about differences between men and women to differences in their brains, the data are more consistent with a view of gender similarity than with gender difference. Furthermore, the public understanding of gender differences in the brain are marred by inaccurate reporting, spurious findings, publication bias, and media attention to differences instead of similarities. Even if there is a difference between the brains of men and women, it is more likely to be a result of differential gender socialization than a cause of gender differences.

CHALLENGING ASSUMPTIONS ABOUT GENDER

While actual differences between men and women may be small and primarily rooted in social experiences rather than differences in biology, people clearly hold strong gender stereotypes about men and women.[51] Men and women are seen as members of the "opposite sex," implying that they are completely different from each other. Women are considered to be warm and kind, interested in children, sensitive, friendly, patient, cheerful, wholesome, cooperative, and emotionally expressive. It is also seen as less desirable for a woman to be intelligent, decisive, ambitious, have leadership ability, or be principled, efficient, self-reliant, persuasive, and assertive. Men, in contrast, are described as having good business sense, being athletic, having good leadership ability, as well as being more ambitious, assertive, competitive, and decisive. It is also seen as less important and desirable for a man to be friendly, helpful, clean, kind, cooperative, show interest in children, and express emotion.

There can be considerable pressure for people to conform to these stereotypes, which works to increase and maintain gender differences. However, it is also possible to actively defy these stereotypes. Social-role theory proposes that gender may be better considered something that people do or a role that people enact rather than an essential part of who they are. However, if gender is something people *do* it is also something they can *undo*.[52] There are both challenges and possibilities that come about when men and women challenge gender stereotypes, effectively *undoing* gender.

Women as Leaders

Leadership is associated with stereotypically masculine traits.[53] People typically rate men and leaders as having similar traits and women as having different traits.[54] These associations have negative consequences for women who desire to fulfill leadership positions. If a woman believes that she does not have the personal qualities to become a leader, she may be less likely to put herself forth as a leader—resulting in a self-fulfilling prophesy. Another consequence of these stereotypes is known as the double bind (a concept covered in more detail in chapter 7). On the one hand, women are not viewed as good leaders, but if they act in a traditionally masculine fashion as leaders they are often criticized for not being nice enough. Based on the results of sixty-one studies of leadership and gender, women who used a directive or commanding leadership style were found to be evaluated less favorably than men who used that style.[55] Men who acted in a forceful manner were seen as strong leaders while women were seen as being pushy and unlikable. However, when female leaders acted in a more stereotypically feminine manner (e.g., warm and kind), they were criticized for not being tough enough.[56]

Challenging Female Stereotypes

Despite these pressures of the double bind, there is evidence that women can be outstanding leaders. A study combining the results of 162 studies on men's and women's leadership styles found them to be quite similar and identified only one small difference. On average, women tended to use a more democratic and participatory style of leadership while men tended to use a more directive or autocratic style.[57] Other differences have been found in men's and women's use of "transformative" leadership, which is considered the most effective style. Transformative leaders mentor others in the organization, communicate the value of and exhibit optimism for the organization, and encourage new perspectives for problem solving.[58] These practices are associated with high levels of employee motivation, job satisfaction, and organizational performance.[59] Transformative leadership is often contrasted with transactional leadership, which focuses on rewarding good—and punishing poor—employee performance.[60]

A review of the results of forty-five studies found small differences between men and women on these leadership styles.[61] Specifically, women were more likely than men to use transformational approaches—especially mentoring other members of the organization. Again, the differences in leadership style were small and a large percentage of both men (47.5%) and women (52.5%) were transformational leaders. Therefore, knowing a leader's sex would not allow someone to accurately guess what leadership style they were more likely to use.

The authors of this study proposed several explanations as to why women may exhibit more effective leadership styles than men.[62] First, the transformational leadership style incorporates traditionally feminine qualities. This style allows women to avoid some of the negative social consequences of acting either too masculine or too feminine in the work environment (i.e., the double bind). Another explanation is that fewer women than men are promoted to top leadership positions. Those who obtain these positions are likely to be particularly skilled leaders. Furthermore, the fact that there are only small differences between male and female leaders is consistent with social-role theory—people in similar situations (e.g., a leadership role) generally act in similar ways regardless of whether they are male or female. Nevertheless, these data should give people who claim that women's natural abilities are best suited to home and family life some reason for pause. If anything, the research has found that differences between men and women may make women better suited to lead than men.

Men as Caretakers

Gender stereotypes suggest that women are the primary caregivers.[63] Thus men who violate this stereotype experience negative reactions. Stay-at-home fathers are viewed as less competent than stay-at-home mothers.[64] In addition, almost half (45%) of stay-at-home fathers reported experiencing some sort of stigmatizing event, such as people expressing negative reactions to the fact that they stay at home or expressing distrust or suspicion of seeing a man at a playground.[65]

Stereotypes and beliefs about gender roles can make it difficult for men and women who are forced into reverse caretaker/breadwinner roles due to economic conditions. One study investigated twenty-one families in which the father stayed at home and the mother worked, largely due to economic forces.[66] Men struggled with their loss of the breadwinning role and experienced social sanctions for staying at home. One noted that: "[The] perception [among] most of my friends is like . . . get a damn job." Nevertheless, the men interviewed for this study emphasized the way in which staying at home had changed them despite their discomfort in reversing gender roles. Men described the increased value they placed on their children and family as well as how being in charge of childcare increased their skills of nurturing and communication.

Men who go into traditionally female careers face stereotypes as well. Men who are early childhood educators fear suspicion of being pedophiles if they are too nurturing. They are warned by their principals to "constantly be on your guard, on your best behavior, constantly presenting yourself as someone who is safe."[67] Furthermore, male teachers are often given the children with the greatest behavioral challenges, putting them in the role of disciplinarian rather than nurturer. One second-grade male teacher said: "Males get the harder children a lot of times. The behavior problems will usually be in our classes."[68]

Finally, even when a man takes on a nontraditional role, there is an assumption that it creates tension with his sense of masculinity. Media representations of stay-at-home fathers try to offset the perceived stigma by emphasizing their masculine traits. In an analysis of magazine articles on parenting, stay-at-home fathers were described as men who reject traditional definitions of masculinity, yet their masculine natures were often emphasized. One stay-at-home father was described as "tall . . . husky . . . has muscles on his muscles." Other articles emphasized their previous sports backgrounds (e.g., a high school cornerback) and continued participation in the workforce (e.g., running a business from home) while caring for children.[69] The connotation is that caring for children is an inherently feminine activity and can only be acceptable for men if they actively assert their masculinity.

Challenging Male Stereotypes

Despite the negative connotation associated with men taking on a caregiving role, there is evidence that men undergo biological and psychological changes when they provide care that supports this role. From a biological perspective, men's testosterone levels decrease after becoming fathers.[70] Despite the panic that men may feel at this news, lower levels of testosterone actually have been associated with better health outcomes[71] as well as higher marriage quality and lower rates of divorce.[72] Men who spent more time with their children (more than three hours a day) had lower levels of testosterone than those who spent less time. This drop in testosterone is important because higher levels of testosterone are related to less sympathy for and desire to respond to infant cries.[73] These findings suggest that men change in response to their social role as a caregiver, which in turn helps them provide better care by increasing longevity, marital stability, and the tendency to nurture.

From a psychological perspective, there is considerable evidence that when placed in caregiving roles, men become more nurturing. In interviews with stay-at-home fathers, men described the investment they made in their children, the joy that they got out of parenting, and how being a parent had affected them.[74] One man described how he was better suited to staying at home than his wife. He stated: "I always knew I would make a better parent than my wife. Just because of the way that she handled things and reacted versus how I did." The joy experienced from caretaking was expressed by one man who said: "The best thing I can say is just how rewarding it is when my eight-month-old laughs, giggles, whatever, she just smiles at you from across the room." When asked to reflect on how staying at home influenced their sense of masculinity, the men generally rejected gender stereotypes. One said: "I don't think there should be a huge distinction between masculinity and femininity." Another said: "I don't play those macho mind games, I don't want to fight . . . but I don't consider those things to be what makes me a man." Other men commented on how being in a caretaking role changed their personality, saying for example: "I think I've become a lot softer. I think I've become a better listener." These experiences of the stay-at-home fathers are consistent with social-role theory: When men act as caretakers they develop caring personalities.

Research on the parenting abilities of single fathers paints a similar picture of men who are capable parents providing healthy environments for their children. The mental and physical health of single parents and their children have been found to be good for both single mothers and fathers.[75] In fact, single fathers spend the same amount of time accessible to their children as single mothers and more time than married fathers.[76] Although some research has shown that children of single parents may be at some disadvantage academically compared to two-parent families,[77] the underlying culprit is most likely the decreased economic resources available to children of single-parent families.[78] Single fathers are actually less likely to suffer from the economic impact of single parenting than mothers, due to their greater earning potential.[79]

While in some cases having two parents does appear to provide advantages over having only one, the research has not specified that the two parents must be a man and a woman. Children raised by gay parents generally do not differ from those raised by heterosexual parents on social, emotional, cognitive, or developmental outcomes. The primary difference between children raised by gay parents and those raised by heterosexual parents is that children raised by gay parents seem to conform less to gender stereotypes.[80] Research has found that gay men are nurturing, active, and competent fathers[81] who are less likely to spank their children than heterosexual couples.[82] Gay fathers do not appear to provide a double dose of masculine parenting, but take on more feminine roles.[83] One gay father reflected: "I am more than just a dad. I'm a man, but I am kind of like a mom too!"[84]

CONSEQUENCES OF A BELIEF IN INNATE GENDER DIFFERENCES

The belief that the sexes are inherently different limits the ability for men and women to make autonomous choices. For example, people may not feel free to choose the clothes they want to wear or engage in the activities in which they are most interested. Beliefs about what men and women should be doing may keep people from working in the occupation of their choice or prevent them from working at all. It will be impossible to find work-family balance if people do not feel free to choose the work, family, and leisure activities they desire. If men cannot be caring and women cannot be leaders then it truly limits both in their ability to have complete and fulfilled lives.

In addition, a belief in innate gender differences can interfere with people's sense of competence. If girls are told long enough that a woman's place is in the home, how will they develop a sense of competence in the work environment? There is research indicating that girls perform worse on tests of math abilities if they are reminded that they are girls before taking them[85]— the gender stereotype that girls are not good at math is that powerful. One of our students told a story of how, at the end of her high school math class, all students received superlative awards for their performance in class. She received "likely to be the best mom" because she always remembered to bring pencils to lend to other students. That was the last challenging math class she took. Similarly, if men are not allowed to play with dolls due to gender norms, how will they develop the skills necessary to demonstrate competence in childcare?

Adhering to rules about gender can undermine a sense of relatedness to others that is essential to well-being. Men and women have stronger relationships when they share experiences and learn to take each other's perspectives.[86] Men may be at increased risk for not meeting their relatedness needs if they are cut off from the caregiver role that nurtures relationships. Although women may build their relationships with their children through their caregiving role, it may come at the expense of their other relationships.[87]

Research we conducted linked the belief that women are inherently better parents than men to a host of negative mental health outcomes.[88] Mothers who held these beliefs (e.g., "although fathers may mean well, they generally are not as good at parenting as mothers") had higher levels of stress and decreased satisfaction with life. Believing that women are inherently better parents was also related to having lower levels of social support. If women are seen as better parents than men, then they generally end up doing more of the parenting and have less time for developing and maintaining relationships. However, even among women with the same amount of social support, those who held stronger beliefs about women's superior parenting capacity had lower levels of life satisfaction. Thus the belief that women are natural parents appears to have damaging effects for maternal mental health.

Many women are taught to believe that they should have a natural maternal instinct.[89] According to this notion, women should look into their baby's eyes and feel a rush of love and joy.[90] They should immediately know what their children need and provide it automatically. These notions assume that women have competence (either innate or learned) in caregiving. So what happens if new mothers fail to experience this rush of maternal instinct? According to self-determination theory, they should experience decreased well-being.

In fact approximately 80% of women have some sort of negative feelings after the birth of their children, referred to as the "baby blues," while 10 to 15% have more serious postpartum depression. The expectation that motherhood should be easy, natural, and stress-free has been implicated as one of the primary causes of postpartum depression.[91] Belief in innate gender differences also contributes to gender inequality in childcare and serves to discourage mothers from seeking social support, which are also risk factors for postpartum depression.

However, maternal instincts may be more myth than reality. Sandra Hrdy, in her book *Mother Nature*,[92] draws on animal research as well as anthropological and historical research to demonstrate that women are not "natural mothers" with special instincts about what to do as parents. Rather, women learn to be mothers through experience and through the help of others. Hrdy contends that across cultures women have had a great deal of help raising children from their own mothers, sisters, and other women in the community. It is through interacting with these role models that new mothers learn how to parent. Furthermore, there are no data suggesting that women make *inherently* better parents than men. Rather, as predicted by the social-role theory, maternal behaviors (e.g., recognizing their own baby's cry) are elicited by spending time caring for children.[93] One classic study found that male rats would act just as maternal as female rats if put in extended contact with rat pups.[94] As Cordelia Fine wryly put it: "If a male *rat*, without even the aid of a William Sears baby-care manual, can be inspired to parent then I would suggest that the prospects for human fathers are pretty good."[95]

CONCLUSION

Most of the discussion of work-family balance has been described as a choice for only women to make. The assumption appears to be that women are biologically more equipped to parent. Research on gender stereotypes shows that the idea that men and women are and should be different is commonplace, and there are social pressures to act in accordance with traditional gender roles. However, the differences between men and women on a wide variety of traits, including those related to both leadership and nurturing, are small and change in response to changing social environments. For example, as women take on more leadership roles, they have had the opportunity to demonstrate excellent leadership skills. Similarly, as men take on more caregiving roles, they have the opportunity to demonstrate superb caregiving traits. Finally, the belief that men and women are inherently different has been linked to reduced self-determination and decreased well-being for mothers. Perhaps it is time to reevaluate the ideas that women are better equipped to be mothers and work-family balance is an issue only women need to wrestle with.

Chapter Six

Balance at Home

The idea of having it all never meant doing it all. Men are parents, too, and actually women will never be equal outside the home until men are equal inside the home.[1] —Gloria Steinem

This chapter is about the nitty-gritty of who does what in the family: the cooking, the cleaning, the laundry, the shopping, the diapers, the baths, the driving around, etc. Although women are increasingly working outside of the home, they continue to do the majority of work inside the home. The fact that many women spend an entire day working and then come home to a second job of working in the house was first documented in the groundbreaking work *The Second Shift*.[2] However, inequities in the division of household labor and childcare are a problem for both families with stay-at-home mothers and those who work outside of the home. Although it may seem that men benefit from the inequality, they also experience negative consequences in terms of decreased marital satisfaction and well-being. Disagreement and irritation between spouses about who is doing what and who is not doing enough can create a seething irritation that erodes even the most loving of marriages. The problem is not just how women and men can share work around the house more equitably, but how both women and men can have happier marriages. Inequality in the division of household labor and childcare represents a major barrier to achieving work-family balance for both men and women.

WOMEN DO MORE THAN MEN

In many ways, things have gotten better and are a lot closer to being equal than they used to be. Women's household labor has declined over the past forty years while men's contribution to housework has increased.[3] Although from 1965 to 2005 the number of hours women spent doing housework was nearly cut in half (from 30 hours a week to 17.5 hours a week) and the number of hours men spent doubled (from 4.9 hours to 10 hours a week), women still do almost twice as much housework as men. Unfortunately, the decline in women's household labor and increase in men's has not been consistent. The biggest decrease in women's relative contributions to household labor occurred between 1965 and 1975. During these years, women went from doing 6.1 times more household labor than men to doing only 3.3 times as much. But movement toward equality has declined with each passing decade. In 1985 women were doing twice as much housework as men, whereas ten years later they were doing 1.8 times as much. What started off as a fast trend toward equality seems to have stagnated.

THE REASONS FOR INEQUITY

Why is there so much inequality between men and women? There is a large body of research literature attempting to answer this question. The conclusion is that it almost all comes down to power. The person with less power in the relationship, usually the woman, gets stuck with the dirty work.

Who Earns More Money?

Generally, men have more power than women in relationships largely due to their greater earning potential (see chapter 7). As a result, women may have a tit-for-tat mentality, whereby they do most of the work around the house to compensate for their spouse's higher wages. Even same-sex couples, who typically have a more even division of household labor and childcare, show a similar pattern: The person who earns less does more of the traditionally feminine household chores (e.g., cooking, cleaning, and laundry).[4] This is known as social exchange theory—each person tries to contribute to the household in such a way that the benefits outweigh the costs so that the other person remains committed to the relationship.[5]

Having the man be the primary provider and the woman do the majority of the work around the house may seem fair on the surface, but women are often dissatisfied with the arrangement. When couples were interviewed about the division of labor in the household, men contended that because they contributed more financially to the household, it was fair for their wife to do most of the work around the house.[6] The wives agreed . . . sort of. While some agreed that, technically, it was fair that they did more because their husbands earned more, they were often quite upset about it. One wife had resigned herself to doing more around the house because her husband earned double what she did. However, she also expressed that she was unhappy in the marriage and seeking marital counseling. The "I earn more, so she should do more" line of justification may seem like a good deal for husbands who earn more than their wives. However, such an arrangement often creates resentment, anger, and decreased marital satisfaction—so maybe it is not such a good deal after all!

Research has suggested one exception to the idea that women who make more money do less labor. Some studies have suggested that when women outearn men, they actually tend to do *more* household labor. Greater earnings by women is related to greater equality in household labor up to the point where the wife outearns the husband—then the more she earns, the less he does.[7] In one study, unemployed men, who presumably had the most time to do household chores, were the group that actually did the least around the house. Why would this be so? When wives do not work they generally see it as their responsibility to do the vast majority of household labor and child-care. However, men may view being unemployed or underemployed as a threat to their masculinity, and their wives worry about these threats. Researchers have suggested that wives do more around the house so their husbands do not feel emasculated.[8] However, more recent research has suggested that this may only be the case for lower-income women in more traditional households, and that it may have been the case more in the 1980s than today. More recent data suggest that for women who earn higher incomes, a "her money, her time" model may come into play, especially as much of the day-to-day labor is outsourced.[9]

Who Works Longer Hours?

Another way of dividing up household responsibilities is based on time availability rather than who earns more money. In general, the person who works longer hours outside the home does less work in the home.[10] Wives find time availability to be a more equitable way to share the household labor than basing it on who makes more money because women typically earn less than men even when doing the same job (see chapter 7). Research has shown that as women work more hours outside of the home, the contribution their husbands make to household chores increases.[11] For example, my (HS) husband is an attorney who earns considerably more than I do as an educator. However, he also has a much more flexible schedule, so he is the one who meets the bus and gets the kids off to their activities the majority of the time.

Unfortunately, the amount of time spent at work is not an entirely objective measure because people often have some flexibility in when and where they complete their work. Women are more likely than men to take advantage of telecommuting or flex-time to increase time at home.[12] Women are also more likely than men to take work home to do after the kids go to bed so that they can spend more time with their children.[13] I (ML) remember when I was coming into the office at 1:00 p.m. during the two years that my husband and I were trying to avoid paying for double full-time day care. Even though chitchatting in the halls is one of my favorite parts of the job, I stopped socializing altogether. I would come in to work, teach my classes, go to meetings, and leave. I often brought piles of papers home to grade. While this kind of efficiency may be admirable in some sense, research has suggested that when women forgo social networking opportunities they are often penalized by being passed up for promotions or raises.[14] By changing their approach to work to maximize family time, women may suffer at work as well as at home because the extra time at home often translates into doing more household and childcare chores.

Who Wants the Relationship More?

Although financial power is an important reason why women do more around the house than men, relationship power is also influential in this process. Generally, the person who wants the relationship more has more power.[15] So who wants the relationship more? The media often portrays women as the ones who want to get married and have children, while men are presented as the ones who fear the loss of their freedom. This theme permeates almost every romantic comedy in Hollywood. For example, in *He's Just Not That into You*,[16] Ben Affleck does not want to marry Jennifer Aniston after many years of living together in a committed relationship, and she has to leave him to get him to propose. If Jennifer Aniston can't easily get a man to commit it leaves little hope for the rest of us!

If a woman feels as though she wanted the relationship and marriage more than her husband, she may believe she needs to do more of the housework to make marriage more palatable for her reluctant spouse. Similarly, a woman may do the majority of the childcare if she feels that having children was primarily her idea. There is some evidence that young men also buy into this sentiment as well. A typical male college student explained why his future wife would probably do most of the household labor by saying: "Well, if she is the one who wants the family, there it goes right there."[17]

But do women really want marriage and children more than men, or is this just another inaccurate stereotype perpetuated by the media? There is some evidence that men tend to fall in love faster than women do and are actually the ones who push for escalation early in the relationship.[18] My colleagues and I (ML) conducted a study to examine how much young men and women desired both marriage and children as well as how much they thought the typical man and the typical women did.[19] Both men and women believed in the stereotype that the typical man was relatively uninterested in marriage and children, but the typical woman really desired them. However, there was absolutely no difference between men's and women's actual desire for marriage and children. For women, but not for men, wanting marriage and children was related to willingness to do chores and childcare in their future relationships. Men may have figured "she will want marriage and children more than me" so his desire for marriage and children did not translate into willingness to do chores. Women and men had a misperception of how much the typical person of the opposite sex wants a family, which resulted in a perceived, but inaccurate, power imbalance that would give men the upper hand in a marriage. Therefore, women may do more (and men do less) around the house to make marriage and having kids "worth it" for their, supposedly, reluctant husbands.[20]

Beyond Power: Vaginas and Dirty Socks

In addition to the power differential, some people argue that women do more of the household chores and childcare then men because their standards for cleanliness are higher—they just care more. There may be some truth to this sentiment. Even when all of the measures of power we discussed are taken into consideration, simply being a woman is related to doing more around the house.[21] In other words, even when women make equal money to men and have an equal amount of time available, they still do more around the house. Furthermore, women tend to care more about the status of their house, have higher standards for cleanliness, and feel more responsible for keeping the house clean.[22] Research has found that individuals who have higher standards generally do most of the work.[23]

Women's higher standards are a big factor driving inequity in the division of labor. Women, so the theory goes, have a lower tolerance for things being dirty.[24] So a woman will see a pair of socks on the floor, it will bother her, and she will put them in the hamper. She will see an overflowing laundry basket and start a load. Most men are simply not as bothered by these things. In interviews, men have expressed the sentiment that it is not fair that they should have to do housework up to the high standards of their wives. They are happy with the house being a little messy, so why should they have to clean it up? They might say: "If she wants to keep the house squeaky clean then she can go ahead and do it." One study found that 34% of men felt as though it was too difficult to keep the house clean enough to meet the standards of their wives.[25]

This difference in cleanliness standards creates a self-perpetuating cycle. As women start to do more tasks around the house they take "ownership" of the tasks[26] and develop standards about how to do them properly. Furthermore, men who are extremely intelligent and competent in many domains of their life may display a certain level of incompetence around certain chores that they are not comfortable doing. We frequently hear women complain that it is easier to do everything around the house because when their husbands try to "help" they mess everything up. One study found that women spend an average of three hours a week redoing chores (e.g., laundry, dishes, and vacuuming) that their partners did not complete "properly."[27] One story shared with us was about a woman who complained that her husband could not even make frozen fish sticks, which does not exactly take a degree in culinary science. The directions on the box specify: Step 1—Preheat oven. Step 2—Take fish sticks out of box (the manufacturers do not even assume that people know they have to take the sticks out of the box). Another woman we know decided it would be easier to do the cooking herself after her fiancé ruined a few nonstick pans because he could not remember to use a plastic utensil rather than a fork. Still other women we know resort to playing a game of "chicken" with their husbands over who will pick the dirty socks up off the floor and put them in the hamper—usually the women lose. All of these women expressed particular frustration because their husbands are educated men who hold professional jobs. Men's ability to pay attention to detail at work, but not home, suggests something other than lack of ability may at the root of the problem.

Evolution versus Social-Role Theory (Revisited)

It is worth taking a moment to think about where women's higher standards for household work and greater attention to detail come from when it comes to domestic tasks. Why is it, exactly, that having a vagina is related to noticing a pair of dirty socks and having a penis is related to a certain amount of dirt blindness? Evolutionary theorists might suggest that it is encoded into people's genes. Perhaps when women were out gathering fruit, those who had a better sense of smell were more likely to survive because they avoided potential poisons. We think this explanation is unlikely and would venture that there is nothing inherent about having a vagina that makes women more sensitive to dirt. There are certainly women who are slobs and many couples where the husband is cleaner than his wife. We can think of a few, including my (ML's) own marriage. While neither of us are neat freaks, I am easily the messier member of the family.

We would argue that the cultural expectations about what it means to be a man and a woman (see social-role theory in chapter 5) are the reasons that women are generally more sensitive to mess than men. For example, many men and women grew up in families where the women do the majority of the domestic tasks and men may learn that these tasks are a woman's role.[28] During a typical Thanksgiving dinner, the women usually do the majority of the cooking. After dinner the men generally watch football and drink beer, while the women gather in the kitchen talking and cleaning up. When men and women grow up in families where this is the pattern, the gender roles of who does what are rarely questioned.

Images of women in domestic roles are pervasive in the media. Snow White went into the forest and was rescued by seven dirty men for whom she happily cooked and cleaned. Cinderella demonstrated "good" values by spending her day cleaning while her lazy stepsisters lounged around the house. Probably the ultimate icon is June Cleaver who was perfectly coiffed at all times, kept the house spotless and had dinner on the table when her husband got home from work. Not surprisingly, a content analysis of women's and men's magazines show that women's magazines, especially women's home magazines, have many advertisements demonstrating women engaging in traditional domestic roles. Men are rarely, if ever, displayed doing anything domestic around the house.[29]

When men *are* portrayed doing work around the house they are almost always portrayed as idiots and clowns who simply cannot get things right. Huggies decided to pull ads that suggested their diapers and wipes were "dad proof" after dads protested that they were insulting.[30] Movies like *Mr. Mom* and *Daddy Daycare* portray fathers as completely incompetent, at least initially, in the realms of childcare and housework. When Michael Keaton's character loses his job, he becomes *Mr. Mom* by staying home to take care of the kids while his wife goes to work. Unfortunately, he's never done any of the childcare or household tasks before, so he makes a complete mess of everything.

Another social pressure created by assumptions about gender roles involves fears about the social evaluation and judgment from others. I (ML) know if people come into my home and it is a mess, they would not think, "Wow, Julian [my husband] is a real slacker; he should pick up more around the house." They are more likely to think, "I can't believe she keeps her home so messy." It is generally considered a woman's responsibility to keep the house clean, so when it is dirty, it is the wife who experiences the potential social repercussions. Another example about how this plays out in my (HS) life is that my husband likes to invite people over to watch sports on the weekends. I frequently do not want to entertain because I have not had time to go shopping for food and clean the house. He thinks the house is fine as it is, and we can just order pizza when people come over. Our compromise is that we allow his friends to come over when the house is messy, because they are less likely to care. We only invite my friends over when the house is clean.

Finally, cultural expectations about gender particularly affect men. Men are under a great deal of pressure not to seem in any way "feminine." Young men are constantly attempting to bolster their sense of masculinity among their peers because the punishment for acting feminine, including expressing emotions or expressing physical pain, is to be called "gay" or "girly."[31] Given the relentless pressure on men to maintain their masculinity and the social sanctions for being perceived as not masculine, it may not be surprising that doing "women's work" around the house may be a source of shame for men, even if they do not fully realize it. When men and women are not educated about the pressures they are under to conform to gender roles, they do not have the tools to fight against those pressures—it is hard to resist an unnamed pressure.

No One Likes Housework, but Only Men Get Thanked

Another argument for women's greater participation in household labor is that women simply *like* housework more than men. However, there is not much research to suggest that this is true. While some aspects of household work can be rewarding (at least when it is over), most people do not enjoy the actual act of cleaning toilets. Women do feel more responsibility for household chores, but there is no indication that they enjoy them more. One study showed that women did enjoy both laundry and childcare more than men. [32] However, men actually enjoyed grocery shopping, kitchen cleanup, and housecleaning more than women. Men may have reported enjoying some household tasks more than women because they felt they had some choice in whether or not they had to do these tasks, while women felt more of an obligation.

There is some evidence that the person who enjoys doing a task more is more likely to do that task; however, men's preferences take precedence over women's. [33] It makes sense for women to defer to men if men have more power in relationships—if they particularly like a chore, they will do it, but women generally have to do the rest of the chores, including the ones that nobody likes. Given that men generally feel less obligated to do chores, they are generally thanked and appreciated more when they do them. [34] He vacuums the house once, proudly announces it, and expects lavish praise. But she has vacuumed the house ten times as often without comment. Women are generally less likely to be thanked or shown appreciation for doing chores because it is just seen as "what women do." One study found that the feeling of being appreciated and mattering in a relationship was one of the most important predictors of perceptions of fairness in the relationship and relationship satisfaction. [35]

Another reason that men may receive more gratitude for their contributions to the household is that the tasks they do are often larger and more visible, such as mowing the lawn or shoveling the walk. [36] Sometimes a man takes on an even more impressive project like building a play set or laying down a hardwood floor. This type of project can take days or weeks to complete, which reduces the time he has to contribute to cooking, cleaning, or childcare. At the end of such a project, he will get a great deal of praise. Neighbors will come to "ooh and aah" and admire his handiwork. But people rarely get praised and thanked for the smaller everyday chores like cooking, cleaning, and laundry. Children on television may beam and say, "Thanks for the great meal, Mom," but that does not happen very often in everyday life. Rarely do moms hear, "Wow, that was a really great load of laundry you did" or "The toilet looks particularly bright and shiny today." One reason these tasks rarely get noticed is that they happen every day in a similar fashion.

There is another difference between the type of larger, infrequent household tasks that men typically do and the daily repetitive tasks that women generally do and that is the amount of control that people typically have over when to do them. There is generally some leeway about when to mow the lawn or work on some house project. But there is a lot less leeway about when and how often dinner is put on the table, cleaning the resulting dishes, and packing daily lunches. These tasks need to happen pretty much every day and, generally, at specific times of the day. In other words, people generally have less autonomy over when they do these tasks; thus they are called "low-control tasks." Women generally spend three times more on these tasks than men; and it is these tasks that make women feel as though the division of labor in their household is unfair—these tasks are usually boring, repetitive, and underappreciated. [37]

Managing and Organizing Is Labor Too

Even when both members of a couple have high-paying jobs and share the work around the house relatively equally, women often have the additional task of managing and organizing everything that has to be done. Research has found that this is a common pattern in couples. It is almost always the wife who keeps the mental "to do" list. [38] Often husbands are perfectly willing to do a load of laundry or unload the dishwasher if they are asked to do so; however, they may not realize what has to be done in the first place. There is more to running a household than just doing chores. It involves planning and organization. What will be cooked for dinner this week? What needs to be put on the grocery list? Are we out of milk or toilet paper? How long has it been since the toilets have been scrubbed? Even when household labor is outsourced—someone else is paid to do it—it is usually the woman who organizes the outsourcing. Rarely do you hear men sitting around discussing whether or not they are happy with their hired household help. It is generally up to the woman to organize such things.

In one study wives were asked what husbands could do better around the house to make them more satisfied with the division of labor in the household. [39] One of the principle things that wives wished their husbands did more of was to share in the management, organization, and delegation of household tasks. It was only women with husbands who did virtually nothing around the house who wished that their husbands would help more with daily repetitive tasks like dishes and laundry. Many husbands were already doing that. Women did not want "helpers"; they wanted partners. What the women really wanted was somebody to share the mental burden of planning and organization.

Women are generally also in charge of what has been called emotion work.[40] Who remembers to buy Mother's Day cards? Who remembers to call Aunt Sally on her birthday? Who remembers to tip the mailman and write thank-you notes for presents? It is almost always the woman. All of this work takes time and effort, but it is rarely rewarded or appreciated. It is just seen as something that women are supposed to do to maintain relationships. Consider what happens if a couple walks into a party without a present or side dish when everyone else has brought something. It is generally the woman who will be judged for the social faux pas and bear the repercussions.

Having Children Increases Inequality

Although couples without children may enjoy an equitable division of labor, research has shown consistently that relationships start to become more and more unequal after the birth of a child.[41] Both men and women start to hold more traditional beliefs about gender roles and are more likely to think that women are better suited to take care of children than men.[42] When men and women believe that women are naturally predisposed to motherhood (a belief we challenged in chapter 5),[43] there is a more traditional division of household labor and childcare (i.e., the woman does the majority). The inequality is often justified by references to women's "natural" abilities to parent. One mother who took on the majority of the household labor and childcare claimed: "The woman has it more in her genes to be more equipped for nurturing."[44] When fathers believe that women have a natural ability to parent, mothers are considerably more likely to spend time as the sole provider of childcare.[45] Conversely, when mothers reject the belief that women are inherently better parents then men, fathers are more likely to be involved in childcare. Thus belief in inherent gender differences has consistently been found to be related to inequity in the division of labor.[46]

All of the task management and emotion work increases when children enter the picture. There are playdates to schedule, after-school activities to organize, birthday parties to attend, gifts to buy, doctor's appointments to schedule, and the list goes on and on. Men are usually very willing to complete these tasks when asked, as long as it does not conflict with their work schedule. But they are rarely the ones who organize the activities, schedule the playdates, or make the doctor's appointments.

Inequity in the division of labor can sneak up on couples after the birth of the child, largely due to issues associated with the pay gap, leave availability, and difficulty finding adequate childcare—all issues that we will cover in chapter 7.[47] When inequality sets in, resentment can breed. Judith Warner interviewed women who had opted out of the workforce. These women were disturbed by the fact that while they were once equal to their partner, they came to be seen as the one primarily responsible for all of the domestic tasks. One woman said: "I had the sense of being in an unequal marriage. . . . I think he preferred the house to be 'kept' in a different kind of way than I was prepared to do it. If I had any angst about being an overeducated stay-at-home mom, it was not about raising the kids, but it was about sweeping."[48] They also felt the loss of power acutely, noting that at times they had to negotiate with their husbands about money for childcare.[49] Even when women decided to return to the workforce after many years staying at home either part time or full time, the patterns of inequality remained entrenched. One woman noted: "When I worked at KPMG we did 50/50," she said. "We were making equal money. Then once I started staying home, I was doing laundry, dinner . . ." But, once she started working again, the expectations remained the same. "There just doesn't seem to be a way to go back."[50]

CONSEQUENCES OF UNEQUAL DIVISION OF HOUSEHOLD LABOR

Why should both men and women work toward greater equality in the division of labor within their relationships? There is research evidence to suggest that this inequity is detrimental to both men and women. First and foremost, it clearly damages a couple's relationship with each other. It also decreases the amount of time that women have for leisure activities, which is bad for their health, relationships, and well-being. Finally, it undermines both men's and women's ability to meet their need for the autonomy, competence, and relatedness required for well-being.

Unhappy Marriages

One of the strongest findings about the consequences of unequal division of labor is that people, especially women who perceive the division of labor to be unfair, are more distressed[51] and less satisfied in their marriage.[52] Feeling that things are inequitable was also related to a greater likelihood for divorce, especially if it was the woman who felt things were unfair, and it usually was.[53] In fact, women initiate divorce at least twice as often as men.[54] The relationship between unfair division of labor and marital dissatisfaction is exacerbated during the transition to motherhood. One longitudinal study found that when women became mothers, they did more housework, which led to a sense that the work load was unfair and subsequent marital dissatisfaction.[55]

Having a wife who is dissatisfied with how labor is divided in the household is no fun for husbands either. A beautiful, fun, engaging wife has started to become an angry and dissatisfied nag. "You need to take out the trash," "you are not changing that diaper right," "how could you have forgotten to brush the kids' teeth?" Eyes are rolled, sighs are heaved, and couples grow more distant. None of this is good for a couple's sex life either.[56] It is hard to want to have sex with someone when there is deep-seated resentment because he never remembers to pick up his socks and never unloads the dishwasher. The idea that he "never" does this only adds to his resentment: "Whaddya mean? "he might say. "I did it last week." Of course, men likely become less interested in having sex with women who they view as being nagging critics.

The data relating participation in household labor to sexual frequency actually paint a bit of a mixed picture. One study found that couples have more sex when men do more traditionally masculine chores—women found it sexy when men helped in masculine ways such as yard work and fixing things.[57] Although this study was recently published, it was based on data collected over twenty years ago when men helping at all was probably considered sexy and men doing traditionally feminine chores may have been less accepted. Another study, also using an older data set, which looked at the relationship between marital and sexual satisfaction among married couples, painted a more optimistic picture for couples who shared household labor. This study found that couples where both members worked and participated in household labor actually had more sex, even though you might think that they would have less time.[58] The authors determined that those who work hard also play hard. We would argue that as expectations about gender have shifted, men who vacuum and do dishes are increasingly sexy. We think sharing chores is good foreplay!

Consequences of Inequity: No Time to Play

One of the consequences of the inequitable division of labor is the fact that men tend to have more leisure time than women. It is estimated that married women have several hours less leisure time per week than married men.[59] When men get home from work they often take time to themselves doing activities that help them unwind. On weekends, many husbands decompress after a long week of work with a four- or five-hour game of golf. The disparity in the amount of leisure time that men and women have has been identified in some studies as one of the biggest sources of marital dissatisfaction.[60] I (ML) can certainly identify with this as I sometimes find myself calculating the amount of time my husband and I have to ourselves. These calculations can get tricky of course. What counts as leisure time? Does it count if I am reading blogs on the computer while simultaneously watching my children practice gymnastics? It certainly does not count if I have to intervene when my son's handstand results in him kicking my daughter, and I comfort her while listening to ear-deafening screams. Does it count as leisure if I take the children on a playdate if I am friends with the parents? If I choose to use my alone time doing research or writing this book, does it count as leisure time?

Leisure time has important implications for people's health and relationships. In one study, researchers examined what husbands and wives did with their time after work.[61] They confirmed that men engaged in more leisure activities, while women did more household chores. However, they also measured production of the stress hormone cortisol. Cortisol is produced when people are stressed and leads to all sorts of health problems including increased body fat—particularly the kind of fat that accumulates around the belly[62] as well as even more dire consequences such as increased likelihood of death.[63] Furthermore, if the body is producing too much cortisol people are unable to fall asleep.[64] Men who were able to have leisure time after work had decreased cortisol production over the course of the evening. Women, who were less likely to have a chance to relax and engage in leisure activities, continued to have high levels of cortisol throughout the night.[65] So inequity in the division of labor and the leisure gap between men and women may be literally killing women (as well as making them fatter, more stressed, and sleep deprived). In addition, women who were able to unwind after work and allow their cortisol production to decrease had higher marital satisfaction.[66]

Decreased Well-Being

The negative consequences associated with unequal division of labor in the household can reduce an individual's well-being by interfering with their basic needs of autonomy, competence, and relatedness.[67] When men make more money than women, it gives them more power in the relationship.[68] The person with the money and power has more autonomy, not only in terms of making financial decisions (e.g., whether to hire someone to help with household chores), but also in terms of how to spend their time. As a result, women spend more time doing housework and childcare[69] and have less leisure time[70] than men. Women also have less autonomy over which chores they do. Men select the tasks they find more enjoyable, while women do whatever remains.[71] In addition, men typically have more autonomy in when they complete their chores while women perform more low-control tasks that have to be done on a specific schedule.[72] It is clear that women have much to gain by reducing these inequities. However, research suggests that men will also benefit if they work toward equality, even though it may not seem appealing at first to have to do more around the house.[73] In a study of thirty-one countries, men reported higher family satisfaction when they were more involved in household labor and childcare.[74] In addition, inequity was associated with increased negative emotions and decreased positive emotions for both members of the couple. The person doing more experienced distress and anger, while the person doing less experienced fear and self-reproach at the exploitive relationship.[75]

Inequity in the division of household labor can also adversely impact men's and women's sense of competence. Women frequently express frustration that men just mess things up when they try to "help."[76] So they often take on the majority of the household tasks to ensure the chores are completed to their standards.[77] Rather than bolstering women's sense of competence, however, the additional burden seems to create stress and reduce well-being.[78] In addition to the negative feedback men may get from their wives about their competence regarding household chores and childcare, men are also bombarded with messages of their incompetence from the media. Although there has been pushback against these stereotypes (e.g., against the Huggies ad campaign),[79] negative messages from the media can certainly undermine men's competence and decrease their motivation to contribute equally in the household sphere.[80] It is detrimental to women and insulting to men for people to assume men cannot contribute equally to housework and childcare.

Finally, inequality in the household damages men's and women's relationships with each other. In fact it is a strong predictor of marriage dissatisfaction and divorce.[81] The lack of gratitude displayed for doing household chores exacerbates the problem because gratitude has been found to strengthen relationships.[82] In addition, the reduction in leisure time for women, who do the majority of the housework, can negatively impact their relatedness. Participation in leisure activities is one of the primary ways that people develop their relationships with others[83] and build social support networks.[84] However, it is not only women's relationships that are negatively affected. If women are doing the majority of the emotion work for a couple, it means that men may not be building and maintaining their own relationships with friends and family. Given the importance of social support for well-being,[85] men's reliance on their wives to maintain their relationships seems shortsighted.

INCREASING EQUALITY IN THE HOME

Men and women, especially those from the millennial generation, want equality in their marriages.[86] In a study my colleague and I (ML) did assessing the expectations of division of labor among college students, both men and women ideally wanted equality. However, while men thought equality in their future relationships would actually happen, women believed that they would have to do the majority of household labor and childcare.[87] We think it is encouraging that the young men wanted and expected equality. It may be a more challenging goal than they anticipate, but working toward marital equality is worth the effort. Couples who both wanted equality and were actually able to achieve it have been identified as the most satisfied with their relationships.[88]

How can couples increase equality in their home? To some extent, the problem is much larger than the two individuals in a relationship. It stems from the view that men and women are inherently different (see chapter 5). If women are caregivers and men are providers, then it is only natural that women do more of the household labor. It also stems from expectations about the ideal worker that do not allow family obligations to interfere with work (see chapter 4), making it difficult for men who take on the ideal-worker role to equitably contribute to family life. Furthermore, the inequality stems from social barriers such as the pay gap that we will discuss further in chapter 7. Given that men earn more than women, their employment contributes more toward supporting the family and gives men more power in the relationship. These issues make it more likely for mothers to cut back on work or stop working altogether, even if they would have been happier finding a way to combine work and family. Although there are these larger problems to address, there are many changes that can be made within people's relationships to reduce inequity in the division of household labor.

First, partners in a relationship have to decide how they are going to define "equal." Should people put a scoreboard in the living room? "And she has just spent twenty minutes folding laundry, he is down by twenty folks, wait, he is unloading the dishwasher, this is getting closer . . . closer. Oh, broken glass, that's five penalty points." We think one of the biggest misunderstandings about how to share household labor fairly is that everything needs to be done fifty-fifty, and that conversations should revolve around calculating the exact amount of labor each member puts into tasks. Couples who have egalitarian divisions of labor are often more fluid and flexible than this in their approach. One person likes to cook more; the other is more likely to do laundry. The person who gets home earlier starts dinner; the other one cleans up. Some couples may try to share all of the chores while others may have specializations.[89] Couples need to figure out what works best for them.

One way couples can increase the equity in division of labor is to communicate and be clear about their expectations. Although the majority of married women (53%) want to change the division of labor in the family, very few (less than 13%) actually talk to their husbands about it.[90] Women who are assertive and talk with their husbands about what they want are more likely to have a division of labor closer to their personal ideal. One working mother whose husband stays at home described how better communication improved her marriage:

We'd sit down weekly to discuss our finances, to make a weekly menu plan, to create a family to-do list. We created a budget and agreed to consult one another on any non-essential purchases. Sharing that burden has been a relief. We talk about what the coming week will bring, who needs a flu shot and when to call the electrician. [91]

One study found that couples who had the lowest levels of conflict had clear distinctions about who does what, did not interfere in the others' tasks, made few demands, and demonstrated respect for each other's contributions to the household. [92] In addition, women might benefit from lowering their standards about how work needs to be done. [93] Given that a great deal of the inequity in the division of labor may stem from women feeling as though their husbands do not live up to their standards of cleanliness, women who are less concerned about these standards are more likely to have equality. [94] A *New York Times* article titled "In Defense of Filth" concluded with the following: "A clean house is a sign of a wasted life, truly. Hope is messy: Eventually we'll all be living in perfect egalitarian squalor." [95]

It may also be helpful for women to remember that the reason men are hesitant to participate equally in household labor may be complex and connected to internalized beliefs about what it means to be masculine. Men who do not do chores properly are not incompetent. They simply have not had as much practice, and there is a learning curve. In addition, when a man does a chore improperly it may be a sign that, on some level, he is uncomfortable doing the chore. However, when women become frustrated and take on the tasks themselves, this perpetrates the inequality. [96] Appreciation is important for relationship satisfaction. Women who actively appreciate when men participate in household labor will be likely to have husbands who continue to do so. [97]

Men would also benefit from increasing the equality in the division of labor, especially considering the costs of inequity for marital satisfaction. Men should do more than simply take on tasks when assigned, but should participate in the management and organization of the household. [98] Men should also pay attention to leisure time. One of the biggest negative effects of inequity stems from the leisure gap, so husbands would benefit from working to make sure that wives have enough time to unwind after a long day and have other opportunities to participate in leisure activities. [99] Husbands would also do well to remember the importance of appreciation, [100] although not as a substitute for being a true partner in the household.

CONCLUSION

We believe the inequity of household labor between men and women is a major barrier to finding work-family balance. Despite progress, women are still doing significantly more of the housework and childcare than men. This inequity is fueled by beliefs about gender differences that pervade the home (i.e., women are natural caretakers) as well as work environments (e.g., leave policy and the wage gap). These conditions result in a power imbalance that contributes to unequal division of household labor. Although the social roles of being a spouse and parent have important benefits for people (see chapter 2), the advantages of having multiple roles depend on the quality of each role.[101] Unequal division of household labor decreases role quality and has serious consequences. When inequity in the division of labor interferes with people's ability to meet their needs for autonomy, competence, and relatedness, their overall well-being declines. Fortunately, better understanding the causes and consequences of unequal division of labor can help couples become motivated to find ways to increase equality.

Chapter Seven

Societal Barriers to Balance

The barriers that make it difficult to balance work and family responsibilities are often difficult to see because they are built into the structure of society. Thus when women make the decision to leave the workplace to care for their children, it is generally framed as a privileged choice. For example, in the *New York Times Magazine* article on the "opt out" revolution, the author asks why women do not run the world. The conclusion she came to was because they do not want to.[1] The implication was that when high-powered, highly educated women leave the workforce, their choices are free and unconstrained. These women simply chose family over career—end of story.

THE ILLUSION OF CHOICE

But are these choices really free and unconstrained? Pamela Stone interviewed women to understand the reasons why they had left the workforce after having children.[2] She found that women overwhelmingly did not want to leave the workplace, but felt forced out. Women found it hard to leave their jobs and give up their professional identity—for many the "choice" was agonizing. Many felt that their work environments were "all or nothing." If they did manage to gain a part-time position, they reported being put on a "mommy track" that kept them from getting interesting work assignments and promotions. The mothers she interviewed also noted that their husbands' careers had taken priority in the family, which resulted in women contributing more to the childcare and housework. One woman noted: "My husband has always said to me, 'You can do whatever you want to do,' but he's not there to pick up any load."

Most women do not actually have a true choice about whether to work or stay at home. Although approximately 8% of professional women with ad-

vanced degrees "opt out" of the workplace to care for their children,[3] it is a
myth that the vast majority of women who stay at home with their children
are highly educated and wealthy. As described in chapter 2, women with
lower levels of education are actually more likely to leave the workplace
when they have children because they are faced with impossible choices—
the jobs that are open to them often do not pay enough to cover the childcare
expenses of working outside of the home.[4]

This chapter describes the barriers in society that affect the ability of
people to balance work and family. In chapter 4, we described how inflexible
work environments make balance difficult for all. In chapter 5, we described
how pervasive gender stereotypes shape beliefs about male and female roles.
Now we will explore how these beliefs in the fundamental differences between men and women manifest themselves in the work environment, creating gender inequality in hiring and compensation. In addition, we will address how parental-leave policies and lack of affordable, high-quality childcare contribute to the problem of work-family balance.

THE PAY GAP

Over the past forty years, women's participation in the labor force has increased dramatically. According to the Pew Research Center, women com-
prised just over a third (38%) of the paid labor force in 1970 but made up
almost half of it (47%) in 2013.[5] Women with children under the age of six
have increased their labor force participation from 39% to 65% over the
same period. Women are also graduating from college at higher rates than
men, while more women than ever are getting professional degrees such as in
law or medicine, and being elected to public office.[6] In fact, a Gallup poll
found that 53% of Americans (61% of men and 45% of women) believe that
women have the same job opportunities as men.[7]

Despite women's increased labor force participation and the perception of
gender equality in the job market, there is still considerable inequity in the
workplace. In 2011, women earned only seventy-seven cents for every dollar
earned by men, based on annual median earnings.[8] This pay gap is experienced by women of every race, although it is highest for Hispanic and Latina
women, who earned only 59% of what white males earned. The pay gap
cannot simply be accounted for by differences in education levels. The truth
is that men outearn women at every level of education. Women earn approximately three-fourths of what comparably educated men earn, ranging from a
low of 72% for women with a professional degree to a high of 80% for
women with a doctoral degree. Furthermore, the pay gap is not specific to the
United States—women's earnings universally lag behind men's based on
statistics from 150 countries.[9]

The pay gap between women and men can be seen immediately after college graduation and increases over time. One year after college women earned only 82% of what men made. Even when almost every single demographic variable was controlled for (including college major, occupation, economic sector, hours worked, months unemployed since graduation, GPA, type of undergraduate institution, institution selectivity, age, geographical region, and marital status), a 7% gap in pay between women and men remained unexplained. [10] This pay gap widens as people age. Women earn only 69% of what their male counterparts do ten years after graduation with 12% of the difference remaining unexplained. [11] Finally, even though wives had more education than their husbands, on average, men still outearned their wives as newlyweds. [12]

Despite this evidence some people have tried to discredit the pay gap. For example, in May 2013 Fox News ran a story calling the pay gap a "myth." According to Fox: "The gender pay gap is not a result of discrimination, coercion, or anything like that. To put it simply, it's a matter of women's choices." [13] The language of choice seems to be used as a way to disguise discrimination and inequity. In fact, it may be that encouraging people to view women's decisions to leave the workplace as a choice actually *causes* people to become less aware of continued gender discrimination. When college undergraduates were shown a poster about a fictional book, *Choosing to Leave: Women's Experiences away from the Workplace*, they were significantly more likely to believe that opportunities for men and women were equal and that gender discrimination was nonexistent than were students who saw an almost identical book poster, *Women at Home: Experiences away from the Workplace*, that did not frame the issue as one of choice. [14] Although women and men do make different decisions that affect their salaries, the relevant question remains: How free and unconstrained are those choices in light of gender inequality in the workplace?

In Pamela Stone's interviews with women who decided to leave their job, it was apparent that their lower pay in comparison to their husband's contributed to their decision to opt out of the workforce. [15] This perception that the wives' salaries were not important relative to the needs of the family was especially salient because women generally perceived the cost of childcare as coming out of their salary, not the family income. One woman explained how she was spending up to 90% of "her" salary on childcare. Thus women's lower salaries create an environment whereby the motivation to continue working decreases. Simply put, making more money motivates people to stay in the workforce.

The pay gap adversely affects not only women, but also children. A 2013 Pew Research report found that 40% of the children in the United States were primarily supported by their mothers. This included 8.6 million children living with single mothers and 5.1 million children living in families where the woman was the primary breadwinner.[16] Therefore, the pay gap puts children at risk of poor living conditions and inadequate nutrition and health care.[17] Given the magnitude of the problem for women and children, it is important to understand the factors that contribute to the pay gap so that solutions can be identified.

Teachers Make Less than Architects

One of the biggest sources of the pay gap is occupational gender segregation. In other words, women tend to work in occupations that pay less. According to the U.S. Bureau of Labor Statistics, relatively low-paying jobs (e.g., personal care and service, office and administrative support, health-care support, and education or library staff) are occupied over 70% by women.[18] Higher-paying jobs, such as architects, engineers, chief executive officers, and protective service occupations, are dominated by men.

These wage differences may exist because many occupational wages were set during a time when explicit discrimination against women was the norm, and the relative wages of different occupations has stayed consistent over time.[19] For example, a memo sent by the California Civil Service in 1930 to many companies explicitly instructed officials to set wages for jobs dominated by women at a lower rate than jobs dominated by men, even if those jobs required the same credentials and experience.[20] A 1936 California memo discussing whether to give clerical workers or janitors pay increases noted that only janitors should get the pay increase: "The clerical workers are more generally the younger single persons not having the same degree of family responsibility."[21] Thus early assumptions that women do not need as much money because they are either single or have a husband supporting them were codified into the pay structure of many jobs, and those pay differentials have remained constant to this day.

Given that traditionally feminine jobs generally pay less, why do women continue to track themselves into those jobs? It could be argued that women are choosing these jobs, knowing that they involve lower pay, and should not complain if they earn less than men. However, considering the gendered messages that children receive throughout their lives, can it truly be considered a choice when women track themselves into these lower-paying careers? Notice that the lower-paying careers tend to be those that emphasize interpersonal relationships and care for others. As mentioned in chapter 5, young girls and women are taught from a very early age that caring for others is something that women, not men, do.[22] For example, analyses of prime-time television shows have found that male characters are more likely to be portrayed in work contexts, and female characters are more often portrayed in caretaking roles or jobs that involve serving others.[23] Research has even shown that when young women are exposed to commercials that show gender-stereotyped roles, they are less likely to strive toward leadership and take leadership positions in subsequent tasks.[24] So repeated exposure to these media images takes a toll.

One major reason for inequality in the workplace is that male-dominated jobs tend to pay more than jobs traditionally held by women. Another reason is that women have moved into traditionally masculine spheres as they strive for equality in the workplace, but men have not moved into traditionally feminine jobs, due to lack of status and pay.[25] Men also have not increased their contributions to housework and childcare at a rate comparable to women's increased involvement in work outside the home (see chapter 6). Despite these changing conditions, the work environment still operates under the assumption that there is an individual at home who is responsible for the home and childcare. This approach may have worked in 1960 when only 20% of mothers worked (although not for those working mothers).[26] But the current realities are quite different, and the workplace culture has not adjusted to these differences.

Yet, the pay gap between men and women is not fully accounted for by occupational gender segregation. Even within the same field, men are paid more than women. Female financial managers make 70% of what male financial managers make and female computer programmers make 84% of what their male counterparts earn. Even men who enter predominately female occupations make more money, although the gap does tend to be smaller. Female high school teachers make only 93% of what their male counterparts earn, and female nurses make 91% of what male nurses are paid.[27]

Salary Negotiation and the Double Bind

Another factor that contributes to the pay gap is that women generally expect lower salaries than men. One study found that undergraduate women expected to earn $4,000 less than men for their initial salaries and a whopping $33,000 less than men at their peak salaries.[28] These salary expectations matter because the expectation of a higher salary can lead to negotiation and, ultimately, higher pay. One study of newly hired employees found that those who negotiated received a starting salary $5,000 higher than those who did not—a starting salary difference of $5,000 can translate into a lifetime earnings differential of $600,000.[29]

Research has suggested that women generally do not have confidence in themselves when they enter a negotiation. One study asked men and women to simulate a negotiation for a starting salary and then asked them their thoughts and feelings after the discussion.[30] The majority of the men reported that they felt as though they knew their worth and felt entitled to more money. In contrast, the majority of women reported that they were unsure of their worth and felt entitled to the same salary as everyone else. For example, a male participant said: "Well it's fine that that's what your standard offer is but I'm not a standard student and I don't think that I should be categorized in that same range of capability and therefore salary." In contrast, a female participant responded: "As long as I was making the average, that's all I really cared about."[31]

Negotiating for a higher salary can be challenging for women who are socialized to believe that being "feminine" involves being modest and avoiding self-promotion.[32] It seems as though an easy response to this problem would be to encourage women to negotiate more like men. In other words, if a woman wants a higher salary, she needs to feel entitled to more money and assertively ask for it. Unfortunately, the solution is not that easy. The truth is that when women do negotiate like men, they are perceived as unlikeable. One study found that female job candidates who negotiated were perceived as less likeable than candidates who accepted the given salary, especially by male evaluators. These women were perceived as more demanding and not very nice, which accounted for their decreased likeability. Men who negotiated, however, were not seen as more demanding, less nice, or less likable.[33] Women are in a bit of a "damned if you do, damned if you don't" situation. If they negotiate they are seen as unlikable and if they do not negotiate they receive a lower salary.

The issue women have with salary negotiations is part of a larger problem experienced by women working in high-status or leadership positions known as the double bind.[34] The double bind is a catch-22 for women in the workplace. People expect women to be interpersonally warm, kind to others, modest, and not self-promoting—this is known as being communal. However, people associate leadership with traditionally masculine qualities such as being direct, assertive, and confident—this is known as being agentic. When women act agentic they are viewed negatively. In the words of a female executive: "People often had to speak up to defend their turf, but when the women did so, they were vilified. They were labeled 'control freaks'; men acting the same way were called 'passionate.'"[35] Of course, if women conform to their gender roles and act communally, they are seen as less competent and are likely to receive lower pay. What is the path out of this conundrum? Alice Eagly and Linda Carli, in their book *Through the Labyrinth: The Truth about How Women Become Leaders*, advise: "A woman can finesse the double bind to some extent by combining assertive task behavior with kindness, niceness, and helpfulness."[36] Although this advice cannot solve the pay gap entirely, it indicates a potential way out of the double bind associated with salary negotiation: Women must project confidence about their worth and skills without appearing self-promoting or unlikeable.

Starting Salary Is Only Half the Battle

Assuming women can successfully walk the tightrope between being assertive and communal enough to negotiate a starting salary equivalent to their
male peers, the battle is still not over. Research has suggested that, once
hired, women are less likely than men to be promoted.[37] This discrepancy
may be due to the fact that women have a harder time finding mentors and
informal networks that help them climb the corporate ladder.[38] Success is
often more about "who you know than what you know." The persistence of
"old boys' networks" can make it difficult for women to enter positions of
power. Many organizations are run by men who pursue social networks
through masculine activities. A business journalist and former CEO wrote:
"It's still hard to resist the feeling that at meetings, at conferences, on golf
courses, women are gatecrashers."[39] Another woman in finance noted:
"There was a big social network there that revolved around men's sports and
men's activities, and to be on the outside of that really impacted my ability to
develop relationships with people."[40] A female executive at Walmart was
told that she would probably not advance because she did not hunt or fish,
and that middle managers' meetings often took place at strip clubs and Hoot-
ers.[41] Women also have difficulty with social networking because these activities often take place after traditional work hours and can interfere with
responsibilities at home.

The Motherhood Wage Penalty

The pay gap reflects not only that women earn less than men, but also that
mothers earn less than non-mothers—there is a motherhood wage penalty.
The penalty gets more severe with each additional child. The first child is
associated with being paid 3% less than non-mothers, the second child with
9-11% less, and having three or more children with 12-16% less.[42] In fact,
for women under the age of thirty-five, the gap between mothers and non-
mothers is larger than the gap between women and men.[43] In contrast, when
men become fathers, there is no negative effect on their employment. For a
man, becoming a parent can even result in a fatherhood bonus.[44] This fatherhood bonus is especially large for white professional men, whose salaries are
approximately 12% higher than those of non-fathers. This fatherhood wage
bonus cannot be fully accounted for by men being more invested in work and
working longer hours after having children. However, a big portion of the
wage bonus can be explained by the fact that fathers are more likely to be
married, and studies have shown that simply having a wife results in a wage
increase.[45] Interestingly, one study showed that the motherhood wage penalty does not apply to lesbians, who actually receive a motherhood wage advantage of up to 20%.[46] Although it is not entirely clear why lesbians have a

wage advantage similar to that of fathers, they may be viewed as also having a "wife" who is responsible for the childcare and household management.

There have been many hypotheses about the causes of the motherhood wage penalty. It may be that mothers are discriminated against both in initial hiring processes as well as in starting salaries. One study found that when women were described as being a "mother" on a job application for a consultant, they were evaluated as less educated and competent. They were also less likely to be hired or promoted as well as more likely to be offered a lower starting salary than when they were not described as being a mother.[47] In another study, researchers sent fake résumés of equally qualified women and men to actual employers advertising for jobs. The cover letter indicated either that the applicant was the chair of the elementary parent-teacher association (implying that they were a parent) or that the applicant was the chair of the college alumni organization. The non-mothers were contacted at twice the rate of the mothers. Fathers, on the other hand, were actually called back slightly more than non-fathers.

Other research has suggested that discrimination against mothers increases when motherhood is seen as a choice that women make. When participants read an essay about all the free choices that people are able to make in the world, including motherhood, they were less likely to want to hire a mother and tended to offer mothers a lower starting salary. However, when participants read an essay about all the constraints that limit people's freedom, including motherhood, the effect was reversed.[48] Thus when people are asked to think about women "choosing" to leave the workplace, they are not only less likely to acknowledge that gender discrimination exists,[49] but also more likely to discriminate in hiring practices and salary negotiations for mothers.[50]

Discrimination against mothers in salaries and promotions are not just found in research studies, but are reported by mothers in the workplace. One attorney explained that after she had become a mother she was repeatedly passed up for promotions that were given to less qualified men with children and to women with no children. The assumption made by the company was that she would not want to work long hours because she was a mother. Instead of giving her the opportunity to make that decision herself, they simply did not promote her. In another case, a sales representative was passed up for a promotion "because she had children and he didn't think she'd want to relocate her family"[51] despite the fact that she had repeatedly applied for a promotion and had indicated that she was willing to move. Court records indicate that women from a variety of professions, including "a bank vice president, an attorney on a partner track, an assistant medical director, a hotel regional manager, and a national sales director" have been denied promotions or demoted because they were mothers.[52] For every mother who has sued on the grounds of discrimination, it is likely that there are numerous other women experiencing similar treatment who have not. A graduate of Harvard Law School protested the assumptions made about her after she had a baby, saying "I had a baby, not a lobotomy."[53]

Another explanation for the motherhood wage penalty is that mothers choose jobs that pay less in order to have more flexibility. However, the motherhood wage penalty has been found to be especially large in predominantly female professions. In addition, these jobs are actually no more likely to have flexible work hours, good health insurance, paid sick or vacation time, or job-protected maternity leave.[54] Thus the idea that women choose jobs that have greater flexibility in exchange for lower pay is not supported by the data.

In sum, the pay gap represents a bit of a chicken-and-egg problem. Do women leave the workplace, especially when they become mothers, because their pay is low, or is their pay low because they leave the workplace? The answer is likely both. The research shows that women are more likely to leave the workplace if their wages are proportionally less than that of their husband's.[55] Of course, leaving the workplace negatively impacts wages. As Hilary Lips, a professor at Radford University and an expert in the pay gap, reflected:

> If we were to deliberately design a society in which there was a virtual guarantee that women would work fewer hours and choose part-time work and lower-paid occupations more often than men, what would we do? We would probably reward women less than men for their work, make it difficult for them to combine family and full-time employment responsibilities and identify certain lower-paid occupations with femininity and higher paid ones with masculinity.[56]

PARENTAL LEAVE

Another barrier to the ability to balance work and family is the lack of national policies to support families. Unlike most industrialized countries, the United States does not offer paid leave after the birth of a child. According to a Human Rights Watch survey of 190 countries around the world, in 2011 the United States was one of only three countries that did not provide any paid maternity leave—the others were Papua New Guinea and Swaziland.[57] There are several international treaties that recommend at least some mandatory paid parental leave. The United Nations adopted the Convention on the Elimination of All Forms of Discrimination against Women (CEDAW) in 1979,[58] which explicitly recommended paid leave for new parents.[59] Despite ratification by 186 countries, the United States is one of the few countries and the only industrialized Western democracy that has not approved CEDAW.[60]

The United States did enact the Family Medical Leave Act (FMLA) in 1993, which provides twelve weeks of unpaid leave for eligible workers, which can be used for the birth, adoption, or foster-care placement of a child; the care of a sick family member; or personal illness. However, in order to be eligible for FMLA, a person must have worked over 1,250 hours for a public agency or a company that employees fifty or more people and have been employed there for at least one year. Although a recent law did expand the childcare provision to allow same-sex partners to care for children that are not biologically their own, FMLA does not apply to sick care for a same-sex partner unless they are legally married and reside in a state that recognizes the marriage of same-sex couples.[61] Given these restrictions, FMLA only applies to approximately half of the U.S. workforce.[62]

In the mid-2000s, both California and New Jersey started a paid-leave program funded by withholding payroll taxes. Both programs allow up to six weeks of paid leave for the same care activities covered by FMLA. In 2013 New Jersey allowed workers to earn two-thirds of their wages up to $584 per week,[63] while California workers could earn up to 55% of their wages up to $1067 per week.[64] Both programs were opposed by many in the business community, out of fear that they would create undue burdens and taxes. However, a report on the California paid-leave program found that businesses generally reported no effects or positive effects on profitability, morale, and employee turnover. The vast majority of businesses also reported no cost increases. The results for workers indicated that many still did not know about the program or felt as though the wage replacement was too low to make it worth using. However, those who used it experienced an increased ability to bond with their children and to arrange childcare when they did return to work.

Lack of Leave Is Bad for Mothers

Despite a few model state programs, the majority of workers in the United States have no access to paid parental leave. The decision to grant paid leave is left up to individual employers, and only 11% of the workforce has access to any paid leave.[65] Lack of access to both adequate leave and paid leave has consistently negative effects on the mental and physical health of parents, especially mothers. Having less than twelve weeks of maternal leave and having less than eight weeks of paid maternal leave were associated with increased depression and decreased overall health for new mothers.[66] Short maternal leave (six weeks or less) has been considered a risk factor for depression, especially in combination with other risks (e.g., marital discord).[67] Interviews with sixty-four parents by the Human Rights Watch illustrated the negative consequences of not having paid parental leave.[68] Mothers reported experiencing health problems, mental health problems, financial problems, and strain at work, including being fired or demoted. For example, one mother had to return to work one week after suffering from a hemorrhage because she could not afford to take unpaid time off. Other parents reported that they were unable to seek treatment for severe postpartum depression because they had to return to work. Many parents reported significant debt associated with taking unpaid time off from work. Finally, women reported experiencing hostility at work when they asked for leave and when they returned. An attorney who returned to work after five weeks of maternity leave found that her office had been given to someone else and was asked to use the conference room. Other women reported that they were demoted, or at least not promoted, after they had children.

Here is a profile reported by the Human Rights Report:

> Hannah C. worked close to 38 hours a week in a bank when she became pregnant—just short of full-time. As a result she had no benefits, and did not take a day off during her nine months of pregnancy even though she was ill throughout. Instead, she was allocated the station closest to the restroom so that she could take two steps to throw up, freshen up, and come back out. Hannah was not offered paid maternity leave and she left her job when her son was born. She started babysitting other children and doing odd jobs when her baby was about a month old, and struggled for many months after the birth to pay for rent and food. She eventually resorted to food stamps.[69]

The impact of unpaid leave was even more disastrous for lower-income women. Women reported going into bankruptcy and having to take on large amounts of debt in order to meet the basic needs of the family after the birth of a child.[70] Having children is a precipitating factor for falling below the poverty line, especially for single mothers. The birth of a child initiated a spell of poverty in 12.9% of families and in 24.6% of families headed by a single mother.[71]

Lack of Leave Is Bad for Children

Paid parental leave also has been associated with better children's health. Across eighteen countries, paid leave was associated with decreased infant mortality. For every ten weeks that paid leave was extended, infant mortality rates were predicted to decrease by 4.1%. However, unpaid leave did not impact infant mortality rates because the majority of people, the authors speculated, cannot afford to take advantage of unpaid opportunities.[72] A comprehensive study of the effect of the FMLA act in the United States came to similar conclusions. Child-outcome statistics improved in states with short leave policies after the introduction of FMLA.[73] Specifically, college-educated married women had lower rates of premature birth and low-birth-weight children as well as decreased infant mortality rates. The authors suggested that child outcomes improved due to decreased maternal stress during pregnancy over the availability of leave as well as due to the actual time off after childbirth. However, there was no positive effect of FMLA policies for less-educated and single women, which is likely because they could not afford to take unpaid leave. These two studies suggest that the positive benefits associated with leave policies are only found when people can actually afford to take leave—either the leave is paid or families can afford to forgo some income for a period of time.

In addition, child health can be adversely affected due to the impact of inadequate leave policies on breastfeeding. The earlier women return to work after childbirth, the less likely they are to initiate breastfeeding; and if they do breastfeed they are likely to do so for shorter periods of time.[74] The problem may be exacerbated by poor conditions for pumping breast milk at work. Women described pumping in "bathrooms, copy rooms, shared kitchens, bulk closets, a gymnasium, a phone booth, an equipment storage room, a photography studio, a mail truck, and an exam room."[75] Many women who had to pump in uncomfortable or public locations stopped breastfeeding after a few weeks despite intentions to breast feed for six months or more, as recommended by the American Academy of Pediatrics.

Inadequate leave may also impact child health through access to health insurance. Although FMLA requires that health insurance be maintained, health insurance can be a huge concern for the 50% of the workforce that is not eligible for FMLA. Even if parents have health insurance, lack of adequate leave can interfere with parents' ability to obtain adequate medical care for their children. Women who returned to work before their infants were twelve weeks old were more likely to have children who missed immunizations and well-visit appointments.[76] Parents who had paid leave were five times as likely as those who did not to stay home and care for their sick children, which is associated with faster recovery times.[77] A physician interviewed by Human Rights Watch noted: "It boils down to people making choices based on finances rather than health. . . . We need to recognize that having a healthy population means investing in parents and caregivers."[78]

When Too Much Leave Is a Problem

It is clear that lack of paid leave has a detrimental effect on U.S. workers and their families, which may make U.S. employees look wistfully at countries that offer long paid leaves funded by the government. Sweden offers 480 days of parental leave at 80% pay that can be divided between the mother and the father with the stipulation that two months are reserved for mothers and two months are reserved for fathers.[79] In Hungary women are paid for three years to care for their children at 70% of their wages. While this may seem ideal, these policies can have unintended consequences that can be quite detrimental for gender equality. Countries that have longer maternal leave times also have a larger pay gap between males and females,[80] fewer women in managerial positions, and more women in traditionally feminine jobs with lower pay (e.g., secretary), suggesting that employers may discriminate against women who take extremely long leave.[81]

Specifically, in Hungary where women typically take three years leave, employers are reluctant to hire women because they fear women will leave to have children. Executives openly discussed their discomfort during interviews, with one noting: "A 25-year-old is okay, she probably won't give birth for another five years . . . a 30-year-old is problematic already, she is likely to have kids soon."[82] Another executive at a bank stated: "If you decide to have a baby, your job is over because no one will wait for you for three years." Employers also mentioned automatically screening out women who had three-year gaps in their résumé and explicitly asking women about their childbearing plans, even though it violated Hungarian law. Furthermore, they reported that firms generally restructured jobs so that they were no longer available after a woman returned from three years of maternity leave.

It seems that when leaves are too long, it reduces the incentive of an employer to hire women and to give them jobs with significant responsibilities. Thus the relationship of leave length to women's pay and employment status can be best understood in terms of the inverted U-shaped curve. If maternity leave is too short, women are left with the options of decreasing or ceasing work to care for their children versus going back to work quickly and risking the potentially negative maternal and child outcomes described above. However, when women take leaves that are "too long" there is a detrimental effect as well. Research on the relationship between leave length and wages has actually demonstrated this inverted U-shaped relationship. In an investigation of twenty-one countries, when parental leave was moderate as in Australia and Israel (i.e., forty to ninety weeks), there were smaller wage penalties for having children. The benefits of moderate leave lengths were especially large in countries that had egalitarian attitudes about gender. However, in countries where leave was either very short or very long, mothers experienced larger wage penalties.[83] Women suffered the greatest wage penalties in countries with very long leaves and a lack of public childcare (such as Hungary). Research has generally suggested that leave policies of up to six months have no negative effect on women's wages.[84]

Is Leave Only for Women?

The other problem with long-leave policies is that, while they do allow people to balance work and family life, they are generally only taken by women. "If women have social rights that do not apply to men or are seldom

used by men and the practices of these rights are unprofitable for the employers, employers may choose to discriminate against female job applicants."[85]
What happens when men also are encouraged to take leave?

Despite the fact that Sweden allows parents to share the allotted 480 days
of leave after the birth of the child, women take much more leave than men.
During the 1970s, fathers used only 1% of the leave available, and in 1991
men took only 6% of it.[86] The barriers to men taking leave included workplaces that were unsupportive of paternal leave, and the belief that taking
leave would interfere with men's sense of masculinity—in the 1970s men
who took leave were called "velvet dads."[87] Sweden addressed the issue of
fathers not taking leave by designating a portion as only being available to
fathers (e.g., two months).[88] The Swedish government also instituted a public
service campaign to help men associate childcare with masculinity. Government ads featured pictures of muscular men holding babies, including a well-
known weightlifter with a baby sitting on his bicep. The policies and public
service campaigns have made a big difference. Currently 85% of Swedish
fathers take some parental leave, with 80% using up to a third of the total
leave allocated.[89] Corporate attitudes toward fathers taking leave remain one
of the biggest barriers to fathers taking more time off. A study of some of the
largest companies in Sweden found that corporate support for men taking
leave rose dramatically between 1993 and 2006, but the majority of corporations still did not formally support men taking extended leave.[90]

Sharing leave between parents has had a positive effect on Swedish families. Shared leave results in increased earnings for mothers (one study found
a 7% increase in mother's earnings for every month that a father took off) as
well as greater marital satisfaction and lower divorce rates.[91] Similar results
have been found in Norway, where the father's use of leave has been associated with higher incomes for mothers as well as more equality between the
incomes of the partners.[92] Studies have also found that Swedish fathers who
use more of their allocated leave spent more time interacting with their
children and were more satisfied with the relationship that they had with their
children.[93]

Other countries have also introduced policies that reserve leave days that
can only be taken by men. Portugal has twenty days of paternity leave,
Poland has one week, Belgium has ten days, and Brazil has five days—all
paid leave that can only be taken by fathers.[94] However, the United States
does not have a formal policy, so paternity leave is at the discretion of the
employer. Although a small minority of men have the opportunity to take
paid leave in the United States, very few take advantage of this opportunity.
According to a survey from the Society for Human Resource Management,
15% of companies offer leave to new fathers. For example, Yahoo recently
instituted a policy whereby men can take up to eight weeks of paid leave.[95]

Yet even when men are fortunate enough to work for companies with paid leave available to them, they rarely take it.

The *Wall Street Journal* reported that while Ernst & Young offers up to six weeks of paid leave for fathers, the vast majority only take two weeks.[96] Men in higher-level positions feel as though they are too important to their company to take leave and worry that they will be seen as less committed to their jobs if they take significant time off. When the *Wall Street Journal* asked for comments on their Facebook page about paternity leave, they noticed an interesting generational divide. Younger men seemed more comfortable with taking leave and seemed to care less about living up to the image of an ideal worker. One commented: "If you value the opinion of some middle-manager who won't remember your name two years after he's sacked you for putting your family first, over the opportunity to bond with your own child, I'd say your priorities are all wrong. But then, my kids have much cuter smiles than any of my bosses ever did, so I'm biased." On the other hand, another noted: "The stigma is real. Every person I know that took more than two weeks for their child's birth lost their former job or were forced out of their company within the next six months." The *Wall Street Journal* article concluded that men will not feel comfortable taking advantage of leave until it becomes an inherent part of corporate culture.

The lack of corporate support and the stigma associated with paternity leave is unfortunate because research has found positive outcomes when fathers take time off to care for their children. One study looked at over forty-five hundred families with children born in 2001.[97] They measured whether the amount of leave that fathers took influenced how involved they were with their children. Men who took two or more weeks off were significantly more involved, at nine months, in all childcare tasks including diapering, feeding, bathing, dressing, and getting up with the baby during the night.

Children with more involved fathers experienced decreased behavior problems as well as increased cognitive development and social competence. These positive effects of paternal involvement were found above and beyond the effects of the mother's involvement.[98] Thus increased availability of paternal leave may have significant long-term benefits for U.S. families. The results of this study are particularly interesting because men commented on the *Wall Street Journal*'s article on paternity leave that they felt there was not much they could do during the first few weeks after childbirth.[99] The baby is mostly sleeping and eating, so if the mother is breastfeeding, she is doing the bulk of the work in those weeks. It may be that leave taken when the baby is somewhat older and can more readily interact with the father is more beneficial. In Sweden, the leave allocation can be taken any time until the child turns eight years old.[100]

Another interesting theme that emerged from the comments about the *Wall Street Journal* article on paternity leave was that some people were irritated that parents receive a leave benefit that is not available to nonparents.[101] Just as rights that are only given to women can disadvantage women in the workplace (e.g., the motherhood wage penalty), rights only available to parents could disadvantage parents by causing resentment from people without children or discrimination by employers against parents in hiring, salary, and promotion decisions. Corporations may need to consider how work-life flexibility policies apply to all employees. Recent university graduates without children still report difficulty balancing workplace commitments with leisure time, building friendships, and maintaining health.[102] Therefore, policies that allow everyone to balance work and their personal life can challenge the notion that ideal workers are solely dedicated to work and have no life or responsibilities outside of their jobs.

LACK OF AFFORDABLE CHILDCARE

Difficulty finding high-quality and affordable childcare is another barrier to work-family balance that impacts the entire income spectrum. According to the 2013 report of Child Care Aware of America, the annual cost of full-time infant care is high, ranging from $4,863 in Mississippi to $16,430 in Massachusetts.[103] In thirty-eight states and the District of Columbia, the cost of infant care exceeded 10% of the median income of a married couple, which is considered the benchmark for affordable care by the U.S. Department of Health and Human Services.[104] In twenty-one states childcare costs are more expensive than median rent payments, and in all fifty states childcare for two children is more expensive than rent payments.

Although the federal government provides block grants to states to help low-income residents pay for childcare through Child Care Development Block Grants (CCDBG), only 1.7 million children get aid through this program, which is only one out of every six eligible children. These block grants are often used on unregulated and unlicensed childcare facilities because there is no regulation stipulating that money obtained through CCDBG grants be used in a licensed childcare facility. In fact, money received through CCDBG grants is often insufficient to pay the cost of a licensed high-quality childcare facility, and families receiving these grants are unable to make up the difference.[105]

Parents earning lower incomes tend to rely on a patchwork of care, utilizing family, friends, and neighbors. Consider the case of Emily, a divorced single mother of a seven- and nine-year-old who works outside of Boston.[106] In a given week, Emily relies on nine different adults, including her sister, her children's teacher, a neighbor, and a grandmother, to implement a carefully constructed childcare plan. However, this plan is so tenuous that if anyone becomes ill or is unable to help, the system falls apart. One welfare-to-work mother left her children with a neighbor who watched several children in exchange for their childcare vouchers. One day she came home early from her job-training program and reported: "I got there and she wasn't there. There was five children lying around in their pissy diapers, crying, hungry, dirty. I waited forty-five minutes before she came back."[107] This mother left the job-training program, noting: "Do they want me to make it or don't they? No self-respecting woman leaves her child in danger. Not even if they say you have to."

As a result of the precarious nature of their childcare arrangements, approximately 30% of low-income workers report having to disrupt their work schedules to accommodate childcare. In addition, half of all low-wage workers have been sanctioned at work for performing duties related to family care.[108] Another consequence of the lack of affordable childcare is that many children are left home alone. One study found that in families below the poverty level, 7.5% of children aged five to eight and 14% of children aged nine to eleven were left home alone. These children often lived in dangerous neighborhoods and were instructed to stay indoors for their own safety, even on hot summer days without air conditioning.[109]

Although there are some small subsidies for childcare for the poor, there is no help for the middle or professional class other than income tax credits for childcare expenses. High-quality and affordable childcare is a struggle for everyone to find and the lack of a national childcare system hurts families across all income groups. However, the middle class may be struck particularly hard. One study found that the poorest-quality childcare centers were those serving families in the middle-income range.[110] On the one hand, middle-class families are not eligible for government childcare subsidies available to lower-income families. On the other hand, they may not have the option for one parent to stop working and stay home with the children, which is available to some higher-income families. Therefore, the cost and uncertain quality of childcare remains a constant source of stress and frustration.[111]

Although childcare costs are less of a pressing financial burden for upper-middle- and high-income families, the lack of consistent and affordable high-quality childcare affects these families as well. The cost of childcare is generally calculated out of the woman's, rather than the family's, income,[112] which affects her employment decisions after birth. Approximately one-fourth (23%) of professional women who left their careers cited the lack of high-quality affordable childcare as a key factor in why they quit.[113] Women who "opt out" of the workforce miss out on the benefits of having multiple roles, which we described in chapter 2 (e.g., increased physical and mental health), and may have a difficult time obtaining a similar level of employment and pay when they return to work.

The benefits of providing affordable, high-quality childcare are not limited to the financial impact on parents. The studies reviewed in chapter 2 indicated how children in these settings have higher academic achievement throughout their educational career. Economists have concluded that investing in early education is more effective than investing in job training and literacy programs to produce a healthy workforce. Early childhood education can even decrease crime rates. Early education programs have been found to reduce future costs associated with crime by 6 to 10% (given that crime costs taxpayers $1 trillion dollars a year, this is indeed a significant savings).[114] A recent report from the NAACP noted that while education spending has been decreasing, prison spending has been increasing.[115] Diverting money into early childhood education that could have long-term positive outcomes in terms of the crime rate is a good investment.

What to Do about Childcare

The history of poor support for childcare in the United States can be traced to the failure of the Comprehensive Childcare Development Act of 1971. This bill was passed by both houses of Congress, but was eventually vetoed by President Nixon. It proposed free childcare for low-income families and on a sliding scale based on income for other families. The bill provided for the establishment of high-quality childcare centers and would have put the United States on a path toward accessible childcare for all. Unfortunately, no other legislation has been brought forth that even comes close to the scope of that bill.[116] Despite some subsidies given to lower-income parents, the government support for childcare and early childhood education is minimal. Even Head Start, which involves high-quality early childhood education, is not helpful for working parents as the hours of Head Start centers do not correspond to the work day.[117]

There have been many recommendations about how to improve our national childcare policy. One of the recommendations of the organization Child Care Aware of America is that existing federal grant money for childcare should only be used in settings where workers have been trained and where there is oversight to ensure quality of care. Of course, it is difficult to hire high-quality, trained childcare providers, given that the pay is so poor. One study found that 25% of center-based caregivers and 35% of home-based childcare providers had incomes less than double the poverty line (which is only about $37,000 for a family of three).[118] Low wages can lead to low morale, high turnover, and ultimately bad-quality childcare.

Many other countries have successful model childcare programs. Sweden has had a system of high-quality childcare in place since the mid-1960s.[119] Children are guaranteed childcare beginning at age one, for which parents pay a maximum of 13% of the costs depending on their income.[120] France also provides highly subsidized childcare for children under two (parents pay less than 30%) and free preschool for children over two; they have almost

100% participation in preschool. These and other countries view preschool as an important public service that prepares children academically and socially for school and adult life. Government involvement in childcare operations allows greater control over quality as well,[121] ensuring that children will experience the benefits associated with high-quality childcare as described in chapter 2. Mothers and their families also benefit from affordable, high-quality childcare through greater labor force participation and higher wages.[122] France and many Nordic countries have strong parental leave and childcare policies that allow parents autonomy in determining how to provide care for their young children in a manner that best meets the needs of the family.[123]

In sum, lack of high-quality and affordable childcare is a key barrier to work-family balance across the income spectrum. Although the United States government was once on track to help families afford high-quality childcare, that goal was derailed in the early 1970s and the current system of childcare is inadequate. The Obama administration has taken some steps to increase the availability of early childhood education, including increasing funding for Head Start, reauthorizing and slightly expanding the CCDBG grants, and initiating "Race to the Top" initiatives so that states can work to improve their early learning programs.[124] However, the United States would benefit from following the example of other countries that implement policies that support families' access to high-quality, affordable childcare.

CONCLUSION

In sum, this chapter has covered a number of barriers that make balancing work and family difficult and constrain people's choices. Gender inequality in the workplace in terms of hiring, starting salaries, and promotions work to push mothers out of the workforce, robbing them of the benefits associated with the employee role. Moving toward greater egalitarianism will not simply involve changing individual minds, but will necessitate a change in corporate culture and a change in government policies. Other barriers include the lack of national policies that support work-family balance. The limited availability of paid parental leave and high-quality, affordable childcare make it difficult for parents and children to achieve optimum physical and mental health outcomes. The key to tackling these barriers, however, is to consider the issues as important for both men and women—not simply as issues important to mothers. The goal to balance work and personal life is not something that should be seen as only relevant to parents. If work-life policies are viewed as beneficial to everyone, whether they have children or not, they are more likely to be wholeheartedly supported and the stigma involved in using them will diminish.

Chapter Eight

Beyond Balance

Finding Happiness and Meaning

Being out of balance, overwhelmed, and living a life in which the basic needs for competence, autonomy, and relatedness are not met can have serious mental health consequences. In the book *Maxed Out*, Katrina Alcorn described how feeling out of balance led to an emotional breakdown.[1] She described how the desire to be both a good worker and a good parent led to feeling constant guilt over not doing either one as well as she wanted, which took a toll on her: "I fell into a profound despair, plagued by panic attacks, insomnia, shame, and dread."[2] When people experience conflict among their social roles (e.g., employee, spouse, and parent), they experience stress and depression.[3] When parents become overinvolved in their children's lives, they feel less satisfaction with their own.[4] When people work too much, they experience decreased health and well-being.[5] When people fail to view men and women as equal partners in taking care of the home and children, they experience more stress and less satisfaction with life.[6]

If the mental health statistics in the United States are any indication of how well people are doing with work-family balance, things are not going very well. One in every five people in the United States is diagnosed with depression.[7] Not only is depression a significant mental health problem, but also it interferes with the ability to participate in other social roles such as working[8] and parenting.[9] Anxiety disorders are even more common than depression, and people often experience both at the same time.[10] In addition to experiencing poor mental health, feeling negative emotions is associated with increased risk of physical health problems (e.g., heart disease, diabetes, smoking, unhealthy diet) as well as death.[11]

If you asked people what their goal in life is, they probably would not say: "I want to just get by in life without being diagnosed with depression. If I accomplish that, my life will be complete." Instead, people want to be happy[12] and happier than they currently are.[13] This desire for happiness seems to be universal. In a study of college students in forty-two countries, happiness was considered a very important goal and was a frequent focus of attention.[14] In fact, almost 70% of the sample rated the importance of happiness as "extraordinarily important and valuable"—the highest rating possible.

There is actually a great deal of evidence that being happier is associated with numerous positive physical and psychological benefits.[15] In fact, people who are happier actually live longer.[16] Women who expressed the highest number of different positive emotions in an essay they wrote in their early twenties lived over ten years longer than women who expressed the fewest different positive emotions. The differences in longevity cannot be explained by lifestyle differences (e.g., diet, exercise, or health care) because all of the women in this study became nuns and lived in a convent for the remainder of their lives. There's some evidence that experiencing positive emotions helps people live longer by undoing the physical stress that negative emotions have on the body (e.g., increased heart rate).[17] In addition to better physical health, people who are happier have better performance at work, problem-solving skills, coping skills, self-esteem, and relationships.[18] Thus people who are happier are also more likely to live their lives to the fullest and flourish. They want to experience positive emotions (e.g., happiness) and make meaningful contributions at home, work, and the world. In other words, people want to "not only feel good but also do good."[19] So how do people do that?

HAPPY AS PIE

It *is* possible to increase happiness, but the path to happiness is not what most people might think. People tend to believe that they will finally be happy when they meet some external goal such as getting that promotion at work, buying their dream home, or sending their kids off to college. Accomplishing these goals may affect happiness to some extent, but they are really a fairly small piece of the overall picture. Research is converging on the idea that there are three major pieces of the happiness pie—genetics, circumstances, and intentional activity.[20]

Genetics

About half of how happy people feel is actually due to the genes they have inherited, although estimates range from 30% to 80%.[21] These estimates are made by comparing the similarity in happiness among identical twins, fraternal twins, siblings, and adopted children. Generally, research has found that the more closely people are related, the more similar their happiness levels are. The genes people inherit provide them with a baseline level of happiness known as the genetic set point. Think of this genetic set point as something like a thermostat that is set to keep the house at a specific temperature. On a hot day, the temperature in the house rises (e.g., happiness increases in response to some positive event). Then, the air conditioning comes on to cool the house down to the temperature set on the thermostat (e.g., the happiness set point). Although the set point tends to keep happiness somewhat constant, even identical twins who have identical genes are *not* completely identical in their levels of happiness.

Circumstances

The high rate of heritability of happiness led some researchers to suggest that: "trying to be happier is as futile as trying to be taller."[22] However, if about half of happiness is genetic, then about half is not—it is affected by the environment. But what aspects of the environment are important? If people were asked what they needed to be happier, their first response might be something like: "Winning a million dollars" or "Moving to a tropical island." However, we saw in chapter 4 that money really only increases happiness up to the point that people have enough to pay for their basic needs with enough extra to feel comfortable.[23] Earning more money does increase people's satisfaction with life. However, it is important to remember that the circumstances of life, such as money, only account for about 10% of people's happiness. So, even if there are some benefits of earning more and more money, it may not have as much of an impact on people's overall well-being as they think.

It turns out that where people live doesn't have that much impact on how happy they are either. People may think living somewhere where the weather is always nice (e.g., California) or where there are more cultural opportunities (e.g., a big city) will make them happier. However, people who live in places with nice weather do not score higher on measures of satisfaction with life than people living in other places.[24] Living on that tropical island won't increase your happiness as much as you might imagine.

Although people think the circumstances of their life play a major role in how happy they are, research suggests that many relatively stable aspects of life such as how much money people make, where they live, and demographic factors (e.g., gender, racial/ethnic background, and age) have very little impact on happiness.[25] For example, men and women do not tend to differ much in how happy they are. People from different racial and ethnic backgrounds tend to have similar levels of happiness. People who are more intelligent are not any happier than those who are less intelligent. Although people with more education do tend to have greater psychological well-being, it is attributed to their greater sense of purpose in life rather than feelings of happiness per se.[26] Similarly, being more attractive does not seem to buy people any greater access to happiness—apparently, blondes don't really have more fun! Although people might think that they will be less happy as they get older, that does not seem to be the case. There is some evidence that people experience *more* positive emotions as they age,[27] however, other aspects associated with well-being (e.g., purpose in life) may decline.[28] Although there have been individual studies that have found differences in happiness among some of these groups, taken as a whole the research indicates few differences by gender, race, intelligence, attractiveness, or age. In other words, happiness does not discriminate—it is equally available to all people!

Some life circumstances do have an impact on happiness and well-being. For example, religious belief or spirituality seems to be associated with greater well-being.[29] Highly spiritual people who view their faith as the most important influence in their life report that they are "very happy" at twice the rate of people who are low in spiritual commitment.[30] However, the relationship between religion and aspects of well-being, such as feeling that life has meaning and purpose, is stronger than it is with actual feelings of happiness.[31] Finally, as we mentioned in chapter 2, being employed is related to greater well-being.[32]

Although some life circumstances seem to affect happiness (e.g., money, religiosity, and employment), these circumstances still only account for about 10% of people's overall happiness. In addition, it is important to remember that the majority of these studies are correlational in nature—meaning that while people who are more religious are also happier, it is possible that people who are happy are more likely to be religious. It just isn't possible to randomly assign people to be religious or not and then follow them throughout their lives to see who is happier to determine a causal relationship. Even if there is a causal relationship between some circumstances and happiness, there's another problem with trying to change life circumstances to increase happiness—people adapt.

Why Most Circumstances Don't Matter That Much

In general, people are remarkably good at adapting to new circumstances, which is one of the human strengths that has ensured their survival over time. To understand adaptation better, think about a time when you might have been in class or at work and the fluorescent light overhead was flickering. At first, this may have been distracting and annoying; however, you probably quickly tuned it out and focused on the material at hand. In this case, habituation to the light flickering was beneficial, as it is in many cases. However, the human tendency to adapt means that people gain considerably less pleasure from their surrounding circumstances than they think they will. This process is known as hedonic adaptation (hedonism is the pursuit of pleasurable experiences) or the hedonic treadmill, because people have to keep working and working to keep the same level of happiness, so they never really get ahead. Remember, from chapter 4, the people who won the lottery sometime during the past year who were not any happier than those who hadn't won?[33] In fact, some research has suggested that people adapt to most life events, good or bad, within about three months.[34] There are some exceptions, such as major life events—unemployment, divorce, the death of a spouse, and the onset of a disability.[35] These major events do decrease people's satisfaction with life over the long term, although not necessarily their day-to-day experiences of happiness.[36] So it is possible that people continue to experience numerous positive emotions on a daily basis, but still judge that they may not be entirely satisfied because their lives did not end up the way they had envisioned.

Thus circumstances don't matter as much as people think they do. So why do people think circumstances matter so much? Basically people are not very good at predicting how they will feel when something happens. They predict that positive events will make them happier (or that negative events will make them sadder) and that they will feel this way longer than they actually will.[37] For example, people fail to recognize that the increase in well-being they anticipate from buying a big new house might be offset by having a larger house to clean, higher heating bills, a bigger yard to mow, and a longer commute to work. Conversely, when people imagine what it would be like to be poor or have a disability, they tend to overemphasize the negative without taking into account the positive, such as enjoying time with family and friends or watching a beautiful sunset. Remember, as pointed out in chapter 4, that people who do not make a lot of money are happier than you would think.[38]

In sum, circumstances play a small role in happiness, but they are less important than people think. Many relatively stable life circumstances have very little impact on happiness at all (e.g., our race, gender, and age). Even when circumstances do matter initially, people tend to adapt to them fairly quickly, so they have little impact on happiness after the initial boost they give. Overall, circumstances account for only about 10% of people's happiness.

Intentional Activities

If where people live, how much money they have, or other circumstances of their lives only plays a small role in their happiness, what aspects of the environment really matter? The last piece of the happiness pie is made up of the things that people do—their intentional activities—which accounts for about 40% of people's happiness.[39] Thus a lot of people's happiness is actually under their control. The key to increasing happiness is to pursue activities that bring inherent joy for their own sake. In other words, when people do activities because they are intrinsically motivated to do them—activities that meet their needs for autonomy, competence, and relatedness—greater well-being is a natural by-product.

Self-Care

One extremely important building block for well-being is good self-care. People need to get adequate rest, nutrition, and exercise. The good news is that each of these is also independently associated with feeling happier, in addition to providing the foundation for completing other activities associated with autonomy, competence, and relatedness. Adequate rest is essential for health and well-being.[40] Sleep deprivation negatively affects people's moods even more than it does their ability to think or react quickly.[41] People who do not get enough sleep tend to have more stress, anxiety, and anger in response to relatively mild stressors.[42] My family (HS) got a new puppy while I was working on this book. I had to get up and let him out twice a night for the first few weeks we had him and was feeling extremely sleep deprived. I know that I definitely had a much shorter fuse with everyone in my family until he was old enough to sleep through the night.

Eating is also generally associated with positive feelings.[43] The majority of research on eating and well-being has focused on increased eating due to stress.[44] However, there is some evidence that eating unhealthily (e.g., highly processed foods that are high in trans fat) increases people's chances of developing depression.[45] Conversely, people who eat several servings of fruits and vegetables per day are more satisfied with their lives.[46] However, it is possible that happier people eat healthier, so one study had people keep a diary of their food for three weeks. People who ate more fruits and vegetables not only experienced more positive emotions that day, but felt happier the next day as well.[47] These data suggest that healthy eating really is good for people's well-being.

There is a lot of research showing that exercise improves people's moods. A review of over a hundred studies found that people who regularly get aerobic activity (three to five times per week for about thirty minutes), such as walking, jogging, swimming, or dancing, experience significantly more positive emotions.[48] Exercise improves well-being by decreasing negative emotions. In fact, exercise has been found to be as effective in treating depression as taking antidepressants,[49] and people who exercise are less likely than those taking antidepressants to experience depression six months later.[50] Meanwhile, people who are happier are more likely to exercise. So exercise makes people feel good, and feeling good makes people want to exercise even more.[51] In addition to self-care, happiness can be found by actively pursuing activities that are inherently enjoyable—specifically activities that meet the needs for autonomy, competence, and relatedness.

Increasing Autonomy

We have already reviewed a significant amount of research in previous chapters that links the ability to make autonomous choices (e.g., at work, when doing chores, choosing to be a parent) to greater well-being. In a classic study of people living in nursing homes, some participants were given more responsibility and choice in their day-to-day lives than others. They were told that they were responsible for taking care of themselves. If there was anything they were unhappy with at the facility, then they were responsible for reporting it so that it could be changed. They were also given choices in how they wanted their room arranged, what activities they participated in, and whether or not they wanted a plant in their room that they would be responsible for taking care of (which they all did). Residents on a different floor were told about the activity choices available at the nursing home, but emphasis was placed on how the staff was there to help the residents with anything they needed. They were also given a plant as a gift and told that the staff would take care of it for them. The nursing home residents who were given more responsibility and choice in their daily lives had better health, higher participation in activities, and greater well-being than those on the other floor.[52] Although all residents had the same opportunities available to them, people who were told that they could make their own choices about whether or not to participate were healthier and happier than those who were told they could have all the help they needed.

As with many things we have described in this book, more is not always better. While making autonomous choices is associated with greater happiness and well-being, it does not mean that having more and more choices will lead to greater and greater happiness. While it is true that having no choice will decrease well-being,[53] it is not true that having more choices will lead to steadily increasing happiness—there is that inverted, U-shaped relationship again. Barry Schwartz, professor of psychology at Swarthmore College, has written extensively on the paradox that, although people tend to think that having more choices will inherently make them happier, it typically does not.[54] Researchers have consistently found that there is an optimal number, typically between three and seven choices, that is associated with better outcomes.[55] Researchers have found that people are more likely to make a purchase (e.g., jam or chocolate) if they are given a limited number of choices (as opposed to none or too many) and were more satisfied with their purchase afterward.[56] Similarly, college students were more motivated to write, and wrote higher quality extra-credit essays, when given a choice of six topics rather than thirty topics.[57] Finally, employees were more likely to enroll in a 401k savings plan for retirement if there were fewer, rather than more, funds to select from.[58]

Sometimes having more choices feels overwhelming.[59] Imagine trying to buy a car. There are so many choices of makes, models, and features, and with all of the information that is available at your fingertips on the Internet, it may seem impossible to do an exhaustive search of every possible option. When people feel overloaded by choices, it can actually inhibit decision making rather than enhance freedom and well-being.[60] In addition, the more choices people have, the more regret they may feel over selecting one option over another.[61] People tend to revisit the decision they made, questioning whether it really was the best decision or not, which detracts from the enjoyment of the choice they made. To receive the benefits of making an autonomous choice, people should set criteria for making a selection, select an option that meets those criteria, stop looking at other options after a decision is made, make the decision irreversible (e.g., go ahead and book the nonrefundable vacation), and focus on the benefits of the choice that was made.[62]

Increasing Competence

Engaging in activities (e.g., work, parenting, etc.) that provide people with the opportunity to demonstrate their competence and abilities has been associated with greater well-being. People feel more positive emotion and vitality when they have a high level of competence in completing their daily activities.[63] What can people do to increase their sense of competence? Research has identified numerous ways of developing and demonstrating competence that are associated with increased well-being. For example, people can develop competence by being fully engaged in their activities, living mindfully in the present, as well as identifying and using their strengths.

Flow

Have you ever been so absorbed in what you were doing that you lost complete track of time? Maybe it was while you were at work or maybe it was while you were doing something you love like playing the piano, running, or painting. If so, you were experiencing a state of flow. Flow tends to occur when a task is done for its own sake because it is enjoyable and meaningful.[64] It is more common when tasks provide a level of challenge that matches people's skill level.[65] Too little challenge results in boredom, while too much challenge results in anxiety. Another important prerequisite to experiencing flow is that the activity needs to provide clear and immediate feedback. You do not have to stop the activity, step back, and evaluate your performance, which would break the feeling of flow. If you hit the wrong note on the piano, you know right away. As a result of immediate feedback and opportunity for correction, people's skills tend to increase over time. Tasks must become increasingly more challenging to match skill level. Thus the experience of flow increases people's competence as skills increase to match the challenge of the task.

A lot of people experience flow during their leisure activities. A classic example is in the movie *For the Love of the Game*.[66] Kevin Costner's character is a professional baseball player who is pitching a perfect game. However, he doesn't even realize it until the bottom of the eighth inning—he's been in "the zone" until that point. Once he becomes consciously aware of how close he is to pitching a perfect game, he immediately throws two balls and almost jeopardizes his lifelong goal. I (HS) know that I experience flow most frequently when I'm working. When I'm doing research to prepare a lecture, write an article, or work on this book, I get lost in thought. I enjoy reading challenging material, thinking about how it all fits together, and figuring out how to present it in a way that makes sense to other people. I become so engaged in what I'm doing that I lose all track of time and hours pass like minutes.

These experiences of flow have been associated consistently with greater well-being.[67] Although people often report an absence of emotion while experiencing flow, people who experience flow more frequently are happier and feel their life has meaning. Flow can occur during many activities, including leisure, work, or socializing, which suggests many routes to increasing happiness.

Mindfulness

The ability to "live in the moment," known as mindfulness, seems to be associated with greater well-being even if people are not experiencing flow. Mindfulness involves a nonjudgmental awareness of the present moment.[68] People can be mindful of sensations in their bodies (e.g., how do your toes, fingers, etc. feel right now) as well as their thoughts and emotions. When people simply acknowledge that thoughts or feelings exist without evaluating them, they can view them as passing events that do not necessarily require further thought or action. If you have ever had a negative thought, you may realize how liberating it can be to have the thought without judging it. If you feel angry at someone, you can simply feel the anger without adding other emotions such as guilt, denial, or fear. Thus, nonjudgmental awareness can keep negative thoughts from escalating into spirals of misery.

Mindfulness has been associated with greater competence as well as greater self-knowledge.[69] People who are mindful know more about themselves and their motivations because they pay attention to their current experience and are more aware and accepting of all of the different parts of themselves—even the parts people may not be particularly proud of. [70] They can better focus and sustain their attention as well as hold more information in working memory, suggesting there are intellectual advantages to being mindful. [71] People who had just two weeks of mindfulness training performed significantly better on the reading comprehension portion of the Graduate Record Examinations. [72] Mindfulness is also associated with greater emotional competence. People who are mindful have a better sense of their own emotions as well as the emotions of others. They are better able to handle their own negative emotions. [73] They are able to feel more empathy with others, have better communication skills, and better social relationships. [74]

There is accumulating data that mindfulness has significant benefits for both physical and psychological health. Mindfulness is associated with decreased emotional reactivity and faster recovery from stress, which improves cardiovascular health as well as immune response to viruses. [75] Mindfulness is also associated with greater well-being, fewer mental health problems such as anxiety and depression, as well as decreased alcohol and drug use. [76] People who are able to accept their negative emotions are less likely to experience depression. [77] In fact, people are more likely to flourish—not only lack mental health problems, but also experience positive emotions—if they observe their own experiences without judging them. [78]

An attitude of mindful acceptance has been identified as an extremely useful approach to parenting. When people approach their children with awareness and a nonjudgmental attitude, it has a positive effect on both parent and child. People who practice mindful parenting have compassion and acceptance for themselves and their children, are aware of their own emotional responses, and listen to their children with attention and awareness. [79] Although this is a relatively new area where more research is needed, evidence for the benefits of taking a mindful approach to child rearing is growing. [80] Mindfulness may help parenting in a variety of ways. For example, when people focus their attention on their reactions in a nonjudgmental manner, it may reduce parenting stress. When your toddler throws herself on the floor and refuses to put on her shoes, it may be more useful for you to take a moment to notice your own physiological reaction and observe it without judgment before you decide how to respond. Taking just that moment to be mindful can decrease your own stress response and allow you to make a calmer decision about what to do next. The self-acceptance that comes from mindfulness can also help reduce guilt parents may feel about being "bad parents" when they do not live up to their internalized expectations for how they are "supposed" to be or feel.

The benefits of parents accepting themselves and their children for who they are can also be seen in taking a nonjudgmental approach to when children reach developmental milestones. This is especially important if a child has developmental challenges, such as autism or attention deficit/hyperactivity disorder.[81] Having a mindful approach to parenting can help take the pressure off the desire to have perfect children, which can be liberating. Little Johnny may not be a math genius, no matter how many tutors are hired. To a large extent children are going to become who they are going to become. Parents' desire for their children to be the best and achieve the most is similar to the materialistic desire to have more than others and impress others with accomplishments and achievements. This type of pressure can lead to overparenting or a type of parenting that can interfere with a child's sense of autonomy—the negative results of which we reviewed in chapter 3. However, parents who practice mindful acceptance can reduce this pressure.

Mindfulness can also help people achieve balance at work. Imagine someone in a very demanding job who is earning a great deal of money. However, that job may not be satisfying on a variety of other levels. Mindful people would be aware of their dissatisfaction with their job without being judgmental of themselves for disliking a job that may seem desirable from the outside. One study found that people who were materialistic tended to avoid their emotions, likely because they were often concerned with impression management and wanted to avoid looking weak to other people.[82] Researchers have directly linked being mindful with being less materialistic and more satisfied with the amount of money acquired instead of constantly wanting more.[83] Because materialism is one of the factors that can inspire people to overwork, mindfulness can be an important antidote, helping to achieve balance.

If one of the big predictors of happiness is to find out what is intrinsically and truly motivating, mindfulness can help people figure out what that is. Being aware of and accepting of thoughts can help people truly know themselves as well as what their interests and passions are, even if their passions are things that society has told them are not worth valuing. Figuring out who you are and what you truly want to do necessarily involves accepting all of the aspects of yourself—even the negative parts.

Identifying and Using Strengths

Another way that people can develop competence and increase their well-being is by identifying their strengths and using them. The way most of life operates (e.g., school and work) is that someone who knows more (e.g., a teacher or supervisor) evaluates people's work and identifies what they are doing wrong so they can try to remediate their weaknesses and do better. However, there is another option: People could identify their strengths and develop them further to enhance future performance and well-being.

People may have strengths in many areas, including intellectual (e.g., creativity or curiosity), emotional (e.g., honesty, loyalty), interpersonal (e.g., ability to love and be loved), civic (e.g., fairness or leadership), or strengths that connect people to something larger than themselves (e.g., religiousness or appreciation of beauty). Once people identify their strengths (and there are online tests for doing that),[84] they can make a point of using their most fundamental signature strengths in their daily lives. Research has shown that people with and without depression experience decreased depressive symptoms and increased happiness for up to six months after participating in an intervention that helped them identify and use their strengths.[85] It is important for people to vary the way they use their strengths to keep experiencing the benefits; otherwise, they may adapt to using the strength and stop receiving the boost in mood. For example, if one of your strengths is kindness and you decide to buy someone a cup of coffee every day to utilize that kindness, you might eventually adapt to this act and stop receiving a happiness boost from it. However, if you do something different each day to help different people, then you are likely to experience long-term benefits from using that strength.

There has been some research to suggest that even when people just think about using their strengths, it increases their well-being. People who wrote about a time in the past when they used what they considered to be their most important quality felt less negative about their body, were more open to information, and expressed a greater desire to make positive changes in their behavior.[86] People who were told to imagine and write about being their "best possible self" in the future also experienced greater well-being, including more positive feelings and better health.[87]

There is a great deal of research suggesting that people who are more optimistic about themselves and how things will turn out tend to be happier and healthier.[88] People who are naturally optimistic live longer and are less likely to get sick. They have more energy and make more friends. Optimists are more likely to persevere in the face of difficulty and try harder after they fail, which builds their skills and competence further. They also have better coping skills and experience fewer mental health problems such as depression.

What if you're not naturally optimistic? Are pessimistic people doomed to a short and miserable life? The good news is that it is possible for people who are not born with a "glass is half full" kind of mentality to develop skills possessed by their optimistic peers. Martin Seligman wrote a book called *Learned Optimism*, which describes a five-step method for becoming more optimistic and reaping the benefits associated with it.[89] The ABCDE model suggests that when an **a**dverse event occurs (e.g., I lost the expensive earrings my friend loaned me), people have automatic negative **b**eliefs (e.g., I'm so irresponsible. She's going to hate me), which have behavioral **c**onsequences (e.g., I feel terrible, so I'm going to avoid her). However, Seligman asks people to **d**ispute those beliefs (e.g., While she'll probably be upset, she won't hate me. I am not completely irresponsible; I've always returned things I've borrowed from her in the past) and notice the energizing effects of this disputation (e.g., I was able to relax enough to call her to explain what had happened). People sometimes allow their inner voices to say really mean things about themselves (e.g., I'm irresponsible, stupid, etc.) that they would never dream of saying to another person. So people need to learn to defend themselves against their own negative self-talk the same way they would defend a friend who was being attacked in a similar manner.

Now that you know that developing your strengths and thinking positively about yourself is associated with greater well-being, it is time for us to remind you that there are limitations on these benefits. Just because using a strength or being optimistic benefits well-being does not mean that more and more is better and better. In fact, there is research that suggests that the optimal amount of each strength is a moderate amount, while the complete absence or excess is associated with poor outcomes—the inverted U-shaped curve.[90] Even optimism seems to be more beneficial in moderation.[91] While it has physical and mental health benefits at optimal levels, too much optimism can also be detrimental. There is some evidence that people who are highly optimistic are not realistic in their assessment of the risks. Thus they may experience more injuries or even death associated with risk taking (e.g., smoking, drinking, or skydiving).[92] After all, they think everything is going to work out just fine. While wearing rose-colored glasses and having positive illusions that everything will be OK has been found to be beneficial to physical and mental health to an extent,[93] it is possible to reach a tipping point beyond which optimism is no longer protective, but destructive.

Increasing Relatedness

Research has consistently shown that social relationships—or meeting the intrinsic need for relatedness—are crucial for both physical and mental well-being.[94] People who have close personal relationships, including friendships and being married, have been found to be happier and more satisfied with their lives than those who do not. In a study comparing the top 10% of happiest people to the bottom 10%, happier people had better social relationships than did unhappy people.[95] One study looking at well-being levels of people living in the slums of Calcutta, India, found that while their life satisfaction was lower than middle-class students in India, many of them were quite satisfied with their social relationships and identified their love for friends and family as central to their sense of well-being in life. For example, a woman with two deceased daughters, who lived in the slums, said that her relationship with her son gave her great joy. A sex worker enjoyed visits with her family, and a man who lived on the street said that his only regret was that he did not see his family more.[96] If good social relationships are a necessary condition for happiness, what can people do to foster and strengthen their relationships?

Spending Money to Foster Relationships

In chapter 4 we challenged the idea that money is the path to happiness. Indeed, purchasing material items does little to increase happiness because people quickly adapt to having something new and always want more— unfortunately, "retail therapy" is not the answer. However, there are ways people can spend money that do increase well-being.[97] Some have argued that if money is not making you happy then you are not using it right![98] The primary way to use money to increase well-being is to use it to foster relationships. When people spend money on others, rather than themselves, it enhances relationships and increases happiness.[99] In a nationally representative sample in the United States, people who spent more of their income on others reported being happier than those who spent more on themselves, regardless of income level.[100] Spending money on others increases well-being across a variety of countries, cultures, and socioeconomic levels.[101]

It's not just that happier people spend more on others either. Experimental studies have found that spending money on others actually causes an increase in happiness. People who were given money and told to spend it on other people were happier than people who were allowed to spend it on themselves. People benefited more when spending money on those they were closer to compared to those they interacted with less.[102] However, people still experienced positive benefits of spending money on others even if they did not interact with the receiver, such as making charitable donations.[103] Given that people who spend money on others are happier and people who are happier are also more likely to spend money on others, this may be one potential method for achieving sustainable increases in well-being over time.

Spending money on experiences (e.g., a vacation), particularly experiences spent with others, has also been found to be related to increased well-being.[104] In fact, spending money on shared experiences is valued over both solitary experiences and material purchases.[105] If I (HS) go out of town by myself on business, I certainly enjoy staying in a nice hotel, eating out, and having a bit of peace and quiet while I'm gone. On the other hand, if my husband can come on the trip with me, then it's like a mini-vacation. We take time to go sightseeing, eat at some of the best restaurants in the area, and really strengthen our relationship by building memories together. Experiences also increase happiness because people are less likely to habituate to the memory of an experience than they are to the presence of a material good.[106]

The interesting thing about how spending money on experiences can enhance happiness is that the anticipation of the experience can boost happiness more than the experience itself. Think about the last time you booked a vacation. In the weeks and months before the vacation, you may have spent a great deal of time thinking and fantasizing about the upcoming trip. The anticipation of the vacation increases happiness. The emotional intensity of anticipating a future event has been shown to be stronger than how people feel emotionally when they remember an event.[107] Thus vacations or other experiences may be more beneficial before they occur than after!

Spending (Interesting) Time Together

Spending money to have vacations or experiences with loved ones can also help relationships because they can help overcome boredom. Couples who were bored after seven years of marriage had considerably less relationship satisfaction nine years later than those who were excited about their relationship.[108] Research on overcoming boredom in relationships has indicated that when couples engage in new and exciting experiences together (whether or not on vacation), they have higher relationship satisfaction, which is directly linked to a decrease in relationship boredom.[109] Researchers have also conducted experiments with couples to see if participating in interesting activities together helped their relationship. Couples were brought into the research lab and randomly assigned to engage in an exciting task, such as completing an obstacle course Velcro-ed together, or a boring task of crawling on mats separately to retrieve a ball. Couples who completed the exciting task spoke to each other in an accepting, rather than hostile, tone and reported greater relationship satisfaction and less boredom. The couples who completed the boring task did not experience these positive outcomes.

People who engage in exciting experiences with their spouse are likely to increase relationship satisfaction and overall life satisfaction. We are not suggesting that people should find evermore creative activities to do while Velcro-ed to their spouse, but you get the idea. People who share exciting or new activities with their spouse feel connected to their life partner and fulfill their fundamental need for relatedness. Taking time to go dancing or tandem skydiving is a good way to increase relationship satisfaction. My husband (ML) and I make an effort to go on a date night every single week and have done so ever since our children were infants. That was one of the promises we made to each other before we had children. Those date nights are not always spent having major adventures, and we have never actually been Velcro-ed together, but good conversation, going to movies, or enjoying a wine tasting together has greatly enhanced our relationship satisfaction and well-being. The money we spend on babysitters is well worth it. I suppose if we really wanted to spice things up we could try using Velcro!

Being Happy with What You Have: Savoring and Gratitude

Another way to build social relationships is to savor the experiences you have with other people and express gratitude on a regular basis. Savoring is the intentional effort to prolong a positive experience and can slow down the habituation that generally occurs to material goods and even to experiences. Not surprisingly, savoring is associated with greater well-being.[110] People can savor by anticipating an upcoming event, enjoying the event in the moment (e.g., stop to appreciate the beautiful sunset), or by reminiscing about past events. Savoring is associated with increases in individual well-being— people experience more positive emotions as well as get more enjoyment from the event.[111] It can also build social bonds with other people.[112] Relationships seem to especially benefit when someone tells another person about a positive experience and the person responds in an enthusiastic and supportive manner.[113] People who savor the good times with each other have greater relationship satisfaction, more intimacy, and higher levels of trust. When people take the time to celebrate each others' successes, they also report liking each other more and being more committed to the relationship. The next time your spouse or friend wants to reminisce about a funny memory from your past or share some good news, it is important to take the time to stop and listen intently. Show enthusiastic interest by asking questions to find out more details and complimenting the person on their accomplishments.

In addition to savoring everyday experiences, people can strengthen their relationships with others by showing gratitude. There is a great deal of psychological literature that has pointed to the physical and mental health benefits of having an attitude of gratitude—people who are grateful experience more positive emotion, greater satisfaction with life, and overall well-being.[114] Beyond the individual benefits, gratitude has been likened to the glue that holds relationships together—in other words, gratitude finds, reminds, and binds relationships. Feeling gratitude toward someone is a signal that the person has the potential to be (*find*) or already is (*remind*) a good relationship partner and strengthens the connection (*bind*) between the two people.[115] Both the person who expresses gratitude as well as the recipient experience a closer relationship with the other as a result.[116]

Some people feel and express gratitude on a regular basis, while others are less naturally inclined. What are some ways that you can increase your feelings of gratitude to reap the personal and interpersonal benefits? There are several fairly simple activities that research has found people can do to increase gratitude and promote individual feelings of happiness as well as strengthen relationships. You can count your blessings—taking time to notice the big and small things in life increases well-being.[117] Keeping a gratitude journal to write down a few things each day, or even once a week, that you are thankful for is associated with feeling more positive emotions and fewer depressive symptoms.[118] People who actually sent a letter of gratitude to another person experienced increases in happiness and satisfaction with life.[119] I (HS) frequently have my students write a gratitude letter when we are studying the effects of gratitude on well-being. It is always one of their favorite activities and clearly strengthens their relationship with the recipient. Here is how one student described the experience in her journal:

> After completing this letter to my prior swim coach, I realized how much the little things meant. Everything I mentioned in the letter was day-to-day interaction we had, such as him making a funny face and it making me smile. . . . I realized that I should appreciate the people that can make me smile when it is one of the last things I want to do. I sent this letter to my coach, and he called me the next day. He said that after reading this he had tears of joy in his eyes. Together we recalled many other memories and were laughing for almost an hour over the phone. His overall well being was amplified hearing how much of an impact he made on my life. The day after sending the letter and talking to my coach, I couldn't stop smiling after recalling how important he was and I felt great that I had finally let him know how important he was and still is to me.

Helping Others

Another way to strengthen relationships and increase happiness is to help other people in nonmonetary ways. There is a substantial amount of research suggesting that there is a strong relationship between helping others and happiness. For example, volunteering is associated with better physical and mental well-being. People who volunteered more hours were happier, more satisfied with life, and less depressed than people who volunteered less.[120] Helping others can not only increase individual well-being, but also build and strengthen relationships with other people. Research has shown that performing random acts of kindness three to five times per week (e.g., holding the door for someone, helping them clean up a mess, or paying for a stranger's coffee) increases people's happiness[121] and enhances how much other people want to spend time with them.[122] Happy people are more likely to help others and helping others increases happiness as well as strengthens relationships with the people helped, which further increases happiness.[123] So helping others seems to be a good way to increase and sustain gains in happiness. However, there is some evidence that helping others should be done in moderation. People who provided informal care to a friend or relative who was sick or disabled were happier than those who did not, but only if they provided less than six hours of care per week. People who provided more than eleven hours of care per week were less happy than non-caregivers.[124] Putting others' needs before your own self-care seems to decrease well-being.

Forgiveness

While gratitude is a way of responding to help from others that builds relationships and increases well-being, forgiveness in response to harm from
others has a similar effect.[125] All relationships inevitably experience some
level of insult and injury. People can respond to those instances in a way that
strengthens or weakens the relationship. Forgiveness is a decision to replace
negative thoughts, feelings, and behaviors about a person or situation with
positive ones.[126] Deciding to forgive someone puts the needs of another
person or the relationship itself before the needs of the individual, which
strengthens the relationship.[127] The inability to forgive has been associated
with decreased well-being, including decreased health and satisfaction with
life as well as higher levels of stress and depression.[128] Conversely, forgiveness is associated with better health and well-being.[129] Forgiveness is likely
associated with greater health and well-being because of its role in repairing
and maintaining relationships.[130] People are more likely to forgive others
when they feel close to them as well as when they are committed to and
satisfied with their relationship. People are also more likely to forgive if they
are able to empathize with the offender and if the offender offers a sincere
apology.

Although grudges tend to fade naturally over time, some people have a
great deal of difficulty forgiving others.[131] The good news is that there are
several models that research has shown are effective for helping people learn
to forgive,[132] including Worthington's REACH model of forgiveness[133] as
well as Enright's forgiveness training.[134] The REACH model consists of five
steps. **R**ecalling the transgression in an objective manner, trying to **e**mpathize
or understand the other person's point of view, viewing forgiveness as an
altruistic gift by thinking about how good it feels to be forgiven, **c**ommitting
yourself to forgive by making it public (e.g., telling another person you plan
to forgive even if it's not the person who hurt you), and **h**olding on to the
decision to forgive. Enright's model has four steps, the first of which is to
uncover or bring to light the negative effects of not forgiving (e.g., anger,
poor health, or difficulty concentrating on anything else). Then you need to
make a conscious *decision* to forgive and *work* toward that decision by trying
to feel empathy toward the transgressor. Finally, try to *discover* why you
went through the experience and how you have grown as a result. Both of
these models view forgiveness as a decision that people make and must
actively work toward rather than something that people passively wait to
feel. People who approach forgiveness in this way are two to three times
more likely to be able to forgive than those who don't.[135] Thus they are more
likely to experience the physical and mental health benefits associated with
forgiveness.

Many of the elements included in these approaches to forgiveness can be found in the reaction of the Amish community after a tragic shooting. In 2006 Charles Roberts entered an Amish elementary school and shot ten young girls, killing five of them and himself. Just hours after the shooting, members of the Amish community went to the home of the shooter to console his family and let them know they had forgiven him. Members of the Amish community also attended the funeral of the shooter and formed a human shield around his family to protect them from the media covering the story. In an interview several years later, the shooter's widow indicated she had forgiven her husband, but did not excuse what he had done. "It's not like I could forgive him once for what he did and never have to think about it again. It's something that I think about all the time," she said. "But I don't have to just forgive Charlie for him. I have to forgive him so that I can be whole, and so that it doesn't eat away inside of me the same way that he allowed anger to eat away inside of him."[136] In this example, the Amish truly gave an altruistic gift of forgiveness and committed to it publicly. The widow made a conscious decision to forgive, and worked to hold onto that decision over time without excusing her husband's behavior, while at the same time acknowledging the negative consequences of failing to forgive.

Although extending this level of forgiveness seems very difficult, when people refuse to forgive someone, they actually allow that person to continue hurting them because holding onto a grudge is so bad for mental and physical health. However, forgiveness does not necessarily mean that people have to reconcile the relationship with the offender. Some transgressions are beyond reconciliation and, in fact, would be unhealthy to reconcile (e.g., an abusive relationship). Just the process of letting go of negative feelings and making a decision to see things differently is enough to impact well-being.[137] Forgiveness does not mean forgetting the past, but rather framing it in a way such that your own health and well-being do not suffer.

Social Comparisons: The Downside of Relationships

Although relationships are beneficial, a potential downside is that people have the tendency to compare themselves to others. People may feel perfectly content about their own work and family life until they look at their neighbor's house, which is bigger and nicer than their own. People may feel satisfied with their children until they notice that their neighbor's children are reading better and never seem to whine.

People compare themselves to others to obtain accurate evaluations of themselves;[138] however, who they chose to compare themselves to has an impact on their self-esteem and well-being. People who make downward social comparisons (i.e., compare themselves to people who are less fortunate) tend to increase their well-being.[139] One study interviewed survivors of a tsunami two years after the event and found that they tended to compare themselves to those who were less fortunate (e.g., didn't survive). As a result, almost all of the survivors (95%) considered themselves to be "lucky" and experienced increased well-being.[140] As mentioned in chapter 4, people who thought they were better off financially than a close relative reported greater satisfaction with life.[141] Comparing yourself to people who have less than you do can instill a sense of gratitude for what you already have.[142]

In contrast, making upward social comparisons—comparing yourself to people who have more or are better at something—has been linked to depression, shame, and resentment.[143] Research comparing happy and unhappy people has revealed that unhappy people are extremely sensitive to people who do better than they do. In a series of studies, participants were asked to engage in difficult tasks. Strikingly, unhappy people who did poorly, but knew others did worse, felt better than if they had done fairly well, but found out others did better.[144] Happy people were more likely to feel good based on their own performance rather than how their performance stacked up against others. Even just making upward comparisons to images in the media can decrease people's sense of self-esteem and physical attractiveness.[145]

While comparing yourself to people who are worse off may temporarily increase well-being, a general tendency to compare yourself to others is problematic. People who compare themselves to others are more likely to feel negative and destructive emotions such as guilt, envy, regret, defensiveness, and blaming others for their problems.[146] Although social comparison may result in short-term benefits, such as increasing self-esteem when people perceive themselves as better off than others, the long-term consequences of living life based on how you compare to others can be extremely damaging.

Research has also suggested that the emotion of envy can hijack our attention.[147] One study found that people were more likely to pay attention and remember details from newspaper articles about people that they envied and were less able to concentrate on completing other tasks. Women were particularly envious of physically attractive women, while both men and women were likely to be envious of people who were wealthy. This study concluded that envious people tend to note and remember details about the lives of those they envy. However, all this attention spent envying others reduces the resources and skills available for other tasks.

The widespread use of social media magnifies the problem of envy. People are constantly bombarded with social media that presents idealized views of other people's lives. For example, on Facebook people post adorable pictures of their children frolicking in the woods accompanied by charming quotes their children have said. One blogger contrasted what she posted on Facebook with the reality of her life in her blog titled "We Need to Quit Telling Lies on Facebook."[148] She described a morning where her children woke at the crack of dawn, screamed at each other, watched television, and found her tampons. They also briefly played backgammon before the kids started arguing and stopped playing. They took a walk in the orchards before they became muddy and started complaining. Her Facebook status posts from that day, on the other hand, painted a picture of an idyllic day: "My children and I woke up with the sun, smiling. . . . We played backgammon, our skin mottled by drops of shade in the morning light. . . . We went for a walk in the orchards, and we danced between emerald leaves like fairies." In other words, she claimed, her Facebook posts were full of s**t as she was attempting to paint a picture of a family who is happy: "Look everyone! Look! My kids are happy! I'm happy! We're happy!"

The destructiveness of idealized social media presentation is twofold. When people read the glowing status updates of others, they are likely to feel worse about their own flawed lives, especially if they are the type of people who tend to judge their self-worth in comparison to others. In addition, when people put forth a version of themselves that is not genuine, they can actually feel bad about themselves.[149] In one study some college students had to pretend to understand made-up words (e.g., besionary) to complete a test, while others did not. Afterward, both groups were praised for their performance. The praise raised the self-esteem of those who did not have to fake understanding of nonwords, but lowered the self-esteem of the students who pretended to understand them.[150] In other words, when people portray their life as better than it actually is on social media, all of the "likes" they get for their status updates and pictures may actually make them feel worse about themselves.

Mindfulness, being both aware and nonjudgmental of experiences, may be a solution to the negative consequences of social comparison. When people are able to mindfully accept both the positive and negative parts of themselves, they may be less likely to put forward fake self-presentations and worry less about the negative evaluation of others.[151] It might be impossible for people not to notice at all when other people have more (or less) than they do. However, when social comparisons are made mindfully they can be a source of information (That person is a great public speaker; what are her techniques?) or inspiration, rather than an opportunity to feel bad.

SUSTAINING HAPPINESS

As you can see, there are many specific activities and frames of mind that have been found to increase happiness. The desire to be happy seems to be a fundamental human goal across time and culture.[152] While people's general propensity for happiness may be inherited (50%), that does not mean that it is predetermined. Happiness is also not left up to the fate of people's circumstances. Many circumstances have very little impact on people's happiness.

People who attempt to pursue happiness through their circumstances (e.g., earning the most money, having the biggest house, marrying the ideal spouse, having the perfect children, etc.) may find some increased satisfaction with their lives, but are not likely to experience more day-to-day feelings of happiness. People will adapt to many of these circumstances within a relatively short period of time, so life circumstances only account for about 10% of happiness. The remaining 40% is within people's control, determined by what they do and how they do it.

In some ways, happiness is a lot like weight loss. In other words, there is generally a "set point" that people's weights will naturally hover around. If you want to weigh less than this, you have to participate in intentional activities to decrease your weight such as diet and exercise. However, if you stop dieting and exercising, you will drift back toward your weight set point. So, to maintain weight loss, you have to keep participating in these intentional activities. In fact, your body might even get used to a particular exercise and you find that you either have to do more (e.g., run farther) or vary the type of exercise you do in order to maintain the desired lower weight. Happiness works similarly. You inherit a "set point" or natural level of happiness. If you want to be happier than that, you have to intentionally work at it. You have to diet, or cut back on things that are not associated with happiness (e.g., comparing yourself to others), and exercise, by participating in intentional behaviors that do increase happiness (e.g., gratitude, mindfulness, savoring, etc.). You need to vary the types of happiness "exercises" that you do to avoid adapting to them. You can use your strengths in novel ways each day or vary the types of activities you do to express gratitude so that you don't get used to them and stop receiving the benefit. It is likely that the fit between the person and the exercise matters. Certain exercises may work better for some people than others.[153] Finally, it helps people succeed if they actually want to be happier because they are more likely to "stick to the program."[154] It seems that "becoming happier takes both a will and a proper way."[155]

The good news is that there is also evidence that, similar to exercise—the more you do it, the more you want to do it, and the more you get out of it. People who are in a good mood are more likely to want to be around other people, and being around others puts people in an even better mood. Expressing gratitude to others increases feelings of positive emotions, and people who are happy feel more grateful. So feeling positive emotions leads to exactly the types of behaviors that generate even more positive emotions. This *upward spiral* of positive emotions allows people to flourish.[156]

CONCLUSION: GOING BEYOND BALANCE

In order to lead a more balanced life, people may need to reevaluate their values and goals. In prior chapters, we have discussed ways in which people can get out of balance and how that may interfere with well-being. People can over-parent and overwork. There can be gender inequality both at home and in the office. However, it is possible to have balance and even to have gender equality, and still not feel very happy. In a *Forbes* article on work-life balance, the author describes the phenomenon by saying:

> Happiness is still the ultimate goal—but happiness and work-life balance aren't the same thing. You can have perfect work-life balance and a dead-end job that leaves you exhausted. Those who are able to lead inspired, engaging lives in various spheres—from work, to family, to personal well-being—have something greater than balance. They have fulfillment. Their life fits. [157]

This chapter addresses how to make your life fit. Our advice to you is to do what you love to do, even if you do not become rich and famous doing it. Carve out a life in which you have choices about what you do. Participate in activities that help you build and demonstrate your competence in a variety of settings—working outside the home, volunteering, engaging in hobbies, or doing activities inside the home. Look for opportunities to challenge yourself in meaningful ways and become fully absorbed in the activities you're doing. Finally, be sure to foster meaningful relationships with other people. Take time to connect with others by participating in leisure activities together, expressing gratitude for what they have done, forgiving them for what they haven't done, and celebrating their successes with them. Living a life where there are multiple opportunities to experience autonomy, relatedness, and competence is the path to happiness.

Chapter Nine

Balance and Beyond

Finding the Sweet Spot

In this book, we have been advocating for people to strive for work-family balance and a meaningful and satisfying life. How do we get there? We have argued that there are four answers to that question. People need to:

1. Find balance among their roles by doing all things in moderation.
2. Make each social role an opportunity to experience autonomy, competence, and relatedness—the three basic needs according to self-determination theory.
3. View work-family balance as a goal for both men and women, rather than a women's issue. Men and women should strive for equality both at home and at work.
4. Get involved and work toward structural support for families such as parental-leave benefits, flexible work schedules, and affordable high-quality childcare.

FINDING BALANCE: THERE CAN BE TOO MUCH OF A GOOD THING

What, exactly, does it mean to lead a meaningful and balanced life? We argued that balance involves a sense of moderation—finding the sweet spot on the inverted U-shaped curve. Being overinvolved in either work or family life is limiting. Children need love, but they do not need *constant* attention and intellectual stimulation. They do not benefit, and may even suffer, if the level of parental involvement becomes controlling and interfering. Work can be satisfying and rewarding, but overwork can lead to stress and illness.

People need money, but too much money and the pursuit of money can have harmful effects.

A lot of the advice people, especially women, are given is to "do more and to be more." To strive to "have it all." But having it all does not mean doing it all. When being instructed to "lean in," women may feel pressured if they can't or simply do not want to work that hard. Similarly, women are asked if they are "mom enough"—the message is that if they don't constantly carry their children or breastfeed until the age of four, then they are inadequate. This contrasting set of pressures between work and home is paralyzing, stressful, and demoralizing. Women feel guilt and shame when they don't live up to the ideal parenting standards. Their attempts to "lean in" do not usually result in a rocketing path to corporate success. Women often look at others who have made difference choices—whether it is women who have the time to grow organic food and keep spotless homes or women who have achieved incredible corporate and financial success. They wonder if they are failing . . . if they are failures.

It is time to let go of these pressures and to realize that you don't have to be "all in" in every domain of your life. Good enough is good enough. In fact, it is better. Instead of striving for perfection, try to strive for the sweet spot in the inverted U. We are not advocating that you slack off at work or neglect your children. We are saying that there is a wide range of "good enough," so you don't have to worry so much about whether you are doing it "right." The house is clean enough, the children are read to enough, your career is successful enough, and there is enough money. Enough is actually enough. You are enough.

WHAT REALLY MATTERS: AUTONOMY, COMPETENCE, AND RELATEDNESS

Of course, balance is not a guaranteed path to happiness. It is possible to be balanced but miserable. What really matters is whether people involve themselves in activities that allow them to meet their needs for autonomy, competence, and relatedness. Balance can help people do that. Being meaningfully involved in both work and family life creates more opportunities to feel a sense of autonomy, to feel competent, and to make meaningful social connections. For some people, these basic needs may be met by focusing more in one domain or another.

For many, the debate about work-family balance becomes framed as the "mommy wars." In the media, mothers who work outside the home are pitted against those who do not. Which is better for women? Which is better for children? In our view, the issue is not which choice is inherently better, but whether there's a choice at all. Research has shown that when mothers are happy with their decision, whether they work or stay home, their children are better off.[1] The key factor seems to be the mother's sense of autonomy. However, many times the decision to work or stay home is not an autonomous choice. When the choice is between staying home and working in an inflexible work environment with substandard childcare, then it is not an autonomous choice. When a couple decides that it is the wife who should stay home because she earns less money, even though she loves her job more, then it is not an autonomous choice. If a man or woman truly wants to stay home but cannot because the family needs his or her income, then the choice to work is not a fully autonomous choice. If it is only women having to make choices between work and family, if staying at home or reducing hours is not even considered as a viable option for men, then the choices are not truly autonomous. If society is structured in such a way (e.g., lack of support for working parents) that it limits the options that parents have for how to combine work and family, then the choices they make are not fully autonomous. When this happens people's well-being can be adversely affected.

There is no magic level of involvement in work and family that works for everyone because everyone differs on what choices meet their needs. There is no one-size-fits-all approach to work-family balance—we are not suggesting that every person should devote 50% of their time to each area and they will magically feel at peace. If you love your job, feel competent and challenged by it, and enjoy being with your coworkers, then a higher investment in work may make sense to meet your needs for autonomy, competence, and relatedness. If staying at home is what you autonomously choose to do, and you have the financial means to be able to do it, that choice will be right for you. Of course, not earning an income may put people at risk in the case of divorce, illness, or death of a spouse. The choice to stay at home may result in someone's autonomy being limited in the future, and people making that choice need to be aware of this potential risk. However, people who are able to meet their needs for autonomy, competence, and relatedness, regardless of whether that's at work or at home, are likely to experience greater well-being.

Unfortunately, many people are motivated by extrinsic goals and have lost touch with what really motivates them. They may not even know what it is that they truly love to do. Many people are, instead, motivated by external factors. Money, success, and admiration certainly do have their advantages. People who are wealthy and have the best of everything may feel more satisfied with their lives. However, this sense of satisfaction does not necessarily lead to everyday experiences of happiness and joy. People who own a lot of material possessions typically get over the initial excitement of a new purchase fairly quickly and return to their baseline level of happiness. Finally, even people who are respected and admired by others may have poor self-esteem if they feel as though that respect and admiration is based on a fake self-presentation. The pursuit of materialistic goals almost always comes at the expense of spending quality time sharing experiences and pursuing meaningful social relationships, which are critical to well-being.

In the search for well-being there is another, more modest, path to consider. In this path, having less may result in actually having more. Instead of focusing on having more money, people can achieve true well-being through focusing their energies on tasks that they truly enjoy—tasks that bring them a sense of competence and challenge as well as those that promote their sense of connection with others. They can also savor, be mindful, and be grateful for what they have. This path involves people being aware and accepting of their thoughts and feelings—taking the good with the bad. People who do not know what it is that they truly love to do may wish to practice mindful self-acceptance, which can help them enhance their self-awareness and figure out what truly inspires them. Focusing on intrinsic motivational needs does not necessarily mean having lowered aspirations. A lawyer can focus on forging meaningful relationships with clients or growing from challenging cases rather than focusing on billable hours or becoming a partner.[2] For many people, jobs that are intrinsically motivating may pay less than jobs selected for external goals. This may mean that you earn less than others around you, which could make you feel bad. By avoiding comparing yourself to others (e.g., my house is not as nice as the Joneses') and by focusing on what you love to do, you can avoid the trap of feeling as though you do not have enough, when, in fact, you do.

In sum, achieving true happiness and a sense that life has meaning involves a shift in values. Instead of evaluating life based on how it stacks up against others or some set of external criteria, both men and women would benefit from focusing on meeting their intrinsic needs for autonomy, competence, and relatedness. This focus will ensure that whatever social roles people participate in are high quality and contribute to their well-being.

BALANCE IS NOT JUST FOR WOMEN: WORK-FAMILY BALANCE IS AN ISSUE FOR EVERYONE

For so long, balance has been framed as an issue that only women need to address. Women have made great strides toward social equality with men since the second-wave feminist movement of the 1960s. They have entered the workplace in unprecedented numbers and now constitute 46% of workers.[3] Furthermore, women have made significant progress in terms of leadership and occupied 14.3% of executive officer positions in the Fortune 500 rankings in 2012.[4] However, the progress toward gender equality has stalled. Although there was great initial momentum, not much progress has been made since the 1990s. In 2012, 59% of managerial positions were still occupied by men while 41% were held by women.[5] Women only hold 4.2% of Fortune 500 CEO positions, which is up from 0.2% in 1996.[6] As we discussed in chapter 7, there is still a considerable pay gap that shows no sign of disappearing. Thus women are still not equal to men in the workplace or in positions of power.

We think the main reason that gender inequality has stalled is that it has been a largely one-sided movement. Women have moved into management and high-level corporate positions, but men have not moved into traditionally feminine occupations such as teaching and nursing at the same pace.[7] Despite taking on more traditionally masculine roles, women continue to do the lion's share of work at home, as discussed in chapter 6. The increased workload outside of the home, combined with little reduction in workload at home, contributes to women's difficulty balancing work and family.

The belief that men and women are inherently different fuels the continued existence of gender inequality. In addition, men are under a great deal of social pressure to avoid looking feminine.[8] However, as we have seen in chapter 5, the differences between men and women have been vastly overstated. Men and women are considerably more similar than different. Furthermore, young men and women typically want the same things. Both desire marriage and children equally.[9] Both want to combine work and family in a loving and egalitarian relationship.[10] Both complain of difficulty balancing work and family.[11]

The ability of everyone to lead satisfied, meaningful, and balanced lives largely rests on the people who are in power realizing that the status quo does not work for them anymore. Change can certainly occur when more women enter positions of power. Sheryl Sandberg, COO of Facebook, described her push to create a work environment where women had resources to pump breast milk and felt comfortable leaving the office in order to be with a child.[12] Indeed, some have argued that change will only occur when a critical mass of women gain positions of power. But there is no reason why men in power cannot advocate for change as well. When men in power make leaving the office at a reasonable time an expected and normal part of office life, change is more likely to occur. When men see housework and childcare as something that they are equally responsible for (because they live in the house and are parents to their children just as much as their wives are), balance and egalitarian relationships become possible.

When men enter professions such as teaching and nursing, the status of those professions will rise and men will be able to enjoy the flexibility that these jobs can offer. As I (ML) mentioned in the introduction, my husband is a guidance counselor at a high school. This job is excellent for work-family balance—he is home to get our children off the bus every single day. Not to mention that he is an outstanding influence for the male students—many of whom are lacking a male role model. But he is the only male guidance counselor in the school and one of the very few in the district.

Women have made great strides toward equality and can continue to work on social change. Much of the conversation has focused on how women should work on "leaning in" and achieving more positions of power. However, social change for gender equality and work-family balance is not something for only women to be concerned about. Instead of seeing themselves as engaged in a "battle of the sexes," men and women need to see themselves as being on the same team. When they do, they can work together for conditions that will allow both of them to lead meaningful, satisfying, and balanced lives.

BALANCE: MORE THAN JUST AN INDIVIDUAL PROBLEM

Work-family balance is not simply a problem that can be solved on the individual level. There are many barriers to equality that need to be solved through organizational change. Yes, it is possible for high-status and highly educated women to individually work toward increasing their own personal level of equality. Women can be encouraged to negotiate for higher salaries, to "sit at the table," and to combine niceness with authority in order to be both liked and respected as leaders.[13] But this only solves the problem for those who are successful and leaves most people still struggling. Instead, change will have to involve collective action. The city of Boston has recently committed to ending the pay gap between men and women.[14] As of November 2013, forty-four organizations have made pledges to close the wage gap. They will each take three steps, out of a list of thirty-three possible choices including wage transparency, actively recruiting women for top positions, offering paid family leave, promoting a results-oriented work environment (ROWE), providing subsidized childcare, and eliminating the wage history on applications (because women generally have a history of lower wages, which sets them up to earn lower wages in the future). The report on closing the wage gap states that its goal is for Boston to become the best city in America for working women. It outlines changes that can be made at each stage of the pipeline where women are lost. These include women's choice of major and career path, their ability to be hired into top-level positions and negotiate for top salaries, performance evaluations that may contain unconscious gender stereotypes, workplace flexibility issues that push women out of the workplace, and lack of women in senior positions.[15]

Other states are taking positive steps toward gender equality as well. The state of Minnesota requires employees from the public sector to do a study every few years examining pay equity and to eliminate pay disparities.[16] In 2009, New Mexico passed an initiative in which businesses that seek contracts with the state government need to provide information on salaries by gender in order to eliminate any possible gender bias.[17]

Companies are also making the move toward gender equality. Edge Certified is a global organization that provides companies with the information and resources that they need to eliminate the pay gap and create an equal playing field for men and women. On their website, they note that companies with the most women on their boards outperform those with the least by 26%. In addition, promoting equality will have added advantages of increasing financial stability and lowering turnover rates.[18] The data we reviewed in chapter 4 showed that companies can enhance employee satisfaction and well-being as well as productivity if they take steps to promote workplace flexibility and a positive work environment. Companies want workers who are intrinsically motivated to work at their organizations. Providing workers with autonomy over their schedules and over the way in which they get their tasks done, giving workers tasks that will make them feel competent and challenged, and creating a supportive workplace environment where relationships between employees are encouraged will promote workers who truly enjoy the jobs that they are doing. This approach will result in workers that are happier, more productive, and less likely to leave the organization.

There are other signs of positive social change. For example, Oklahoma has had a universal, publically funded preschool program since 1998, which currently educates approximately three-fourths of the students in that state. President Obama has praised that program as a model for a national prekindergarten program. The Oklahoma program has been a success, boosting scores for children in reading, writing, and math.[19] Although the long-term financial benefits of providing universal pre-K have not been established, it is estimated that the return on investment will be 3:1 or 4:1 based on increased earnings and decreased use of the criminal justice system.[20]

Other policy changes that can help with work-family balance are also under discussion. For example, raising the minimum wage is essential to helping lower-income workers balance work and family. In chapter 4 we discussed the negative effects of wage inequality on people's physical and mental health. Great disparity in wages negatively affects entire communities as it encourages envy and social comparison from those in lower wage groups, a certain amount of callousness from those in higher wage groups,[21] and distrust all around. Thus efforts to raise the minimum wage are essential to helping everyone balance work and family and lead truly meaningful lives.

IMAGINE

Imagine a world where both men and women have equal opportunities to work and to spend time with family; where work, childcare, and housework are seen as truly shared responsibilities.[22] Imagine a world where workplace flexibility is the norm and the expectation is that all workers will be happier and, ultimately, more productive if they have some control over how they do their jobs and when and where they are able to work. Imagine a world where people choose jobs that they find meaningful, rather than jobs they feel they are supposed to have, or ones that pay the most money. Imagine a world where high-quality childcare is available to all; where minimum wage jobs provide a salary that allows workers to support themselves and their families. Imagine a world where people can lead truly meaningful lives—lives where people's own autonomy and those around them are respected, where people strive to achieve because of the joy that comes from a job well done, and where people are encouraged to build and nurture meaningful relationships with others. This world is possible, but we are going to have to work together to get there.

Notes

1. THE SEARCH FOR BALANCE

1. Sheryl Sandberg, *Lean In: Women, Work, and the Will to Lead* (New York: Random House, 2013).

2. Brigid Schulte, *Overwhelmed: Work, Love and Play When No One Has the Time* (New York: Sarah Crichton / Farrar, Straus & Giroux, 2014).

3. Katrina Alcorn, *Maxed Out: American Moms on the Brink* (Berkeley: Seal Press, 2013).

4. Adam M. Grant and Barry Schwartz, "Too Much of a Good Thing: The Challenge and Opportunity of the Inverted U," *Perspectives on Psychological Science* 6, no. 1 (2011): 61–76.

5. Anne-Marie Slaughter, "Why Women Still Can't Have It All," *The Atlantic*, July/August 2012, http://www.theatlantic.com/magazine/archive/2012/07/why-women-still-cant-have-it-all/309020.

6. Richard M. Ryan and Edward L. Deci, "Self-Determination Theory and the Facilitation of Intrinsic Motivation, Social Development, and Well-Being," *American Psychologist* 55, no. 1 (2000): 68–78.

7. Ibid.

8. Ibid.

9. Harry T. Reis et al., "Daily Well-Being: The Role of Autonomy, Competence, and Relatedness," *Personality and Social Psychology Bulletin* 26, no. 4 (2000): 419–435.

10. Kim Parker and Wendy Wang, "Modern Parenthood: Roles of Moms and Dads Converge as They Balance Work and Family," Pew Research Social and Demographic Trends, posted March 14, 2013, http://www.pewsocialtrends.org/2013/03/14/modern-parenthood-roles-of-moms-and-dads-converge-as-they-balance-work-and-family.

11. Catherine Rampell, "Working Parents, Wanting Fewer Hours," *Economix* (blog), *New York Times*, July 10, 2013, http://economix.blogs.nytimes.com/2013/07/10/working-parents-wanting-fewer-hours/?src=rechp.

12. Richard Dorment, "Why Men Still Can't Have It All," *Esquire,* May 28, 2013, http://www.esquire.com/features/why-men-still-cant-have-it-all-0613?click=pp.

13. Harry Chapin, "The Cat's in the Cradle" on *Verities and Balderdash* album, released 1974, compact disc.

14. Kathleen Gerson, *The Unfinished Revolution: How a New Generation Is Reshaping Family, Work, and Gender in America* (New York: Oxford University Press, 2010).

15. Ibid., 111.

16. Ibid.

17. Pamela Stone, *Opting Out? Why Women Really Quit Careers and Head Home* (Berkeley: University of California Press, 2007), 51.

2. BALANCING MULTIPLE ROLES

1. Jennifer Senior, "All Joy and No Fun: Why Parents Hate Parenting," *New York*, July 4, 2010, http://nymag.com/news/features/67024.

2. Daniel Kahneman et al., "A Survey Method for Characterizing Daily Life Experience: The Day Reconstruction Method," *American Association for the Advancement of Science* 306, no. 5702 (2004): 1776–1780.

3. Kei M. Nomaguchi and Melissa A. Milkie, "Costs and Rewards of Children: The Effects of Becoming a Parent on Adults' Lives," *Journal of Marriage and Family* 65, no. 2 (2003): 356–374; Denise B. Kandel, Mark Davies, and Victoria H. Raveis, "The Stressfulness of Daily Social Roles for Women: Marital, Occupational and Household Roles," *Journal of Health and Social Behavior* 26, no. 1 (1985): 64–78.

4. Maike Luhmann et al., "Subjective Well-Being and Adaptation to Life Events: A Meta-Analysis," *Journal of Personality and Social Psychology* 102, no. 3 (2012): 592–615.

5. Ranae J. Evenson and Robin W. Simon, "Clarifying the Relationship between Parenthood and Depression," *Journal of Health and Social Behavior* 46, no. 4 (2005): 341–358.

6. Sara McLanahan and Julia Adams, "The Effect of Children on Adults' Psychological Well-Being: 1957–1976," *Social Forces* 68, no. 1 (1989): 124–146.

7. Victor J. Callan, "The Personal and Marital Adjustment of Mothers and of Voluntarily and Involuntarily Childless Wives," *Journal of Marriage and the Family* 49, no. 4 (1987): 847–856.

8. Ibid.

9. Amitai Etzioni, "Does Having Kids Make You Less Happy?," *CNN Opinion*, August 16, 2012, http://www.cnn.com/2012/07/30/opinion/etzioni-children.

10. Amy Claxton and Maureen Perry-Jenkins, "No Fun Anymore: Leisure and Marital Quality across the Transition to Parenthood," *Journal of Marriage and Family* 70, no. 1 (2008): 28–43.

11. Callan, "The Personal and Marital," 847–856.

12. Frances K. Grossman, "Affiliation and Autonomy in the Transition to Parenthood," *Family Relations* 36, no. 3 (1987): 263–269; Courtney Pierce Keeton, Maureen Perry-Jenkins, and Aline G. Sayer, "Sense of Control Predicts Depressive and Anxious Symptoms across the Transition to Parenthood," *Journal of Family Psychology* 22, no. 2 (2008): 212–221.

13. Ramona T. Mercer and Sandra L. Ferketich, "Experienced and Inexperienced Mothers' Maternal Competence during Infancy," *Research in Nursing and Health* 18, no. 4 (1995): 333–343.

14. Albert Bandura et al., "Impact of Family Efficacy Beliefs on Quality of Family Functioning and Satisfaction with Family Life," *Applied Psychology* 60, no. 3 (2011): 421–448.

15. Senior, "All Joy and No Fun."

16. Jean M. Twenge, W. Keith Campbell, and Craig A. Foster, "Parenthood and Marital Satisfaction: A Meta-Analytic Review," *Journal of Marriage and Family* 65, no. 3 (2003): 574–583.

17. Lisa S. Hackel and Diane N. Ruble, "Changes in the Marital Relationship after the First Baby Is Born: Predicting the Impact of Expectancy Disconfirmation," *Journal of Personality and Social Psychology* 62, no. 6 (1992): 944–957; Kate Harwood, Neil McLean, and Kevin Durkin, "First-Time Mothers' Expectations of Parenthood: What Happens When Optimistic Expectations Are Not Matched by Later Experiences?," *Developmental Psychology* 43, no. 1 (2007): 1–12.

18. Hackel and Ruble, "Changes in the Marital," "944–957.

19. Tone Ahlborg and Margaretha Strandmark, "Factors Influencing the Quality of Intimate Relationships Six Months after Delivery: First-time Parents' Own Views and Coping Strategies," *Journal of Psychosomatic Obstetrics & Gynecology* 27, no. 3 (2006): 163–172.

20. Senior, "All Joy and No Fun."

21. Twenge, Campbell, and Foster, "Parenthood and Marital Satisfaction," 574–583.

22. Ibid.

23. S. Katherine Nelson et al., "In Defense of Parenthood: Children Are Associated with More Joy than Misery," *Psychological Science* 24, no. 1 (2013): 1–8.

24. Evenson and Simon, "Clarifying the Relationship," 341–358; Debra Umberson and Walter R. Gove, "Parenthood and Psychological Well-Being: Theory, Measurement, and Stage in the Family Life Course," *Journal of Family Issues* 10, no. 4 (1989): 440–462; Mathew P. White and Paul Dolan, "Accounting for the Richness of Daily Activities," *Psychological Science* 20, no. 8 (2009): 1000–1008; Michele Hoffnung and Michelle A. Williams, "Balancing Act: Career and Family during College-Educated Women's 30s," *Sex Roles* 68, no. 5–6 (2012): 321–334.

25. Thomas Hansen, Britt Slagsvold, and Torbjørn Moum, "Childlessness and Psychological Well-Being in Midlife and Old Age: An Examination of Parental Status Effects across a Range of Outcomes," *Social Indicators Research* 94, no. 2 (2009): 343–362.

26. Kandel, Davies, and Raveis, "The Stressfulness of Daily," 64–78.

27. Steve Wiens, "To Parents of Small Children: Let Me Be the One Who Says It Out Loud," *The Blog* (blog), *Huffington Post*, May 3, 2013, http://www.huffingtonpost.com/steve-wiens/let-me-be-the-one-who-says-it-out-loud_b_3209305.html.

28. Karen Henwood and Joanne Procter, "The 'Good Father:' Reading Men's Accounts of Paternal Involvement during the Transition to First-Time Fatherhood," *British Journal of Social Psychology* 42, no. 3 (2003): 337–355.

29. S. Katherine Nelson et al., "In Defense of Parenthood," 1–8.

30. Holly S. Schindler, "The Importance of Parenting and Financial Contributions in Promoting Fathers' Psychological Health," *Journal of Marriage and Family* 72, no. 2 (2010): 318–332.

31. Chris Knoester, Richard J. Petts, and David J. Eggebeen, "Commitments to Fathering and the Well-Being and Social Participation of New, Disadvantaged Fathers," *Journal of Marriage and Family* 69, no. 4 (2007): 991–1004.

32. Nelarine Cornelius and Denise Skinner, "The Careers of Senior Men and Women: A Capabilities Theory Perspective." *British Journal of Management* 19, no. S1 (2008): S141–S149.

33. Jan-Emmanuel De Neve, James H. Fowler, and Bruno S. Frey, "Genes, Economics, and Happiness" (CESIFO working paper no. 2946, Category 12, Empirical and Theoretical Methods, Ifo Institute, Leibniz Institute for Economic Research at the University of Munich, Germany, 2010); Richard E. Lucas, "Adaptation and the Set-Point Model of Subjective Well-Being: Does Happiness Change after Major Life Events?," *Current Directions in Psychological Science* 16, no. 2 (2007): 75–79; Richard E. Lucas et al., "Reexamining Adaptation and the Set Point Model of Happiness: Reactions to Changes in Marital Status," *Journal of Personality and Social Psychology* 84, no. 3 (2003): 527–539; Luhmann et al., "Subjective Well-Being and Adaptation," 592–615.

34. Lisa Rosenthal et al., "The Importance of Full-Time Work for Urban Adults' Mental and Physical Health," *Social Science and Medicine* 75, no. 9 (2012): 1692–1696.

35. Lisa Belkin, "The Opt-Out Revolution," *New York Times Magazine*, October 26, 2003, http://www.nytimes.com/2003/10/26/magazine/26WOMEN.html.

36. David Cotter and Paula England, "Moms and Jobs: Trends in Mothers' Employment and Which Mothers Stay Home," *Council on Contemporary Families*, May 10, 2007, http://www.contemporaryfamilies.org/work-family/momsjobs.html.

37. Paula England, Janet Gornick, and Emily Fitzgibbons Shafer, "Women's Employment, Education, and the Gender Gap in 17 Countries," *Monthly Labor Review* 135 (2012): 3–12.

38. Elizabeth Mendes, Lydia Saad, and Kyley McGeeney, "Stay-at-Home Moms Report More Depression, Sadness, Anger: But Low-Income Stay-at-Home Moms Struggle the Most," *Gallup Wellbeing* (blog), Gallup, May 18, 2012, http://www.gallup.com/poll/154685/Stay-Home-Moms-Report-Depression-SadnessAnger.aspx?utm_source=alert&utm_medium=email&utm_campaign=syndication&utm_content_morelink&utm_term=All%20Gallup%20Headlines.

39. Keva Glynn et al., "The Association between Role Overload and Women's Mental Health," *Journal of Women's Health* 18, no. 2 (2009): 217–223.

40. Mendes, Saad, and McGeeney, "Stay-at-Home Moms."

41. Cheryl Buehler and Marion O'Brien, "Mother's Part-Time Employment: Associations with Mother and Family," *Journal of Family Psychology* 25, no. 6 (2011): 895–906.

42. Rosalind Chait Barnett and Janet Shibley Hyde, "Women, Men, Work, and Family," *American Psychologist* 56, no. 10 (2001): 781–796.

43. Marnie Dobson and Peter L. Schnall, "From Stress to Distress: The Impact of Work on Mental Health," in *Unhealthy Work: Causes, Consequences, Cures*, ed. Peter L. Schnall, Marnie Dobson, and Ellen Rosskam, Critical Approaches in the Health Social Sciences Series, ed. Ray H. Elling (Amityville, NY: Baywood, 2009), 113–132.

44. Barbara C. Ilardi et al., "Employee and Supervisor Ratings of Motivation: Main Effects and Discrepancies Associated with Job Satisfaction and Adjustment in a Factory Setting," *Journal of Applied Social Psychology* 23, no. 21 (1993): 1789–1805.

45. Dobson and Schnall, "From Stress to Distress," 113–132.

46. Matthew J. Grawitch, Melanie Gottschalk, and David C. Munz, "The Path to a Healthy Workplace: A Critical Review Linking Healthy Workplace Practices, Employee Well-Being, and Organizational Improvements," *Consulting Psychology Journal: Practice and Research* 58, no. 3 (2006): 129–147.

47. Sarah-Geneviève Trépanier, Claude Fernet, and Stéphanie Austin, "The Moderating Role of Autonomous Motivation in the Job Demands-Strain Relation: A Two Sample Study," *Motivation and Emotion* 37, no. 1 (2013): 93–105.

48. Ibid.

49. Paul P. Baard, Edward L. Deci, and Richard M. Ryan, "Intrinsic Need Satisfaction: A Motivational Basis of Performance and Well-Being in Two Work Settings," *Journal of Applied Social Psychology* 34, no. 10 (2004): 2045–2068.

50. Ilardi et al., "Employee and Supervisor Ratings," 1789–1805.

51. Amy Wrzesniewski et al., "Jobs, Careers, and Callings: People's Relations to Their Work," *Journal of Research in Personality* 31, no. 1 (1997): 21–33.

52. Ibid.

53. Satoris S. Culbertson, Maura J. Mills, and Clive J. Fullager, "Work Engagement and Work-Family Facilitation: Making Homes Happier through Positive Affective Spillover," *Human Relations* 65, no. 9 (2012): 1155–1177.

54. Yessenia Castro and Kathryn H. Gordon, "A Review of Recent Research on Multiple Roles and Women's Mental Health," in *Women and Mental Disorders*, ed. Paula K. Lundberg-Love, Kevin L. Nadal, and Michele A. Paludi (Santa Barbara, CA: Praeger, 2012), 1: 37–54.

55. Marian N. Ruderman, "Benefits of Multiple Roles for Managerial Women," *Academy of Management Journal* 45, no. 2 (2002): 369–386.

56. Jeffrey H. Greenhaus and Nicholas J. Beutell, "Sources of Conflict between Work and Family Roles," *Academy of Management Review* 10, no. 2 (1985): 76–88.

57. Suzanne M. Bianchi and Melissa A. Milkie, "Work and Family Research in the First Decade of the 21st Century," *Journal of Marriage and Family* 72, no. 3 (2010): 705–725.

58. Tammy D. Allen et al., "Consequences Associated with Work-To-Family Conflict: A Review and Agenda for Future Research," *Journal of Occupational Health Psychology* 5, no. 2 (2000): 278–308.

59. Kei M. Nomaguchi, "Change in Work-Family Conflict among Employed Parents between 1977 and 1997," *Journal of Marriage and Family* 71, no. 1 (2009): 15–32.

60. Kei M. Nomaguchi, Melissa A. Milkie, and Suzanne M. Bianchi, "Time Strains and Psychological Well-Being: Do Dual-Earner Mothers and Fathers Differ?," *Journal of Family Issues* 26, no. 6 (2005): 756–792.

61. Leslie B. Hammer et al., "The Longitudinal Effects of Work-Family Conflict and Positive Spillover on Depressive Symptoms among Dual-Earner Couples," *Journal of Occupational Health Psychology* 10, no. 2 (2005): 138–154.

62. Ibid.

63. Castro and Gordon, "Multiple Roles and Women's Mental Health," 37–54; Sam D. Sieber, "Toward a Theory of Role Accumulation," *American Sociological Review* 39, no. 4

(1974): 567–578; Stephen R. Marks, "Multiple Roles and Role Strain: Some Notes on Human Energy, Time and Commitment," *American Sociological Review* 42, no. 6 (1977): 921–936.

64. Barnett and Hyde, "Women, Men, Work," 781–796.

65. Robert T. Brennan, Rosalind Chait Barnett, and Karen C. Gareis, "When She Earns More than He Does: A Longitudinal Study of Dual-Earner Couples," *Journal of Marriage and Family* 63, no. 1 (2001): 168–182.

66. Barnett and Hyde, "Women, Men, Work," 781–796.

67. Castro and Gordon, "Multiple Roles and Women's Mental Health," 37–54.

68. Barnett and Hyde, "Women, Men, Work," 788–789.

69. Castro and Gordon, "Multiple Roles and Women's Mental Health," 37–54.

70. Sheldon Cohen and Thomas A. Wills, "Stress, Social Support, and the Buffering Hypothesis," *Psychological Bulletin* 98, no. 2 (1985): 310–357.

71. Sonja Lyubomirsky, Laura King, and Ed Diener, "The Benefits of Frequent Positive Affect: Does Happiness Lead to Success?," *Psychological Bulletin* 131, no. 6 (2005): 803–855.

72. Rosalind C. Barnett, Nancy L. Marshall, and Joseph H. Pleck, "Men's Multiple Roles and Their Relationship to Men's Psychological Distress," *Journal of Marriage and Family* 54, no. 2 (1992): 358–367.

73. Ibid.

74. Jeffrey H. Greenhaus and Gary N. Powell, "When Work and Family Are Allies: A Theory of Work-Family Enrichment," *Academy of Management Review* 31, no. 1 (2006): 72–92.

75. Barbara L. Fredrickson and Thomas Joiner, "Positive Emotions Trigger Upward Spirals toward Emotional Well-Being," *Psychological Science* 13, no. 2 (2002): 172–75.

76. Greenhaus and Powell, "When Work and Family Are Allies," 72–92.

77. Ruderman, "Benefits of Multiple Roles," 369–386.

78. Ibid.

79. Ibid.

80. Laurel A. McNall, Jessica M. Nicklin, and Aline D. Masuda, "A Meta-Analytic Review of the Consequences Associated with Work-Family Enrichment," *Journal of Business and Psychology* 25, no. 3 (2010): 381–396; Joseph G. Grzywacz and Brenda L. Bass, "Work, Family, and Mental Health: Testing Different Models of Work-Family Fit," *Journal of Marriage and Family* 65, no. 1 (2003): 248–262.

81. Karen C. Gareis et al., "Work-Family Enrichment and Conflict: Additive Effects, Buffering, or Balance?," *Journal of Marriage and Family* 71, no. 3 (2009): 696–707.

82. Culbertson, Mills, and Fullager, "Work Engagement," 1155–1177.

83. Lori L. Wadsworth and Bradley P. Owens, "The Effects of Social Support on Work-Family Enhancement and Work-Family Conflict in the Public Sector," *Public Administration Review* 67, no. 1 (2007): 75–87.

84. Hammer et al., "Longitudinal Effects of Work-Family Conflict," 138–154.

85. Stewart D. Friedman and Jeffrey H. Greenhaus, *Work and Family—Allies or Enemies?: What Happens When Business Professionals Confront Life Choices* (New York: Oxford University Press, 2000), 200.

86. Kim Parker and Wendy Wang, "Modern Parenthood: Roles of Moms and Dads Converge as They Balance Work and Family," Pew Research Social and Demographic Trends, posted March 14, 2013, http://www.pewsocialtrends.org/2013/03/14/modern-parenthood-roles-of-moms-and-dads-converge-as-they-balance-work-and-family.

87. Belkin, "The Opt-Out Revolution."

88. Pamela Stone, *Opting Out? Why Women Really Quit Careers and Head Home* (Berkeley: University of California Press, 2007), 51.

89. Jay Belsky et al., "Are There Long-Term Effects of Early Child Care?," *Child Development* 78, no. 2 (2007): 681–701.

90. Noam Shpancer, "The Effects of Daycare: Persistent Questions, Elusive Answers," *Early Childhood Research Quarterly* 21, no. 2 (2006): 227–237.

91. Rachel G. Lucas-Thompson, Wendy A. Goldberg, and JoAnn Prause, "Maternal Work Early in the Lives of Children and Its Distal Associations with Achievement and Behavior Problems: A Meta-Analysis," *Psychological Bulletin* 136, no. 6 (2010): 915–942.

92. Ibid.

93. Belsky et al., "Effects of Early Child Care," 681–701.

94. Lucas-Thompson, Goldberg, and Prause, "Maternal Work," 915–942.

95. Wendy A. Goldberg et al., "Maternal Employment and Children's Achievement in Context: A Meta-Analysis of Four Decades of Research," *Psychological Bulletin* 134, no. 1 (2008): 77–108.

96. Ibid.; Lucas-Thompson, Goldberg, and Prause, "Maternal Work," 915–942.

97. Goldberg et al., "Maternal Employment," 77–108.

98. Lucas-Thompson, Goldberg, and Prause, "Maternal Work," 915–942; Wen-Jui Han, Jane Waldfogel, and Jeanne Brooks-Gunn, "The Effects of Early Maternal Employment on Later Cognitive and Behavioral Outcomes," *Journal of Marriage and Family* 63, no. 2 (2001): 336–354; Lawrence Berger et al., "First-Year Maternal Employment and Child Outcomes: Differences across Racial and Ethnic Groups," *Children and Youth Services Review* 30, no. 4 (2008): 365–387.

99. Goldberg et al., "Maternal Employment," 77–108.

100. Belsky et al., "Effects of Early Child Care," 681–701; Deborah Lowe Vandell, "Do Effects of Early Child Care Extend to Age 15 Years? Results from the NICHD Study of Early Child Care and Youth Development," *Child Development* 81, no. 3 (2010): 737–756.

101. Belsky et al., "Effects of Early Child Care," 681–701; Vandell, "Early Child Care Extend," 737–756.

102. Ellen S. Peisner-Feinberg et al., "The Relation of Preschool Child-Care Quality to Children's Cognitive and Social Developmental Trajectories through Second Grade," *Child Development* 72, no. 5 (2001): 1534–1553.

103. Robert H. Bradley and Deborah Lowe Vandell, "Child Care and the Well-Being of Children," *Archives of Pediatrics & Adolescent Medicine* 161, no. 7 (2007): 669–676; Vandell, "Early Child Care Extend," 737–756.

104. Bradley and Vandell, "Child Care and Well-Being," 669–676; Vandell, "Early Child Care Extend," 737–756.

105. Henrik D. Zachrisson et al., "Little Evidence That Time in Child Care Causes Externalizing Problems during Early Childhood in Norway," *Child Development* 84, no. 4 (2013): 1152–1170.

106. Brenda L. Volling and Lynne V. Feagans, "Infant Day Care and Children's Social Competence," *Infant Behavior and Development* 18, no. 2 (1995): 177–188.

107. Kei M. Nomaguchi, "Maternal Employment, Nonparental Care, Mother-Child Interactions, and Child Outcomes during Preschool Years," *Journal of Marriage and Family* 68, no. 5 (2006): 1341–1369.

108. Anne McMunn et al., "Maternal Employment and Child Socio-Emotional Behaviour in the UK: Longitudinal Evidence from the UK Millennium Cohort Study," *Journal of Epidemiology & Community Health* 66, no. 7 (2011).

109. Lawrence L. Schweinhart, David P. Weikart, and Mary B. Larner, "Consequences of Three Preschool Curriculum Models through Age 15," *Early Childhood Research Quarterly* 1, no. 1 (1986): 15–45.

110. Jenet I. Jacob, "The Socio-Emotional Effects of Non-Maternal Childcare on Children in the USA: A Critical Review of Recent Studies," *Early Child Development and Care* 179, no. 5 (2009): 559–570.

111. Young Eun Chang, "The Relation between Mothers' Attitudes toward Maternal Employment and Social Competence of 36-Month-Olds: The Role of Maternal Psychological Well-Being and Sensitivity," *Journal of Child and Family Studies* 22, no. 7 (2013): 987–999.

112. Jay Belsky, "The 'Effects' of Infant Day Care Reconsidered," *Early Childhood Research Quarterly* 3, no. 3 (1988): 235–272.

113. Sarah L. Friedman and D. Ellen Boyle, "Attachment in US Children Experiencing Nonmaternal Care in the Early 1990s," *Attachment and Human Development* 10, no. 3 (2008): 225–261.

114. Cathryn L. Booth, "Child-Care Usage and Mother-Infant 'Quality Time,'" *Journal of Marriage and Family* 64, no. 1 (2002): 16–26.

115. Ibid.

116. Bradley and Vandell, "Child Care and Well-Being," 669–676.

117. Nomaguchi, "Maternal Employment," 1341–1369.

118. Lucas-Thompson, Goldberg, and Prause, "Maternal Work," 915–942.

3. BALANCE AS A PARENT

1. Elizabeth Kolbert, "Spoiled Rotten: Why Do Kids Rule the Roost?," *New Yorker,* July 2, 2012, http://www.newyorker.com/arts/critics/books/2012/07/02/120702crbo_books_kolbert? currentPage=all.

2. Gloria DeGaetano, *Parenting Well in a Media Age: Keeping Our Kids Human* (Fawnskin, CA: Personhood Press, 2004), 5.

3. Garey Ramey and Valerie A. Ramey, "The Rug Rat Race" (working paper no. 15284, National Bureau of Economic Research, Cambridge, MA, 2009).

4. Suzanne M. Bianchi, John P. Robinson, and Melissa A. Milkie, *Changing Rhythms of American Family Life,* Rose Series in Sociology (New York: Russell Sage, 2006), 77.

5. Katherine S. Nelson et al., "In Defense of Parenthood: Children Are Associated with More Joy than Misery," *Psychological Science* 24, no. 1 (2013): 1–8.

6. Rachel M. Martin, "To the Tired Mom," *HuffPost Parents* (blog), *Huffington Post,* October 21, 2013, http://www.huffingtonpost.com/rachel-m-martin/to-the-tired-mom_b_ 4104515.html.

7. Pamela Stone, *Opting Out? Why Women Really Quit Careers and Head Home* (Berkeley: University of California Press, 2007), 40–60.

8. Terry Arendell, "Conceiving and Investigating Motherhood: The Decade's Scholarship," *Journal of Marriage and Family* 62, no. 4 (2000): 1192–1207; Sharon Hays, *The Cultural Contradictions of Motherhood* (New Haven, CT: Yale University Press, 1996).

9. Suzanne M. Bianchi, "Maternal Employment and Time with Children: Dramatic Change or Surprising Continuity?," *Demography* 37, no. 4 (2000): 401–414.

10. Judith Warner, *Perfect Madness: Motherhood in the Age of Anxiety* (New York: Riverhead, 2005), 4.

11. Lauren S. Aaronson, Carol Macnee Mural, and Susan K. Pfoutz, "Seeking Information: Where Do Pregnant Women Go?," *Health Education & Behavior* 15, no. 3 (1988): 335–345.

12. Warner, *Perfect Madness,* 23.

13. Terri Combs-Orme et al., "Context-Based Parenting in Infancy: Background and Conceptual Issues," *Child and Adolescent Social Work Journal* 20, no. 6 (2003): 437–472; Randal D. Day and Laura M. Padilla-Walker, "Mother and Father Connectedness and Involvement During Early Adolescence," *Journal of Family Psychology* 23, no. 6 (2009): 900–904; Mireille Joussemet, Renée Landry, and Richard Koestner, "A Self-Determination Theory Perspective on Parenting," *Canadian Psychology / Psychologie Canadienne* 49, no. 3 (2008): 194–200; Eva M. Pomerantz, Elizabeth A. Moorman, and Scott D. Litwack, "The How, Whom, and Why of Parents' Involvement in Children's Academic Lives: More Is Not Always Better," *Review of Educational Research* 77, no. 3 (2007): 373–410.

14. Harry T. Chugani et al., "Local Brain Functional Activity Following Early Deprivation: A Study of Postinstitutionalized Romanian Orphans," *Neuroimage* 14, no. 6 (2001): 1290–1301.

15. Xitao Fan and Michael Chen, "Parental Involvement and Students' Academic Achievement: A Meta-Analysis," *Educational Psychology Review* 13, no. 1 (2001): 1–22; Pomerantz, Moorman, and Litwack, "Parents' Involvement in Children's Academic," 373–410.

16. Wendy S. Grolnick and Richard M. Ryan, "Parent Styles Associated with Children's Self-Regulation and Competence in School," *Journal of Educational Psychology* 81, no. 2 (1989): 143–154.

17. Dante Cicchetti and Sheree L. Toth, "The Development of Depression in Children and Adolescents," *American Psychologist* 53, no. 2 (1998): 221–241.

18. Brian K. Barber, Joseph E. Olsen, and Shobha C. Shagle. "Associations between Parental Psychological and Behavioral Control and Youth Internalized and Externalized Behaviors," *Child Development* 65, no. 4 (1994): 1120–1136.

19. Day and Padilla-Walker, "Connectedness and Involvement," 900–904.

20. Harry Frederick Harlow, "The Nature of Love," 13 (1958): 673–685.

21. Heon-Jin Lee et al., "Oxytocin: The Great Facilitator of Life, *Progress in Neurobiology* 88, no. 2 (2009): 127–151.

22. Regine A. Schön and Maarit Silvén, "Natural Parenting: Back to Basics in Infant Care," *Evolutionary Psychology* 5, no. 1 (2007): 102–183.

23. Chugani et al., "Local Brain Functional Activity," 1290–1301.

24. William Sears and Martha Sears, *The Attachment Parenting Book: A Commonsense Guide to Understanding and Nurturing Your Baby* (Boston: Little, Brown, 2001).

25. Schön and Silvén, "Natural Parenting," 102–183.

26. Kate Pickert, "The Man Who Remade Motherhood," *Time*, May 21, 2012, http://content.time.com/time/magazine/article/0,9171,2114427,00.html.

27. Katherine E. Green and Melissa M. Groves, "Attachment Parenting: An Exploration of Demographics and Practices,"*Early Child Development and Care* 178, no. 5 (2008): 513–525.

28. Hanna Rosin, "The Case against Breast-Feeding," *The Atlantic*, April 1, 2009, http://www.theatlantic.com/magazine/archive/2009/04/the-case-against-breast-feeding/307311/?single_page=true.

29. Schön and Silvén, "Natural Parenting," 102–183.

30. Urs A. Hunziker and Ronald G. Barr, "Increased Carrying Reduces Infant Crying: A Randomized Controlled Trial," *Pediatrics* 77, no. 5 (1986): 641–648.

31. Elizabeth Anisfeld et al., "Does Infant Carrying Promote Attachment? An Experimental Study of the Effects of Increased Physical Contact on the Development of Attachment," *Child Development* 61, no. 5 (1990): 1617–1627.

32. Marianne S. De Wolff and Marinus H. Ijzendoorn, "Sensitivity and Attachment: A Meta-Analysis on Parental Antecedents of Infant Attachment," *Child Development* 68, no. 4 (1997): 571–591.

33. Hunziker and Barr, "Increased Carrying Reduces Crying," 641–648.

34. Anisfeld et al., "Infant Carrying Promote Attachment," 1617–1627.

35. Jessica Valenti, *Why Have Kids?: A New Mom Explores the Truth about Parenting and Happiness* (Seattle, WA: Amazon, 2012): 19.

36. Schön and Silvén, "Natural Parenting," 102–183.

37. Suad Nakamura, Marilyn Wind, and Mary Ann Danello, "Review of Hazards Associated with Children Placed in Adult Beds," *Archives of Pediatrics & Adolescent Medicine* 153, no. 10 (1999): 1019–1023; N. J. Scheers, George W. Rutherford, and James S. Kemp, "Where Should Infants Sleep? A Comparison of Risk for Suffocation of Infants Sleeping in Cribs, Adult Beds, and Other Sleeping Locations," *Pediatrics* 112, no. 4 (2003): 883–889.

38. James J. McKenna and Thomas McDade, "Why Babies Should Never Sleep Alone: A Review of the Co-Sleeping Controversy in Relation to SIDS, Bedsharing and Breast Feeding," *Paediatric Respiratory Reviews* 6, no. 2 (2005): 134–152; Edmund Anthony Severn Nelson et al., "International Child Care Practices Study: Infant Sleeping Environment," *Early Human Development* 62, no. 1 (2001): 43–55.

39. Meret A. Keller and Wendy A. Goldberg, "Co-Sleeping: Help or Hindrance for Young Children's Independence?," *Infant and Child Development* 13, no. 5 (2004): 369–388.

40. Ibid.

41. Kathleen Dyer Ramos, Davin Youngclarke, and Jane E. Anderson, "Parental Perceptions of Sleep Problems among Co-Sleeping and Solitary Sleeping Children," *Infant and Child Development* 16, no. 4 (2007): 417–431.

42. June J. Pilcher and Allen J. Huffcutt, "Effects of Sleep Deprivation on Performance: A Meta-Analysis," *Journal of Sleep Research & Sleep Medicine* 19, no. 4 (1996): 318–326.

43. Rachel Conrad, "Desiring Relation: Mothers' and Children's Agency, Subjectivity, and Time," *Studies in Gender and Sexuality* 10, no. 1 (2009): 12–20.

44. McKenna and McDade, "Babies Should Never Sleep Alone," 134.

45. Schön and Silvén, "Natural Parenting," 102–183.

46. American Academy of Pediatrics, "Breastfeeding and the Use of Human Milk," *Pediatrics: Official Journal of the American Academy of Pediatrics* 129, no. 3 (2012): e827–e841.

47. W. Jonas et al., "Short- and Long-Term Decrease of Blood Pressure in Women during Breastfeeding," *Breastfeeding Medicine* 3, no. 2 (2008): 103–109.

48. Maureen Wimberly Groer, Mitzi Wilkinson Davis, and Jean Hemphill, "Postpartum Stress: Current Concepts and the Possible Protective Role of Breastfeeding," *Journal of Obstetric, Gynecologic, & Neonatal Nursing* 31, no. 4 (2002): 411–417; Elizabeth Sibolboro Mezzacappa, Robert M. Kelsey, and Edward S. Katkin, "Breast Feeding, Bottle Feeding, and Maternal Autonomic Responses to Stress," *Journal of Psychosomatic Research* 58, no. 4 (2005): 351–365.

49. Tiffany Field, Maria Hernandez-Reif, and Larissa Feijo, "Breastfeeding in Depressed Mother-Infant Dyads," *Early Child Development and Care* 172, no. 6 (2002): 539–545.

50. Susan Flagler Virden, "The Relationship between Infant Feeding Method and Maternal Role Adjustment," *Journal of Nurse-Midwifery* 33, no. 1 (1988): 31–35.

51. Jessica Nihlén Fahlquist and Sabine Roeser, "Ethical Problems with Information on Infant Feeding in Developed Countries," *Public Health Ethics* 4, no. 2 (2011): 192–202.

52. Ellie J. Lee, "Living with Risk in the Age of 'Intensive Motherhood': Maternal Identity and Infant Feeding," *Health, Risk & Society* 10, no. 5 (2008): 467.

53. Ibid., 475.

54. Ibid., 467–477; Maggie Redshaw and Jane Henderson, "Learning the Hard Way: Expectations and Experiences of Infant Feeding Support," *Birth* 39, no. 1 (2012): 21–29.

55. Yvonne Hauck, Wendy A. Hall, and Christine Jones, "Prevalence, Self-efficacy and Perceptions of Conflicting Advice and Self-Management: Effects of a Breastfeeding Journal," *Journal of Advanced Nursing* 57, no. 3 (2007): 306–317; Pat Hoddinott and Roisin Pill, "A Qualitative Study of Women's Views about How Health Professionals Communicate about Infant Feeding," *Health Expectations* 3, no. 4 (2000): 224–233.

56. Rosin, "Case against Breast-Feeding."

57. Valenti, *Why Have Kids?*, 38.

58. Michelle Healy, "Buying Breast Milk Online? It May Be Contaminated," *USA Today*, October 21, 2013, http://www.usatoday.com/story/news/nation/2013/10/21/breast-milk-bacteria/3002973.

59. Sarah A. Keim et al., "Microbial Contamination of Human Milk Purchased via the Internet," *Pediatrics* 132, no. 5 (2013): e1227–e1235.

60. Richard M. Martin et al., "Effects of Promoting Longer-Term and Exclusive Breastfeeding on Adiposity and Insulin-Like Growth Factor-I at Age 11.5 Years: A Randomized Trial," *JAMA* 309, no. 10 (2013): 1005–1013.

61. Jarno Jansen, Carolina de Weerth, and J. Marianne Riksen-Walraven, "Breastfeeding and the Mother-Infant Relationship: A Review," *Developmental Review* 28, no. 4 (2008): 503–521.

62. Lawrence Aber, Pamela Morris, and Cybele Raver, "Children, Families and Poverty: Definitions, Trends, Emerging Science and Implications for Policy," *Social Policy Report* 26, no. 3 (2012): 1–29.

63. Eirik Evenhouse and Siobhan Reilly, "Improved Estimates of the Benefits of Breastfeeding Using Sibling Comparisons to Reduce Selection Bias," *Health Services Research* 40, no. 6, pt. 1 (2005): 1781–1802.

64. Jansen, de Weerth, and Riksen-Walraven, "Breastfeeding and Mother-Infant Relationship," 503–521.

65. Miriam Liss and Mindy J. Erchull, "Feminism and Attachment Parenting: Attitudes, Stereotypes, and Misperceptions," *Sex Roles* 67, no. 3–4 (2012): 131–142.

66. Erica Jong, "Mother Madness," *Wall Street Journal*, November 6, 2010, http://online.wsj.com/article/SB10001424052748704462704575590603553674296.html.

67. Valenti, *Why Have Kids?*, 21.

68. William T. Greenough, "Experiential Modification of the Developing Brain: The Environment and the Organism's Interactions with It May Play an Important Part in the Formation of Synapses between Nerve Cells in the Brain," *American Scientist* 63, no. 1 (1975): 37–46.

69. "Brain Development," *Zero to Three: National Center for Infants, Toddlers, and Families*, http://www.zerotothree.org/child-development/brain-development.

70. Glenda Wall, "Mothers' Experiences with Intensive Parenting and Brain Development Discourse," *Women's Studies International Forum* 33, no. 3 (2010): 253–263.

71. Warner, *Perfect Madness*, 6.

72. Brigid Schulte, *Overwhelmed: Work, Love and Play When No One Has the Time* (New York: Sarah Crichton / Farrar, Straus & Giroux, 2014).

73. "Can a Video Teach Babies to Read?," ABC News, March 6, 2013, http://abc-news.go.com/GMA/AmericanFamily/story?id=126294.

74. Ulric Neisser et al., "Intelligence: Knowns and Unknowns," *American Psychologist* 51, no. 2 (1996): 77–101; Betty Hart and Todd R. Risley, *Meaningful Differences in the Everyday Experience of Young American Children* (Baltimore, MD: Paul H. Brookes, 1995).

75. Neisser et al., "Intelligence: Knowns and Unknowns," 77–101.

76. John Protzko, Joshua Aronson, and Clancy Blair, "How to Make a Young Child Smarter: Evidence from the Database of Raising Intelligence," *Perspectives on Psychological Science* 8, no. 1 (2013): 25–40.

77. Don Campbell, *The Mozart Effect for Children: Awakening Your Child's Mind, Health, and Creativity with Music* (New York: William Morrow, 2000).

78. E. Glenn Schellenberg, "Music and Cognitive Abilities," *Current Directions in Psychological Science* 14, no. 6 (2005): 317–320; E. Glenn Schellenberg, "Long-Term Positive Associations between Music Lessons and IQ," *Journal of Educational Psychology* 98, no. 2 (2006): 457–468.

79. Schellenberg, "Music Lessons and IQ," 457–468.

80. Frances H. Rauscher et al., "Music Training Causes Long-Term Enhancement of Preschool Children's Spatial-Temporal Reasoning," *Neurological Research* 19, no. 1 (1997): 2–8; E. Glenn Schellenberg, "Music Lessons Enhance IQ," *Psychological Science* 15, no. 8 (2004): 511–514.

81. Ari Brown, "Media Use by Children Younger than 2 Years," *Pediatrics* 128, no. 5 (2011): 1040–1045.

82. Tamar Lewin, "No Einstein in Your Crib? Get a Refund," *New York Times,* October 23, 2009, http://www.nytimes.com/2009/10/24/education/24baby.html.

83. Frederick J. Zimmerman, Dimitri A. Christakis, and Andrew N. Meltzoff, "Television and DVD/Video Viewing in Children Younger than 2 Years," *Archives of Pediatrics & Adolescent Medicine* 161, no. 5 (2007): 473–479.

84. Frederick J. Zimmerman, Dimitri A. Christakis, and Andrew N. Meltzoff, "Associations between Media Viewing and Language Development in Children Under Age 2 Years," *Journal of Pediatrics* 151, no. 4 (2007): 364–368.

85. Marina Krcmar, "Word Learning in Very Young Children from Infant-Directed DVDs," *Journal of Communication* 61, no. 4 (2011): 780–794; Michael B. Robb, Rebekah A. Richert, and Ellen A. Wartella, "Just a Talking Book? Word Learning From Watching Baby Videos," *British Journal of Developmental Psychology* 27, no. 1 (2009): 27–45.

86. Ramey and Ramey, "The Rug Rat Race."

87. Jennifer A. Fredricks and Jacquelynne S. Eccles, "Extracurricular Involvement and Adolescent Adjustment: Impact of Duration, Number of Activities, and Breadth of Participation," *Applied Developmental Science* 10, no. 3 (2006): 132–146.

88. Boaz Shulruf, "Do Extra-Curricular Activities in Schools Improve Educational Outcomes? A Critical Review and Meta-Analysis of the Literature," *International Review of Education* 56, no. 5-6 (2010): 591–612.

89. Amy Feldman Farb and Jennifer L. Matjasko, "Recent Advances in Research on School-Based Extracurricular Activities and Adolescent Development," *Developmental Review* 32, no. 1 (2012): 1–48.

90. Jennifer A. Fredricks, "Extracurricular Participation and Academic Outcomes: Testing the Over-Scheduling Hypothesis," *Journal of Youth and Adolescence* 41, no. 3 (2012): 295–306.

91. Casey A. Knifsend and Sandra Graham, "Too Much of a Good Thing? How Breadth of Extracurricular Participation Relates to School-Related Affect and Academic Outcomes During Adolescence," *Journal of Youth and Adolescence* 41, no. 3 (2012): 379–389.

92. Shari Melman, Steven G. Little, and K. Angeleque Akin-Little, "Adolescent Overscheduling: The Relationship between Levels of Participation in Scheduled Activities and Self-Reported Clinical Symptomology," *High School Journal* 90, no. 3 (2007): 18–30.

93. Maimone Attia, *Race to Nowhere,* directed by Vicki Abeles and Jessica Congdon (Lafayette, CA: Reel Link Films, 2009), DVD.

94. Suniya S. Luthar and Bronwyn E. Becker, "Privileged but Pressured? A Study of Affluent Youth," *Child Development* 73, no. 5 (2002): 1593–1610.

95. Alvin Rosenfeld and Nicole Wise, *The Over-Scheduled Child: Avoiding the Hyper-Parenting Trap* (New York: St. Martin's Press, 2000).

96. Michael Thompson, *The Pressured Child: Freeing Our Kids from Performance Overdrive and Helping Them Find Success in School and Life* (New York: Ballantine, 2011).

97. Bruce Feiler, "Over-Scheduled Children: How Big a Problem?," *New York Times,* October 11, 2013, http://www.nytimes.com/2013/10/13/fashion/over-scheduled-children-how-big-a-problem.html?pagewanted=1&_r=2&adxnnlx=1381690935-sXqxj/nHxywe2wqj0eOHqQ.

98. Lisa Catherine Harper, "The Crazy, Intense Schedule of Competitive Youth Soccer? Bring It On," *Motherlode: Adventures in Parenting* (blog), *New York Times,* October 7, 2013, http://parenting.blogs.nytimes.com/2013/10/07/the-crazy-intense-schedule-of-competitive-youth-soccer-bring-it-on/?hp&_r=0.

99. Diana Baumrind, "Current Patterns of Parental Authority," *Developmental Psychology* 4, no. 1p2 (1971): 1. Note: These parenting styles also differ in how responsive and warm they are to their children as well with permissive and authoritative parents exhibiting high levels of responsiveness, while authoritarian parents are low on this dimension. See Eleanor E. Maccoby and John A. Martin, "Socialization in the Context of the Family: Parent-Child Interaction," in *Handbook of Child Psychology* (Hoboken, NJ: Wiley, 1983), 4: 37–39.

100. Diana Baumrind, Robert E. Larzelere, and Elizabeth B. Owens, "Effects of Preschool Parents' Power Assertive Patterns and Practices on Adolescent Development," *Parenting: Science and Practice* 10, no. 3 (2010): 157–201.

101. Ibid.

102. Brian Barber and Mingzhu Xia, "The Centrality of Control to Parenting and Its Effects," in *Parenting: Synthesizing Nurturance and Discipline for Optimal Child Development,* ed. Robert E. Larzelere, Amanda Sheffield Morris, and Amanda W. Harrist (Washington, DC: American Psychological Association, 2013), 61–87.

103. Ibid.

104. Ibid.; Kaisa Aunola and Jari-Erik Nurmi, "The Role of Parenting Styles in Children's Problem Behavior," *Child Development* 76, no. 6 (2005): 1144–1159, Susanne Frost Olsen et al., "Maternal Psychological Control and Preschool Children's Behavioral Outcomes in China, Russia, and the United States," in *Intrusive Parenting: How Psychological Control Affects Children and Adolescents,* ed. Brian K. Barber (Washington, DC: American Psychological Association, 2002), 235–262.

105. Aunola and Nurmi, "Parenting Styles," 1144–1159.

106. Barber and Xia, "Centrality of Control to Parenting," 61–87.

107. Wendy Grolnick, Ann Frodi, and Lisa Bridges, "Maternal Control Style and the Mastery Motivation of One-Year-Olds," *Infant Mental Health Journal* 5, no. 2 (1984): 72–82; Mireille Joussemet et al., "A Longitudinal Study of the Relationship of Maternal Autonomy Support to Children's Adjustment and Achievement in School," *Journal of Personality* 73, no. 5 (2005): 1215–1236; Catherine F. Ratelle, Karine Simard, and Frédéric Guay, "University Students' Subjective Well-Being: The Role of Autonomy Support from Parents, Friends, and the Romantic Partner," *Journal of Happiness Studies* 14, no. 3 (2012): 893–910; Bart Soenens and Maarten Vansteenkiste, "Antecedents and Outcomes of Self-Determination in 3 Life Domains: The Role of Parents' and Teachers' Autonomy Support," *Journal of Youth and Adolescence* 34, no. 6 (2005): 589–604.

108. Richard Koestner et al., "Setting Limits on Children's Behavior: The Differential Effects of Controlling vs. Informational Styles on Intrinsic Motivation and Creativity," *Journal of Personality* 52, no. 3 (1984): 233–248.

109. Grolnick, Frodi, and Bridges, "Maternal Control Style," 72–82; Joussemet et al., "Maternal Autonomy Support," 1215–1236; Ratelle, Simard, and Guay, "University Students' Subjective Well-Being," 893–910; Soenens and Vansteenkiste, "Antecedents and Outcomes of Self-Determination," 589–604.

110. Grolnick, Frodi, and Bridges, "Maternal Control Style," 72–82.

111. Joussemet et al., "Maternal Autonomy Support," 1215–1236.

112. Soenens and Vansteenkiste, "Antecedents and Outcomes of Self-Determination," 589–604.

113. Ratelle, Simard, and Guay, "University Students' Subjective Well-Being," 893–910.

114. Soenens and Vansteenkiste, "Antecedents and Outcomes of Self-Determination," 589–604.

115. Valery I. Chirkov and Richard M. Ryan, "Parent and Teacher Autonomy-Support in Russian and US Adolescents: Common Effects on Well-Being and Academic Motivation," *Journal of Cross-Cultural Psychology* 32, no. 5 (2001): 618–635; Ratelle, Simard, and Guay, "University Students' Subjective Well-Being," 893–910; Bart Soenens et al., "Conceptualizing Parental Autonomy Support: Adolescent Perceptions of Promotion of Independence Versus Promotion of Volitional Functioning," *Developmental Psychology* 43, no. 3 (2007): 633–646; Grolnick and Ryan, "Children's Self-Regulation and Competence," 143–154; Gwen A. Kenney-Benson and Eva M. Pomerantz, "The Role of Mothers' Use of Control in Children's Perfectionism: Implications for the Development of Children's Depressive Symptoms," *Journal of Personality* 73, no. 1 (2005): 23–46.

116. Soenens et al., "Conceptualizing Parental Autonomy Support," 633–646.

117. Rick Shoup, Robert M. Gonyea, and George D. Kuh, "Helicopter Parents: Examining the Impact of Highly Involved Parents on Student Engagement and Educational Outcomes" (paper presented at the 49th Annual Forum of the Association for Institutional Research, Atlanta, GA, 2009).

118. Karen L. Fingerman et al., "Helicopter Parents and Landing Pad Kids: Intense Parental Support of Grown Children," *Journal of Marriage and Family* 74, no. 4 (2012): 880–896.

119. Shoup, Gonyea, and Kuh, "Helicopter Parents."

120. Terri LeMoyne and Tom Buchanan, "Does 'Hovering' Matter? Helicopter Parenting and Its Effect on Well-Being," *Sociological Spectrum* 31, no. 4 (2011): 399–418.

121. Chris Segrin et al., "Parent and Child Traits Associated with Overparenting," *Journal of Social and Clinical Psychology* 32, no. 6 (2013): 569–595.

122. Laura M. Padilla-Walker and Larry J. Nelson, "Black Hawk Down? Establishing Helicopter Parenting as a Distinct Construct from Other Forms of Parental Control during Emerging Adulthood," *Journal of Adolescence* 35, no. 5 (2012): 1177–1190.

123. Amy Chua, "Why Chinese Mothers Are Superior," *Wall Street Journal,* January 8, 2011,http://online.wsj.com/news/articles/
SB10001424052748704111504576059713528698754.

124. Su Yeong Kim et al., "Does 'Tiger Parenting' Exist? Parenting Profiles of Chinese Americans and Adolescent Developmental Outcomes," *Asian American Journal of Psychology* 4, no. 1 (2013): 7–18.

125. Gráinne M. Fitzsimons and Eli J. Finkel, "Outsourcing Self-Regulation," *Psychological Science* 22, no. 3 (2011): 369–375.

126. Elinor Ochs and Carolina Izquierdo, "Responsibility in Childhood: Three Developmental Trajectories," *Ethos* 37, no. 4 (2009): 400.

127. Fingerman et al., "Helicopter Parents," 880–896.

128. Anna Rotkirch and Kristiina Janhunen, "Maternal Guilt," *Evolutionary Psychology: An International Journal of Evolutionary Approaches to Psychology and Behavior* 8, no. 1 (2009): 90–106.

129. Ylva Elvin-Nowak, "The Meaning of Guilt: A Phenomenological Description of Employed Mothers' Experiences of Guilt," *Scandinavian Journal of Psychology* 40, no. 1 (1999):

73–83; Jackie Guendouzi, "'The Guilt Thing': Balancing Domestic and Professional Roles," *Journal of Marriage and Family* 68, no. 4 (2006): 901–909.

130. Samantha Seagram and Judith C. Daniluk, "'It Goes with the Territory': The Meaning and Experience of Maternal Guilt for Mothers of Preadolescent Children," *Women & Therapy* 25, no. 1 (2002): 69.

131. Stacey E. Rubin and H. Ray Wooten, "Highly Educated Stay-at-Home Mothers: A Study of Commitment and Conflict," *Family Journal* 15, no. 4 (2007): 336–345.

132. Ibid.

133. Rotkirch and Janhunen, "Maternal Guilt," 90–106.

134. Hays, *Cultural Contradictions of Motherhood*, 98–108; Seagram and Daniluk, "It Goes with the Territory," 61–88; Jean-Anne Sutherland, "Mothering, Guilt and Shame," *Sociology Compass* 4, no. 5 (2010): 310–321; Wall, "Intensive Parenting and Brain Development," 253–263.

135. Jackie Guendouzi, "'I Feel Quite Organized This Morning': How Mothering Is Achieved Through Talk," *Sexualities, Evolution & Gender* 7, no. 1 (2005): 17–35.

136. Miriam Liss, Holly H. Schiffrin, and Kathryn M. Rizzo, "Maternal Guilt and Shame: The Role of Self-Discrepancy and Fear of Negative Evaluation," *Journal of Child and Family Studies* 22, no. 8 (2012): 1112–1119.

137. Sangmoon Kim, Ryan Thibodeau, and Randall S. Jorgensen, "Shame, Guilt, and Depressive Symptoms: A Meta-Analytic Review," *Psychological Bulletin* 137, no. 1 (2011): 68–96; Annmarie Callahan Churchill and Christopher G. Davis, "Realistic Orientation and the Transition to Motherhood," *Journal of Social and Clinical Psychology* 29, no. 1 (2010): 39–67.

138. Hays, *Cultural Contradictions of Motherhood*, 120.

139. Kathryn M. Rizzo, Holly H. Schiffrin, and Miriam Liss, "Insight into the Parenthood Paradox: Mental Health Outcomes of Intensive Mothering," *Journal of Child and Family Studies* 22, no. 5 (2012): 614–620.

140. Claire E. Ashton-James, Kostadin Kushlev, and Elizabeth W. Dunn, "Parents Reap What They Sow: Child-Centrism and Parental Well-Being," *Social Psychological and Personality Science* 4, no. 6 (2013): 635–642.

141. Rizzo, Schiffrin, and Liss, "Mental Health Outcomes of Intensive Mothering," 614–620.

142. Margaret K. Nelson, *Parenting out of Control: Anxious Parents in Uncertain Times* (New York: New York University Press, 2010).

143. Ibid., 87–106; Segrin et al., "Overparenting," 1–10.

144. Nelson, *Parenting out of Control*, 48–69.

145. Peter Gray, "The Play Deficit," *AEON*, September 18, 2013, http://www.aeonmagazine.com/being-human/children-today-are-suffering-a-severe-deficit-of-play.

146. Nelson, *Parenting out of Control*, 23–47.

147. Schulte, *Overwhelmed*.

148. Wendy S. Grolnick et al., "Antecedents and Consequences of Mothers' Autonomy Support: An Experimental Investigation," *Developmental Psychology* 38, no. 1 (2002): 143–155.

149. Suzanne T. Gurland and Wendy S. Grolnick, "Perceived Threat, Controlling Parenting, and Children's Achievement Orientations," *Motivation and Emotion* 29, no. 2 (2005): 103–121.

150. Nelson, *Parenting out of Control*, 113–127.

151. Barbara K. Hofer, "The Electronic Tether: Parental Regulation, Self-Regulation, and the Role of Technology in College Transitions," *Journal of the First-Year Experience & Students in Transition* 20, no. 2 (2008): 9–24.

152. Wendy S. Grolnick et al., "Evaluative Pressure in Mothers: Effects of Situation, Maternal, and Child Characteristics on Autonomy Supportive versus Controlling Behavior," *Developmental Psychology* 43, no. 4 (2007): 99–1002.

153. Annette Lareau, "Invisible Inequality: Social Class and Childrearing in Black Families and White Families," *American Sociological Review* 67, no. 5 (2002): 747–776.

154. Aber, Morris, and Raver, "Children, Families and Poverty," 1–29.

155. Renée Landry et al., "Trust in Organismic Development, Autonomy Support, and Adaptation among Mothers and Their Children," *Motivation and Emotion* 32, no. 3 (2008): 173–188.

156. Renée Landry et al., "Trust in Organismic Development," 173–188.

157. Lareau, "Invisible Inequality," 747–776.

158. Natasha J. Cabrera, "Positive Development of Minority Children," *Social Policy Report* 27, no. 2 (2013): 1–30.

159. Mireille Joussemet, Renée Landry, and Richard Koestner, "Self-Determination Theory Perspective," 194–200.

160. Donald W. Winnicott, "Transitional Objects and Transitional Phenomena: A Study of the First Not-Me Possession," *International Journal of Psychoanalysis* 34 (1953): 89–97.

4. BALANCE AT WORK

1. Christopher Kilmartin, *The Masculine Self*, 4th ed. (Cornwall-on-Hudson, NY: Sloan, 2010), 204–208.

2. Sheryl Sandberg, *Lean In: Women, Work, and the Will to Lead* (New York: Random House, 2013).

3. Erin Zlomek, "Women and Work: A Harvard Prof's Take," *Bloomberg Business Week*, May 10, 2013, http://www.businessweek.com/articles/2013-05-10/women-and-work-a-harvard-profs-take.

4. Jan-Emmanuel De Neve et al., "Genes, Economics, and Happiness," *Journal of Neuroscience, Psychology, and Economics* 5, no. 4 (2012): 193–211; Richard E. Lucas, "Adaptation and the Set-Point Model of Subjective Well-Being: Does Happiness Change after Major Life Events?," *Current Directions in Psychological Science* 16, no. 2 (2007): 75–79. Richard E. Lucas et al., "Reexamining Adaptation and the Set Point Model of Happiness: Reactions to Changes in Marital Status," *Journal of Personality and Social Psychology* 84, no. 3 (2003): 527–539; Maike Luhmann et al., "Subjective Well-Being and Adaptation to Life Events: A Meta-Analysis," *Journal of Personality and Social Psychology* 102, no. 3 (2012): 592–615.

5. Barbara C. Ilardi et al., "Employee and Supervisor Ratings of Motivation: Main Effects and Discrepancies Associated with Job Satisfaction and Adjustment in a Factory Setting," *Journal of Applied Social Psychology* 23, no. 21 (1993): 1789–1805.

6. Satoris S. Culbertson, Maura J. Mills, and Clive J. Fullager, "Work Engagement and Work-Family Facilitation: Making Homes Happier through Positive Affective Spillover," *Human Relations* 65, no. 9 (2012): 1155–1177.

7. Shelley E. Taylor, Rena L. Repetti, and Teresa Seeman, "Health Psychology: What Is an Unhealthy Environment and How Does It Get under the Skin?," *Annual Review of Psychology* 48, no. 1 (1997): 411–447.

8. Marianna Virtanen et al., "Long Working Hours and Symptoms of Anxiety and Depression: A 5-Year Follow-Up of the Whitehall II Study," *Psychological Medicine* 41, no. 12 (2011): 2485–2494.

9. Ibid.

10. Ibid.

11. June J. Pilcher and Allen J. Huffcutt, "Effects of Sleep Deprivation on Performance: A Meta-Analysis," *Journal of Sleep Research & Sleep Medicine* 19 (May 1996): 318–326; Robert-Paul Juster, Bruce S. McEwen, and Sonia J. Lupien, "Allostatic Load Biomarkers of Chronic Stress and Impact on Health and Cognition," *Neuroscience & Biobehavioral Reviews* 35, no. 1 (2010): 2–16.

12. Akinori Nakata, "Work Hours, Sleep Sufficiency, and Prevalence of Depression among Full-Time Employees: A Community-Based Cross-Sectional Study," *Journal of Clinical Psychiatry* 72, no. 5 (2011): 605–614.

13. Atsuko Kanai, "'Karoshi (Work to Death)' in Japan," *Journal of Business Ethics* 84 (January 2009): 209–216.

14. Juster, McEwen, and Lupien, "Allostatic Load Biomarkers," 2–16.

15. Kenji Iwasaki, Masaya Takahashi, and Akinori Nakata, "Health Problems Due to Long Working Hours in Japan: Working Hours, Workers' Compensation (*Karoshi*), and Preventive Measures," *Industrial Health* 44, no. 4 (2006): 537–540; Kanai, "Karoshi," 209–216.

16. Keva Glynn et al., "The Association between Role Overload and Women's Mental Health," *Journal of Women's Health* 18, no. 2 (2009): 217–223.

17. Sarah-Geneviève Trépanier, Claude Fernet, and Stéphanie Austin, "The Moderating Role of Autonomous Motivation in the Job Demands-Strain Relation: A Two Sample Study," *Motivation and Emotion* 37, no. 1 (2013): 93–105.

18. Ilardi et al., "Employee and Supervisor Ratings," 1789–1805.

19. Marianna Virtanen and Mika Kivimäki, "Saved by the Bell: Does Working Too Much Increase the Likelihood of Depression?," *Expert Review of Neurotherapeutics* 12, no. 5 (2012): 497–499.

20. Joan C. Williams and Holly Cohen Cooper, "The Public Policy of Motherhood," *Journal of Social Issues* 60, no. 4 (2004): 849–865.

21. Peter Kuhn and Fernando Lozano, "The Expanding Workweek? Understanding Trends in Long Work Hours among US Men, 1979–2004" (IZA discussion paper no. 1924, Institute for the Study of Labor (IZA), Bonn, Germany, 2006), 1–51.

22. European Union Council Directive 93/104/EC, "Concerning Certain Aspects of the Organization of Working Time," *Official Journal of the European Union* L 307, 13.12.1993.

23. Joseph G. Altonji and Jennifer Oldham, "Vacation Laws and Annual Work Hours," *Economic Perspectives-Federal Reserve Bank of Chicago* 27, no. 3 (2003): 19–29.

24. "OECD Better Life Index: Work-Life Balance," http://www.oecdbetterlifeindex.org/topics/work-life-balance.

25. Joan C. Williams and Heather Boushey, "The Three Faces of Work-Family Conflict: The Poor, the Professionals, and the Missing Middle," *Work Life Law: UC Hastings College of the Law*, Center for American Progress (2010): 1–86.

26. Jeanne M. Brett and Linda K. Stroh, "Working 61 Plus Hours a Week: Why Do Managers Do It?," *Journal of Applied Psychology* 88, no. 1 (2003): 67–78.

27. "Employment Characteristics of Families—2012," Bureau of Labor Statistics: U.S. Department of Labor, April 26, 2013, http://www.bls.gov/news.release/pdf/famee.pdf.

28. "America's Children: Key National Indicators of Well-Being, 2013: Family Structure and Children's Living Arrangements," ChildStats.gov: Forum on Child and Family Statistics, http://www.childstats.gov/americaschildren/famsoc1.asp.

29. Williams and Boushey, "Work-Family Conflict," 1–86.

30. Ibid.

31. Ibid.

32. Marianne Cooper, "Being the 'Go-To Guy': Fatherhood, Masculinity, and the Organization of Work in Silicon Valley," *Qualitative Sociology* 23, no. 4 (2000): 382.

33. Sandberg, *Lean In*, 128.

34. Lonnie Golden, "The Effects of Working Time on Productivity and Firm Performance: A Research Synthesis Paper," *Conditions of Work and Employment Series No. 33* (Geneva, Switzerland: International Labor Organization, 2012), 1–34.

35. Ibid.

36. Emily Fitzgibbons Shafer, "Wives' Relative Wages, Husbands' Paid Work Hours, and Wives' Labor-Force Exit," *Journal of Marriage and Family* 73, no. 1 (2011): 250–263.

37. Brad Harrington, Fred Van Deusen, and Beth Humberd, *The New Dad: Caring, Committed and Conflicted* (Chestnut Hill, MA: Boston College Center for Work & Family, 2011): 1–41.

38. Williams and Boushey, "Work-Family Conflict," 1–86.

39. Matthew J. Grawitch, Melanie Gottschalk, and David C. Munz, "The Path to a Healthy Workplace: A Critical Review Linking Healthy Workplace Practices, Employee Well-Being, and Organizational Improvements," *Consulting Psychology Journal: Practice and Research* 58, no. 3 (2006): 129–147.

40. E. Jeffrey Hill et al., "Finding an Extra Day a Week: The Positive Influence of Perceived Job Flexibility on Work and Family Life Balance," *Family Relations* 50, no. 1 (2001): 49–58.; E. Jeffrey Hill et al., "Workplace Flexibility, Work Hours, and Work-Life Conflict: Finding an Extra Day or Two," *Journal of Family Psychology* 24, no. 3 (2010): 349–358.

41. Golden, "The Effects of Working Time," 1–34.

42. Richard M. Ryan and Edward L. Deci, "Self-Determination Theory and the Facilitation of Intrinsic Motivation, Social Development, and Well-Being," *American Psychologist* 55, no. 1 (2000): 68–78.

43. Ravi S. Gajendran and David A. Harrison, "The Good, the Bad, and the Unknown about Telecommuting: Meta-Analysis of Psychological Mediators and Individual Consequences," *Journal of Applied Psychology* 92, no. 6 (2007): 1524–1541.

44. R. Pruncho, L. Litchfield, and M. Fried, *Measuring the Impact of Workplace Flexibility: Findings from the National Work/Life Measurement Project* (Chestnut Hill, MA: Center for Work and Family at Boston College, 2000).

45. Gajendran and Harrison, "The Good, the Bad," 1524–1541.

46. Mahmoud M. Watad, Gregory T. Jenkins, and William Paterson, "The Impact of Telework on Knowledge Creation and Management," *Journal of Knowledge Management Practice* 11, no. 4 (2010).

47. Gajendran and Harrison, "The Good, the Bad," 1524–1541.

48. Ibid.

49. Susan C. Eaton, "If You Can Use Them: Flexibility Policies, Organizational Commitment, and Perceived Performance," *Industrial Relations: A Journal of Economy and Society* 42, no. 2 (2003): 145–167.

50. Jennifer Glass, "Blessing or Curse? Work-Family Policies and Mother's Wage Growth over Time," *Work and Occupations* 31, no. 3 (2004): 367–394.

51. Lisa M. Leslie et al., "Flexible Work Practices: A Source of Career Premiums or Penalties?," *Academy of Management Journal* 55, no. 6 (2012): 1407–1428.

52. Pamela Stone and Meg Lovejoy, "Fast-Track Women and the 'Choice' to Stay Home," *The Annals of the American Academy of Political and Social Science* 596, no. 1 (2004): 70.

53. Williams and Boushey, "Work-Family Conflict," 54.

54. Pamela Stone and Lisa Ackerly Hernandez, "The All-or-Nothing Workplace: Flexibility Stigma and 'Opting Out' among Professional-Managerial Women," *Journal of Social Issues* 69, no. 2 (2013): 235–256.

55. Emma Cahusac and Kanji Shireen, "Giving Up: How Gendered Organizational Cultures Push Mothers Out," *Gender, Work & Organization* 21, no. 1 (2014): 61.

56. Lisa Dodson, "Stereotyping Low-Wage Mothers Who Have Work and Family Conflicts," *Journal of Social Issues* 69, no. 2 (2013): 257–278.

57. Shelley J. Correll, Stephen Benard, and In Paik, "Getting a Job: Is There a Motherhood Penalty?" *American Journal of Sociology* 112, no. 5 (2007): 1297–1339.

58. Scott Coltrane et al., "Fathers and the Flexibility Stigma," *Journal of Social Issues* 69, no. 2 (2013): 279–302.

59. Adam B. Butler and Amie Skattebo, "What Is Acceptable for Women May Not Be for Men: The Effect of Family Conflicts with Work on Job-Performance Ratings," *Journal of Occupational and Organizational Psychology* 77, no. 4 (2004): 553–564.

60. Julie Holliday Wayne and Bryanne L. Cordeiro, "Who Is a Good Organizational Citizen? Social Perception of Male and Female Employees Who Use Family Leave," *Sex Roles* 49 (September 2003): 233–246.

61. Jennifer L. Berdahl and Sue H. Moon, "Workplace Mistreatment of Middle Class Workers Based on Sex, Parenthood, and Caregiving," *Journal of Social Issues* 69, no. 2 (2013): 341–366; Joseph A. Vandello et al., "When Equal Isn't Really Equal: The Masculine Dilemma of Seeking Work Flexibility," *Journal of Social Issues* 69, no. 2 (2013): 303–321.

62. Laurie A. Rudman and Kris Mescher, "Penalizing Men Who Request a Family Leave: Is Flexibility Stigma a Femininity Stigma?," *Journal of Social Issues* 69, no. 2 (2013): 322–340.

63. Vandello et al., "When Equal Isn't Really," 303–321.

64. Harrington, Van Deusen, and Humberd, *The New Dad,* 1–41.

65. Timothy D. Golden, John F. Veiga, and Zeki Simsek, "Telecommuting's Differential Impact on Work-Family Conflict: Is There No Place like Home?," *Journal of Applied Psychology* 91, no. 6 (2006): 1340–1350.

66. E. Jeffrey Hill, Alan J. Hawkins, and Brent C. Miller, "Work and Family in the Virtual Office: Perceived Influences of Mobile Telework," *Family Relations* 45, no. 3 (1996): 293–301.

67. Hill et al., "Finding an Extra Day," 49–58.

68. Cath Sullivan and Suzan Lewis, "Home-Based Telework, Gender, and the Synchronization of Work and Family: Perspectives of Teleworkers and Their Co-Residents," *Gender, Work and Organization* 8 (April 2001): 123–145.

69. Phyllis Moen and Erin L. Kelly, *Flexible Work and Well-Being Study* (Minneapolis, MN: Flexible Work and Well-Being Center, University of Minnesota, 2007), iv–viii.

70. Erin L. Kelly, Phyllis Moen, and Eric Tranby, "Changing Workplaces to Reduce Work-Family Conflict: Schedule Control in a White-Collar Organization," *American Sociological Review* 76, no. 2 (2011): 265–290.

71. Ibid.

72. "Gap Inc. Case Study: Quality and Productivity through Trust: Gap Inc. Boosts Quality, Accountability and Productivity through the Adoption of Results-Only Work Environment (ROWE)" Culture Rx, LLC (2012).

73. Suzan Lewis, Rhona Rapoport, and Richenda Gambles, "Reflections on the Integration of Paid Work and the Rest of Life," *Journal of Managerial Psychology* 18, no. 8 (2003): 824–841; Williams and Boushey, "Work-Family Conflict," 1–86.

74. Lewis, Rapoport, and Gambles, "Integration of Paid Work," 824–841.

75. Stephen Marche, "Home Economics: The Link between Work-Life Balance and Income Equality," *The Atlantic*, July/August 2013, http://www.theatlantic.com/magazine/archive/2013/07/the-masculine-mystique/309401/2.

76. Tess Vigeland and Jolie Myers, "Tough Choices: How the Poor Spend Money," *Marketplace*, American Public Media, October 5, 2012, http://www.marketplace.org/topics/wealth-poverty/tough-choices-how-poor-spend-money.

77. Pamela Stone, *Opting Out? Why Women Really Quit Careers and Head Home* (Berkeley: University of California Press, 2007), 73–76.

78. Nancy E. Adler et al., "Socioeconomic Status and Health: The Challenge of the Gradient," *American Psychologist* 49, no. 1 (1994): 15–24; Arline T. Geronimus et al., "'Weathering' and Age Patterns of Allostatic Load Scores among Blacks and Whites in the United States," *American Journal of Public Health* 96, no. 5 (2006): 826–833.

79. Daniel Kahneman and Angus Deaton, "High Income Improves Evaluation of Life but Not Emotional Well-Being," *Proceedings of the National Academy of Sciences* 107, no. 38 (2010): 16489–16493.

80. Moises Velasquez-Manoff, "Status and Stress," *The Opinion Pages* (blog), *New York Times*, July 27, 2013, http://opinionator.blogs.nytimes.com/2013/07/27/status-and-stress/?hpw&_r=0.

81. Kelly D. Martin and Ronald Paul Hill, "Life Satisfaction, Self-Determination, and Consumption Adequacy at the Bottom of the Pyramid," *Journal of Consumer Research* 38, no. 6 (2012): 1155–1168.

82. Kahneman and Deaton, "Income Improves Evaluation of Life," 16489–16493.

83. Philip Brickman, Dan Coates, and Ronnie Janoff-Bulman, "Lottery Winners and Accident Victims: Is Happiness Relative?," *Journal of Personality and Social Psychology* 36, no. 8 (1978): 917.

84. Lara B. Aknin, Elizabeth W. Dunn, and Michael I. Norton, "Happiness Runs in a Circular Motion: Evidence for a Positive Feedback Loop between Prosocial Spending and Happiness," *Journal of Happiness Studies* 13, no. 2 (2012): 347–355.

85. Ed Diener and Robert Biswas-Diener, "Will Money Increase Subjective Well-Being?," *Social Indicators Research* 57, no. 2 (2002): 119–169; Ed Diener et al., "Wealth and Happiness across the World: Material Prosperity Predicts Life Evaluation, Whereas Psychosocial Prosperity Predicts Positive Feeling," *Journal of Personality and Social Psychology* 99, no. 1 (2010): 52–61; Kahneman and Deaton, "Income Improves Evaluation of Life," 16489–16493; Richard E. Lucas, Portia S. Dyrenforth, and Ed Diener, "Four Myths about Subjective Well-Being," *Social and Personality Psychology Compass* 2, no. 5 (2008): 2001–2015; Richard E. Lucas and Ulrich Schimmack, "Income and Well-Being: How Big Is the Gap between the Rich and the Poor?," *Journal of Research in Personality* 43, no. 1 (2009): 75–78; Daniel W. Sacks, Betsey Stevenson, and Justin Wolfers, "The New Stylized Facts about Income and Subjective Well-Being," *Emotion* 12, no. 6 (2012): 1181–1187.

86. Lucas and Schimmack, "Income and Well-Being," 75–78.

87. Ed Diener and Shigehiro Oishi, "Money and Happiness: Income and Subjective Well-Being Across Nations," in *Culture and Subjective Well-Being*, ed. Ed Diener and Eunkook M. Suh, (Cambridge, MA: MIT Press, 2000), 185–218; Richard Easterlin and Onnicha Sawangfa, "Happiness and Economic Growth: Does the Cross Section Predict Time Trends? Evidence from Developing Countries" (IZA discussion paper no. 4000, Institute for the Study of Labor (IZA), Bonn, Germany, 2009), 1–44; Sacks, Stevenson, and Wolfers, "Income and Subjective Well-Being," 1181–1187.

88. Carol Graham, Andrew Eggers, and Sandip Sukhtankar, "Does Happiness Pay?: An Exploration Based on Panel Data from Russia," *Journal of Economic Behavior & Organization* 55, no. 3 (2004): 319–342; Wendy Johnson and Robert F. Krueger, "How Money Buys Happiness: Genetic and Environmental Processes Linking Finances and Life Satisfaction," *Journal of Personality and Social Psychology* 90, no. 4 (2006): 680–691; Michael McBride, "Relative-Income Effects on Subjective Well-Being in the Cross-Section," *Journal of Economic Behavior & Organization* 45, no. 3 (2001): 251–278.

89. Richard A. Easterlin, "Does Economic Growth Improve the Human Lot? Some Empirical Evidence," *Nations and Households in Economic Growth* 89 (1974): 89–125; Easterlin and Sawangfa, "Happiness and Economic Growth," 1–44; Mary Steffel and Daniel M. Oppenheimer, "Happy by What Standard? The Role of Interpersonal and Intrapersonal Comparisons in Ratings of Happiness," *Social Indicators Research* 92, no. 1 (2009): 69–79.

90. Wayne M. Usui, Thomas J. Keil, and K. Robert Durig, "Socioeconomic Comparisons and Life Satisfaction of Elderly Adults," *Journal of Gerontology* 40, no. 1 (1985): 110–114.

91. Michael R. Hagerty, "Social Comparisons of Income in One's Community: Evidence from National Surveys of Income and Happiness," *Journal of Personality and Social Psychology* 78, no. 4 (2000): 764–771.

92. Robert Biswas-Diener, Joar Vittersø, and Ed Diener, "Most People Are Pretty Happy, but There Is Cultural Variation: The Inughuit, the Amish, and the Maasai," *Journal of Happiness Studies* 6, no. 3 (2005): 205–226.

93. Richard G. Wilkinson and Kate E. Pickett, "The Problems of Relative Deprivation: Why Some Societies Do Better than Others," *Social Science & Medicine* 65, no. 9 (2007): 1967.

94. Ibid., 1768–1784.

95. Ibid., 1965.

96. Max Fisher, "Map: How the World's Countries Compare on Income Inequality (The U.S. Ranks below Nigeria)," *Washington Post,* September 27, 2013, http://www.washingtonpost.com/blogs/worldviews/wp/2013/09/27/map-how-the-worlds-countries-compare-on-income-inequality-the-u-s-ranks-below-nigeria.

97. 1 Tim. 6:10 (New International Version).

98. Emily C. Solberg, Edward Diener, and Michael D. Robinson, "Why Are Materialists Less Satisfied?," in *Psychology and Consumer Culture: The Struggle for a Good life in a Materialistic World,* ed. Tim Kasser and Allen D. Kanner (Washington, DC: American Psychological Association, 2004), 29–48.

99. Tim Kasser and Aaron Ahuvia, "Materialistic Values and Well-Being in Business Students," *European Journal of Social Psychology* 32, no. 1 (2002): 137–146; Tim Kasser and Richard M. Ryan, "A Dark Side of the American Dream: Correlates of Financial Success as a Central Life Aspiration," *Journal of Personality and Social Psychology* 65, no. 2 (1993): 410–422; Tim Kasser and Richard M. Ryan, "Further Examining the American Dream: Differential Correlates of Intrinsic and Extrinsic Goals," *Personality & Social Psychology Bulletin* 22, no. 3 (1996): 280–287.

100. Diener and Oishi, "Money and Happiness," 185–218.

101. Carol Nickerson et al., "Zeroing in on the Dark Side of the American Dream: A Closer Look at the Negative Consequences of the Goal for Financial Success," *Psychological Science* 14, no. 6 (2003): 531–536.

102. Christopher K. Hsee et al., "Overearning," *Psychological Science* 24, no. 6 (2013): 852–859.

103. Sanford E. DeVoe and Julian House, "Time, Money, and Happiness: How Does Putting a Price on Time Affect Our Ability to Smell the Roses?," *Journal of Experimental Social Psychology* 48, no. 2 (2012): 466–474.

104. Todd B. Kashdan and William E. Breen, "Materialism and Diminished Well-Being: Experiential Avoidance as a Mediating Mechanism," *Journal of Social and Clinical Psychology* 26, no. 5 (2007): 521–539; Kasser and Ryan, "A Dark Side of the American Dream," 410–422; José Manuel Otero-López et al., "Materialism, Life-Satisfaction and Addictive Buying: Examining the Causal Relationships," *Personality and Individual Differences* 50, no. 6 (2011): 772–776; Maarten Vansteenkiste et al., "Materialistic Values and Well-Being among Business Students: Further Evidence of Their Detrimental Effect," *Journal of Applied Social Psychology* 36, no. 12 (2006): 2892–2908.

105. Jeffrey J. Froh et al., "Gratitude and the Reduced Costs of Materialism in Adolescents," *Journal of Happiness Studies* 12, no. 2 (2011): 289–302.

106. Otero-López et al., "Materialism, Life-Satisfaction and Addictive Buying," 772–776.

107. Kennon M. Sheldon and Sonja Lyubomirsky, "The Challenge of Staying Happier: Testing the Hedonic Adaptation Prevention Model," *Personality and Social Psychology Bulletin* 38, no. 5 (2012): 670–680.

108. Ryan and Deci, "Self-Determination Theory," 521–539.

109. Vansteenkiste et al., "Materialistic Values and Well-Being," 2892–2908.

110. Kathleen D. Vohs, Nicole L. Mead, and Miranda R. Goode, "The Psychological Consequences of Money," *Science* 314, no. 5802 (2006): 1154–1156.

111. Kasser and Ryan, "A Dark Side of the American Dream," 410–422; Kasser and Ryan, "Further Examining the American Dream," 280–287.

112. Monika A. Bauer, James E. B. Wilkie, Jung K. Kim, and Galen V. Bodenhausen, "Cuing Consumerism Situational Materialism Undermines Personal and Social Well-Being," *Psychological Science* 23, no. 5 (2012): 517–523.

113. Rik Pieters, "Bidirectional Dynamics of Materialism and Loneliness: Not Just a Vicious Cycle," *Journal of Consumer Research* 40, no. 4 (2013): 615–631.

114. "Storyline: From Workaholics Anonymous," Workaholics Anonymous World Service Organization, Summer 2012, http://www.workaholics-anonymous.org/pdf_files/news_summer2012.pdf.

115. Tim Kasser et al., "Changes in Materialism, Changes in Psychological Well-Being: Evidence from Three Longitudinal Studies and an Intervention Experiment," *Motivation and Emotion* (2013): 1–22.

116. Paul K. Piff et al., "Having Less, Giving More: The Influence of Social Class on Prosocial Behavior," *Journal of Personality and Social Psychology* 99, no. 5 (2010): 771–784; Paul K. Piff et al., "Higher Social Class Predicts Increased Unethical Behavior," *Proceedings of the National Academy of Sciences* 109, no. 11 (2012): 4086–4091.

117. Piff et al., "Higher Social Class," 4086–4091.

118. Stanley Weiser and Oliver Stone, *Wall Street*, directed by Oliver Stone (Los Angeles, CA: Twentieth Century Fox Film Corporation, 1987), DVD.

119. Diener et al., "Wealth and Happiness," 52–61.

120. Sonja Lyubomirsky, Laura King, and Ed Diener, "The Benefits of Frequent Positive Affect: Does Happiness Lead to Success?," *Psychological Bulletin* 131, no. 6 (2005): 803–855.

121. Ed Diener at al., "Dispositional Affect and Job Outcomes," *Social Indicators Research* 59, no. 3 (2002): 229–259; Ed Diener and Martin E. P. Seligman, "Beyond Money toward an Economy of Well-Being," *Psychological Science in the Public Interest* 5, no. 1 (2004): 1–31; Lyubomirsky, King, and Diener, "Benefits of Frequent Positive Affect," 803–855.

122. Lyubomirsky, King, and Diener, "Benefits of Frequent Positive Affect," 803–855.

123. Diener, Nickerson, Lucas, and Sandvik, "Dispositional Affect and Job Outcomes," 229–259.

124. Barry M. Straw, Robert I. Sutton, and Lisa H. Pelled, "Employee Positive Emotion and Favorable Outcomes at the Workplace," *Organization Science* 5, no. 1 (1994): 51–71.

125. Noel Murray et al., "The Influence of Mood on Categorization: A Cognitive Flexibility Interpretation," *Journal of Personality and Social Psychology* 59, no. 3 (1990): 411–425.

126. Yessenia Castro and Kathryn H. Gordon, "A Review of Recent Research on Multiple Roles and Women's Mental Health," in *Women and Mental Disorders*, ed. Paula K. Lundberg-Love, Kevin L. Nadal, and Michele A. Paludi (Santa Barbara, CA: Praeger, 2012), 1: 37–54.

127. Straw, Sutton, and Pelled, "Employee Positive Emotion," 51–71.

128. Joseph Chancellor and Sonja Lyubomirsky, "Happiness and Thrift: When (Spending) Less is (Hedonically) More," *Journal of Consumer Psychology* 21, no. 2 (2011): 131–138.

5. BALANCE IS FOR BOTH MEN AND WOMEN

1. Glenda Wall and Stephanie Arnold, "How Involved Is Involved Fathering?: An Exploration of the Contemporary Culture of Fatherhood," *Gender & Society* 21, no. 4 (2007): 508–527.

2. Stephen Marche, "Home Economics: The Link between Work-Life Balance and Income Equality," *The Atlantic*, July/August 2013, http://www.theatlantic.com/magazine/archive/2013/07/the-masculine-mystique/309401.

3. Tanvi Gautam, "Real Men Don't Need Work Life Balance," *Forbes*, May 23, 2012, http://www.forbes.com/sites/forbeswomanfiles/2012/05/23/real-men-dont-need-work-life-balance/2.

4. Anne-Marie Slaughter, "Why Women Still Can't Have It All," *The Atlantic*, July/August 2012, http://www.theatlantic.com/magazine/archive/2012/07/why-women-still-cant-have-it-all/309020.

5. Slaughter, "Have It All."

6. Wendy Wang, Kim Parker, and Paul Taylor, "Breadwinner Moms: Moms Are the Sole or Primary Provider in Four-in-Ten Households with Children; Public Conflicted about Growing Trend," Pew Research Social and Demographic Trends, posted May 29, 2013, http://www.pewsocialtrends.org/2013/05/29/breadwinner-moms.

7. Jack Mirkinson, "All-Male Fox Panel Freaks Out about Female Breadwinners" (video), *HuffPost Media* (blog), *Huffington Post*, May 30, 2013, http://www.huffingtonpost.com/2013/05/30/fox-female-breadwinners_n_3358926.html.

8. Mirkinson, "Fox Panel Freaks Out."

9. Margaret Wheeler Johnson, "Bryan Fischer, Conservative Radio Host, Claims 'Men Are Designed To Be the Breadwinners,'" *Huff Post Women*, May 31, 2013, http://www.huffingtonpost.com/2013/05/31/bryan-fischer-men-designed-to-be-breadwinners_n_3367765.html.

10. Lisa Miller, "The Retro Wife: Feminists Who Say They're Having It All—By Choosing to Stay Home," *New York*, March 17, 2013, http://nymag.com/news/features/retro-wife-2013-3.

11. Jane Sunderland, "Baby Entertainer, Bumbling Assistant and Line Manager: Discourses of Fatherhood in Parentcraft Texts," *Discourse & Society* 11, no. 2 (2000): 249–274.

12. Sunderland, "Discourses of Fatherhood," 249–274.

13. Jane Sunderland, "'Parenting' or 'Mothering'? The Case of Modern Childcare Magazines," *Discourse & Society* 17, no. 4 (2006): 503–528.

14. Wall and Arnold, "Involved Fathering," 508–527.

15. Robert P. Jones, Daniel Cox, and Juhem Navarro-Rivera, "The 2012 American Values Survey: How Catholics and the Religiously Unaffiliated Will Shape the 2012 Election and Beyond," Public Religion Research Institute, October 23, 2012, 66–67. American Public Religion Research Institute.

16. Alice H. Eagly and Wendy Wood, "The Origins of Sex Differences in Human Behavior: Evolved Dispositions versus Social Roles," *American Psychologist* 54, no. 6 (1999): 408–423.

17. Miller, "The Retro Wife."

18. Anthony Gottlieb, "It Ain't Necessarily So: How Much Do Evolutionary Stories Reveal about the Mind?," *New Yorker*, September 17, 2012, http://www.newyorker.com/arts/critics/books/2012/09/17/120917crbo_books_gottlieb.

19. John Gray, *Men Are from Mars, Women Are from Venus* (New York: J. G. Productions, 2012).

20. Bobbi J. Carothers and Harry T. Reis, John Gray, "Men Are from Mars, Women Are from Venus" (New York: J. G. Productions, 2012); Christopher Kilmartin, *The Masculine Self*, 4th ed. (Cornwall-on-Hudson, NY: Sloan, 2010), 38–42.

21. Lise Eliot, *Pink Brain Blue Brain: How Small Differences Grow into Troublesome Gaps—And What We Can Do about It* (New York: Houghton Mifflin Harcourt, 2009).

22. Ibid., 55–64, 26.

23. Janet Shibley Hyde, "The Gender Similarities Hypothesis," *American Psychologist* 60, no. 6 (2005): 581–592.

24. Ibid.

25. Sara M. Lindberg et al., "New Trends in Gender and Mathematics Performance: A Meta-Analysis," *Psychological Bulletin* 136, no. 6 (2010): 1123–1135.

26. Alice H. Eagly and Maureen Crowley, "Gender and Helping Behavior: A Meta-Analytic Review of the Social Psychological Literature," *Psychological Bulletin* 100, no. 3 (1986): 283.

27. Marianne LaFrance, Marvin A. Hecht, and Elizabeth Levy Paluck, "The Contingent Smile: A Meta-Analysis of Sex Differences in Smiling," *Psychological Bulletin* 129, no. 2 (2003): 305–334.

28. Carothers and Reis, "Men and Women Are from Earth," 385–407.

29. Hyde, "The Gender Similarities Hypothesis," 581–592.

30. Carothers and Reis, "Men and Women Are from Earth," 385–407.

31. John Condry and Sandra Condry, "Sex Differences: A Study of the Eye of the Beholder," *Child Development* 47, no. 3 (1976): 812–819.

32. Hugh Lytton and David M. Romney, "Parents' Differential Socialization of Boys and Girls: A Meta-Analysis," *Psychological Bulletin* 109, no. 2 (1991): 267–296.

33. Barbara A. Morrongiello and Kerri Hogg, "Mothers' Reactions to Children Misbehaving in Ways That Can Lead to Injury: Implications for Gender Differences in Children's Risk Taking and Injuries," *Sex Roles* 50, no. 1–2 (2004): 103–118.

34. Eliot, *Pink Brain Blue Brain*, 103–143.

35. Candace West and Don H. Zimmerman, "Doing Gender," *Gender and Society* 1, no. 2 (1987): 125–151.

36. Deborah A. Prentice and Erica Carranza, "What Women and Men Should Be, Shouldn't be, Are Allowed to Be, and Don't Have to Be: The Contents of Prescriptive Gender Stereotypes," *Psychology of Women Quarterly* 26, no. 4 (2002): 269–281.

37. Eagly and Wood, "The Origins of Sex Differences," 408–423.

38. Ibid.

39. Jean M. Twenge, "Changes in Masculine and Feminine Traits over Time: A Meta-Analysis," *Sex Roles* 36, no. 5–6 (1997): 305–325.

40. Jessica Fischer and Veanne N. Anderson, "Gender Role Attitudes and Characteristics of Stay-at-Home and Employed Fathers," *Psychology of Men & Masculinity* 13, no. 1 (2012). 16–31.

41. Cordelia Fine, *Delusions of Gender: How Our Minds, Society, and Neurosexism Create Difference of Gender* (New York: W.W. Norton, 2010).

42. Ibid., 139.

43. Katherine M. Bishop and Douglas Wahlsten, "Sex Differences in the Human Corpus Callosum: Myth or Reality?," *Neuroscience & Biobehavioral Reviews* 21, no. 5 (1997): 581–601.

44. Mikkel Wallentin, "Putative Sex Differences in Verbal Abilities and Language Cortex: A Critical Review," *Brain and Language* 108, no. 3 (2009): 175–183.

45. Janet Shibley Hyde, "New Directions in the Study of Gender Similarities and Differences," *Current Directions in Psychological Science* 16, no. 5 (2007): 259–263; Anelis Kaiser et al., "On Sex/Gender Related Similarities and Differences in fMRI Language Research," *Brain Research Reviews* 61, no. 2 (2009): 49–59.

46. Lutz Jäncke et al., "Short-Term Functional Plasticity in the Human Auditory Cortex: An fMRI Study," *Cognitive Brain Research* 12, no. 3 (2001): 479–485.

47. Eleanor A. Maguire et al., "Navigation-Related Structural Change in the Hippocampi of Taxi Drivers," *Proceedings of the National Academy of Sciences* 97, no. 8 (2000): 4398–4403.

48. Shira Offer and Barbara Schneider, "Revisiting the Gender Gap in Time-Use Patterns—Multitasking and Well-Being among Mothers and Fathers in Dual-Earner Families," *American Sociological Review* 76, no. 6 (2011): 809–833.

49. Craig M. Bennett et al., "Neural Correlates of Interspecies Perspective Taking in the Post-Mortem Atlantic Salmon: An Argument for Multiple Comparisons Correction," *Neuroimage* 47, no. 1 (2009): S125.

50. Kaiser et al., "On Sex/Gender," 49–59.

51. Prentice and Carranza, "What Women and Men Should Be," 269–281.

52. Francine M. Deutsch, "Undoing Gender," *Gender and Society* 21, no. 1 (2007): 106–127.

53. Prentice and Carranza, "What Women and Men Should Be," 269–281.

54. Alice H. Eagly and Linda L. Carli, *Through the Labyrinth: The Truth about How Women Become Leaders* (Boston, MA: Harvard Business School, 2007), 90.

55. Alice H. Eagly, Mona G. Makhijani, and Bruce G. Klonsky, "Gender and the Evaluation of Leaders: A Meta-Analysis," *Psychological Bulletin* 111, no. 1 (1992): 3–22.

56. Eagly and Carli, *Through the Labyrinth*, 117.

57. Alice H. Eagly and Blair T. Johnson, "Gender and Leadership Style: A Meta-Analysis," *Psychological Bulletin* 108, no. 2 (1990): 233–256.

58. Alice H. Eagly, Mary C. Johannesen-Schmidt, and Marloes L. van Engen, "Transformational, Transactional, and Laissez-Faire Leadership Styles: A Meta-Analysis Comparing Women and Men," *Psychological Bulletin* 129, no. 4 (2003): 569–591.

59. Timothy A. Judge and Ronald F. Piccolo, "Transformational and Transactional Leadership: A Meta-Analytic Test of Their Relative Validity," *Journal of Applied Psychology* 89, no. 5 (2004): 755–768.

60. Eagly, Johannesen-Schmidt, and van Engen, "Leadership Styles," 569–591.

61. Ibid.

62. Ibid.

63. Prentice and Carranza, "What Women and Men Should Be," 269–281.

64. Ruth Gaunt, "Breadwinning Moms, Caregiving Dads: Double Standard in Social Judgments of Gender Norm Violators," *Journal of Family Issues* 34, no. 1 (2013): 3–24.

65. Aaron B. Rochlen, Ryan A. McKelley, and Tiffany A. Whittaker, "Stay-at-Home Fathers' Reasons for Entering the Role and Stigma Experiences: A Preliminary Report," *Psychology of Men & Masculinity* 11, no. 4 (2010): 279–285.

66. Noelle Chesley, "Stay-at-Home Fathers and Breadwinning Mothers: Gender, Couple Dynamics, and Social Change," *Gender & Society* 25, no. 5 (2011): 642–664.

67. Paul Sargent, "The Gendering of Men in Early Childhood Education," *Sex Roles* 52, no. 3-4 (2005): 256.

68. Ibid.

69. Wall and Arnold, "Involved Fathering," 521.

70. Lee T. Gettler et al., "Longitudinal Evidence That Fatherhood Decreases Testosterone in Human Males," *Proceedings of the National Academy of Sciences* 108, no. 39 (2011): 16194–16199.

71. Ibid.; Shohreh Shahabi et al., "Free Testosterone Drives Cancer Aggressiveness: Evidence from US Population Studies," ed. Lars Berglund, *PLoS ONE* 8, no. 4 (2013): e61955.

72. Alan Booth and James M. Dabbs, "Testosterone and Men's Marriages," *Social Forces* 72, no. 2 (1993): 463–477.

73. Alison S. Fleming et al., "Testosterone and Prolactin Are Associated with Emotional Responses to Infant Cries in New Fathers," *Hormones and Behavior* 42, no. 4 (2002): 399–413.

74. Aaron B. Rochlen et al., "'I'm Just Providing for My Family': A Qualitative Study of Stay-at-Home Fathers," *Psychology of Men & Masculinity* 9, no. 4 (2008): 193–206.

75. Shirley M. H. Hanson, "Healthy Single Parent Families," *Family Relations* 35, no. 1 (1986): 125–132.

76. Jennifer L. Hook and Satvika Chalasani, "Gendered Expectations? Reconsidering Single Fathers' Child-Care Time," *Journal of Marriage and Family* 70, no. 4 (2008): 978–990.

77. Susan L. Brown, "Marriage and Child Well-Being: Research and Policy Perspectives," *Journal of Marriage and Family* 72, no. 5 (2010): 1059–1077.

78. David M. Fergusson, Joseph M. Boden, and L. John Horwood, "Exposure to Single Parenthood in Childhood and Later Mental Health, Educational, Economic, and Criminal Behavior Outcomes," *Archives of General Psychiatry* 64, no. 9 (2007): 1089.

79. Gretchen Livingston, "The Rise of Single Fathers: A Ninefold Increase Since 1960," Pew Research Social and Demographic Trends, posted July 2, 2013, http://www.pewsocialtrends.org/2013/07/02/the-rise-of-single-fathers.

80. Dana Berkowitz and Katherine A. Kuvalanka, "Gay Fathers' Involvement in Their Young Children's Lives," in *Father Involvement in Young Children's Lives: A Global Analysis*, ed. Jyotsna Pattnaik (London: Springer, 2013), 89–106.

81. Ibid.

82. Suzanne M. Johnson and Elizabeth O'Connor, *The Gay Baby Boom: The Psychology of Gay Parenthood* (New York: New York University Press, 2002).

83. Timothy J. Biblarz and Judith Stacey, "How Does the Gender of Parents Matter?," *Journal of Marriage and Family* 72, no. 1 (2010): 3–22.

84. Gerald P. Mallon, *Gay Men Choosing Parenthood* (New York: Columbia University Press, 2004), 24.

85. Steven J. Spencer, Claude M. Steele, and Diane M. Quinn, "Stereotype Threat and Women's Math Performance," *Journal of Experimental Social Psychology* 35, no. 1 (1999): 4–28.

86. Rosalind Chait Barnett and Janet Shibley Hyde, "Women, Men, Work, and Family," *American Psychologist* 56, no. 10 (2001): 781–796; Pepper Schwartz, *Peer Marriage: How Love between Equals Really Works* (New York: Free Press, 1994); Sheldon Cohen and Thomas A. Wills, "Stress, Social Support, and the Buffering Hypothesis," *Psychological Bulletin* 98, no. 2 (1985): 310–357.

87. Cornelia Wrzus et al., "Social Network Changes and Life Events across the Life Span: A Meta-Analysis," *Psychological Bulletin* 139, no. 1 (2013): 53–80.

88. Kathryn M. Rizzo, Holly H. Schiffrin, and Miriam Liss, "Insight into the Parenthood Paradox: Mental Health Outcomes of Intensive Mothering," *Journal of Child and Family Studies* 22, no. 5 (2012): 614–620.

89. Regine A. Schön and Maarit Silvén, "Natural Parenting: Back to Basics in Infant Care," *Evolutionary Psychology* 5, no. 1 (2007): 102–183.

90. Sharon Hays, *The Cultural Contradictions of Motherhood* (New Haven, CT: Yale University Press, 1996), 97–131.

91. Christina Lee, "Social Context, Depression, and the Transition to Motherhood," *British Journal of Health Psychology* 2, no. 2 (1997): 93–108.

92. Sarah Blaffer Hrdy, *Mother Nature: A History of Mothers, Infants, and Natural Selection* (New York: Ballantine Books, 1999).

93. Erik Gustafsson et al., "Fathers Are Just as Good as Mothers at Recognizing the Cries of Their Baby," *Nature Communications* 4 (2013): 1698.

94. J. S. Rosenblatt, "Nonhormonal Basis of Maternal Behavior in the Rat," *Science* 156, no. 3781 (1967): 1512–1513.

95. Fine, *Delusions of Gender*, 88.

6. BALANCE AT HOME

1. Cordelia Fine, *Delusions of Gender: How Our Minds, Society, and Neurosexism Create Difference of Gender* (New York: W.W. Norton, 2010), 89.

2. Arlie Hochschild and Anne Machung, *The Second Shift: Working Parents and the Revolution at Home* (New York: Penguin, 1989).

3. Suzanne M. Bianchi et al., "Is Anyone Doing the Housework? Trends in the Gender Division of Household Labor," *Social Forces* 79, no. 1 (2000): 191–228; Mylène Lachance-Grzela and Geneviève Bouchard, "Why Do Women Do the Lion's Share of Housework? A Decade of Research," *Sex Roles* 63, no. 11–12 (2010): 767–780.

4. Abbie E. Goldberg, JuliAnna Z. Smith, and Maureen Perry-Jenkins, "The Division of Labor in Lesbian, Gay, and Heterosexual New Adoptive Parents," *Journal of Marriage and Family* 74, no. 4 (2012): 812–828.

5. Paul A. Nakonezny and Wayne H. Denton, "Marital Relationships: A Social Exchange Theory Perspective," *American Journal of Family Therapy* 36, no. 5 (2008): 402–412.

6. Constance T. Gager, "What's Fair Is Fair? Role of Justice in Family Labor Allocation Decisions," *Marriage and Family Review* 44, no. 4 (2008): 511–545.

7. Julie Brines, "Economic Dependency, Gender, and the Division of Labor at Home," *American Journal of Sociology* 100, no. 3 (1994): 652–688.; Theodore N. Greenstein, "Economic Dependence, Gender, and the Division of Labor in the Home: A Replication and Extension," *Journal of Marriage and Family* 62, no. 2 (2000): 322–335.

8. Maxine P. Atkinson and Jacqueline Boles, "WASP (Wives as Senior Partners)," *Journal of Marriage and Family* 46, no. 4 (1984): 861–870.; Michael Bittman, Paula England, and Liana Sayer, "When Does Gender Trump Money? Bargaining and Time in Household Work," *American Journal of Sociology* 109, no. 1 (2003): 185–214.

9. Oriel Sullivan, "An End to Gender Display through the Performance of Housework? A Review and Reassessment of the Quantitative Literature Using Insights from the Qualitative Literature," *Journal of Family Theory & Review* 3, no. 1 (2011): 1–13.

10. Gager, "What's Fair Is Fair," 511–545.

11. Scott Coltrane, "Research on Household Labor: Modeling and Measuring the Social Embeddedness of Routine Family Work," *Journal of Marriage and the Family* 62 (November 2000): 1208–1233; Scott Coltrane and Masako Ishii-Kuntz, "Men's Housework: A Life Course Perspective," *Journal of Marriage and the Family* 54 (February 1992): 43–57; Amy Kroska, "Divisions of Domestic Work," *Journal of Marriage and Family* 65 (2004): 456–473.

12. Alice H. Eagly and Linda L. Carli, *Through the Labyrinth* (Boston: Harvard Business School, 2007), 152–154.

13. Anne-Marie Slaughter, "Why Women Still Can't Have It All," *The Atlantic*, July/August 2012, http://www.theatlantic.com/magazine/archive/2012/07/why-women-still-cant-have-it-all/309020.

14. Eagly and Carli, *Through the Labyrinth*, 144–146.

15. Willard Waller, *The Family: A Dynamic Interpretation* (New York: Gordon, 1938).

16. *He's Just Not That into You*, directed by Ken Kwapis (Los Angeles, CA: New Line Cinema, 2009), DVD.

17. Anne Machung, "Talking Career, Thinking Job: Gender Differences in Career and Family Expectations of Berkeley Seniors," *Feminist Studies* 15, no. 1 (1989): 35–58.

18. T. L. Huston and R. D. Ashmore, "Women and Men in Personal Relationships," in *The Social Psychology of Female-Male Relations,* ed. Richard D. Ashmore and Frances K. Del Boca (New York: Academic Press, 1986).

19. Mindy J. Erchull et al., "Well . . . She Wants It More: Perceptions of Social Norms about Desires for Marriage and Children and Anticipated Chore Participation," *Psychology of Women Quarterly* 34, no. 2 (2010): 253–260.

20. Ibid.

21. Kroska, "Divisions of Domestic Work," 456–473.

22. Anne-Rigt Poortman and Tanja Van Der Lippe, "Attitudes toward Housework and Child Care and the Gendered Division of Labor," *Journal of Marriage and Family* 71, no. 3 (2009): 526–541.

23. Jess K. Alberts, Sarah J. Tracy, and Angela Trethewey, "An Integrative Theory of the Division of Domestic Labor: Threshold Level, Social Organizing and Sensemaking," *Journal of Family Communication* 11, no. 1 (2011): 21–38.

24. Ibid.

25. Myra Marx Ferree, "The Gender Division of Labor in Two-Earner Marriages: Dimensions of Variability and Change," *Journal of Family Issues* 12, no. 2 (1991): 158–180.

26. Robin Patric Clair, "The Rhetoric of Dust: Toward a Rhetorical Theory of the Division of Domestic Labor," *Journal of Family Communication* 11, no. 1 (2011): 50–59.

27. Deborah Arthurs, "Women Spend THREE HOURS Every Week Redoing Chores Their Men Have Done Badly," Mail Online, March 19, 2012, http://www.dailymail.co.uk/femail/article-2117254/Women-spend-hours-week-redoing-chores-men-badly.html.

28. Christopher Kilmartin, *The Masculine Self*, 4th ed. (Cornwall-on-Hudson, NY: Sloan Publishing, 2010), 79–80.

29. Terri D. Conley and Laura R. Ramsey, "Killing Us Softly? Investigating Portrayals of Women and Men in Contemporary Magazine Advertisements," *Psychology of Women Quarterly* 35, no. 3 (2011): 469–478.

30. Lisa Belkin, "Huggies Pulls Ads after Insulting Dads," *HuffPost Parents* (blog), *Huffington Post*, March 12, 2012, http://www.huffingtonpost.com/lisa-belkin/huggies-pulls-diaper-ads_b_1339074.html.

31. Matthew Oransky and Jeanne Marecek, "'I'm Not Going to Be a Girl': Masculinity and Emotions in Boys' Friendships and Peer Groups," *Journal of Adolescent Research* 24, no. 2 (2009): 218–241.

32. Kroska, "Divisions of Domestic Work," 456–473.

33. Jane Riblett Wilkie, Myra Marx Ferree, and Kathryn Strother Ratcliff, "Gender and Fairness: Marital Satisfaction in Two-Earner Couples," *Journal of Marriage and the Family* 60 (August 1998): 577–594.

34. Alberts, Tracy, and Trethewey, "Division of Domestic Labor," 21–38.

35. Sayaka Kawamura and Susan L. Brown, "Mattering and Wives' Perceived Fairness of the Division of Household Labor," *Social Science Research* 39, no. 6 (2010): 976–986.

36. Mikael Nordenmark and Charlott Nyman, "Fair or Unfair? Perceived Fairness of Household Division of Labour and Gender Equality among Women and Men: The Swedish Case," *European Journal of Women's Studies* 10, no. 2 (2003): 181–209.

37. Sharon J. Bartley, Priscilla W. Blanton, and Jennifer L. Gilliard, "Husbands and Wives in Dual-Earner Marriages: Decision-Making, Gender Role Attitudes, Division of Household Labor, and Equity," *Marriage & Family Review* 37, no. 4 (2005): 69–94.

38. Gager, "What's Fair Is Fair," 511–545.

39. Ibid.

40. Marjorie L. Devault, "Comfort and Struggle: Emotion Work in Family Life," *ANNALS of the American Academy of Political and Social Science* 561, no. 1 (1999): 52–63.

41. Jeffrey Dew and W. Bradford Wilcox, "If Momma Ain't Happy: Explaining Declines in Marital Satisfaction among New Mothers," *Journal of Marriage and Family* 73, no. 1 (2011): 1–12.

42. Sabra L. Katz-Wise, Heather A. Priess, and Janet S. Hyde, "Gender-Role Attitudes and Behavior across the Transition to Parenthood," *Developmental Psychology* 46, no. 1 (2010): 18–28.

43. Sharon Hays, *The Cultural Contradictions of Motherhood* (New Haven, CT: Yale University Press, 1996), 98–108.

44. Scott Coltrane, "Household Labor and the Routine Production of Gender," *Social Problems* 36, no. 5 (1989): 485.

45. Ruth Gaunt, "Biological Essentialism, Gender Ideologies, and Role Attitudes: What Determines Parents' Involvement in Child Care," *Sex Roles* 55, no. 7-8 (2006): 523–533.

46. Thoroddur Bjarnason and Andrea Hjalmsdottir, "Egalitarian Attitudes Towards the Division of Household Labor Among Adolescents in Iceland," *Sex Roles* 59, no. 1–2 (2008): 49–60; Francine M. Deutsch, Amy P. Kokot, and Katherine S. Binder, "College Women's Plans for Different Types of Egalitarian Marriages," *Journal of Marriage and Family* 69, no. 4 (2007): 916–929.; Miriam Liss et al., "Development and Validation of a Quantitative Measure of Intensive Parenting Attitudes," *Journal of Child and Family Studies* 22, no. 5 (2013): 621–636.

47. Joan C. Williams and Holly Cohen Cooper, "The Public Policy of Motherhood," *Journal of Social Issues* 60, no. 6 (2004): 851.

48. Judith Warner, "The Opt-Out Generation Wants Back In," *New York Times Magazine*, August 7, 2013, http://www.nytimes.com/2013/08/11/magazine/the-opt-out-generation-wants-back-in.html?pagewanted=5&adxnnl=1&adxnnlx=1381955314-mp25GLFR4GCaal0MAZktDg.

49. Ibid.

50. Ibid.

51. Sharon T. Claffey and Kristin D. Mickelson, "Division of Household Labor and Distress: The Role of Perceived Fairness for Employed Mothers," *Sex Roles* 60, no. 11–12 (2009): 819–831.

52. Michelle L. Frisco and Kristi Williams, "Perceived Housework Equity, Marital Happiness, and Divorce in Dual-Earner Households," *Journal of Family Issues* 24, no. 1 (2003): 51–73.

53. Ibid.

54. Margaret F. Brinig and Douglas W. Allen, "'These Boots Are Made for Walking': Why Most Divorce Filers Are Women," *American Law and Economics Review* 2, no. 1 (2000): 126–169.

55. Dew and Wilcox, "If Momma Ain't Happy," 1–12.

56. Constance T. Gager and Scott T. Yabiku, "Who Has the Time? The Relationship between Household Labor Time and Sexual Frequency," *Journal of Family Issues* 31, no. 2 (2010): 135–163; Lisa S. Hackel and Diane N. Ruble, "Changes in the Marital Relationship after the First Baby Is Born: Predicting the Impact of Expectancy Disconfirmation," *Journal of Personality and Social Psychology* 62, no. 6 (1992): 944–957.

57. Sabino Kornrich, Julie Brines, and Katrina Leupp, "Egalitarianism, Housework, and Sexual Frequency in Marriage," *American Sociological Review* 78, no. 1 (2013): 26–50.

58. Gager and Yabiku, "Who Has the Time?," 135–163.

59. Suzanne M. Bianchi, John P. Robinson, and Melissa A. Milkie, *Changing Rhythms of American Family Life*, Rose Series in Sociology (New York: Russell Sage, 2006), 97–99.

60. Nordenmark and Nyman, "Fair or Unfair," 181–209.

61. Darby E. Saxbe, Rena L. Repetti, and Anthony P. Graesch, "Time Spent in Housework and Leisure: Links with Parents' Physiological Recovery from Work," *Journal of Family Psychology* 25, no. 2 (2011): 271–281.

62. Anne E. Moyer et al., "Stress-Induced Cortisol Response and Fat Distribution in Women," *Obesity Research* 2, no. 3 (1994): 255–262.

63. Sandra E. Sephton et al., "Diurnal Cortisol Rhythm as a Predictor of Breast Cancer Survival," *Journal of the National Cancer Institute* 92, no. 12 (2000): 994–1000.

64. Anne Helene Garde et al., "Bi-Directional Associations between Psychological Arousal, Cortisol, and Sleep," *Behavioral Sleep Medicine* 10, no. 1 (2012): 28–40.

65. Saxbe, Repetti, and Graesch, "Time Spent in Housework and Leisure," 271–281.

66. Darby E. Saxbe, Rena L. Repetti, and Adrienne Nishina, "Marital Satisfaction, Recovery from Work, and Diurnal Cortisol among Men and Women," *Health Psychology* 27, no. 1 (2008): 15–25.

67. Richard M. Ryan and Edward L. Deci, "Self-Determination Theory and the Facilitation of Intrinsic Motivation, Social Development, and Well-Being," *American Psychologist* 55, no. 1 (2000): 68–78.

68. Nakonezny and Denton, "Marital Relationships," 402–412.

69. Bianchi et al., "Is Anyone Doing the Housework?," 191–228.

70. Nordenmark and Nyman, "Fair or Unfair," 181–209.

71. Wilkie, Ferree, and Ratcliff, "Gender and Fairness," 577–594.

72. Bartley, Blanton, and Gilliard, "Husbands and Wives," 69–94.

73. Alberts, Tracy, and Trethewey, "Division of Domestic Labor," 21–38.

74. Renata Forste and Kiira Fox, "Search Types," *Journal of Comparative Family Studies* 43 (2012): 613–631.

75. Kathryn J. Lively, Lala Carr Steelman, and Brian Powell, "Equity, Emotion, and Household Division of Labor Response," *Social Psychology Quarterly* 73, no. 4 (2010): 358–379.

76. Hays, *Cultural Contradictions of Motherhood*, 98–108.

77. Poortman and Van Der Lippe, "Gendered Division of Labor," 526–541.

78. Claffey and Mickelson, "Division of Household Labor," 819–832.

79. Belkin, "Huggies Pulls Ads."

80. Timothy Allen Pehlke II et al., "Does Father Still Know Best? An Inductive Thematic Analysis of Popular TV Sitcoms," *Fathering: A Journal of Theory, Research, and Practice about Men as Fathers* 7, no. 2 (2009): 114–139.

81. Frisco and Williams, "Perceived Housework Equity," 51–73.

82. Sara B. Algoe, "Find, Remind, and Bind: The Functions of Gratitude in Everyday Relationships," *Social and Personality Psychology Compass* 6, no. 6 (2012): 455–469.

83. Amy Claxton and Maureen Perry-Jenkins, "No Fun Anymore: Leisure and Marital Quality across the Transition to Parenthood," *Journal of Marriage and Family* 70, no. 1 (2008): 28–43.

84. Cornelia Wrzus et al., "Social Network Changes and Life Events across the Life Span: A Meta-Analysis," *Psychological Bulletin* 139, no. 1 (2013): 53–80.

85. Sonja Lyubomirsky, Laura King, and Ed Diener, "The Benefits of Frequent Positive Affect: Does Happiness Lead to Success?," *Psychological Bulletin* 131, no. 6 (2005): 803–855; Julianne Holt-Lunstad and Timothy B. Smith, "Social Relationships and Mortality," *Social and Personality Psychology Compass* 6 (2012): 41–53.

86. Sabrina F. Askari et al., "Men Want Equality, But Women Don't Expect It: Young Adults' Expectations for Participation in Household and Child Care Chores," *Psychology of Women Quarterly* 34, no. 2 (2010): 243–252; Melissa A. Milkie et al., "Gendered Division of Childrearing: Ideals, Realities, and the Relationship to Parental Well-Being," *Sex Roles* 47, no. 1–2 (2002): 21–38.

87. Askari et al., "Men Want Equality," 243–252.

88. Rosemary Crompton and Clare Lyonette, "The New Gender Essentialism: Domestic and Family 'Choices' and Their Relation to Attitudes," *British Journal of Sociology* 56, no. 4 (2005): 601–620.

89. Gager, "What's Fair Is Fair," 511–545.

90. Clelia Anna Mannino and Francine M. Deutsch, "Changing the Division of Household Labor: A Negotiated Process between Partners," *Sex Roles* 56, no. 5–6 (2007): 309–324.

91. Hanna Otero, "Resentment: How an Equal Division of Labor Almost Destroyed My Marriage," Babble, January 22, 2009, http://www.babble.com/mom/working-mom-and-stay-at-home-shared-parenting-marriage-trouble.

92. Elinor Ochs and Tamar Kremer-Sadlik, eds., *Fast-Forward Family: Home, Work, and Relationships in Middle-Class America* (Berkeley: University of California Press, 2013), 106–110.

93. Julia T. Wood, "Which Ruler Do We Use? Theorizing the Division of Domestic Labor," *Journal of Family Communication* 11, no. 1 (2011): 39–49.

94. Alberts, Tracy, and Trethewey, "Division of Domestic Labor," 21–38.

95. Stephen Marche, "The Case for Filth," *The Opinion Pages* (blog), *New York Times*, December 7, 2013, http://www.nytimes.com/2013/12/08/opinion/sunday/the-case-for-filth.html?pagewanted=3&_r=0&hp&rref=opinion.

96. Clair, "The Rhetoric of Dust," 50–59.

97. Alberts, Tracy, and Trethewey, "Division of Domestic Labor," 21–38.

98. Kawamura and Brown, "Division of Household Labor," 976–986.

99. Saxbe, Repetti, and Nishina, "Marital Satisfaction," 15–25.

100. Kawamura and Brown, "Division of Household Labor," 976–986.

101. Yessenia Castro and Kathryn H. Gordon, "A Review of Recent Research on Multiple Roles and Women's Mental Health," in *Women and Mental Disorders*, ed. Paula K. Lundberg-Love, Kevin L. Nadal, and Michele A. Paludi (Santa Barbara, CA: Praeger, 2012), 1:37–54.

7. SOCIETAL BARRIERS TO BALANCE

1. Lisa Belkin, "The Opt-Out Revolution," *New York Times Magazine*, October 26, 2003, http://www.nytimes.com/2003/10/26/magazine/26WOMEN.html.

2. Pamela Stone, *Opting Out? Why Women Really Quit Careers and Head Home* (Berkeley: University of California Press, 2007), 105–131.

3. Christine Percheski, "Opting Out? Cohort Differences in Professional Women's Employment Rates from 1960 to 2005," *American Sociological Review* 73 (June 2008): 497–517.

4. Elizabeth Mendes, Lydia Saad, and Kyley McGeeney, "Stay-at-Home Moms Report More Depression, Sadness, Anger: But Low-Income Stay-at-Home Moms Struggle the Most," *Gallup Wellbeing* (blog), Gallup, May 18, 2012, http://www.gallup.com/poll/154685/Stay-Home-Moms-Report-Depression-SadnessAnger.aspx?utm_source=alert&
utm_medium=email&utm_campaign=syndication&utm_content_morelink&
utm_term=All%20Gallup%20Headlines.

5. Wendy Wang, Kim Parker, and Paul Taylor, "Breadwinner Moms: Moms Are the Sole or Primary Provider in Four-in-Ten Households with Children; Public Conflicted about Growing Trend," Pew Research Social and Demographic Trends, posted May 29, 2013, http://www.pewsocialtrends.org/2013/05/29/breadwinner-moms.

6. Paula England, "The Gender Revolution: Uneven and Stalled," *Gender and Society* 24 (April 2010): 149–166.

7. Jeffrey M. Jones, "Gender Differences in Views of Job Opportunity: Fifty-Three Percent of Americans Believe Opportunities are Equal," Gallup, posted August 2, 2005, http://www.gallup.com/poll/17614/gender-differences-views-job-opportunity.aspx.

8. Hilary M. Lips, "The Gender Pay Gap: Challenging the Rationalizations. Perceived Equality, Discrimination, and the Limits of Human Capital Models," *Sex Roles* 68, no. 3–4 (2012): 169–185.

9. Ibid.

10. "The Simple Truth about the Gender Pay Gap: 2013 Edition," American Association of University Women (AAUW) report, posted in 2013, http://www.aauw.org/files/2013/03/the-simple-truth-about-the-gender-pay-gap-2013.pdf.

11. Judy Goldberg Dey and Catherine Hill, "Behind the Pay Gap," American Association of University Women (AAUW) (Washington, DC: American Association of University Women Educational Foundation, 2007), 1–54.

12. Wang, Parker, and Taylor, "Breadwinner Moms."

13. Steve Tobak, "The Gender Pay Gap Is a Myth," FoxBusiness, May 3, 2013, http://www.foxbusiness.com/business-leaders/2013/05/03/gender-pay-gap-is-myth/
#ixzz2UtaMK5La.

14. Nicole M. Stephens and Cynthia S. Levine, "Opting Out or Denying Discrimination? How the Framework of Free Choice in American Society Influences Perceptions of Gender Inequality," *Psychological Science* 22, no. 10 (2011): 1231–1236.

15. Stone, *Opting Out?*, 74.

16. Wang, Parker, and Taylor, "Breadwinner Moms."

17. U.S. Senate Joint Economic Committee, *Invest in Women, Invest in America: A Comprehensive Review of Women in the U.S. Economy*, a report by the Majority Staff of the Joint Economic Committee, Representative Carolyn B. Maloney, Chair (Washington, DC: Joint Economic Committee, 2010), 1–252.

18. Lips, "The Gender Pay Gap," 169–185.

19. Paula England, Paul Allison, and Yuxiao Wu, "Does Bad Pay Cause Occupations to Feminize, Does Feminization Reduce Pay, and How Can We Tell with Longitudinal Data?," *Social Science Research* 36, no. 3 (2007): 1237–1256.

20. Marlene Kim, "Inertia and Discrimination in the California State Civil Service," *Industrial Relations: A Journal of Economy and Society* 38, no. 1 (1999): 46–68.

21. Ibid., 54.

22. Christopher Kilmartin, *The Masculine Self*, 4th ed. (Cornwall-on-Hudson, NY: Sloan, 2010), 272–273.

23. Scott Coltrane and Michele Adams, "Work-Family Imagery and Gender Stereotypes: Television and the Reproduction of Difference," *Journal of Vocational Behavior* 50, no. 2 (1997): 323–347.

24. Paul G. Davies, Steven J. Spencer, and Claude M. Steele, "Clearing the Air: Identity Safety Moderates the Effects of Stereotype Threat on Women's Leadership Aspirations," *Journal of Personality and Social Psychology* 88, no. 2 (2005): 276–287.

25. England, "The Gender Revolution," 149–166.

26. Joan C. Williams and Heather Boushey, "The Three Faces of Work-Family Conflict: The Poor, the Professionals, and the Missing Middle," *Work Life Law: UC Hastings College of the Law*, Center for American Progress (2010): 1–86.

27. "The Simple Truth," American Association of University Women (AAUW) report.

28. Mary Hogue, Cathy L. Z. DuBois, and Lee Fox-Cardamone, "Gender Differences in Pay Expectations: The Roles of Job Intention and Self-View," *Psychology of Women Quarterly* 34, no. 2 (2010): 215–227.

29. Michelle Marks and Crystal Harold, "Who Asks and Who Receives in Salary Negotiation?," *Journal of Organizational Behavior* 32, no. 3 (2011): 371–394.

30. Lisa A. Barron, "Ask and You Shall Receive? Gender Differences in Negotiators' Beliefs about Requests for a Higher Salary," *Human Relations* 56, no. 6 (2003): 635–662.

31. Ibid., 647.

32. Mary E. Wade, "Women and Salary Negotiation: The Costs of Self-Advocacy," *Psychology of Women Quarterly* 25, no. 1 (2001): 65–76.

33. Hannah Riley Bowles, Linda Babcock, and Lei Lai, "Social Incentives for Gender Differences in the Propensity to Initiate Negotiations: Sometimes It Does Hurt to Ask," *Organizational Behavior and Human Decision Processes* 103, no. 1 (2007): 84–103.

34. Alice H. Eagly and Linda L. Carli, *Through the Labyrinth* (Boston: Harvard Business School, 2007), 169–171.

35. Debra Meyerson and Joyce K. Fletcher, "A Modest Manifesto for Shattering the Glass Ceiling," *Harvard Business Review* 78, no. 1 (2000): 127–136.

36. Eagly and Carli, *Through the Labyrinth*, 164.

37. David W. Johnston and Wang-Sheng Lee, "Climbing the Job Ladder: New Evidence of Gender Inequality," *Industrial Relations: A Journal of Economy and Society* 51, no. 1 (2012): 129–151.

38. Eagly and Carli, *Through the Labyrinth*, 169–171.

39. Ibid., 145.

40. Ibid.

41. Liza Featherstone, *Selling Women Short: The Landmark Battle for Workers' Rights at Wal-Mart* (New York: Basic Books, 2004), 81.

42. Michelle J. Budig and Paula England, "The Wage Penalty for Motherhood," *American Sociological Review* 66 (April 2001): 204–225; Rebecca Glauber, "Women's Work and Working Conditions: Are Mothers Compensated for Lost Wages?," *Work and Occupations* 39, no. 2 (2012): 115–138.

43. Ann Crittenden, *The Price of Motherhood: Why the Most Important Job in the World Is Still the Least Valued* (New York: Metropolitan Books, 2001), 94.

44. Budig and England, "The Wage Penalty," 204–225; Amanda K. Baumle, "The Cost of Parenthood: Unraveling the Effects of Sexual Orientation and Gender on Income," *Social Science Quarterly* 90, no. 4 (2009): 983–1002.

45. Melissa J. Hodges and Michelle J. Budig, "Who Gets the Daddy Bonus?: Organizational Hegemonic Masculinity and the Impact of Fatherhood on Earnings," *Gender and Society* 24 (December 2010): 717–745.

46. Baumle, "The Cost of Parenthood," 983–1002.

47. Amy J. C. Cuddy, Susan T. Fiske, and Peter Glick, "When Professionals Become Mothers, Warmth Doesn't Cut the Ice," *Journal of Social Issues* 60, no. 4 (2004): 701–718.

48. Tamar Kricheli-Katz, "Choice, Discrimination, and the Motherhood Penalty," *Law & Society Review* 46, no. 3 (2012): 557–587.

49. Stephens and Levine, "Opting Out or Denying Discrimination?," 1231–1236.

50. Kricheli-Katz, "Choice, Discrimination," 557–587.

51. Williams and Boushey, "Work-Family Conflict," 59.

52. Ibid., 1–86.

53. Ibid., 58.

54. Glauber, "Women's Work and Working Conditions," 115–138.

55. Emily Fitzgibbons Shafer, "Wives' Relative Wages, Husbands' Paid Work Hours, and Wives' Labor-Force Exit," *Journal of Marriage of Family* 73 (February 2011): 250–263.

56. Lips, "The Gender Pay Gap," 181.

57. Janet Walsh and Human Rights Watch, *Failing Its Families: Lack of Paid Leave and Work-Family Support in the US* (New York: Human Rights Watch, 2011), 1–79.

58. "Convention on the Elimination of All Forms of Discrimination against Women," United Nations Entity for Gender Equality and the Empowerment of Women, 2000–2009, http://www.un.org/womenwatch/daw/cedaw/.

59. Walsh and Human Rights Watch, *Failing Its Families*, 1–79.

60. "A Fact Sheet on CEDAW: Treaty for the Rights of Women," Amnesty International, 2005, http://www.amnestyusa.org/sites/default/files/pdfs/cedaw_fact_sheet.pdf.

61. "Fact Sheet #28F: Qualifying Reasons for Leave under the Family Medical Leave Act," U.S. Department of Labor Wage and Hour Division, August 2013, http://www.dol.gov/whd/regs/compliance/whdfs28f.pdf.

62. Walsh and Human Rights Watch, *Failing Its Families*, 1–79.

63. "Your Guide to Family Leave Insurance in New Jersey," Division of Temporary Disability Insurance, http://lwd.state.nj.us/labor/forms_pdfs/tdi/WPR-119.pdf.

64. "Paid Family Leave Benefits," State of California Employment Development Department, http://www.edd.ca.gov/disability/PFL_Benefit_Amounts.htm.

65. Walsh and Human Rights Watch, *Failing Its Families*, 1–79.

66. Pinka Chatterji and Sarah Markowitz, "Family Leave after Childbirth and the Mental Health of New Mothers," *Journal of Mental Health Policy and Economics* 15, no. 2 (2012): 61.

67. Janet Shibley Hyde et al., "Maternity Leave and Women's Mental Health," *Psychology of Women Quarterly* 19, no. 2 (1995): 257–285.

68. Walsh and Human Rights Watch, *Failing Its Families*, 1–79.

69. Ibid., 8.

70. Ibid., 1–79.

71. Ibid., 38.

72. Sakiko Tanaka, "Parental Leave and Child Health across OECD Countries," *Economic Journal* 115, no. 501 (2005): F7–F28.

73. Maya Rossin, "The Effects of Maternity Leave on Children's Birth and Infant Health Outcomes in the United States," *Journal of Health Economics* 30, no. 2 (2011): 221–239.

74. Lawrence M. Berger, Jennifer Hill, and Jane Waldfogel, "Maternity Leave, Early Maternal Employment and Child Health and Development in the US," *Economic Journal* 115, no. 501 (2005): F29–F47.

75. Walsh and Human Rights Watch, *Failing Its Families*, 55.

76. Berger, Hill, and Waldfogel, "Maternity Leave," F29–F47.

77. Walsh and Human Rights Watch, *Failing Its Families*, 1–79.

78. Walsh and Human Rights Watch, *Failing Its Families*, 47.

79. Michael B. Wells and Anna Sarkadi, "Do Father-Friendly Policies Promote Father-Friendly Child-Rearing Practices? A Review of Swedish Parental Leave and Child Health Centers," *Journal of Child and Family Studies* 21, no. 1 (2011): 25–31.

80. Hadas Mandel and Moshe Semyonov, "Family Policies, Wage Structures, and Gender Gaps: Sources of Earnings Inequality in 20 Countries," *American Sociological Review* 70, no. 6 (2005): 949–967.

81. Ibid.

82. Christy Glass and Eva Fodor, "Public Maternalism Goes to Market: Recruitment, Hiring, and Promotion in Postsocialist Hungary," *Gender and Society* 25, no. 1 (2011): 14

83. Joya Misra, Michelle Budig, and Irene Boeckmann, "The Motherhood Penalty in Cross-National Perspective: The Importance of Work-Family Policies and Cultural Attitudes," *Social Politics* 19, no. 2 (2012): 163–193.

84. Ariane Hegewisch and Janet C. Gornick, "The Impact of Work-Family Policies on Women's Employment: A Review of Research from OECD Countries," *Community, Work & Family* 14, no. 2 (2011): 119–138.

85. M. N. Hansen, "The Vicious Circle of the Welfare State? Women's Labor Market Situation in Norway and Great Britain," *Comparative Social Research* 15 (1995): 1–34.

86. Magnus Bygren and Ann-Zofie Duvander, "Parents' Workplace Situation and Fathers' Parental Leave Use," *Journal of Marriage and Family* 68, no. 2 (2006): 363–372.

87. Katrin Bennhold, "In Sweden, Men Can Have It All," *New York Times*, June 9, 2010, http://www.nytimes.com/2010/06/10/world/europe/10iht-sweden.html?pagewanted=all&_r=0.

88. Ibid.

89. Ibid.

90. Linda Haas and C. Philip Hwang, "Is Fatherhood Becoming More Visible at Work? Trends in Corporate Support for Fathers Taking Parental Leave in Sweden," *Fathering: A Journal of Theory, Research, and Practice about Men as Fathers* 7, no. 3 (2009).

91. Bennhold, "In Sweden."

92. Trude Lappegard, "Couples' Parental Leave Practices: The Role of the Workplace Situation," *Journal of Family and Economic Issues* 33, no. 3 (2012): 298–305.

93. Linda Haas and C. Philip Hwang, "The Impact of Taking Parental Leave on Fathers' Participation in Childcare and Relationships with Children: Lessons from Sweden," *Community, Work & Family* 11, no. 1 (2008): 85–104.

94. Walsh and Human Rights Watch, *Failing Its Families*, 1–79.

95. Allen Smith, "Gender Difference in Yahoo Paid Parental-Leave Program Is OK Legally," *Society for Human Resource Management*, June 4, 2013, http://www.shrm.org/legalissues/federalresources/pages/yahoo-paid-leave.aspx.

96. Lauren Weber, "Why Dads Don't Take Paternity Leave: More Companies Offer New Fathers Paid Time Off, but Many Fear Losing Face Back at the Office," *Wall Street Journal*, June 12, 2013, http://online.wsj.com/news/articles/SB10001424127887324049504578541633708283670.

97. Lenna Nepomnyaschy and Jane Waldfogel, "Paternity Leave and Fathers' Involvement with Their Young Children: Evidence from the American Ecls-B," *Community, Work & Family* 10, no. 4 (2007): 427–453.

98. Paul R. Amato, "Paternal Involvement and Children's Behavior Problems," *Journal of Marriage and the Family* 61 (May 1999): 375–384; Natasha J. Cabrera et al., "Fatherhood in the Twenty-First Century," *Child Development* 71, no. 1 (2000): 127–136.

99. Weber, "Why Dads Don't."

100. Wells and Sarkadi, "Do Father-Friendly Policies," 25–31.

101. Weber, "Why Dads Don't."

102. Jessica Keeney et al., "From 'Work-Family' to 'Work-Life:' Broadening Our Conceptualization and Measurement," *Journal of Vocational Behavior* 82, no. 3 (2013): 221–237.

103. "Parents and the High Cost of Child Care 2013 Report," Child Care Aware of America (2013), 1–67.

104. Ibid.

105. Ibid.

106. Williams and Boushey, "Work-Family Conflict," 14.

107. Ibid., 22.

108. Ibid., 1–86.

109. Ibid., 21–22.

110. Ibid., 47.

111. Ibid., 1–86.

112. Stone, *Opting Out?*, 74.

113. Williams and Boushey, "Work-Family Conflict," 57.

114. Madeleine Kunin, *The New Feminist Agenda: Defining the Next Revolution for Women, Work, and Family* (White River Junction, VT: Chelsea Green, 2012), 121.

115. "Misplaced Priorities: Over Incarcerate, Under Educate: Excessive Spending on Incarceration Undermines Educational Opportunity and Public Safety in Communities," National Association for the Advancement of Colored People (2011).

116. Kunin, *The New Feminist Agenda*, 108.

117. Ibid.

118. Ibid.

119. Siv Gustafsson and Frank Stafford, "Child Care Subsidies and Labor Supply in Sweden," *Journal of Human Resources* 27, no. 1 (1992): 204–230.

120. Jane Waldfogel, "International Policies toward Parental Leave and Child Care," *Future of Children* 11, no. 1 (2001): 99–111.

121. Waldfogel, "International Policies," 99–111.
122. Misra, Budig, and Boeckmann, "The Motherhood Penalty," 163–193.
123. Waldfogel, "International Policies," 99–111.
124. "Education: Knowledge and Skills for the Jobs of the Future," White House: President Barack Obama, http://www.whitehouse.gov/issues/education/early-childhood.

8. BEYOND BALANCE

1. Katrina Alcorn, *Maxed Out: American Moms on the Brink* (Berkeley: Seal Press, 2013).
2. Ibid.,1.
3. Tammy D. Allen et al., "Consequences Associated with Work-to-Family Conflict: A Review and Agenda for Future Research," *Journal of Occupational Health Psychology* 5, no. 2 (2000): 278–308.
4. Karen L. Fingerman, et al., "Helicopter Parents and Landing Pad Kids: Intense Parental Support of Grown Children," *Journal of Marriage and Family* 74, no. 4 (2012): 880–896.
5. Marianna Virtanen et al., "Long Working Hours and Symptoms of Anxiety and Depression: A 5-Year Follow-Up of the Whitehall II Study," *Psychological Medicine* 41, no. 12 (2011): 2485–2494; Shelley E. Taylor, Rena L. Repetti, and Teresa Seeman, "Health Psychology: What Is an Unhealthy Environment and How Does It Get under the Skin?," *Annual Review of Psychology* 48, no. 1 (1997): 411–447.
6. Sharon T. Claffey and Kristin D. Mickelson, "Division of Household Labor and Distress: The Role of Perceived Fairness for Employed Mothers," *Sex Roles* 60, no. 11-12 (2009): 819–831; Kathryn M. Rizzo, Holly H. Schiffrin, and Miriam Liss, "Insight into the Parenthood Paradox: Mental Health Outcomes of Intensive Mothering," *Journal of Child and Family Studies* 22, no. 5 (2013): 614–620.
7. Laura A. Pratt and Debra J. Brody, "Depression in the United States Household Population, 2005–2006," *NCHS Data Brief* 7 (September 2008): 1–8.
8. Ibid.
9. E. Mark Cummings and Patrick T. Davies, "Maternal Depression and Child Development," *Journal of Child Psychology and Psychiatry* 35, no. 1 (1994): 73–122; Frank J. Elgar et al., "Maternal and Paternal Depressive Symptoms and Child Maladjustment: The Mediating Role of Parental Behavior," *Journal of Abnormal Child Psychology* 35, no. 6 (2007): 943–955.
10. Ronald C. Kessler et al., "The Epidemiology of Major Depressive Disorder," *JAMA* 289, no. 23 (2003): 3095–3105; Mark Olfson et al., "Prevalence of Anxiety, Depression, and Substance Use Disorders in an Urban General Medicine Practice," *Archives of Family Medicine* 9, no. 9 (2000): 876.
11. Eric S. Kim et al., "Purpose in Life and Reduced Stroke in Older Adults: The Health and Retirement Study," *Journal of Psychosomatic Research* 74, no. 5 (2013): 427–432; Heiner Maier and Jacqui Smith, "Psychological Predictors of Mortality in Old Age," *Journals of Gerontology Series B: Psychological Sciences and Social Sciences* 54B, no. 1 (1999): P44–P54; Laura A. Pratt and Debra J. Brody, "Depression and Smoking in the U.S. Household Population Aged 20 and Over, 2005–2008," *NCHS Data Brief* 34 (April 2010): 1–8; Andreas von Leupoldt and Bernhard Dahme, "The Impact of Emotions on Symptom Perception in Patients with Asthma and Healthy Controls," *Psychophysiology* 50, no. 1 (2013): 1–4.
12. Ed Diener, "Subjective Well-Being: The Science of Happiness and a Proposal for a National Index," *American Psychologist* 55, no. 1 (2000): 34–43; David G. Myers, "The Funds, Friends, and Faith of Happy People," *American Psychologist* 55, no. 1 (2000): 56–67.
13. Iris B. Mauss et al., "Can Seeking Happiness Make People Unhappy? Paradoxical Effects of Valuing Happiness," *Emotion* 11, no. 4 (2011): 807–815.
14. Diener, "Subjective Well-Being," 34–43.
15. Barbara L. Fredrickson, "What Good Are Positive Emotions?," *Review of General Psychology* 2, no. 3 (1998): 300–319.

16. Deborah D. Danner, David A. Snowdon, and Wallace V. Friesen, "Positive Emotions in Early Life and Longevity: Findings from the Nun Study," *Journal of Personality and Social Psychology* 80, no. 5 (2001): 804–813.

17. Barbara L. Fredrickson and Robert W. Levenson, "Positive Emotions Speed Recovery from the Cardiovascular Sequelae of Negative Emotions," *Cognition & Emotion* 12, no. 2 (1998): 191–220; Barbara L. Fredrickson et al., "The Undoing Effect of Positive Emotions," *Motivation and Emotion* 24, no. 4 (2000): 237–258.

18. Sonja Lyubomirsky, Laura King, and Ed Diener, "The Benefits of Frequent Positive Affect: Does Happiness Lead to Success?," *Psychological Bulletin* 131, no. 6 (2005): 803–855.

19. Lahnna I. Catalino and Barbara L. Fredrickson, "A Tuesday in the Life of a Flourisher: The Role of Positive Emotional Reactivity in Optimal Mental Health," *Emotion* 11, no. 4 (2011): 938–950; Corey L. M. Keyes, "Promoting and Protecting Mental Health as Flourishing: A Complementary Strategy for Improving National Mental Health," *American Psychologist* 62, no. 2 (2007): 95–108.

20. Sonja Lyubomirsky, Kennon M. Sheldon, and David Schkade, "Pursuing Happiness: The Architecture of Sustainable Change," *Review of General Psychology* 9, no. 2 (2005): 111–131.

21. Meike Bartels and Dorret I. Boomsma, "Born to be Happy? The Etiology of Subjective Well-Being," *Behavior Genetics* 39, no. 6 (2009): 605–615; Jan-Emmanuel De Neve et al., "Genes, Economics, and Happiness," *Journal of Neuroscience, Psychology, and Economics* 5, no. 4 (2012): 193–211; David Lykken and Auke Tellegen, "Happiness Is a Stochastic Phenomenon," *Psychological Science* 7, no. 3 (1996): 186–189; R. B. Nes et al., "Subjective Well-Being: Genetic and Environmental Contributions to Stability and Change," *Psychological Medicine* 36, no. 7 (2006): 1033–1042.

22. Lykken and Tellegen, "Happiness Is," 189.

23. Daniel Kahneman and Angus Deaton, "High Income Improves Evaluation of Life but Not Emotional Well-Being," *Proceedings of the National Academy of Sciences* 107, no. 38 (2010): 16489–16493.

24. David A. Schkade and Daniel Kahneman, "Does Living in California Make People Happy? A Focusing Illusion in Judgments of Life Satisfaction," *Psychological Science* 9, no. 5 (1998): 340–346.

25. Ed Diener et al., "Subjective Well-Being: Three Decades of Progress," *Psychological Bulletin* 125, no. 2 (1999): 276–302; Lykken and Tellegen, "Happiness Is,"186–189; David G. Myers and Ed Diener, "Who Is Happy?," *Psychological Science* 6, no. 1 (1995): 10–19.

26. Carol D. Ryff and Burton H. Singer, "Know Thyself and Become What You Are: A Eudaimonic Approach to Psychological Well-Being," *Journal of Happiness Studies* 9, no. 1 (2008): 13–9.

27. Derek M. Isaacowitz and Fredda Blanchard-Fields, "Linking Process and Outcome in the Study of Emotion and Aging," *Perspectives on Psychological Science* 7, no. 1 (2012): 3–17.

28. Ryff and Singer, "Know Thyself," 13–9.

29. De Neve et al., "Genes, Economics, and Happiness," 193–211; Myers and Diener, "Who Is Happy?," 10–19; Dirk van Dierendonck, "Spirituality as an Essential Determinant for the Good Life, Its Importance Relative to Self-Determinant Psychological Needs," *Journal of Happiness Studies* 13, no. 4 (2012): 685–700.

30. Myers and Diener, "Who Is Happy?," 10–19.

31. Dierendonck, "Spirituality as," 685–700.

32. De Neve et al., "Genes, Economics, and Happiness," 193–211; Myers and Diener, "Who Is Happy?," 10–19; Dierendonck, "Spirituality as," 685–700.

33. Philip Brickman, Dan Coates, and Ronnie Janoff-Bulman, "Lottery Winners and Accident Victims: Is Happiness Relative?," *Journal of Personality and Social Psychology* 36, no. 8 (1978): 917–927.

34. Eunkook Suh, Ed Diener, and Frank Fujita, "Events and Subjective Well-Being: Only Recent Events Matter," *Journal of Personality and Social Psychology* 70, no. 5 (1996): 1091–1102.

35. Richard E. Lucas, "Time Does Not Heal All Wounds: A Longitudinal Study of Reaction and Adaptation to Divorce," *Psychological Science* 16, no. 12 (2005): 945–950; Richard E. Lucas, "Adaptation and the Set Point Model of Subjective Well-Being: Does Happiness Change after Major Life Events?" *Current Directions in Psychological Science* 16, no. 2 (2007): 75–79; Richard E. Lucas, "Long-Term Disability Is Associated with Lasting Changes in Subjective Well-Being: Evidence from Two Nationally Representative Longitudinal Studies," *Journal of Personality and Social Psychology* 92, no. 4 (2007): 717–730; Richard E. Lucas et al., "Reexamining Adaptation and the Set Point Model of Happiness: Reactions to Changes in Marital Status," *Journal of Personality and Social Psychology* 84, no. 3 (2003): 527–539; Richard E. Lucas et al., "Unemployment Alters the Set Point for Life Satisfaction," *Psychological Science* 15, no. 1 (2004): 8–13.

36. Lucas, "Adaptation," 78.

37. Timothy D. Wilson and Daniel T. Gilbert, "Affective Forecasting: Knowing What to Want," *Current Directions in Psychological Science* 14, no. 3 (2005): 131–134.

38. Lara B. Aknin, Michael I. Norton, and Elizabeth W. Dunn, "From Wealth to Well-Being? Money Matters, but Less than People Think," *Journal of Positive Psychology* 4, no. 6 (2009): 523–527.

39. Lyubomirsky, Sheldon, and Schkade, "Pursuing Happiness," 111–131.

40. June J. Pilcher and Allen J. Huffcutt, "Effects of Sleep Deprivation on Performance: A Meta-Analysis," *Journal of Sleep Research & Sleep Medicine* 19, no. 4 (1996): 318–326; Robert-Paul Juster, Bruce S. McEwen, and Sonia J. Lupien, "Allostatic Load Biomarkers of Chronic Stress and Impact on Health and Cognition," *Neuroscience & Biobehavioral Reviews* 35, no. 1 (2010): 2–16.

41. Pilcher and Huffcutt, "Effects of Sleep Deprivation," 318–326.

42. Jared D. Minkel et al., "Sleep Deprivation and Stressors: Evidence for Elevated Negative Affect in Response to Mild Stressors When Sleep Deprived," *Emotion* 12, no. 5 (2012): 1015–1020.

43. Michael Macht, Christine Haupt, and Andrea Salewsky, "Emotions and Eating in Everyday Life: Application of the Experience-Sampling Method," *Ecology of Food and Nutrition* 43, no. 4 (2004): 11–21.

44. Deborah J. Wallis and Marion M. Hetherington, "Emotions and Eating: Self-Reported and Experimentally Induced Changes in Food Intake under Stress," *Appetite* 52, no. 2 (2009): 355–362.

45. Felice N. Jacka et al., "Association of Western and Traditional Diets with Depression and Anxiety in Women," *American Journal of Psychiatry* 167, no. 3 (2010): 305–311; Almudena Sánchez-Villegas et al., "Dietary Fat Intake and the Risk of Depression: The SUN Project," ed. Lorraine Brennan, *PLoS ONE* 6, no. 1 (2011): e16268.

46. David G. Blanchflower, Andrew J. Oswald, and Sarah Stewart-Brown, "Is Psychological Well-Being Linked to the Consumption of Fruit and Vegetables?" *Social Indicators Research* 114, no. 3 (2013): 785–801.

47. Bonnie A. White, Caroline C. Horwath, and Tamlin S. Conner, "Many Apples a Day Keep the Blues Away: Daily Experiences of Negative and Positive Affect and Food Consumption in Young Adults," *British Journal of Health Psychology* 18, no. 4 (2013): 782–798.

48. Justy Reed and Sarah Buck, "The Effect of Regular Aerobic Exercise on Positive-Activated Affect: A Meta-Analysis," *Psychology of Sport and Exercise* 10, no. 6 (2009): 581–594.

49. James A. Blumenthal et al., "Exercise and Pharmacotherapy in the Treatment of Major Depressive Disorder," *Psychosomatic Medicine* 69, no. 7 (2007): 587–596.

50. Michael Babyak et al., "Exercise Treatment for Major Depression: Maintenance of Therapeutic Benefit at 10 Months," *Psychosomatic Medicine* 62, no. 5 (2000): 633–638.

51. Barbara L. Fredrickson, "Positive Emotions Broaden and Build," in *Advances in Experimental Social Psychology,* ed. Patricia Devine and Ashby Plant (San Diego, CA: Academic Press, 2013), 47: 1–53.

52. Ellen J. Langer and Judith Rodin, "The Effect of Choice and Enhanced Personal Responsibility for the Aged: A Field Experiment in an Institutional Setting," *Journal of Personality and Social Psychology* 34, no. 2 (1976): 191–198.

53. Richard M. Ryan and Edward L. Deci, "Self-Determination Theory and the Facilitation of Intrinsic Motivation, Social Development, and Well-Being," *American Psychologist* 55, no. 1 (2000): 68–78; Shenna S. Iyengar and Mark R. Lepper, "When Choice Is Demotivating: Can One Desire Too Much of a Good Thing?" *Journal of Personality and Social Psychology* 79, no. 6 (2000): 995–1006; Langer and Rodin, "The Effect of Choice," 191–198.

54. Barry Schwartz, "Self-Determination: The Tyranny of Freedom," *American Psychologist* 55, no. 1 (2000): 79–88.

55. Barry Schwartz, *The Paradox of Choice* (New York: HarperCollins, 2004), 132–137.

56. Iyengar and Lepper, "When Choice Is Demotivating," 995–1006.

57. Ibid.

58. Shenna S. Iyengar, Wei Jiang, and Gur Huberman, "How Much Choice Is Too Much: Determinants of Individual Contributions in 401K Retirement Plans," in *Pension Design and Structure: New Lessons from Behavioral Finance*, ed. Olivia S. Mitchell and Steve Utkus (Oxford: Oxford University Press, 2004), 83–97.

59. Schwartz, "The Tyranny of Freedom," 79–88.

60. Iyengar and Lepper, "When Choice Is Demotivating," 995–1006; Chris M. White and Ulrich Hoffrage, "Testing the Tyranny of Too Much Choice against the Allure of More Choice," *Psychology & Marketing* 26, no. 3 (2009): 280–298.

61. Schwartz, *The Paradox of Choice*, 147–166; White and Hoffrage, "Testing the Tyranny," 280–298.

62. Schwartz, *The Paradox of Choice*, 211–236.

63. Harry T. Reis et al., "Daily Well-Being: The Role of Autonomy, Competence, and Relatedness," *Personality and Social Psychology Bulletin* 26, no. 4 (2000): 419–435.

64. Mihaly Csikszentmihalyi, "If We Are So Rich, Why Aren't We Happy?," *American Psychologist* 54, no. 10 (1999): 821–827.

65. Jeanne Nakamura and Mihaly Csikszentmihalyi, "Flow Theory and Research," in *Handbook of Positive Psychology*, ed. C. R. Snyder and Shane J. Lopez (New York: Oxford University Press, 2009), 195–206.

66. *For the Love of the Game*, directed by Sam Raimi (1999; Universal City, CA: Universal Studios, 2000), DVD.

67. Nakamura and Csikszentmihalyi, "Flow Theory and Research," 195–206.

68. Scott R. Bishop et al., "Mindfulness: A Proposed Operational Definition," *Clinical Psychology: Science and Practice* 11, no. 3 (2004): 230–241.

69. Kirk Warren Brown and Richard M. Ryan, "The Benefits of Being Present: Mindfulness and Its Role in Psychological Well-Being," *Journal of Personality and Social Psychology* 84, no. 4 (2003): 822–848.

70. Erika N. Carlson, "Overcoming the Barriers to Self-Knowledge: Mindfulness as a Path to Seeing Yourself as You Really Are," *Perspectives on Psychological Science* 8, no. 2 (2013). 173–186.

71. Ibid.

72. Michael D. Mrazek et al., "Mindfulness Training Improves Working Memory Capacity and GRE Performance While Reducing Mind Wandering," *Psychological Science* 24, no. 5 (2013): 776–781.

73. Kimberly A. Coffey, Marilyn Hartman, and Barbara L. Fredrickson, "Deconstructing Mindfulness and Constructing Mental Health: Understanding Mindfulness and Its Mechanisms of Action," *Mindfulness* 1, no. 4 (2010): 235–253.

74. Ibid; James W. Carson et al., "Mindfulness-Based Relationship Enhancement," *Behavior Therapy* 35, no. 3 (2004): 471–494.

75. Bethany E. Kok, Christian E. Waugh, and Barbara L. Fredrickson, "Meditation and Health: The Search for Mechanisms of Action," *Social and Personality Psychology Compass* 7, no. 1 (2013): 27–39.

76. Ibid; Shian-Ling Keng, Moria J. Smoski, and Clive J. Robins, "Effects of Mindfulness on Psychological Health: A Review of Empirical Studies," *Clinical Psychology Review* 31, no. 6 (2011): 1041–1056; Stefan G. Hofmann et al., "The Effect of Mindfulness-Based Therapy on Anxiety and Depression: A Meta-Analytic Review," *Journal of Consulting and Clinical Psychology* 78, no. 2 (2010): 169–183; Brown and Ryan, "The Benefits of Being Present,"

822–848; Nancy L. Sin and Sonja Lyubomirsky, "Enhancing Well-Being and Alleviating Depressive Symptoms with Positive Psychology Interventions: A Practice-Friendly Meta-Analysis," *Journal of Clinical Psychology* 65, no. 5 (2009): 467–487.

77. Amanda J. Shallcross et al., "Let It Be: Accepting Negative Emotional Experiences Predicts Decreased Negative Affect and Depressive Symptoms," *Behaviour Research and Therapy* 48, no. 9 (2010): 921–929.

78. Catalino and Fredrickson, "A Tuesday," 938–950; Keyes, "Promoting and Protecting," 95–108.

79. Larissa G. Duncan, J. Douglas Coatsworth, and Mark T. Greenberg, "A Model of Mindful Parenting: Implications for Parent-Child Relationships and Prevention Research," *Clinical Child and Family Psychology Review* 12, no. 3 (2009): 255–270.

80. Jeanette A. Sawyer Cohen and Randye J. Semple, "Mindful Parenting: A Call for Research," *Journal of Child and Family Studies* 19, no. 2 (2010): 145–151.

81. Susan M. Bögels, Annukka Lehtonen, and Kathleen Restifo, "Mindful Parenting in Mental Health Care," *Mindfulness* 1, no. 2 (2010): 107–120.

82. Todd B. Kashdan and William E. Breen, "Materialism and Diminished Well-Being: Experiential Avoidance as a Mediating Mechanism," *Journal of Social and Clinical Psychology* 26, no. 5 (2007): 521–539.

83. Kirk Warren Brown et al., "When What One Has Is Enough: Mindfulness, Financial Desire Discrepancy, and Subjective Well-Being," *Journal of Research in Personality* 43, no. 5 (2009): 727–736.

84. The VIA-Inventory of Strengths can be taken at: "VIA-Inventory of Strengths," *Penn International Strengths Project*, 2006, http://www.authentichappiness.sas.upenn.edu/aiesec/content.aspx?id=821.

85. Martin E. P. Seligman et al., "Positive Psychology Progress: Empirical Validation of Interventions," *American Psychologist* 60, no. 5 (2005): 410–421; Martin E. P. Seligman, Tayyab Rashid, and Acacia C. Parks, "Positive Psychotherapy," *American Psychologist* 61, no. 8 (2006): 774–788.

86. Michaela M. Bucchianeri and Alexandra F. Corning, "An Experimental Test of Women's Body Dissatisfaction Reduction through Self-Affirmation," *Applied Psychology: Health and Well - Being* 4, no. 2 (2012): 188–201.

87. Laura A. King, "The Health Benefits of Writing about Life Goals," *Personality and Social Psychology Bulletin* 27, no. 7 (2001): 798–807; Kennon M. Sheldon and Sonja Lyubomirsky, "Achieving Sustainable Gains in Happiness: Change Your Actions, Not Your Circumstances," *Journal of Happiness Studies* 7, no. 1 (2006): 55–86; Sonja Lyubomirsky et al., "Becoming Happier Takes Both a Will and a Proper Way: An Experimental Longitudinal Intervention to Boost Well-Being," *Emotion* 11, no. 2 (2011): 391–402.

88. Lyubomirsky, King, and Diener, "Benefits of Frequent Positive Affect," 803–855; Christopher Peterson, Martin E. Seligman, and George E. Vaillant, "Pessimistic Explanatory Style Is a Risk Factor for Physical Illness: A Thirty-Five-Year Longitudinal Study," *Journal of Personality and Social Psychology* 55, no. 1 (1988): 23–27.

89. Martin E. Seligman, *Learned Optimism: How to Change Your Mind and Your Life* (New York: Vintage Books, 2006), 207–234.

90. Adam M. Grant and Barry Schwartz, "Too Much of a Good Thing: The Challenge and Opportunity of the Inverted U," *Perspectives on Psychological Science* 6, no. 1 (2011): 61–76.

91. Richard W. Robins and Jennifer S. Beer, "Positive Illusions about the Self: Short-Term Benefits and Long-Term Costs," *Journal of Personality and Social Psychology* 80, no. 2 (2001): 340–352.

92. H. S. Friedman, "Personality and Longevity: Paradoxes," in *The Paradoxes of Longevity*, ed. Jean-Marie Robine et al. (Berlin Heidelberg: Springer, 1999), 115–122.

93. Shelley E. Taylor et al., "Psychological Resources, Positive Illusions, and Health," *American Psychologist* 55, no. 1 (2000): 99–109.

94. Myers and Diener, "Who Is Happy?," 10–19; Lyubomirsky, King, and Diener, "Benefits of Frequent Positive Affect," 803–855.

95. Ed Diener and Martin E. P. Seligman, "Very Happy People," *Psychological Science* 13, no. 1 (2002): 81–84.

96. Robert Biswas-Diener and Ed Diener, "Making the Best of a Bad Situation: Satisfaction in the Slums of Calcutta," *Social Indicators Research* 55, no. 3 (2001): 329–352.

97. Elizabeth W. Dunn, Daniel T. Gilbert, and Timothy D. Wilson, "If Money Doesn't Make You Happy, Then You Probably Aren't Spending It Right," *Journal of Consumer Psychology* 21, no. 2 (2011): 115–125.

98. Ibid.

99. Lara B. Aknin et al., "Prosocial Spending and Well-Being: Cross-Cultural Evidence for a Psychological Universal," *Journal of Personality and Social Psychology* 104, no. 4 (2013): 635–652; Elizabeth W. Dunn, Lara B. Aknin, and Michael I. Norton, "Spending Money on Others Promotes Happiness," *Science* 319, no. 5870 (2008): 1687–1688; Dunn, Gilbert, and Wilson, "If Money Doesn't," 115–125.

100. Aknin, Norton, and Dunn, "From Wealth to Well-Being?," 523–527.

101. Aknin et al., "Prosocial Spending and Well-Being," 635–652.

102. Lara B. Aknin et al., "It's the Recipient That Counts: Spending Money on Strong Social Ties Leads to Greater Happiness than Spending on Weak Social Ties," ed. Matjaz Perc, *PloS ONE* 6, no. 2 (2011): e17018.

103. Lara B. Aknin, Elizabeth W. Dunn, and Michael I. Norton, "Happiness Runs in a Circular Motion: Evidence for a Positive Feedback Loop between Prosocial Spending and Happiness," *Journal of Happiness Studies* 13, no. 2 (2012): 347–355.

104. Travis J. Carter and Thomas Gilovich, "The Relative Relativity of Material and Experiential Purchases," *Journal of Personality and Social Psychology* 98, no. 1 (2010): 146–159; Dunn, Gilbert, and Wilson, "If Money Doesn't," 115–125; Leaf Van Boven, "Experientialism, Materialism, and the Pursuit of Happiness," *Review of General Psychology* 9, no. 2 (2005): 132–142; Leaf Van Boven and Thomas Gilovich, "To Do or to Have? That Is the Question," *Journal of Personality and Social Psychology* 85, no. 6 (2003): 1193–1202.

105. Peter A. Caprariello and Harry T. Reis, "To Do, to Have, or to Share? Valuing Experiences over Material Possessions Depends on the Involvement of Others," *Journal of Personality and Social Psychology* 104, no. 2 (2013): 199–215.

106. Carter and Gilovich, "The Relative Relativity," 146–159.

107. Leaf Van Boven and Laurence Ashworth, "Looking Forward, Looking Back: Anticipation Is More Evocative than Retrospection," *Journal of Experimental Psychology: General* 136, no. 2 (2007): 289–300.

108. Irene Tsapelas, Arthur Aron, and Terri Orbuch, "Marital Boredom Now Predicts Less Satisfaction 9 Years Later," *Psychological Science* 20, no. 5 (2009): 543–545.

109. Arthur Aron et al., "Couples' Shared Participation in Novel and Arousing Activities and Experienced Relationship Quality," *Journal of Personality and Social Psychology* 78, no. 2 (2000): 273–284.

110. Fred B. Bryant, "Savoring Beliefs Inventory (SBI): A Scale for Measuring Beliefs about Savouring," *Journal of Mental Health* 12, no. 2 (2003): 175–196.

111. Jennifer L. Smith and Fred B. Bryant, "Are We Having Fun Yet? Savoring, Type A Behavior, and Vacation Enjoyment," *International Journal of Wellbeing* 3, no. 1 (2013): 1–19; Harry T. Reis et al., "Are You Happy for Me? How Sharing Positive Events with Others Provides Personal and Interpersonal Benefits," *Journal of Personality and Social Psychology* 99, no. 2 (2010): 311–329.

112. Fredrickson, "What Good Are Positive Emotions?," 300–319.

113. Shelly L. Gable and Harry T. Reis, "Good News! Capitalizing on Positive Events in an Interpersonal Context," in *Advances in Experimental Social Psychology*, ed. Mark P. Zanna (San Diego, CA: Academic Press, 2010), 42: 195–257; Reis et al., "Are You Happy for Me?," 311–329.

114. Julianne Holt-Lunstad and Timothy B. Smith, "Social Relationships and Mortality," *Social and Personality Psychology Compass* 6, no. 1 (2012): 41–53; Lyubomirsky et al., "Becoming Happier," 391–402; Loren Toussaint and Philip Friedman, "Forgiveness, Gratitude, and Well-Being: The Mediating Role of Affect and Beliefs," *Journal of Happiness Studies* 10, no. 6 (2009): 635–654; Philip C. Watkins et al., "Gratitude and Happiness: Development of a Measure of Gratitude, and Relationships with Subjective Well-Being," *Social Behavior and Personality: An International Journal* 31, no. 5 (2003): 431–451.

115. Sara B. Algoe, "Find, Remind, and Bind: The Functions of Gratitude in Everyday Relationships," *Social and Personality Psychology Compass* 6, no. 6 (2012): 455–469; Sara B. Algoe, Jonathan Haidt, and Shelly L. Gable, "Beyond Reciprocity: Gratitude and Relationships in Everyday Life," *Emotion* 8, no. 3 (2008): 425–429.

116. Sara B. Algoe, Shelly L. Gable, and Natalya C. Maisel, "It's the Little Things: Everyday Gratitude as a Booster Shot for Romantic Relationships," *Personal Relationships* 17, no. 2 (2010): 217–233; Sara B. Algoe and Jonathan Haidt, "Witnessing Excellence in Action: The 'Other-Praising' Emotions of Elevation, Gratitude, and Admiration," *Journal of Positive Psychology* 4, no. 2 (2009): 105–127; Algoe, Haidt, and Gable, "Beyond Reciprocity," 425–429; Sara B. Algoe, Barbara L. Fredrickson, and Shelly L. Gable, "The Social Functions of the Emotion of Gratitude via Expression," *Emotion* 13, no. 4 (2013): 605–609.

117. Robert A. Emmons and Michael E. McCullough, "Counting Blessings versus Burdens: An Experimental Investigation of Gratitude and Subjective Well-Being in Daily Life," *Journal of Personality and Social Psychology* 84, no. 2 (2003): 377–389; Kennon M. Sheldon and Sonja Lyubomirsky, "How to Increase and Sustain Positive Emotion: The Effects of Expressing Gratitude and Visualizing Best Possible Selves," *Journal of Positive Psychology* 1, no. 2 (2006): 73–82.

118. Seligman et al., "Positive Psychology Progress," 410–421; Kennon M. Sheldon and Sonja Lyubomirsky, "Achieving Sustainable New Happiness: Prospects, Practices, and Prescriptions," in *Positive Psychology in Practice*, ed. P. Alex Linley and Stephen Joseph (Hoboken, NJ: Wiley, 2004), 127–145; Steven M. Toepfer, Kelly Cichy, and Patti Peters, "Letters of Gratitude: Further Evidence for Author Benefits," *Journal of Happiness Studies* 13, no. 1 (2012): 187–201.

119. Seligman et al., "Positive Psychology Progress," 410–421; Toepfer, Cichy, and Peters, "Letters of Gratitude,"187–201.

120. Peggy A. Thoits and Lyndi N. Hewitt, "Volunteer Work and Well-Being," *Journal of Health and Social Behavior* 42, no. 2 (2001): 115–131.

121. Dunn, Aknin, and Norton, "Spending Money on Others," 1687–1688; Sheldon and Lyubomirsky, "Achieving Sustainable New Happiness," 127–145.

122. Kristin Layous et al., "Kindness Counts: Prompting Prosocial Behavior in Preadolescents Boosts Peer Acceptance and Well-Being," ed. Frank Krueger, *PLoS ONE* 7, no. 12 (2012): e51380: 1–7.

123. Lyubomirsky, King, and Diener, "Benefits of Frequent Positive Affect," 803–855.

124. Cretien van Campen, Alice H. de Boer, and Jurjen Ledema, "Are Informal Caregivers Less Happy than Noncaregivers? Happiness and the Intensity of Caregiving in Combination with Paid and Voluntary Work," *Scandinavian Journal of Caring Sciences* 27, no. 1 (2013): 44–50.

125. Toussaint and Friedman, "Forgiveness, Gratitude, and Well-Being," 635–654.

126. Everett L. Worthington Jr. et al., "Forgiveness, Health, and Well-Being: A Review of Evidence for Emotional versus Decisional Forgiveness, Dispositional Forgivingness, and Reduced Unforgiveness," *Journal of Behavioral Medicine* 30, no. 4 (2007): 291–302.

127. Michael E. McCullough, "Forgiveness as Human Strength: Theory, Measurement, and Links to Well-Being," *Journal of Social and Clinical Psychology* 19, no. 1 (2000): 43–55.

128. Majda Rijavec, Lana Jurčec, and Ivana Mijočević, "Gender Differences in the Relationship between Forgiveness and Depression/Happiness," *Psihologijske teme* 19, no. 1 (2010): 189–202; Maria Teresa Muñoz Sastre et al., "Forgivingness and Satisfaction with Life," *Journal of Happiness Studies* 4, no. 3 (2003): 323–335.

129. Michael E. McCullough and Charlotte Vanoyen Witvliet, "The Psychology of Forgiveness," in *Handbook of Positive Psychology,* ed. C. R. Snyder and Shane J. Lopez (New York: Oxford University Press, 2002): 2, 446–455; Sastre et al., "Forgivingness and Satisfaction," 323–335.

130. McCullough, "Forgiveness as Human Strength," 43–55.

131. Alex H. S. Harris et al., "Effects of a Group Forgiveness Intervention on Forgiveness, Perceived Stress, and Trait-Anger," *Journal of Clinical Psychology* 62, no. 6 (2006): 715–733.

132. Thomas W. Baskin and Robert D. Enright, "Intervention Studies on Forgiveness: A Meta-Analysis," *Journal of Counseling & Development* 82, no. 1 (2004): 79–90.

133. Forgiveness Intervention Manuals, VCU Department of Psychology Faculty Page, updated August 2, 2012, http://www.people.vcu.edu/~eworth.

134. Robert D. Enright, *Forgiveness Is a Choice: A Step-By-Step Process for Resolving Anger and Restoring Hope* (Washington, DC: American Psychological Association, 2001).

135. Harris et al., "Group Forgiveness Intervention," 715.

136. Kaitlyn Folmer, Natasha Singh, and Suzan Clarke, "Amish School Shooter's Widow, Marie Monville, Speaks Out," ABC News, September 30, 2013, http://abcnews.go.com/US/amish-school-shooters-widow-marie-monville-remembers-tragedy/story?id=20417790&page=3.

137. Toussaint and Friedman, "Forgiveness, Gratitude, and Well-Being," 635–654.

138. Leon Festinger, "A Theory of Social Comparison Processes," *Human Relations* 7, no. 2 (1954): 117–140.

139. Richard H. Smith, "Assimilative and Contrastive Emotional Reactions to Upward and Downward Social Comparisons," in *Handbook of Social Comparison: Theory and Research*, ed. Jerry Suls and Ladd Wheeler (New York: Kluwer Academic / Plenum, 2000): 173–200; Thomas Ashby Wills, "Downward Comparison Principles in Social Psychology," *Psychological Bulletin* 90, no. 2 (1981): 245–271.

140. Karl Halvor Teigen and Tine K. Jensen, "Unlucky Victims or Lucky Survivors? Spontaneous Counterfactual Thinking by Families Exposed to the Tsunami Disaster," *European Psychologist* 16, no. 1 (2011): 48–57.

141. Wayne M. Usui, Thomas J. Keil, and K. Robert Durig, "Socioeconomic Comparisons and Life Satisfaction of Elderly Adults," *Journal of Gerontology* 40, no. 1 (1985): 110–114.

142. Emmons and McCullough, "Counting Blessings versus Burdens," 377–389.

143. Smith, "Assimilative and Contrastive," 173–200.

144. Sonja Lyubomirsky and Lee Ross, "Hedonic Consequences of Social Comparison: A Contrast of Happy and Unhappy People," *Journal of Personality and Social Psychology* 73, no. 6 (1997): 1141–1157.

145. Charles S. Gulas and Kim McKeage, "Extending Social Comparison: An Examination of the Unintended Consequences of Idealized Advertising Imagery," *Journal of Advertising* 29, no. 2 (2000): 17–28.

146. Judith B. White et al., "Frequent Social Comparisons and Destructive Emotions and Behaviors: The Dark Side of Social Comparisons," *Journal of Adult Development* 13, no. 1 (2006): 36–44.

147. Sarah E. Hill, Danielle J. DelPriore, and Phillip W. Vaughan, "The Cognitive Consequences of Envy: Attention, Memory, and Self-Regulatory Depletion," *Journal of Personality and Social Psychology* 101, no. 4 (2011): 653–666.

148. Sarah Emily Tuttle-Singer, "We Need to Quit Telling Lies on Facebook," *Kveller: A Jewish Twist on Parenting* (blog), February 25, 2013, http://www.kveller.com/blog/parenting/we-need-to-quit-telling-lies-on-facebook/?fb_action_ids=10151785558844225&fb_action_types=og.likes&fb_source=other_multiline&action_object_map=%7B%2210151785558844225%22%3A503877192984086%7D&action_type_map=%7B%2210151785558844225%22%3A%22og.likes%22%7D&action_ref_map=%5B%5Dz.

149. Shelley H. Carson and Ellen J. Langer, "Mindfulness and Self-Acceptance," *Journal of Rational-Emotive & Cognitive-Behavior Therapy* 24, no. 1 (2006): 29–43.

150. Murad S. Hussain and Ellen Langer, "A Cost of Pretending," *Journal of Adult Development* 10, no. 4 (2003): 261–270.

151. Carson and Langer, "Mindfulness and Self-Acceptance," 29–43.

152. Diener, "Subjective Well-Being," 34–43; Myers, "Happy People," 56–67.

153. Sonja Lyubomirsky and Kristin Layous, "How Do Simple Positive Activities Increase Well-Being?" *Current Directions in Psychological Science* 22, no. 1 (2013): 57–62.

154. Lyubomirsky et al., "Becoming Happier," 391–402.

155. Ibid., 391.

156. Barbara L. Fredrickson and Thomas Joiner, "Positive Emotions Trigger Upward Spirals toward Emotional Well-Being," *Psychological Science* 13, no. 2 (2002): 172–175; Barbara L.

Fredrickson and Marcial F. Losada, "Positive Affect and the Complex Dynamics of Human Flourishing," *American Psychologist* 60, no. 7 (2005): 678–686.

157. Kristi Hedges, "R.I.P. Work-Life Balance," *ForbesWoman* (blog), *Forbes*, July 11, 2013, http://www.forbes.com/sites/work-in-progress/2013/07/11/r-i-p-work-life-balance.

9. BALANCE AND BEYOND

1. Young Eun Chang, "The Relation between Mothers' Attitudes toward Maternal Employment and Social Competence of 36-Month-Olds: The Role of Maternal Psychological Well-Being and Sensitivity," *Journal of Child and Family Studies* 22, no. 7 (2013): 987–999.

2. Joseph Chancellor and Sonja Lyubomirsky, "Happiness and Thrift: When (Spending) Less Is (Hedonically) More," *Journal of Consumer Psychology* 21, no. 2 (2011): 131–138.

3. Alice H. Eagly and Linda L. Carli, *Through the Labyrinth: The Truth about How Women Become Leaders* (Boston: Harvard Business School, 2007), 14.

4. "Catalyst Quick Take: Women in U.S. Management and Labor Force" (New York: Catalyst, 2013), http://www.catalyst.org/knowledge/women-us-management-and-labor-force.

5. Philip N. Cohen, "How Can We Jump-Start the Struggle for Gender Equality?" *The Opinion Pages* (blog), *New York Times,* November 23, 2013, http://opinionator.blogs.nytimes.com/2013/11/23/how-can-we-jump-start-the-struggle-for-gender-equality.

6. "Women CEOs of the Fortune 1000," Catalyst, December 10, 2013, http://www.catalyst.org/knowledge/women-ceos-fortune-1000.

7. Paula England, "The Gender Revolution: Uneven and Stalled," *Gender & Society* 24, no. 2 (2010): 149–166.

8. Matthew Oransky and Jeanne Maracek, "'I'm Not Going to Be a Girl': Masculinity and Emotions in Boys' Friendships and Peer Groups," *Journal of Adolescent Research* 24, no. 2 (2009): 218–241.

9. Sabrina F. Askari et al., "Men Want Equality, but Women Don't Expect It: Young Adults' Expectations for Participation in Household and Child Care Chores," *Psychology of Women Quarterly* 34, no. 2 (2010): 243–252.

10. Kathleen Gerson, *The Unfinished Revolution: How a New Generation Is Reshaping Family, Work, and Gender in America* (New York: Oxford University Press, 2010), 103–124.

11. Kim Parker and Wendy Wang, "Modern Parenthood: Roles of Moms and Dads Converge as They Balance Work and Family," Pew Research Social and Demographic Trends, posted March 14, 2013, http://www.pewsocialtrends.org/2013/03/14/modern-parenthood-roles-of-moms-and-dads-converge-as-they-balance-work-and-family.

12. Sheryl Sandberg, *Lean In: Women, Work, and the Will to Lead* (New York: Random House, 2013), 129.

13. Ibid., 39–52.

14. Asma Khalid, "How Boston Is Trying to Eliminate the Gender Wage Gap," 90.9 WBUR, audio, November 26, 2013, http://www.wbur.org/2013/11/26/boston-women-pay-equity-push.

15. "Boston: Closing the Wage Gap: Becoming the Best City in America for Working Women," *Women's Workforce Council,* 2013, http://www.cityofboston.gov/images_ documents/Boston_Closing%20the%20Wage%20Gap_Interventions%20Report_tcm3-41353. pdf.

16. Minnesota Management and Budget: Reporting Forms, Instructions, Software, 2005, http://www.mmb.state.mn.us/reporting-forms-instructions-software.

17. New Mexico Pay Equity Initiative, New Mexico General Services Department. Executive Order #2009-049. December 18, 2009, http://www.generalservices.state.nm.us/statepurchasing/Pay_Equity.aspx.

18. "Closing the Gap: Competitive Advantage from Closing the Corporate Gender Gap," EDGE Certified, http://www.edge-cert.org/CMS/de-CH/Closing%20the%20gap/Competitive%20Advantage.aspx.

19. William T. Gormley, Jr., "Oklahoma's Universal Preschool Program: Better than Ok," *Georgetown Public Policy Review*, May 6, 2013, http://gppreview.com/2013/05/06/oklahomas-universal-preschool-program-better-than-o-k.

20. Timothy J. Bartik, William Gormley, and Shirley Adelstein, "Earnings Benefits of Tulsa's Pre-K Program for Different Income Groups," *Economics of Education Review* 31, no. 6 (2012): 1143–1161.

21. Paul K. Piff et al., "Higher Social Class Predicts Increased Unethical Behavior," *Proceedings of the National Academy of Sciences* 109, no. 11 (2012): 4086–4091.

22. Crawford, Mary E. *Transformations: Women, Gender, and Psychology* (New York: McGraw-Hill, 2006), 477.

Bibliography

Aaronson, Lauren S., Carol Macnee Mural, and Susan K. Pfoutz. "Seeking Information: Where Do Pregnant Women Go?" *Health Education & Behavior* 15, no. 3 (1988): 335–345.

ABC News. "Can a Video Teach Babies to Read?" ABC News, March 6, 2013. http://abc-news.go.com/GMA/AmericanFamily/story?id=126294.

Aber, Lawrence, Pamela Morris, and Cybele Raver. "Children, Families and Poverty: Definitions, Trends, Emerging Science and Implications for Policy." *Social Policy Report* 26, no. 3 (2012): 1–29.

Adler, Nancy E., Thomas Boyce, Margaret A. Chesney, Sheldon Cohen, Susan Folkman, Robert L. Kahn, and S. Leonard Syme. "Socioeconomic Status and Health: The Challenge of the Gradient." *American Psychologist* 49, no. 1 (1994): 15–24.

Ahlborg, Tone, and Margaretha Strandmark. "Factors Influencing the Quality of Intimate Relationships Six Months after Delivery: First-Time Parents' Own Views and Coping Strategies." *Journal of Psychosomatic Obstetrics & Gynecology* 27, no. 3 (2006): 163–172.

Aknin, Lara B., Christopher P. Barrington-Leigh, Elizabeth W. Dunn, John F. Helliwell, Justine Burns, Robert Biswas-Diener, Imelda Kemeza et al. "Prosocial Spending and Well-Being: Cross-Cultural Evidence for a Psychological Universal." *Journal of Personality and Social Psychology* 104, no. 4 (2013): 635–652.

Aknin, Lara B., Elizabeth W. Dunn, and Michael I. Norton. "Happiness Runs in a Circular Motion: Evidence for a Positive Feedback Loop between Prosocial Spending and Happiness." *Journal of Happiness Studies* 13, no. 2 (2012): 347–355.

Aknin, Lara B., Michael I. Norton, and Elizabeth W. Dunn. "From Wealth to Well-Being? Money Matters, but Less than People Think." *Journal of Positive Psychology* 4, no. 6 (2009): 523–527.

Aknin, Lara B., Gillian M. Sandstrom, Elizabeth W. Dunn, and Michael I. Norton. "It's the Recipient That Counts: Spending Money on Strong Social Ties Leads to Greater Happiness than Spending on Weak Social Ties." Edited by Matjaz Perc. *PloS ONE* 6, no. 2 (2011): e17018.

Alberts, Jess K., Sarah J. Tracy, and Angela Trethewey. "An Integrative Theory of the Division of Domestic Labor: Threshold Level, Social Organizing and Sensemaking." *Journal of Family Communication* 11, no. 1 (2011): 21–38.

Alcorn, Katrina. *Maxed Out: American Moms on the Brink*. Berkeley: Seal Press, 2013.

Algoe, Sara B. "Find, Remind, and Bind: The Functions of Gratitude in Everyday Relationships." *Social and Personality Psychology Compass* 6, no. 6 (2012): 455–469.

Algoe, Sara B., Barbara L. Fredrickson, and Shelly L. Gable. "The Social Functions of the Emotion of Gratitude via Expression." *Emotion* 13, no. 4 (2013): 605–609.

Algoe, Sara B., Shelly L. Gable, and Natalya C. Maisel. "It's the Little Things: Everyday Gratitude as a Booster Shot for Romantic Relationships." *Personal Relationships* 17, no. 2 (2010): 217–233.

Algoe, Sara B., and Jonathan Haidt. "Witnessing Excellence in Action: The 'Other-Praising' Emotions of Elevation, Gratitude, and Admiration." *Journal of Positive Psychology* 4, no. 2 (2009): 105–127.

Algoe, Sara B., Jonathan Haidt, and Shelly L. Gable. "Beyond Reciprocity: Gratitude and Relationships in Everyday Life." *Emotion* 8, no. 3 (2008): 425–429.

Allen, Tammy D., David E. L. Herst, Carly S. Bruck, and Martha Sutton. "Consequences Associated with Work-to-Family Conflict: A Review and Agenda for Future Research." *Journal of Occupational Health Psychology* 5, no. 2 (2000): 278–308.

Altonji, Joseph G., and Jennifer Oldham. "Vacation Laws and Annual Work Hours." *Economic Perspectives–Federal Reserve Bank of Chicago* 27, no. 3 (2003): 19–29.

Amato, Paul R. "Paternal Involvement and Children's Behavior Problems." *Journal of Marriage and the Family* 61, no. 2 (1999): 375–384.

American Association of University Women, "The Simple Truth about the Gender Pay Gap: 2013 Edition." American Association of University Women (AAUW) report, posted in 2013. http://www.aauw.org/files/2013/03/the-simple-truth-about-the-gender-pay-gap-2013.pdf.

Amnesty International. "A Fact Sheet on CEDAW: Treaty for the Rights of Women." Amnesty International, 2005. http://www.amnestyusa.org/sites/default/files/pdfs/cedaw_fact_sheet.pdf.

Anisfeld, Elizabeth, Virginia Casper, Molly Nozyce, and Nicholas Cunningham. "Does Infant Carrying Promote Attachment? An Experimental Study of the Effects of Increased Physical Contact on the Development of Attachment." *Child Development* 61, no. 5 (1990): 1617–1627.

Arendell, Terry. "Conceiving and Investigating Motherhood: The Decade's Scholarship." *Journal of Marriage and Family* 62, no. 4 (2000): 1192–1207.

Aron, Arthur, Christina C. Norman, Elaine N. Aron, Colin McKenna, and Richard E. Heyman. "Couples' Shared Participation in Novel and Arousing Activities and Experienced Relationship Quality." *Journal of Personality and Social Psychology* 78, no. 2 (2000): 273–284.

Arthurs, Deborah. "Women Spend Three Hours Every Week Redoing Chores Their Men Have Done Badly." Mail Online, March 19, 2012. http://www.dailymail.co.uk/femail/article-2117254/Women-spend-hours-week-redoing-chores-men-badly.html.

Ashton-James, Claire E., Kostadin Kushlev, and Elizabeth W. Dunn. "Parents Reap What They Sow: Child-Centrism and Parental Well-Being." *Social Psychological and Personality Science* 4, no. 6 (2013): 635–642.

Askari, Sabrina F., Miriam Liss, Mindy J. Erchull, Samantha E. Staebell, and Sarah J. Axelson. "Men Want Equality, but Women Don't Expect It: Young Adults' Expectations for Participation in Household and Child Care Chores." *Psychology of Women Quarterly* 34, no. 2 (2010): 243–252.

Atkinson, Maxine P., and Jacqueline Boles. "WASP (Wives as Senior Partners)." *Journal of Marriage and Family* 46, no. 4 (1984): 861–870.

Attia, Maimone. *Race to Nowhere.* Directed by Vicki Abeles and Jessica Congdon. Lafayette, CA: Reel Link Films, 2009. DVD.

Aunola, Kaisa, and Jari-Erik Nurmi. "The Role of Parenting Styles in Children's Problem Behavior." *Child Development* 76, no. 6 (2005): 1144–1159.

Baard, Paul P., Edward L. Deci, and Richard M. Ryan. "Intrinsic Need Satisfaction: A Motivational Basis of Performance and Well-Being in Two Work Settings." *Journal of Applied Social Psychology* 34, no. 10 (2004): 2045–2068.

Babyak, Michael, James A. Blumenthal, Steve Herman, Parinda Khatri, Murali Doraiswamy, Kathleen Moore, W. Edward Craighead et al. "Exercise Treatment for Major Depression: Maintenance of Therapeutic Benefit at 10 Months." *Psychosomatic Medicine* 62, no. 5 (2000): 633–638.

Bandura, Albert, Gian Vittorio Caprara, Claudio Barbaranelli, Camillo Regalia, and Eugenia Scabini. "Impact of Family Efficacy Beliefs on Quality of Family Functioning and Satisfaction with Family Life." *Applied Psychology* 60, no. 3 (2011): 421–448.

Barber, Brian K., Joseph E. Olsen, and Shobha C. Shagle. "Associations between Parental Psychological and Behavioral Control and Youth Internalized and Externalized Behaviors." *Child Development* 65, no. 4 (1994): 1120–1136.

Barber, Brian, and Mingzhu Xia. "The Centrality of Control to Parenting and Its Effects." In *Parenting: Synthesizing Nurturance and Discipline for Optimal Child Development*, edited by Robert E. Larzelere, Amanda Sheffield Morris, and Amanda W. Harrist, 61–87. Washington, DC: American Psychological Association, 2013.

American Academy of Pediatrics. "Breastfeeding and the Use of Human Milk." *Pediatrics: Official Journal of the American Academy of Pediatrics* 129, no. 3 (2012): e827–e841.

Barnett, Rosalind Chait, and Janet Shibley Hyde. "Women, Men, Work, and Family." *American Psychologist* 56, no. 10 (2001): 781–796.

Barnett, Rosalind C., Nancy L. Marshall, and Joseph H. Pleck. "Men's Multiple Roles and Their Relationship to Men's Psychological Distress." *Journal of Marriage and Family* 54, no. 2 (1992): 358–367.

Barron, Lisa A. "Ask and You Shall Receive? Gender Differences in Negotiators' Beliefs about Requests for a Higher Salary." *Human Relations* 56, no. 6 (2003): 635–662.

Bartels, Meike, and Dorret I. Boomsma. "Born to be Happy? The Etiology of Subjective Well-Being." *Behavior Genetics* 39, no. 6 (2009): 605–615.

Bartik, Timothy J., William Gormley, and Shirley Adelstein. "Earnings Benefits of Tulsa's Pre-K Program for Different Income Groups." *Economics of Education Review* 31, no. 6 (2012): 1143–1161.

Bartley, Sharon J., Priscilla W. Blanton, and Jennifer L. Gilliard. "Husbands and Wives in Dual-Earner Marriages: Decision-Making, Gender Role Attitudes, Division of Household Labor, and Equity." *Marriage & Family Review* 37, no. 4 (2005): 69–94.

Baskin, Thomas W., and Robert D. Enright. "Intervention Studies on Forgiveness: A Meta-Analysis." *Journal of Counseling & Development* 82, no. 1 (2004): 79–90.

Bauer, Monika A., James E. B. Wilkie, Jung K. Kim, and Galen V. Bodenhausen. "Cuing Consumerism Situational Materialism Undermines Personal and Social Well-Being." *Psychological Science* 23, no. 5 (2012): 517–523.

Baumle, Amanda K. "The Cost of Parenthood: Unraveling the Effects of Sexual Orientation and Gender on Income." *Social Science Quarterly* 90, no. 4 (2009): 983–1002.

Baumrind, Diana. "Current Patterns of Parental Authority." *Developmental Psychology* 4, no. 1p2 (1971): 1. Note: These parenting styles also differ in how responsive and warm they are to their children as well with permissive and authoritative parents exhibiting high levels of responsiveness, while authoritarian parents are low on this dimension. See Eleanor E. Maccoby and John A. Martin, "Socialization in the Context of the Family: Parent-Child Interaction," in *Handbook of Child Psychology*, vol. 4. (Hoboken, NJ: Wiley, 1983).

Baumrind, Diana, Robert E. Larzelere, and Elizabeth B. Owens. "Effects of Preschool Parents' Power Assertive Patterns and Practices on Adolescent Development." *Parenting: Science and Practice* 10, no. 3 (2010): 157–201.

Lisa Belkin. "Huggies Pulls Ads after Insulting Dads." *HuffPost Parents* (blog), *Huffington Post*, March 12, 2012. http://www.huffingtonpost.com/lisa-belkin/huggies-pulls-diaper-ads_b_1339074.html.

——. "The Opt-Out Revolution." *New York Times Magazine*, October 26, 2003. http://www.nytimes.com/2003/10/26/magazine/26WOMEN.html.

Belsky, Jay. "The 'Effects' of Infant Day Care Reconsidered." *Early Childhood Research Quarterly* 3, no. 3 (1988): 235–272.

Belsky, Jay, Deborah Lowe Vandell, Margaret Burchinal, K. Alison Clarke-Stewart, Kathleen McCartney, and Margaret Tresch Owen. "Are There Long-Term Effects of Early Child Care?" *Child Development* 78, no. 2 (2007): 681–701.

Bennhold, Katrin. "In Sweden, Men Can Have It All," *New York Times*, June 9, 2010. http://www.nytimes.com/2010/06/10/world/europe/10iht-sweden.html?pagewanted=all&_r=0.

Berdahl, Jennifer L., and Sue H. Moon. "Workplace Mistreatment of Middle Class Workers Based on Sex, Parenthood, and Caregiving." *Journal of Social Issues* 69, no. 2 (2013): 341–366.

Berger, Lawrence, Jeanne Brooks-Gunn, Christina Paxson, and Jane Waldfogel. "First-Year Maternal Employment and Child Outcomes: Differences across Racial and Ethnic Groups." *Children and Youth Services Review* 30, no. 4 (2008): 365–387.

Berger, Lawrence M., Jennifer Hill, and Jane Waldfogel. "Maternity Leave, Early Maternal Employment and Child Health and Development in the US." *Economic Journal* 115, no. 501 (2005): F29–F47.

Berkowitz, Dana, and Katherine A. Kuvalanka. "Gay Fathers' Involvement in Their Young Children's Lives." In *Father Involvement in Young Children's Lives: A Global Analysis*, edited by Jyotsna Pattnaik, 89–106. London: Springer, 2013.

Bianchi, Suzanne M. "Maternal Employment and Time with Children: Dramatic Change or Surprising Continuity?" *Demography* 37, no. 4 (2000): 401–414.

Bianchi, Suzanne M., and Melissa A. Milkie. "Work and Family Research in the First Decade of the 21st Century." *Journal of Marriage and Family* 72, no. 3 (2010): 705–725.

Bianchi, Suzanne M., Melissa A. Milkie, Liana C. Sayer, and John P. Robinson. "Is Anyone Doing the Housework? Trends in the Gender Division of Household Labor." *Social Forces* 79, no. 1 (2000): 191–228.

Bianchi, Suzanne M., John P. Robinson, and Melissa A. Milkie. *Changing Rhythms of American Family Life*. Rose Series in Sociology. New York: Russell Sage, 2006.

Biblarz, Timothy J., and Judith Stacey. "How Does the Gender of Parents Matter?" *Journal of Marriage and Family* 72, no. 1 (2010): 3–22.

Bishop, Katherine M., and Douglas Wahlsten. "Sex Differences in the Human Corpus Callosum: Myth or Reality?" *Neuroscience & Biobehavioral Reviews* 21, no. 5 (1997): 581–601.

Bishop, Scott R., Mark Lau, Shauna Shapiro, Linda Carlson, Nicole D. Anderson, James Carmody, Zindel V. Segal et al. "Mindfulness: A Proposed Operational Definition." *Clinical Psychology: Science and Practice* 11, no. 3 (2004): 230–241.

Biswas-Diener, Robert, and Ed Diener. "Making the Best of a Bad Situation: Satisfaction in the Slums of Calcutta." *Social Indicators Research* 55, no. 3 (2001): 329–352.

Biswas-Diener, Robert, Joar Vittersø, and Ed Diener. "Most People Are Pretty Happy, but There Is Cultural Variation: The Inughuit, the Amish, and the Maasai." *Journal of Happiness Studies* 6, no. 3 (2005): 205–226.

Bittman, Michael, Paula England, and Liana Sayer. "When Does Gender Trump Money? Bargaining and Time in Household Work." *American Journal of Sociology* 109, no. 1 (2003): 185–214.

Bjarnason, Thoroddur, and Andrea Hjalmsdottir. "Egalitarian Attitudes towards the Division of Household Labor among Adolescents in Iceland." *Sex Roles* 59, no. 1–2 (2008): 49–60.

Blanchflower, David G., Andrew J. Oswald, and Sarah Stewart-Brown. "Is Psychological Well-Being Linked to the Consumption of Fruit and Vegetables?" *Social Indicators Research* 114, no. 3 (2013): 785–801.

Blumenthal, James A., Michael A. Babyak, Murali Doraiswamy, Lana Watkins, Benson M. Hoffman, Krista A. Barbour, Steve Herman et al. "Exercise and Pharmacotherapy in the Treatment of Major Depressive Disorder." *Psychosomatic Medicine* 69, no. 7 (2007): 587–596.

Bögels, Susan M., Annukka Lehtonen, and Kathleen Restifo. "Mindful Parenting in Mental Health Care." *Mindfulness* 1, no. 2 (2010): 107–120.

Booth, Alan, and James M. Dabbs. "Testosterone and Men's Marriages." *Social Forces* 72, no. 2 (1993): 463–477.

Booth, Cathryn L. "Child-Care Usage and Mother-Infant 'Quality Time.'" *Journal of Marriage and Family* 64, no. 1 (2002): 16–26.

Boven, Leaf Van. "Experientialism, Materialism, and the Pursuit of Happiness." *Review of General Psychology* 9, no. 2 (2005): 132–142.

Boven, Leaf Van, and Laurence Ashworth. "Looking Forward, Looking Back: Anticipation Is More Evocative than Retrospection." *Journal of Experimental Psychology: General* 136, no. 2 (2007): 289–300.

Boven, Leaf Van, and Thomas Gilovich. "To Do or to Have? That Is the Question." *Journal of Personality and Social Psychology* 85, no. 6 (2003): 1193–1202.

Bowles, Hannah Riley, Linda Babcock, and Lei Lai. "Social Incentives for Gender Differences in the Propensity to Initiate Negotiations: Sometimes It Does Hurt to Ask." *Organizational Behavior and Human Decision Processes* 103, no. 1 (2007): 84–103.

Bradley, Robert H., and Deborah Lowe Vandell. "Child Care and the Well-Being of Children." *Archives of Pediatrics & Adolescent Medicine* 161, no. 7 (2007): 669–676.

Brennan, Robert T., Rosalind Chait Barnett, and Karen C. Gareis. "When She Earns More than He Does: A Longitudinal Study of Dual-Earner Couples." *Journal of Marriage and Family* 63, no. 1 (2001): 168–182.

Brett, Jeanne M., and Linda K. Stroh. "Working 61 Plus Hours a Week: Why Do Managers Do It?" *Journal of Applied Psychology* 88, no. 1 (2003): 67–78.

Brickman, Philip, Dan Coates, and Ronnie Janoff-Bulman. "Lottery Winners and Accident Victims: Is Happiness Relative?" *Journal of Personality and Social Psychology* 36, no. 8 (1978): 917–927.

Brines, Julie. "Economic Dependency, Gender, and the Division of Labor at Home." *American Journal of Sociology* 100, no. 3 (1994): 652–688.

Brinig, Margaret F., and Douglas W. Allen. "'These Boots Are Made for Walking': Why Most Divorce Filers Are Women." *American Law and Economics Review* 2, no. 1 (2000): 126–169.

Brown, Ari. "Media Use by Children Younger than 2 Years." *Pediatrics* 128, no. 5 (2011): 1040–1045.

Brown, Kirk Warren, Tim Kasser, Richard M. Ryan, P. Alex Linley, and Kevin Orzech. "When What One Has Is Enough: Mindfulness, Financial Desire Discrepancy, and Subjective Well-Being." *Journal of Research in Personality* 43, no. 5 (2009): 727–736.

Brown, Kirk Warren, and Richard M. Ryan. "The Benefits of Being Present: Mindfulness and Its Role in Psychological Well-Being." *Journal of Personality and Social Psychology* 84, no. 4 (2003): 822–848.

Brown, Susan L. "Marriage and Child Well-Being: Research and Policy Perspectives." *Journal of Marriage and Family* 72, no. 5 (2010): 1059–1077.

Bryant, Fred B. "Savoring Beliefs Inventory (SBI): A Scale for Measuring Beliefs about Savouring." *Journal of Mental Health* 12, no. 2 (2003): 175–196.

Bucchianeri, Michaela M., and Alexandra F. Corning. "An Experimental Test of Women's Body Dissatisfaction Reduction through Self-Affirmation." *Applied Psychology: Health and Well-Being* 4, no. 2 (2012): 188–201.

Budig, Michelle J., and Paula England. "The Wage Penalty for Motherhood." *American Sociological Review* 66, no. 2 (2001): 204–225.

Buehler, Cheryl, and Marion O'Brien. "Mother's Part-Time Employment: Associations with Mother and Family." *Journal of Family Psychology* 25, no. 6 (2011): 895–906.

Bureau of Labor Statistics. "Employment Characteristics of Families–2012." Bureau of Labor Statistics: U.S. Department of Labor, April 26, 2013. http://www.bls.gov/news.release/pdf/famee.pdf.

Butler, Adam B., and Amie Skattebo. "What Is Acceptable for Women May Not Be for Men: The Effect of Family Conflicts with Work on Job-Performance Ratings." *Journal of Occupational and Organizational Psychology* 77, no. 4 (2004): 553–564.

Bygren, Magnus, and Ann-Zofie Duvander. "Parents' Workplace Situation and Fathers' Parental Leave Use." *Journal of Marriage and Family* 68, no. 2 (2006): 363–372.

Cabrera, Natasha J. "Positive Development of Minority Children." *Social Policy Report* 27, no. 2 (2013): 1–30.

Cabrera, Natasha J., Catherine S. Tamis-LeMonda, Robert H. Bradley, Sandra Hofferth, and Michael E. Lamb. "Fatherhood in the Twenty-First Century." *Child Development* 71, no. 1 (2000): 127–136.

Cahusac, Emma and Shireen, Kanji, "Giving Up: How Gendered Organizational Cultures Push Mothers Out." *Gender, Work & Organization* 21, no. 1 (2014): 57–70.

Callan, Victor J. "The Personal and Marital Adjustment of Mothers and of Voluntarily and Involuntarily Childless Wives." *Journal of Marriage and Family* 49, no. 4 (1987): 847–856.

Campbell, Don. *The Mozart Effect for Children: Awakening Your Child's Mind, Health, and Creativity with Music*. New York: William Morrow, 2000.

Campen, Cretien van, Alice H. de Boer, and Jurjen Ledema. "Are Informal Caregivers Less Happy than Noncaregivers? Happiness and the Intensity of Caregiving in Combination with Paid and Voluntary Work." *Scandinavian Journal of Caring Sciences* 27, no. 1 (2013): 44–50.

Caprariello, Peter A., and Harry T. Reis. "To Do, to Have, or to Share? Valuing Experiences over Material Possessions Depends on the Involvement of Others." *Journal of Personality and Social Psychology* 104, no. 2 (2013): 199–215.

Carlson, Erika N. "Overcoming the Barriers to Self-Knowledge: Mindfulness as a Path to Seeing Yourself as You Really Are." *Perspectives on Psychological Science* 8, no. 2 (2013): 173–186.

Carothers, Bobbi J., and Harry T. Reis. "Men and Women Are from Earth: Examining the Latent Structure of Gender." *Journal of Personality and Social Psychology* 104, no. 2 (2013): 385–407.

Carson, James W., Kimberly M. Carson, Karen M. Gil, and Donald H. Baucom. "Mindfulness-Based Relationship Enhancement." *Behavior Therapy* 35, no. 3 (2004): 471–494.

Carson, Shelley H., and Ellen J. Langer. "Mindfulness and Self-Acceptance." *Journal of Rational-Emotive & Cognitive-Behavior Therapy* 24, no. 1 (2006): 29–43.

Carter, Travis J., and Thomas Gilovich. "The Relative Relativity of Material and Experiential Purchases." *Journal of Personality and Social Psychology* 98, no. 1 (2010): 146–159.

Castro, Yessenia, and Kathryn H. Gordon. "A Review of Recent Research on Multiple Roles and Women's Mental Health." In *Women and Mental Disorders*, vol. 1, edited by Paula K. Lundberg-Love, Kevin L. Nadal, and Michele A. Paludi, 37–54. Santa Barbara, CA: Praeger, 2012.

Catalino, Lahnna I., and Barbara L. Fredrickson. "A Tuesday in the Life of a Flourisher: The Role of Positive Emotional Reactivity in Optimal Mental Health." *Emotion* 11, no. 4 (2011): 938–950.

Catalyst. "Catalyst Quick Take: Women in U.S. Management and Labor Force." New York: Catalyst, 2013. http://www.catalyst.org/knowledge/women-us-management-and-labor-force.

——. "Women CEOs of the Fortune 1000." Catalyst, December 10, 2013. http://www.catalyst.org/knowledge/women-ceos-fortune-1000.

Chancellor, Joseph, and Sonja Lyubomirsky. "Happiness and Thrift: When (Spending) Less Is (Hedonically) More." *Journal of Consumer Psychology* 21, no. 2 (2011): 131–138.

Chang, Young Eun. "The Relation between Mothers' Attitudes toward Maternal Employment and Social Competence of 36-Month-Olds: The Role of Maternal Psychological Well-Being and Sensitivity." *Journal of Child and Family Studies* 22, no. 7 (2013): 987–999.

Chapin, Harry. "The Cat's in the Cradle" on *Verities and Balderdash* album, released 1974, compact disc.

Chatterji, Pinka, and Sarah Markowitz. "Family Leave after Childbirth and the Mental Health of New Mothers." *Journal of Mental Health Policy and Economics* 15, no. 2 (2012): 61–76.

Chesley, Noelle. "Stay-at-Home Fathers and Breadwinning Mothers: Gender, Couple Dynamics, and Social Change." *Gender & Society* 25, no. 5 (2011): 642–664.

Child Care Aware of America. "Parents and the High Cost of Child Care 2013 Report." Child Care Aware of America (2013): 1–67.

Childstats.gov. "America's Children: Key National Indicators of Well-Being, 2013: Family Structure and Children's Living Arrangements." ChildStats.gov: Forum on Child and Family Statistics. http://www.childstats.gov/americaschildren/famsoc1.asp.

Chirkov, Valery I., and Richard M. Ryan. "Parent and Teacher Autonomy-Support in Russian and US Adolescents: Common Effects on Well-Being and Academic Motivation." *Journal of Cross-Cultural Psychology* 32, no. 5 (2001): 618–635.

Chua, Amy. "Why Chinese Mothers Are Superior." *Wall Street Journal,* January 8, 2011. ttp://online.wsj.com/news/articles/SB10001424052748704111504576059713528698754.

Chugani, Harry T., Michael E. Behen, Otto Muzik, Csaba Juhász, Ferenc Nagy, and Diane C. Chugani. "Local Brain Functional Activity Following Early Deprivation: A Study of Postinstitutionalized Romanian Orphans." *Neuroimage* 14, no. 6 (2001): 1290–1301.

Churchill, Annmarie Callahan, and Christopher G. Davis. "Realistic Orientation and the Transition to Motherhood." *Journal of Social and Clinical Psychology* 29, no. 1 (2010): 39–67.

Cicchetti, Dante, and Sheree L. Toth. "The Development of Depression in Children and Adolescents." *American Psychologist* 53, no. 2 (1998): 221–241.

Claffey, Sharon T., and Kristin D. Mickelson. "Division of Household Labor and Distress: The Role of Perceived Fairness for Employed Mothers." *Sex Roles* 60, no. 11–12 (2009): 819–831.

Clair, Robin Patric. "The Rhetoric of Dust: Toward a Rhetorical Theory of the Division of Domestic Labor." *Journal of Family Communication* 11, no. 1 (2011): 50–59.

Claxton, Amy, and Maureen Perry-Jenkins. "No Fun Anymore: Leisure and Marital Quality across the Transition to Parenthood." *Journal of Marriage and Family* 70, no. 1 (2008): 28–43.

Coffey, Kimberly A., Marilyn Hartman, and Barbara L. Fredrickson. "Deconstructing Mindfulness and Constructing Mental Health: Understanding Mindfulness and its Mechanisms of Action." *Mindfulness* 1, no. 4 (2010): 235–253.

Cohen, Jeanette A. Sawyer, and Randye J. Semple. "Mindful Parenting: A Call for Research." *Journal of Child and Family Studies* 19, no. 2 (2010): 145–151.

Cohen, Philip N. "How Can We Jump-Start the Struggle for Gender Equality?" *The Opinion Pages* (blog), *New York Times*, November 23, 2013. http://opinionator.blogs.nytimes.com/ 20.

Cohen, Sheldon, and Thomas A. Wills. "Stress, Social Support, and the Buffering Hypothesis." *Psychological Bulletin* 98, no. 2 (1985): 310–357.

Coltrane, Scott. "Household Labor and the Routine Production of Gender." *Social Problems* 36, no. 5 (1989): 473–489.

———. "Research on Household Labor: Modeling and Measuring the Social Embeddedness of Routine Family Work." *Journal of Marriage and the Family* 62, no. 4 (2000): 1208–1233.

Coltrane, Scott, and Michele Adams. "Work-Family Imagery and Gender Stereotypes: Television and the Reproduction of Difference." *Journal of Vocational Behavior* 50, no. 2 (1997): 323–347.

Coltrane, Scott, and Masako Ishii-Kuntz. "Men's Housework: A Life Course Perspective." *Journal of Marriage and the Family* 54, no. 1 (1992): 43–57.

Coltrane, Scott, Elizabeth C. Miller, Tracy DeHaan, and Lauren Stewart. "Fathers and the Flexibility Stigma." *Journal of Social Issues* 69, no. 2 (2013): 279–302.

Combs-Orme, Terri, Elizabeth E. Wilson, Daphne S. Cain, Timothy Page, and Laura D. Kirby. "Context-Based Parenting in Infancy: Background and Conceptual Issues." *Child and Adolescent Social Work Journal* 20, no. 6 (2003): 437–472.

Condry, John, and Sandra Condry. "Sex Differences: A Study of the Eye of the Beholder." *Child Development* 47, no. 3 (1976): 812–819.

Conley, Terri D., and Laura R. Ramsey. "Killing Us Softly? Investigating Portrayals of Women and Men in Contemporary Magazine Advertisements." *Psychology of Women Quarterly* 35, no. 3 (2011): 469–478.

Conrad, Rachel. "Desiring Relation: Mothers' and Children's Agency, Subjectivity, and Time." *Studies in Gender and Sexuality* 10, no. 1 (2009): 12–20.

Cooper, Marianne. "Being the 'Go-To Guy': Fatherhood, Masculinity, and the Organization of Work in Silicon Valley." *Qualitative Sociology* 23, no. 4 (2000): 379–405.

Cornelius, Nelarine, and Denise Skinner. "The Careers of Senior Men and Women: A Capabilities Theory Perspective." *British Journal of Management* 19, no. S1 (2008): S141–S149.

Correll, Shelley J., Stephen Benard, and In Paik. "Getting a Job: Is There a Motherhood Penalty?" *American Journal of Sociology* 112, no. 5 (2007): 1297–1339.

Cotter, David, and Paula England. "Moms and Jobs: Trends in Mothers' Employment and Which Mothers Stay Home." *Council on Contemporary Families*, May 10, 2007. http:// www.contemporaryfamilies.org/work-family/momsjobs.html.

Craig M. Bennett et al., "Neural Correlates of Interspecies Perspective Taking in the Post-Mortem Atlantic Salmon: An Argument for Multiple Comparisons Correction." *Neuroimage* 47, no. 1 (2009): S125.

Crawford, Mary E. *Transformations: Women, Gender, and Psychology.* New York: McGraw-Hill, 2006.

Crittenden, Ann. *The Price of Motherhood: Why the Most Important Job in the World Is Still the Least Valued.* New York: Metropolitan Books, 2001.

Crompton, Rosemary, and Clare Lyonette. "The New Gender Essentialism: Domestic and Family 'Choices' and Their Relation to Attitudes." *British Journal of Sociology* 56, no. 4 (2005): 601–620.

Csikszentmihalyi, Mihaly. "If We Are So Rich, Why Aren't We Happy?" *American Psychologist* 54, no. 10 (1999): 821–827.

Cuddy, Amy J. C., Susan T. Fiske, and Peter Glick. "When Professionals Become Mothers, Warmth Doesn't Cut the Ice." *Journal of Social Issues* 60, no. 4 (2004): 701–718.

Culbertson, Satoris S., Maura J. Mills, and Clive J. Fullager. "Work Engagement and Work-Family Facilitation: Making Homes Happier through Positive Affective Spillover." *Human Relations* 65, no. 9 (2012): 1155–1177.

Culture Rx. "Gap Inc. Case Study: Quality and Productivity through Trust: Gap Inc. Boosts Quality, Accountability and Productivity through the Adoption of Results-Only Work Environment (ROWE)." Culture Rx, LLC, 2012.

Cummings, Mark E., and Patrick T. Davies. "Maternal Depression and Child Development." *Journal of Child Psychology and Psychiatry* 35, no. 1 (1994): 73–122.

Danner, Deborah D., David A. Snowdon, and Wallace V. Friesen. "Positive Emotions in Early Life and Longevity: Findings from the Nun Study." *Journal of Personality and Social Psychology* 80, no. 5 (2001): 804–813.

Davies, Paul G., Steven J. Spencer, and Claude M. Steele. "Clearing the Air: Identity Safety Moderates the Effects of Stereotype Threat on Women's Leadership Aspirations." *Journal of Personality and Social Psychology* 88, no. 2 (2005): 276–287.

Day, Randal D., and Laura M. Padilla-Walker. "Mother and Father Connectedness and Involvement during Early Adolescence." *Journal of Family Psychology* 23, no. 6 (2009): 900–904.

DeGaetano, Gloria. *Parenting Well in a Media Age: Keeping Our Kids Human.* Fawnskin, CA: Personhood Press, 2004.

De Neve, Jan-Emmanuel, Nicholas A. Christakis, James H. Fowler, and Bruno S. Frey. "Genes, Economics, and Happiness." *Journal of Neuroscience, Psychology, and Economics* 5, no. 4 (2012): 193–211.

Deutsch, Francine M. "Undoing Gender." *Gender and Society* 21, no. 1 (2007): 106–127.

Deutsch, Francine M., Amy P. Kokot, and Katherine S. Binder. "College Women's Plans for Different Types of Egalitarian Marriages." *Journal of Marriage and Family* 69, no. 4 (2007): 916–929.

Devault, Marjorie L. "Comfort and Struggle: Emotion Work in Family Life." *ANNALS of the American Academy of Political and Social Science* 561, no. 1 (1999): 52–63.

DeVoe, Sanford E., and Julian House. "Time, Money, and Happiness: How Does Putting a Price on Time Affect Our Ability to Smell the Roses?" *Journal of Experimental Social Psychology* 48, no. 2 (2012): 466–474.

Dew, Jeffrey, and W. Bradford Wilcox. "If Momma Ain't Happy: Explaining Declines in Marital Satisfaction among New Mothers." *Journal of Marriage and Family* 73, no. 1 (2011): 1–12.

De Wolff, Marianne S., and Marinus H. Ijzendoorn. "Sensitivity and Attachment: A Meta-Analysis on Parental Antecedents of Infant Attachment." *Child Development* 68, no. 4 (1997): 571–591.

Dey, Judy Goldberg, and Catherine Hill. "Behind the Pay Gap." American Association of University Women (AAUW). Washington, DC: American Association of University Women Educational Foundation, 2007.

Diener, Ed. "Subjective Well-Being: The Science of Happiness and a Proposal for a National Index." *American Psychologist* 55, no. 1 (2000): 34–43.

Diener, Ed, and Robert Biswas-Diener. "Will Money Increase Subjective Well-Being?" *Social Indicators Research* 57, no. 2 (2002): 119–169.

Diener, Ed, Weiting Ng, James Harter, and Raksha Arora. "Wealth and Happiness across the World: Material Prosperity Predicts Life Evaluation, Whereas Psychosocial Prosperity Predicts Positive Feeling." *Journal of Personality and Social Psychology* 99, no. 1 (2010): 52–61.

Diener, Ed, Carol Nickerson, Richard E. Lucas, and Ed Sandvik. "Dispositional Affect and Job Outcomes." *Social Indicators Research* 59, no. 3 (2002): 229–259.

Diener, Ed, and Shigehiro Oishi. "Money and Happiness: Income and Subjective Well-Being across Nations." In *Culture and Subjective Well-Being,* edited by Ed Diener and Eunkook M. Suh, 185–218. Cambridge, MA: MIT Press, 2000.

Diener, Ed, and Martin E. P. Seligman. "Beyond Money toward an Economy of Well-Being." *Psychological Science in the Public Interest* 5, no. 1 (2004): 1–31.

——. "Very Happy People." *Psychological Science* 13, no. 1 (2002): 81–84.

Diener, Ed, Eunkook M. Suh, Richard E. Lucas, and Heidi L. Smith. "Subjective Well-Being: Three Decades of Progress." *Psychological Bulletin* 125, no. 2 (1999): 276–302.

Dierendonck, Dirk van. "Spirituality as an Essential Determinant for the Good Life, Its Importance Relative to Self-Determinant Psychological Needs." *Journal of Happiness Studies* 13, no. 4 (2012): 685–700.

Division of Temporary Disability Insurance. "Your Guide to Family Leave Insurance in New Jersey." Division of Temporary Disability Insurance. http://lwd.state.nj.us/labor/forms_pdfs/tdi/WPR–119.pdf13/11/23/how-can-we-jump-start-the-struggle-for-gender-equality.

Dobson, Marnie, and Peter L. Schnall. "From Stress to Distress: The Impact of Work on Mental Health." In *Unhealthy Work: Causes, Consequences, Cures*, edited by Peter L. Schnall, Marnie Dobson, and Ellen Rosskam, 113–132. Critical Approaches in the Health Social Sciences Series, edited by Ray H. Elling. Amityville, NY: Baywood, 2009.

Dodson, Lisa. "Stereotyping Low-Wage Mothers Who Have Work and Family Conflicts." *Journal of Social Issues* 69, no. 2 (2013): 257–278.

Dorment, Richard. "Why Men Still Can't Have It All." *Esquire,* May 28, 2013. http://www.esquire.com/features/why-men-still-cant-have-it-all-0613?click=pp.

Duncan, Larissa G., J. Douglas Coatsworth, and Mark T. Greenberg. "A Model of Mindful Parenting: Implications for Parent-Child Relationships and Prevention Research." *Clinical Child and Family Psychology Review* 12, no. 3 (2009): 255–270.

Dunn, Elizabeth W., Lara B. Aknin, and Michael I. Norton. "Spending Money on Others Promotes Happiness." *Science* 319, no. 5870 (2008): 1687–1688.

Dunn, Elizabeth W., Daniel T. Gilbert, and Timothy D. Wilson. "If Money Doesn't Make You Happy, Then You Probably Aren't Spending It Right." *Journal of Consumer Psychology* 21, no. 2 (2011): 115–125.

Eagly, Alice H., and Linda L. Carli. *Through the Labyrinth.* Boston: Harvard Business School, 2007.

Eagly, Alice H., and Maureen Crowley. "Gender and Helping Behavior: A Meta-Analytic Review of the Social Psychological Literature." *Psychological Bulletin* 100, no. 3 (1986): 283–308.

Eagly, Alice H., Mary C. Johannesen-Schmidt, and Marloes L. van Engen. "Transformational, Transactional, and Laissez-Faire Leadership Styles: A Meta-Analysis Comparing Women and Men." *Psychological Bulletin* 129, no. 4 (2003): 569–591.

Eagly, Alice H., and Blair T. Johnson. "Gender and Leadership Style: A Meta-Analysis." *Psychological Bulletin* 108, no. 2 (1990): 233–256.

Eagly, Alice H., Mona G. Makhijani, and Bruce G. Klonsky. "Gender and the Evaluation of Leaders: A Meta-Analysis." *Psychological Bulletin* 111, no. 1 (1992): 3–22.

Eagly, Alice H., and Wendy Wood. "The Origins of Sex Differences in Human Behavior: Evolved Dispositions versus Social Roles." *American Psychologist* 54, no. 6 (1999): 408–423.

Easterlin, Richard A. "Does Economic Growth Improve the Human Lot? Some Empirical Evidence." *Nations and Households in Economic Growth* 89 (1974): 89–125.

Easterlin, Richard, and Onnicha Sawangfa. "Happiness and Economic Growth: Does the Cross Section Predict Time Trends? Evidence from Developing Countries." IZA Discussion Papers, No. 4000, Institute for the Study of Labor (IZA), Bonn, Germany, 2009, 1–44.

Eaton, Susan C. "If You Can Use Them: Flexibility Policies, Organizational Commitment, and Perceived Performance." *Industrial Relations: A Journal of Economy and Society* 42, no. 2 (2003): 145–167.

Edge Certified. "Closing the Gap: Competitive Advantage from Closing the Corporate Gender Gap." EDGE Certified. http://www.edge-cert.org/CMS/de-CH/Closing%20the%20gap/Competitive%20Advantage.aspx.

Elgar, Frank J., Rosemary S. L. Mills, Patrick J. McGrath, Daniel A. Waschbusch, and Douglas A. Brownridge. "Maternal and Paternal Depressive Symptoms and Child Maladjustment: The Mediating Role of Parental Behavior." *Journal of Abnormal Child Psychology* 35, no. 6 (2007): 943–955.

Eliot, Lise. *Pink Brain Blue Brain: How Small Differences Grow into Troublesome Gaps—And What We Can Do about It*. New York: Houghton Mifflin Harcourt, 2009.

Elvin-Nowak, Ylva. "The Meaning of Guilt: A Phenomenological Description of Employed Mothers' Experiences of Guilt." *Scandinavian Journal of Psychology* 40, no. 1 (1999): 73–83.

Emmons, Robert A., and Michael E. McCullough. "Counting Blessings versus Burdens: An Experimental Investigation of Gratitude and Subjective Well-Being in Daily Life." *Journal of Personality and Social Psychology* 84, no. 2 (2003): 377–389.

England, Paula. "The Gender Revolution: Uneven and Stalled." *Gender & Society* 24, no. 2 (2010): 149–166.

England, Paula, Paul Allison, and Yuxiao Wu. "Does Bad Pay Cause Occupations to Feminize, Does Feminization Reduce Pay, and How Can We Tell with Longitudinal Data?" *Social Science Research* 36, no. 3 (2007): 1237–1256.

England, Paula, Janet Gornick, and Emily Fitzgibbons Shafer. "Women's Employment, Education, and the Gender Gap in 17 Countries." *Monthly Labor Review* 135 (2012): 3–12.

Enright, Robert D. *Forgiveness Is a Choice: A Step-By-Step Process for Resolving Anger and Restoring Hope*. Washington, DC: American Psychological Association, 2001.

Erchull, Mindy J., Miriam Liss, Sarah J. Axelson, Samantha E. Staebell, and Sabrina F. Askari. "Well . . . She Wants It More: Perceptions of Social Norms about Desires for Marriage and Children and Anticipated Chore Participation." *Psychology of Women Quarterly* 34, no. 2 (2010): 253–260.

Etzioni, Amitai. "Does Having Kids Make You Less Happy?" *CNN Opinion*, August 16, 2012. http://www.cnn.com/2012/07/30/opinion/etzioni-children.

European Union Council Directive 93/104/EC. "Concerning Certain Aspects of the Organization of Working Time." *Official Journal of the European Union* L 307, 13.12.1993.

Evenhouse, Eirik, and Siobhan Reilly. "Improved Estimates of the Benefits of Breastfeeding Using Sibling Comparisons to Reduce Selection Bias." *Health Services Research* 40, no. 6, pt.1 (2005): 1781–1802.

Evenson, Ranae J., and Robin W. Simon. "Clarifying the Relationship between Parenthood and Depression." *Journal of Health and Social Behavior* 46, no. 4 (2005): 341–358.

Fahlquist, Jessica Nihlén, and Sabine Roeser. "Ethical Problems with Information on Infant Feeding in Developed Countries." *Public Health Ethics* 4, no. 2 (2011): 192–202.

Fan, Xitao, and Michael Chen. "Parental Involvement and Students' Academic Achievement: A Meta-Analysis." *Educational Psychology Review* 13, no. 1 (2001): 1–22.

Farb, Amy Feldman, and Jennifer L. Matjasko. "Recent Advances in Research on School-Based Extracurricular Activities and Adolescent Development." *Developmental Review* 32, no. 1 (2012): 1–48.

Featherstone, Liza. *Selling Women Short: The Landmark Battle for Workers' Rights at Wal-Mart*. New York: Basic Books, 2004.

Feiler, Bruce. "Overscheduled Children: How Big a Problem?" *New York Times*, October 11, 2013. http://www.nytimes.com/2013/10/13/fashion/over-scheduled-children-how-big-a-problem.html?pagewanted=1&_r=2&adxnnlx=1381690935-sXqxj/nHxywe2wqj0eOHqQ.

Fergusson, David M., Joseph M. Boden, and L. John Horwood. "Exposure to Single Parent-hood in Childhood and Later Mental Health, Educational, Economic, and Criminal Behavior Outcomes." *Archives of General Psychiatry* 64, no. 9 (2007): 1089–1095.

Ferree, Myra Marx. "The Gender Division of Labor in Two-Earner Marriages: Dimensions of Variability and Change." *Journal of Family Issues* 12, no. 2 (1991): 158–180.

Festinger, Leon. "A Theory of Social Comparison Processes." *Human Relations* 7, no. 2 (1954): 117–140.

Field, Tiffany, Maria Hernandez-Reif, and Larissa Feijo. "Breastfeeding in Depressed Mother-Infant Dyads." *Early Child Development and Care* 172, no. 6 (2002): 539–545.

Fine, Cordelia. *Delusions of Gender: How Our Minds, Society, and Neurosexism Create Difference of Gender.* New York: W.W. Norton, 2010.

Fingerman, Karen L., Yen-Pi Cheng, Eric D. Wesselmann, Steven Zarit, Frank Furstenberg, and Kira S. Birditt. "Helicopter Parents and Landing Pad Kids: Intense Parental Support of Grown Children." *Journal of Marriage and Family* 74, no. 4 (2012): 880–896.

Fischer, Jessica, and Veanne N. Anderson. "Gender Role Attitudes and Characteristics of Stay-at-Home and Employed Fathers." *Psychology of Men & Masculinity* 13, no. 1 (2012): 16–31.

Fisher, Max. "Map: How the World's Countries Compare on Income Inequality (the U.S. Ranks below Nigeria)." *Washington Post,* September 27, 2013. http://www.washingtonpost.com/blogs/worldviews/wp/2013/09/27/map-how-the-worlds-coun-tries-compare-on-income-inequality-the-u-s-ranks-below-nigeria.

Fitzsimons, Gráinne M., and Eli J. Finkel. "Outsourcing Self-Regulation." *Psychological Science* 22, no. 3 (2011): 369–375.

Fleming, Alison S., Carl Corter, Joy Stallings, and Meir Steiner. "Testosterone and Prolactin Are Associated with Emotional Responses to Infant Cries in New Fathers." *Hormones and Behavior* 42, no. 4 (2002): 399–413.

Folmer, Kaitlyn, Natasha Singh, and Suzan Clarke. "Amish School Shooter's Widow, Marie Monville, Speaks Out." ABC News, September 30, 2013. http://abcnews.go.com/US/am-ish-school-shooters-widow-marie-monville-remembers-tragedy/story?id=20417790&page=3.

Forgiveness Intervention Manuals. VCU Department of Psychology Faculty Page, updated August 2, 2012. http://www.people.vcu.edu/~eworth.

Forste, Renata, and Kiira Fox. "Search Types." *Journal of Comparative Family Studies* 43 (2012): 613–631.

Fredricks, Jennifer A. "Extracurricular Participation and Academic Outcomes: Testing the Over-Scheduling Hypothesis." *Journal of Youth and Adolescence* 41, no. 3 (2012): 295–306.

Fredricks, Jennifer A., and Jacquelynne S. Eccles. "Extracurricular Involvement and Adolescent Adjustment: Impact of Duration, Number of Activities, and Breadth of Participation." *Applied Developmental Science* 10, no. 3 (2006): 132–146.

Fredrickson, Barbara L. "Positive Emotions Broaden and Build." In *Advances in Experimental Social Psychology*, vol. 47, edited by Patricia Devine and Ashby Plant, 1–53. San Diego: Academic Press, 2013.

———. "What Good Are Positive Emotions?" *Review of General Psychology* 2, no. 3 (1998): 300–319.

Fredrickson, Barbara L., and Thomas Joiner. "Positive Emotions Trigger Upward Spirals toward Emotional Well-Being." *Psychological Science* 13, no. 2 (2002): 172–175.

Fredrickson, Barbara L., and Robert W. Levenson. "Positive Emotions Speed Recovery from the Cardiovascular Sequelae of Negative Emotions." *Cognition & Emotion* 12, no. 2 (1998): 191–220.

Fredrickson, Barbara L., and Marcial F. Losada. "Positive Affect and the Complex Dynamics of Human Flourishing." *American Psychologist* 60, no. 7 (2005): 678–686.

Fredrickson, Barbara L., Roberta A. Mancuso, Christine Branigan, and Michele M. Tugade. "The Undoing Effect of Positive Emotions." *Motivation and Emotion* 24, no. 4 (2000): 237–258.

Friedman, H. S. "Personality and Longevity: Paradoxes." In *The Paradoxes of Longevity*, edited by Jean-Marie Robine, Bernard Forette, Claudio Franceschi, and Michel Allard, 115–122. Berlin, Germany: Springer, 1999.

Friedman, Sarah L., and D. Ellen Boyle. "Attachment in US Children Experiencing Nonmaternal Care in the Early 1990s." *Attachment and Human Development* 10, no. 3 (2008): 225–261.

Friedman, Stewart D., and Jeffrey H. Greenhaus. *Work and Family–Allies or Enemies?: What Happens When Business Professionals Confront Life Choices.* New York: Oxford University Press, 2000.

Frisco, Michelle L., and Kristi Williams. "Perceived Housework Equity, Marital Happiness, and Divorce in Dual-Earner Households." *Journal of Family Issues* 24, no. 1 (2003): 51–73.

Froh, Jeffrey J., Robert A. Emmons, Noel A. Card, Giacomo Bono, and Jennifer A. Wilson. "Gratitude and the Reduced Costs of Materialism in Adolescents." *Journal of Happiness Studies* 12, no. 2 (2011): 289–302.

Gable, Shelly L., and Harry T. Reis. "Good News! Capitalizing on Positive Events in an Interpersonal Context." In *Advances in Experimental Social Psychology,* edited by Mark P. Zanna, vol. 42, 195–257. San Diego: Academic Press, 2010.

Gager, Constance T. "What's Fair Is Fair? Role of Justice in Family Labor Allocation Decisions." *Marriage and Family Review* 44, no. 4 (2008): 511–545.

Gager, Constance T., and Scott T. Yabiku. "Who Has the Time? The Relationship between Household Labor Time and Sexual Frequency." *Journal of Family Issues* 31, no. 2 (2010): 135–163.

Gajendran, Ravi S., and David A. Harrison. "The Good, the Bad, and the Unknown about Telecommuting: Meta-Analysis of Psychological Mediators and Individual Consequences." *Journal of Applied Psychology* 92, no. 6 (2007): 1524–1541.

Garde, Anne Helene, Karen Albertsen, Roger Persson, Åse Marie Hansen, and Reiner Rugulies. "Bi-Directional Associations between Psychological Arousal, Cortisol, and Sleep." *Behavioral Sleep Medicine* 10, no. 1 (2012): 28–40.

Gareis, Karen C., Rosalind Chait Barnett, Karen A. Ertel, and Lisa F. Berkman. "Work-Family Enrichment and Conflict: Additive Effects, Buffering, or Balance?" *Journal of Marriage and Family* 71, no. 3 (2009): 696–707.

Gaunt, Ruth. "Biological Essentialism, Gender Ideologies, and Role Attitudes: What Determines Parents' Involvement in Child Care." *Sex Roles* 55, no. 7–8 (2006): 523–533.

——. "Breadwinning Moms, Caregiving Dads: Double Standard in Social Judgments of Gender Norm Violators." *Journal of Family Issues* 34, no. 1 (2013): 3–24.

Gautam, Tanvi. "Real Men Don't Need Work Life Balance." *Forbes*, May 23, 2012. http://www.forbes.com/sites/forbeswomanfiles/2012/05/23/real-men-dont-need-work-life-balance/2.

Geronimus, Arline T., Margaret Hicken, Danya Keene, and John Bound. "'Weathering' and Age Patterns of Allostatic Load Scores among Blacks and Whites in the United States." *American Journal of Public Health* 96, no. 5 (2006): 826–833.

Gerson, Kathleen. *The Unfinished Revolution: How a New Generation Is Reshaping Family, Work, and Gender in America.* New York: Oxford University Press, 2010.

Gettler, Lee T., Thomas W. McDade, Alan B. Feranil, and Christopher W. Kuzawa. "Longitudinal Evidence That Fatherhood Decreases Testosterone in Human Males." *Proceedings of the National Academy of Sciences* 108, no. 39 (2011): 16194–16199.

Glass, Christy, and Eva Fodor. "Public Maternalism Goes to Market: Recruitment, Hiring, and Promotion in Postsocialist Hungary." *Gender and Society* 25, no. 1 (2011): 5–26.

Glass, Jennifer. "Blessing or Curse? Work-family Policies and Mother's Wage Growth Over Time." *Work and Occupations* 31, no. 3 (2004): 367–394.

Glauber, Rebecca. "Women's Work and Working Conditions: Are Mothers Compensated for Lost Wages?" *Work and Occupations* 39, no. 2 (2012): 115–138.

Glynn, Keva, Heather Maclean, Tonia Forte, and Marsha Cohen. "The Association between Role Overload and Women's Mental Health." *Journal of Women's Health* 18, no. 2 (2009): 217–223.

Goldberg, Abbie E., JuliAnna Z. Smith, and Maureen Perry-Jenkins. "The Division of Labor in Lesbian, Gay, and Heterosexual New Adoptive Parents." *Journal of Marriage and Family* 74, no. 4 (2012): 812–828.

Goldberg, Wendy A., JoAnn Prause, Rachel Lucas-Thompson, and Amy Himsel. "Maternal Employment and Children's Achievement in Context: A Meta-Analysis of Four Decades of Research." *Psychological Bulletin* 134, no. 1 (2008): 77–108.

Golden, Lonnie. "The Effects of Working Time on Productivity and Firm Performance: A Research Synthesis Paper." *Conditions of Work and Employment Series No. 33.* Geneva, Switzerland: International Labor Organization, 2012, 1–34.

Golden, Timothy D., John F. Veiga, and Zeki Simsek. "Telecommuting's Differential Impact on Work-Family Conflict: Is There No Place like Home?" *Journal of Applied Psychology* 91, no. 6 (2006): 1340–1350.

Gormley, William T., Jr. "Oklahoma's Universal Preschool Program: Better than Ok." *Georgetown Public Policy Review*, May 6, 2013. http://gppreview.com/2013/05/06/oklahomas-universal-preschool-program-better-than-ok.

Gottlieb, Anthony. "It Ain't Necessarily So: How Much Do Evolutionary Stories Reveal about the Mind?" *New Yorker*, September 17, 2012. http://www.newyorker.com/arts/critics/books/2012/09/17/120917crbo_books_gottlieb.

Graham, Carol, Andrew Eggers, and Sandip Sukhtankar. "Does Happiness Pay?: An Exploration Based on Panel Data from Russia." *Journal of Economic Behavior & Organization* 55, no. 3 (2004): 319–342.

Grant, Adam M., and Barry Schwartz. "Too Much of a Good Thing: The Challenge and Opportunity of the Inverted U." *Perspectives on Psychological Science* 6, no. 1 (2011): 61–76.

Grawitch, Matthew J., Melanie Gottschalk, and David C. Munz. "The Path to a Healthy Workplace: A Critical Review Linking Healthy Workplace Practices, Employee Well-Being, and Organizational Improvements." *Consulting Psychology Journal: Practice and Research* 58, no. 3 (2006): 129–147.

Gray, John. *Men Are from Mars, Women Are from Venus: The Classic Guide to Understanding the Opposite Sex.* New York: J. G. Productions, 2012.

Gray, Peter. "The Play Deficit." *AEON Magazine*, September 18, 2013. http://www.aeonmagazine.com/being-human/children-today-are-suffering-a-severe-deficit-of-play.

Green, Katherine E., and Melissa M. Groves. "Attachment Parenting: An Exploration of Demographics and Practices." *Early Child Development and Care* 178, no. 5 (2008): 513–525.

Greenhaus, Jeffrey H., and Nicholas J. Beutell. "Sources of Conflict between Work and Family Roles." *Academy of Management Review* 10, no. 2 (1985): 76–88.

Greenhaus, Jeffrey H., and Gary N. Powell. "When Work and Family are Allies: A Theory of Work-Family Enrichment." *Academy of Management Review* 31, no. 1 (2006): 72–92.

Greenough, William T. "Experiential Modification of the Developing Brain: The Environment and the Organism's Interactions with It May Play an Important Part in the Formation of Synapses between Nerve Cells in the Brain." *American Scientist* 63, no. 1 (1975): 37–46.

Greenstein, Theodore N. "Economic Dependence, Gender, and the Division of Labor in the Home: A Replication and Extension." *Journal of Marriage and Family* 62, no. 2 (2000): 322–335.

Groer, Maureen Wimberly, Mitzi Wilkinson Davis, and Jean Hemphill. "Postpartum Stress: Current Concepts and the Possible Protective Role of Breastfeeding." *Journal of Obstetric, Gynecologic, & Neonatal Nursing* 31, no. 4 (2002): 411–417.

Grolnick, Wendy, Ann Frodi, and Lisa Bridges. "Maternal Control Style and the Mastery Motivation of One-Year-Olds." *Infant Mental Health Journal* 5, no. 2 (1984): 72–82.

Grolnick, Wendy S., Suzanne T. Gurland, Wendy DeCourcey, and Karen Jacob. "Antecedents and Consequences of Mothers' Autonomy Support: An Experimental Investigation." *Developmental Psychology* 38, no. 1 (2002): 143–155.

Grolnick, Wendy S., Carrie E. Price, Krista L. Beiswenger, and Christine C. Sauck. "Evaluative Pressure in Mothers: Effects of Situation, Maternal, and Child Characteristics on Autonomy Supportive versus Controlling Behavior." *Developmental Psychology* 43, no. 4 (2007): 991–1002.

Grolnick, Wendy S., and Richard M. Ryan. "Parent Styles Associated with Children's Self-Regulation and Competence in School." *Journal of Educational Psychology* 81, no. 2 (1989): 143–154.

Grossman, Frances K. "Affiliation and Autonomy in the Transition to Parenthood." *Family Relations* 36, no. 3 (1987): 263–269.

Grzywacz, Joseph G., and Brenda L. Bass. "Work, Family, and Mental Health: Testing Different Models of Work-Family Fit." *Journal of Marriage and Family* 65, no. 1 (2003): 248–262.

Guendouzi, Jackie. "'The Guilt Thing': Balancing Domestic and Professional Roles." *Journal of Marriage and Family* 68, no. 4 (2006): 901–909.

——. "'I Feel Quite Organized This Morning': How Mothering Is Achieved through Talk." *Sexualities, Evolution & Gender* 7, no. 1 (2005): 17–35.

Gulas, Charles S., and Kim McKeage. "Extending Social Comparison: An Examination of the Unintended Consequences of Idealized Advertising Imagery." *Journal of Advertising* 29, no. 2 (2000): 17–28.

Gurland, Suzanne T., and Wendy S. Grolnick. "Perceived Threat, Controlling Parenting, and Children's Achievement Orientations." *Motivation and Emotion* 29, no. 2 (2005): 103–121.

Gustafsson, Erik, Florence Levréro, David Reby, and Nicholas Mathevon. "Fathers Are Just as Good as Mothers at Recognizing the Cries of Their Baby." *Nature Communications* 4 (2013): 1698.

Gustafsson, Siv, and Frank Stafford. "Child Care Subsidies and Labor Supply in Sweden." *Journal of Human Resources* 27, no. 1 (1992): 204–230.

Haas, Linda, and C. Philip Hwang. "The Impact of Taking Parental Leave on Fathers' Participation in Childcare and Relationships with Children: Lessons from Sweden." *Community, Work & Family* 11, no. 1 (2008): 85–104.

——. "Is Fatherhood Becoming More Visible at Work? Trends in Corporate Support for Fathers Taking Parental Leave in Sweden." *Fathering: A Journal of Theory, Research, and Practice about Men as Fathers* 7, no. 3 (2009): 303–321.

Hackel, Lisa S., and Diane N. Ruble. "Changes in the Marital Relationship after the First Baby Is Born: Predicting the Impact of Expectancy Disconfirmation." *Journal of Personality and Social Psychology* 62, no. 6 (1992): 944–957.

Hagerty, Michael R. "Social Comparisons of Income in One's Community: Evidence from National Surveys of Income and Happiness." *Journal of Personality and Social Psychology* 78, no. 4 (2000): 764–771.

Hammer, Leslie B., Jennifer C. Cullen, Margaret B. Neal, Robert R. Sinclair, and Margarita V. Shafiro. "The Longitudinal Effects of Work-Family Conflict and Positive Spillover on Depressive Symptoms among Dual-Earner Couples." *Journal of Occupational Health Psychology* 10, no. 2 (2005): 138–154.

Han, Wen-Jui, Jane Waldfogel, and Jeanne Brooks-Gunn. "The Effects of Early Maternal Employment on Later Cognitive and Behavioral Outcomes." *Journal of Marriage and Family* 63, no. 2 (2001): 336–354.

Hansen, Marianne Nordli. "The Vicious Circle of the Welfare State? Women's Labor Market Situation in Norway and Great Britain." *Comparative Social Research* 15 (1995): 1–34.

Hansen, Thomas, Britt Slagsvold, and Torbjørn Moum. "Childlessness and Psychological Well-Being in Midlife and Old Age: An Examination of Parental Status Effects across a Range of Outcomes." *Social Indicators Research* 94, no. 2 (2009): 343–362.

Hanson, Shirley M. H., "Healthy Single Parent Families." *Family Relations* 35, no. 1 (1986): 125–132.

Harlow, Harry Frederick. "The Nature of Love." *American Psychologist* 13 (1958): 673–685.

Harper, Lisa Catherine. "The Crazy, Intense Schedule of Competitive Youth Soccer? Bring It On." *Motherlode: Adventures in Parenting* (blog), *New York Times*, October 7, 2013. http://parenting.blogs.nytimes.com/2013/10/07/the-crazy-intense-schedule-of-competitive-youth-soccer-bring-it-on/?hp&_r=0.

Harrington, Brad, Fred Van Deusen, and Beth Humberd. *The New Dad: Caring, Committed and Conflicted.* Chestnut Hill, MA: Boston College Center for Work & Family, 2011, 1–41.

Harris, Alex H. S., Frederic Luskin, Sonya B. Norman, Sam Standard, Jennifer Bruning, Stephanie Evans, and Carl E. Thoresen. "Effects of a Group Forgiveness Intervention on Forgiveness, Perceived Stress, and Trait-Anger." *Journal of Clinical Psychology* 62, no. 6 (2006): 715–733.

Hart, Betty, and Todd R. Risley. *Meaningful Differences in the Everyday Experience of Young American Children.* Baltimore: Paul H. Brookes, 1995.

Harwood, Kate, Neil McLean, and Kevin Durkin. "First-Time Mothers' Expectations of Parenthood: What Happens When Optimistic Expectations Are Not Matched by Later Experiences?" *Developmental Psychology* 43, no. 1 (2007): 1–12.

Hauck, Yvonne, Wendy A. Hall, and Christine Jones. "Prevalence, Self-Efficacy and Perceptions of Conflicting Advice and Self-Management: Effects of a Breastfeeding Journal." *Journal of Advanced Nursing* 57, no. 3 (2007): 306–317.

Hays, Sharon. *The Cultural Contradictions of Motherhood.* New Haven, CT: Yale University Press, 1996.

Healy, Michelle. "Buying Breast Milk Online? It May Be Contaminated." *USA Today*, October 21, 2013. http://www.usatoday.com/story/news/nation/2013/10/21/breast-milk-bacteria/3002973.

Hedges, Kristi. "R.I.P. Work-Life Balance." *ForbesWoman* (blog), *Forbes*, July 11, 2013. http://www.forbes.com/sites/work-in-progress/2013/07/11/r-i-p-work-life-balance.

Hegewisch, Ariane, and Janet C. Gornick. "The Impact of Work-Family Policies on Women's Employment: A Review of Research from OECD Countries." *Community, Work & Family* 14, no. 2 (2011): 119–38.

Henwood, Karen, and Joanne Procter. "The 'Good Father:' Reading Men's Accounts of Paternal Involvement during the Transition to First-Time Fatherhood." *British Journal of Social Psychology* 42, no. 3 (2003): 337–355.

Hill, Jeffrey E., Jenet Jacob Erickson, Erin K. Holmes, and Maria Ferris. "Workplace Flexibility, Work Hours, and Work-Life Conflict: Finding an Extra Day or Two." *Journal of Family Psychology* 24, no. 3 (2010): 349–358.

Hill, Jeffrey E., Alan J. Hawkins, Maria Ferris, and Michelle Weitzman. "Finding an Extra Day a Week: The Positive Influence of Perceived Job Flexibility on Work and Family Life Balance." *Family Relations* 50, no. 1 (2001): 49–58.

Hill, Jeffrey E., Alan J. Hawkins, and Brent C. Miller. "Work and Family in the Virtual Office: Perceived Influences of Mobile Telework." *Family Relations* 45, no. 3 (1996): 293–301.

Hill, Sarah E., Danielle J. DelPriore, and Phillip W. Vaughan. "The Cognitive Consequences of Envy: Attention, Memory, and Self-Regulatory Depletion." *Journal of Personality and Social Psychology* 101, no. 4 (2011): 653–666.

Hochschild, Arlie, and Anne Machung. *The Second Shift: Working Parents and the Revolution at Home.* New York: Penguin, 1989.

Hoddinott, Pat, and Roisin Pill. "A Qualitative Study of Women's Views about How Health Professionals Communicate about Infant Feeding." *Health Expectations* 3, no. 4 (2000): 224–233.

Hodges, Melissa J., and Michelle J. Budig. "Who Gets the Daddy Bonus?: Organizational Hegemonic Masculinity and the Impact of Fatherhood on Earnings." *Gender and Society* 24, no. 6 (2010): 717–745.

Hofer, Barbara K. "The Electronic Tether: Parental Regulation, Self-Regulation, and the Role of Technology in College Transitions." *Journal of the First-Year Experience & Students in Transition* 20, no. 2 (2008): 9–24.

Hoffnung, Michele, and Michelle A. Williams, "Balancing Act: Career and Family during College Educated Women's 30s." *Sex Roles* 68, no. 5–6 (2012): 321–334.

Hofmann, Stefan G., Alice T. Sawyer, Ashley A. Witt, and Diana Oh. "The Effect of Mindfulness-Based Therapy on Anxiety and Depression: A Meta-Analytic Review." *Journal of Consulting and Clinical Psychology* 78, no. 2 (2010): 169–183.

Hogue, Mary, Cathy L. Z. DuBois, and Lee Fox-Cardamone. "Gender Differences in Pay Expectations: The Roles of Job Intention and Self-View." *Psychology of Women Quarterly* 34, no. 2 (2010): 215–227.

Holt-Lunstad, Julianne, and Timothy B. Smith. "Social Relationships and Mortality." *Social and Personality Psychology Compass* 6, no. 1 (2012): 41–53.

Holy Bible, 1 Tim. 6:10 (New International Version).

Hook, Jennifer L., and Satvika Chalasani. "Gendered Expectations? Reconsidering Single Fathers' Child-Care Time." *Journal of Marriage and Family* 70, no. 4 (2008): 978–990.

Hrdy, Sarah Blaffer. *Mother Nature: A History of Mothers, Infants, and Natural Selection.* New York: Ballantine Books, 1999.

Hsee, Christopher K., Jiao Zhang, Cindy F. Cai, and Shirley Zhang. "Overearning." *Psychological Science* 24, no. 6 (2013): 852–859.

Hunziker, Urs A., and Ronald G. Barr. "Increased Carrying Reduces Infant Crying: A Randomized Controlled Trial." *Pediatrics* 77, no. 5 (1986): 641–648.

Hussain, Murad S., and Ellen Langer. "A Cost of Pretending." *Journal of Adult Development* 10, no. 4 (2003): 261–270.

Huston, T. L., and R. D. Ashmore. "Women and Men in Personal Relationships." In *The Social Psychology of Female-Male Relations,* edited by Richard D. Ashmore and Frances K. Del Boca. New York: Academic Press, 1986.

Hyde, Janet Shibley. "The Gender Similarities Hypothesis." *American Psychologist* 60, no. 6 (2005): 581–592.

——. "New Directions in the Study of Gender Similarities and Differences." *Current Directions in Psychological Science* 16, no. 5 (2007): 259–263.

Hyde, Janet Shibley, Marjorie H. Klein, Marilyn J. Essex, and Roseanne Clark. "Maternity Leave and Women's Mental Health." *Psychology of Women Quarterly* 19, no. 2 (1995): 257–285.

Ilardi, Barbara C., Dean Leone, Tim Kasser, and Richard M. Ryan. "Employee and Supervisor Ratings of Motivation: Main Effects and Discrepancies Associated with Job Satisfaction and Adjustment in a Factory Setting." *Journal of Applied Social Psychology* 23, no. 21 (1993): 1789–1805.

Isaacowitz, Derek M., and Fredda Blanchard-Fields. "Linking Process and Outcome in the Study of Emotion and Aging." *Perspectives on Psychological Science* 7, no. 1 (2012): 3–17.

Iwasaki, Kenji, Masaya Takahashi, and Akinori Nakata. "Health Problems Due to Long Working Hours in Japan: Working Hours, Workers' Compensation (*Karoshi*), and Preventive Measures." *Industrial Health* 44, no. 4 (2006): 537–540.

Iyengar, Shenna S., Wei Jiang, and Gur Huberman. "How Much Choice Is Too Much: Determinants of Individual Contributions in 401K Retirement Plans." In *Pension Design and Structure: New Lessons from Behavioral Finance,* edited by Olivia S. Mitchell and Steve Utkus, 83–97. Oxford: Oxford University Press, 2004.

Iyengar, Shenna S., and Mark R. Lepper. "When Choice Is Demotivating: Can One Desire Too Much of a Good Thing?" *Journal of Personality and Social Psychology* 79, no. 6 (2000): 995–1006.

Jacka, Felice N., Julie A. Pasco, Arnstein Mykletun, Lana J. Williams, Allison M. Hodge, Sharleen Linette O'Reilly, Geoffrey C. Nicholson et al. "Association of Western and Traditional Diets with Depression and Anxiety in Women." *American Journal of Psychiatry* 167, no. 3 (2010): 305–311.

Jacob, Jenet I. "The Socio-Emotional Effects of Non-Maternal Childcare on Children in the USA: A Critical Review of Recent Studies." *Early Child Development and Care* 179, no. 5 (2009): 559–570.

Jansen, Jarno, Carolina de Weerth, and J. Marianne Riksen-Walraven. "Breastfeeding and the Mother-Infant Relationship: A Review." *Developmental Review* 28, no. 4 (2008): 503–521.

Johnson, Margaret Wheeler. "Bryan Fischer, Conservative Radio Host, Claims 'Men Are Designed to be the Breadwinners.'" *HuffPost Women* (blog), *Huffington Post*, May 31, 2013. http://www.huffingtonpost.com/2013/05/31/bryan-fischer-men-designed-to-be-breadwinners_n_3367765.html.

Johnson, Suzanne M., and Elizabeth O'Connor. *The Gay Baby Boom: The Psychology of Gay Parenthood.* New York: New York University Press, 2002.

Johnson, Wendy, and Robert F. Krueger. "How Money Buys Happiness: Genetic and Environmental Processes Linking Finances and Life Satisfaction." *Journal of Personality and Social Psychology* 90, no. 4 (2006): 680–691.

Johnston, David W., and Wang-Sheng Lee. "Climbing the Job Ladder: New Evidence of Gender Inequality." *Industrial Relations: A Journal of Economy and Society* 51, no. 1 (2012): 129–151.

Jonas, W., E. Nissen, A. B. Ransjö-Arvidson, I. Wiklund, P. Henriksson, and K. Uvnäs-Moberg. "Short-and Long-Term Decrease of Blood Pressure in Women during Breastfeeding." *Breastfeeding Medicine* 3, no. 2 (2008): 103–109.

Jones, Jeffrey M. "Gender Differences in Views of Job Opportunity: Fifty-Three Percent of Americans Believe Opportunities Are Equal." Gallup, posted August 2, 2005. http://www.gallup.com/poll/17614/gender-differences-views-job-opportunity.aspx.

Jones, Robert P., Daniel Cox, and Juhem Navarro-Rivera. "The 2012 American Values Survey: How Catholics and the Religiously Unaffiliated Will Shape the 2012 Election and Beyond." Public Religion Research Institute, October 23, 2012, 66–67.

Jong, Erica. "Mother Madness." *Wall Street Journal*, November 6, 2010. http://online.wsj.com/article/SB10001424052748704462704575590603553674296.html.

Joussemet, Mireille, Richard Koestner, Natasha Lekes, and Renée Landry. "A Longitudinal Study of the Relationship of Maternal Autonomy Support to Children's Adjustment and Achievement in School." *Journal of Personality* 73, no. 5 (2005): 1215–1236.

Joussemet, Mireille, Renée Landry, and Richard Koestner. "A Self-Determination Theory Perspective on Parenting." *Canadian Psychology / Psychologie Canadienne* 49, no. 3 (2008): 194–200.

Judge, Timothy A., and Ronald F. Piccolo. "Transformational and Transactional Leadership: A Meta-Analytic Test of Their Relative Validity." *Journal of Applied Psychology* 89, no. 5 (2004): 755–768.

Juster, Robert-Paul, Bruce S. McEwen, and Sonia J. Lupien. "Allostatic Load Biomarkers of Chronic Stress and Impact on Health and Cognition." *Neuroscience & Biobehavioral Reviews* 35, no. 1 (2010): 2–16.

Kahneman, Daniel, and Angus Deaton. "High Income Improves Evaluation of Life but not Emotional Well-Being." *Proceedings of the National Academy of Sciences* 107, no. 38 (2010): 16489–16493.

Kahneman, Daniel, Alan B. Krueger, David A. Schkade, Norbert Schwartz, and Arthur A. Stone. "A Survey Method for Characterizing Daily Life Experience: The Day Reconstruction Method." *American Association for the Advancement of Science* 306, no. 5702 (2004): 1776–1780.

Kaiser, Anelis, Sven Haller, Sigrid Schmitz, and Cordula Nitsch. "On Sex/Gender Related Similarities and Differences in fMRI Language Research." *Brain Research Reviews* 61, no. 2 (2009): 49–59.

Kanai, Atsuko. "'Karoshi (Work to Death)' in Japan." *Journal of Business Ethics* 84, no. 52 (2009): 209–216.

Kandel, Denise B., Mark Davies, and Victoria H. Raveis. "The Stressfulness of Daily Social Roles for Women: Marital, Occupational and Household Roles." *Journal of Health and Social Behavior* 26, no. 1 (1985): 64–78.

Kashdan, Todd B., and William E. Breen. "Materialism and Diminished Well-Being: Experiential Avoidance as a Mediating Mechanism." *Journal of Social and Clinical Psychology* 26, no. 5 (2007): 521–539.

Kasser, Tim, and Aaron Ahuvia. "Materialistic Values and Well-Being in Business Students." *European Journal of Social Psychology* 32, no. 1 (2002): 137–146.

Kasser, Tim, Katherine L. Rosenblum, Arnold J. Sameroff, Edward L. Deci, Christopher P. Niemiec, Richard M. Ryan, Osp Árnadóttir et al. "Changes in Materialism, Changes in Psychological Well-Being: Evidence from Three Longitudinal Studies and an Intervention Experiment." *Motivation and Emotion* (2013): 1–22.

Kasser, Tim, and Richard M. Ryan. "A Dark Side of the American Dream: Correlates of Financial Success as a Central Life Aspiration." *Journal of Personality and Social Psychology* 65, no. 2 (1993): 410–422.

———. "Further Examining the American Dream: Differential Correlates of Intrinsic and Extrinsic Goals." *Personality & Social Psychology Bulletin* 22, no. 3 (1996): 280–287.

Katz-Wise, Sabra L., Heather A. Priess, and Janet S. Hyde. "Gender-Role Attitudes and Behavior across the Transition to Parenthood." *Developmental Psychology* 46, no. 1 (2010): 18–28.

Kawamura, Sayaka, and Susan L. Brown. "Mattering and Wives' Perceived Fairness of the Division of Household Labor." *Social Science Research* 39, no. 6 (2010): 976–986.

Keeney, Jessica, Elizabeth M. Boyd, Ruchi Sinha, Alyssa F. Westring, and Ann Marie Ryan. "From 'Work-Family' to 'Work-Life': Broadening Our Conceptualization and Measurement." *Journal of Vocational Behavior* 82, no. 3 (2013): 221–237.

Keeton, Courtney Pierce, Maureen Perry-Jenkins, and Aline G. Sayer. "Sense of Control Predicts Depressive and Anxious Symptoms across the Transition to Parenthood." *Journal of Family Psychology* 22, no. 2 (2008): 212–221.

Keim, Sarah A., Joseph S. Hogan, Kelly A. McNamara, Vishnu Gudimetla, Chelsea E. Dillon, Jesse J. Kwiek, and Sheela R. Geraghty. "Microbial Contamination of Human Milk Purchased via the Internet." *Pediatrics* 132, no. 5 (2013): e1227–e1235.

Keller, Meret A., and Wendy A. Goldberg. "Co-Sleeping: Help or Hindrance for Young Children's Independence?" *Infant and Child Development* 13, no. 5 (2004): 369–388.

Kelly, Erin L., Phyllis Moen, and Eric Tranby. "Changing Workplaces to Reduce Work-Family Conflict: Schedule Control in a White-Collar Organization." *American Sociological Review* 76, no. 2 (2011): 265–290.

Keng, Shian-Ling, Moria J. Smoski, and Clive J. Robins. "Effects of Mindfulness on Psychological Health: A Review of Empirical Studies." *Clinical Psychology Review* 31, no. 6 (2011): 1041–1056.

Kenney-Benson, Gwen A., and Eva M. Pomerantz. "The Role of Mothers' Use of Control in Children's Perfectionism: Implications for the Development of Children's Depressive Symptoms." *Journal of Personality* 73, no. 1 (2005): 23–46.

Kessler, Ronald C., Patricia Berglund, Olga Demler, Robert Jin, Doreen Koretz, Kathleen R. Merikangas, A. John Rush et al. "The Epidemiology of Major Depressive Disorder." *JAMA* 289, no. 23 (2003): 3095–3105.

Keyes, Corey L. M. "Promoting and Protecting Mental Health as Flourishing: A Complementary Strategy for Improving National Mental Health." *American Psychologist* 62, no. 2 (2007): 95–108.

Khalid, Asma. "How Boston Is Trying to Eliminate the Gender Wage Gap." 90.9 WBUR, audio, November 26, 2013. http://www.wbur.org/2013/11/26/boston-women-pay-equity-push.

Kilmartin, Christopher. *The Masculine Self.* 4th ed. Cornwall-on-Hudson, NY: Sloan, 2010.

Kim, Eric S., Jennifer K. Sun, Nansook Park, and Christopher Peterson. "Purpose in Life and Reduced Stroke in Older Adults: The Health and Retirement Study." *Journal of Psychosomatic Research* 74, no. 5 (2013): 427–432.

Kim, Marlene. "Inertia and Discrimination in the California State Civil Service." *Industrial Relations: A Journal of Economy and Society* 38, no. 1 (1999): 46–68.

Kim, Sangmoon, Ryan Thibodeau, and Randall S. Jorgensen. "Shame, Guilt, and Depressive Symptoms: A Meta-Analytic Review." *Psychological Bulletin* 137, no. 1 (2011): 68–96.

Kim, Su Yeong, Yijie Wang, Diana Orozco-Lapray, Yishan Shen, and Mohammed Murtuza. "Does 'Tiger Parenting' Exist? Parenting Profiles of Chinese Americans and Adolescent Developmental Outcomes." *Asian American Journal of Psychology* 4, no. 1 (2013): 7–18.

King, Laura A. "The Health Benefits of Writing about Life Goals." *Personality and Social Psychology Bulletin* 27, no. 7 (2001): 798–807.

Knifsend, Casey A., and Sandra Graham. "Too Much of a Good Thing? How Breadth of Extracurricular Participation Relates to School-Related Affect and Academic Outcomes during Adolescence." *Journal of Youth and Adolescence* 41, no. 3 (2012): 379–389.

Knoester, Chris, Richard J. Petts, and David J. Eggebeen. "Commitments to Fathering and the Well Being and Social Participation of New, Disadvantaged Fathers." *Journal of Marriage and Family* 69, no. 4 (2007): 991–1004.

Koestner, Richard, Richard M. Ryan, Frank Bernieri, and Kathleen Holt. "Setting Limits on Children's Behavior: The Differential Effects of Controlling vs. Informational Styles on Intrinsic Motivation and Creativity." *Journal of Personality* 52, no. 3 (1984): 233–248.

Kok, Bethany E., Christian E. Waugh, and Barbara L. Fredrickson. "Meditation and Health: The Search for Mechanisms of Action." *Social and Personality Psychology Compass* 7, no. 1 (2013): 27–39.

Kolbert, Elizabeth. "Spoiled Rotten: Why Do Kids Rule the Roost?" *New Yorker*, July 2, 2012. http://www.newyorker.com/arts/critics/books/2012/07/02/120702crbo_books_kolbert?currentPage=all .

Kornrich, Sabino, Julie Brines, and Katrina Leupp. "Egalitarianism, Housework, and Sexual Frequency in Marriage." *American Sociological Review* 78, no. 1 (2013): 26–50.

Krcmar, Marina. "Word Learning in Very Young Children from Infant-Directed DVDs." *Journal of Communication* 61, no. 4 (2011): 780–794.

Kricheli-Katz, Tamar. "Choice, Discrimination, and the Motherhood Penalty." *Law & Society Review* 46, no. 3 (2012): 557–587.

Kroska, Amy. "Divisions of Domestic Work." *Journal of Marriage and Family* 65 (2004): 456–473.

Kuhn, Peter, and Fernando Lozano. "The Expanding Workweek? Understanding Trends in Long Work Hours among US Men, 1979–2004." IZA Discussion Papers, No. 1924, Institute for the Study of Labor (IZA), Bonn, Germany, 2006, 1–51.

Kunin, Madeleine. *The New Feminist Agenda: Defining the Next Revolution for Women, Work, and Family.* White River Junction, VT: Chelsea Green, 2012.

Kwapis, Ken, dir. *He's Just Not That into You.* Los Angeles: New Line Cinema, 2009.

Lachance-Grzela, Mylène, and Geneviève Bouchard. "Why Do Women Do the Lion's Share of Housework? A Decade of Research." *Sex Roles* 63, no. 11–12 (2010): 767–780.

LaFrance, Marianne, Marvin A. Hecht, and Elizabeth Levy Paluck. "The Contingent Smile: A Meta-Analysis of Sex Differences in Smiling." *Psychological Bulletin* 129, no. 2 (2003): 305–334.

Landry, Renée, Natasha Whipple, Geneviève Mageau, Mireille Joussemet, Richard Koestner, Lina DiDio, Isabelle Gingras et al. "Trust in Organismic Development, Autonomy Support, and Adaptation among Mothers and Their Children." *Motivation and Emotion* 32, no. 3 (2008): 173–188.

Langer, Ellen J., and Judith Rodin. "The Effect of Choice and Enhanced Personal Responsibility for the Aged: A Field Experiment in an Institutional Setting." *Journal of Personality and Social Psychology* 34, no. 2 (1976): 191–198.

Lappegard, Trude. "Couples' Parental Leave Practices: The Role of the Workplace Situation." *Journal of Family and Economic Issues* 33, no. 3 (2012): 298–305.

Lareau, Annette. "Invisible Inequality: Social Class and Childrearing in Black Families and White Families." *American Sociological Review* 67, no. 5 (2002): 747–776.

Layous, Kristin, S. Katherine Nelson, Eva Oberle, Kimberly A. Schonert-Reichl, and Sonja Lyubomirsky. "Kindness Counts: Prompting Prosocial Behavior in Preadolescents Boosts Peer Acceptance and Well-Being." Edited by Frank Krueger. *PLoS ONE* 7, no. 12 (2012): e51380: 1–7.

Lee, Christina. "Social Context, Depression, and the Transition to Motherhood." *British Journal of Health Psychology* 2, no. 2 (1997) 93–108.

Lee, Ellie J. "Living with Risk in the Age of 'Intensive Motherhood': Maternal Identity and Infant Feeding." *Health, Risk & Society* 10, no. 5 (2008): 467–477.

Lee, Heon-Jin, Abbe H. Macbeth, Jerome H. Pagani, and W. Scott Young 3rd. "Oxytocin: The Great Facilitator of Life." *Progress in Neurobiology* 88, no. 2 (2009): 127–151.

LeMoyne, Terri, and Tom Buchanan. "Does 'Hovering' Matter? Helicopter Parenting and Its Effect on Well-Being." *Sociological Spectrum* 31, no. 4 (2011): 399–418.

Leslie, Lisa M., Colleen Flaherty Manchester, Tae-Youn Park, and Si Ahn Mehng. "Flexible Work Practices: A Source of Career Premiums or Penalties?" *Academy of Management Journal* 55, no. 6 (2012): 1407–1428.

Leupoldt, Andreas von, and Bernhard Dahme. "The Impact of Emotions on Symptom Perception in Patients with Asthma and Healthy Controls." *Psychophysiology* 50, no. 1 (2013): 1–4.

Lewin, Tamar. "No Einstein in Your Crib? Get a Refund." *New York Times*, October 23, 2009. http://www.nytimes.com/2009/10/24/education/24baby.html.

Lewis, Suzan, Rhona Rapoport, and Richenda Gambles. "Reflections on the Integration of Paid Work and the Rest of Life." *Journal of Managerial Psychology* 18, no. 8 (2003): 824–841.

Lindberg, Sara M., Janet Shibley Hyde, Jennifer L. Petersen, and Marcia C. Linn. "New Trends in Gender and Mathematics Performance: A Meta-Analysis." *Psychological Bulletin* 136, no. 6 (2010): 1123–1135.

Lips, Hilary M. "The Gender Pay Gap: Challenging the Rationalizations. Perceived Equality, Discrimination, and the Limits of Human Capital Models." *Sex Roles* 68, no. 3–4 (2012): 169–185.

Liss, Miriam, and Mindy J. Erchull. "Feminism and Attachment Parenting: Attitudes, Stereotypes, and Misperceptions." *Sex Roles* 67, no. 3–4 (2012): 131–142.

Liss, Miriam, Holly H. Schiffrin, Virginia H. Mackintosh, Haley Miles-McLean, and Mindy J. Erchull. "Development and Validation of a Quantitative Measure of Intensive Parenting Attitudes." *Journal of Child and Family Studies* 22, no. 5 (2013): 621–636.

Liss, Miriam, Holly H. Schiffrin, and Kathryn M. Rizzo. "Maternal Guilt and Shame: The Role of Self-Discrepancy and Fear of Negative Evaluation." *Journal of Child and Family Studies* 22, no. 8 (2012): 1112–1119.

Lively, Kathryn J., Lala Carr Steelman, and Brian Powell. "Equity, Emotion, and Household Division of Labor Response." *Social Psychology Quarterly* 73, no. 4 (2010): 358–379.

Livingston, Gretchen. "The Rise of Single Fathers: A Ninefold Increase since 1960." Pew Research Social and Demographic Trends, posted July 2, 2013. http://www.pewsocialtrends.org/2013/07/02/the-rise-of-single-fathers.

Lucas, Richard E. "Adaptation and the Set-Point Model of Subjective Well-Being: Does Happiness Change after Major Life Events?" *Current Directions in Psychological Science* 16, no. 2 (2007): 75–79.

———. "Long-Term Disability Is Associated with Lasting Changes in Subjective Well-Being: Evidence from Two Nationally Representative Longitudinal Studies." *Journal of Personality and Social Psychology* 92, no. 4 (2007): 717–730.

———. "Time Does Not Heal All Wounds: A Longitudinal Study of Reaction and Adaptation to Divorce." *Psychological Science* 16, no. 12 (2005): 945–950.

Lucas, Richard E., Andrew E. Clark, Yannis Georgellis, and Ed Diener. "Reexamining Adaptation and the Set Point Model of Happiness: Reactions to Changes in Marital Status." *Journal of Personality and Social Psychology* 84, no. 3 (2003): 527–539.

———. "Unemployment Alters the Set Point for Life Satisfaction." *Psychological Science* 15, no. 1 (2004): 8–13.

Lucas, Richard E., Portia S. Dyrenforth, and Ed Diener. "Four Myths about Subjective Well-Being." *Social and Personality Psychology Compass* 2, no. 5 (2008): 2001–2015.

Lucas, Richard E., and Ulrich Schimmack. "Income and Well-Being: How Big Is the Gap between the Rich and the Poor?" *Journal of Research in Personality* 43, no. 1 (2009): 75–78.

Lucas-Thompson, Rachel G., Wendy A. Goldberg, and JoAnn Prause. "Maternal Work Early in the Lives of Children and Its Distal Associations with Achievement and Behavior Problems: A Meta-Analysis." *Psychological Bulletin* 136, no. 6 (2010): 915–942.

Luhmann, Maike, Wilhelm Hofmann, Michael Eid, and Richard E. Lucas. "Subjective Well-Being and Adaptation to Life Events: A Meta-Analysis." *Journal of Personality and Social Psychology* 102, no. 3 (2012): 592–615.

Luthar, Suniya S., and Bronwyn E. Becker. "Privileged but Pressured? A Study of Affluent Youth." *Child Development* 73, no. 5 (2002): 1593–1610.

Lutz Jäncke, Nadine Gaab, Torsten Wüstenberg, Henning Scheich, and H.-J. Heinze. "Short-Term Functional Plasticity in the Human Auditory Cortex: An fMRI Study." *Cognitive Brain Research* 12, no. 3 (2001): 479–585.

Lykken, David, and Auke Tellegen. "Happiness Is a Stochastic Phenomenon." *Psychological Science* 7, no. 3 (1996): 186–189.

Lytton, Hugh, and David M. Romney. "Parents' Differential Socialization of Boys and Girls: A Meta-Analysis." *Psychological Bulletin* 109, no. 2 (1991): 267–296.

Lyubomirsky, Sonja, Rene Dickerhoof, Julia K. Boehm, and Kennon M. Sheldon. "Becoming Happier Takes Both a Will and a Proper Way: An Experimental Longitudinal Intervention to Boost Well-Being." *Emotion* 11, no. 2 (2011): 391–402.

Lyubomirsky, Sonja, Laura King, and Ed Diener. "The Benefits of Frequent Positive Affect: Does Happiness Lead to Success?" *Psychological Bulletin* 131, no. 6 (2005): 803–855.

Lyubomirsky, Sonja, and Kristin Layous. "How Do Simple Positive Activities Increase Well-Being?" *Current Directions in Psychological Science* 22, no. 1 (2013): 57–62.

Lyubomirsky, Sonja, and Lee Ross. "Hedonic Consequences of Social Comparison: A Contrast of Happy and Unhappy People." *Journal of Personality and Social Psychology* 73, no. 6 (1997): 1141–1157.

Lyubomirsky, Sonja, Kennon M. Sheldon, and David Schkade. "Pursuing Happiness: The Architecture of Sustainable Change." *Review of General Psychology* 9, no. 2 (2005): 111–131.

Macht, Michael, Christine Haupt, and Andrea Salewsky. "Emotions and Eating in Everyday Life: Application of the Experience-Sampling Method." *Ecology of Food and Nutrition* 43, no. 4 (2004): 11–21.

Machung, Anne. "Talking Career, Thinking Job: Gender Differences in Career and Family Expectations of Berkeley Seniors." *Feminist Studies* 15, no. 1 (1989): 35–58.

Maguire, Eleanor A., David G. Gadian, Ingrid S. Johnsrude, Catriona D. Good, John Ashburner, Richard S. J. Frackowiak, and Christopher D. Frith. "Navigation-Related Structural Change in the Hippocampi of Taxi Drivers." *Proceedings of the National Academy of Sciences* 97, no. 8 (2000): 4398–4403.

Maier, Heiner, and Jacqui Smith. "Psychological Predictors of Mortality in Old Age." *Journals of Gerontology Series B: Psychological Sciences and Social Sciences* 54B, no. 1 (1999): P44–P54.

Mallon, Gerald P. *Gay Men Choosing Parenthood.* New York: Columbia University Press, 2004.

Mandel, Hadas, and Moshe Semyonov. "Family Policies, Wage Structures, and Gender Gaps: Sources of Earnings Inequality in 20 Countries." *American Sociological Review* 70, no. 6 (2005): 949–967.

Mannino, Clelia Anna, and Francine M. Deutsch. "Changing the Division of Household Labor: A Negotiated Process between Partners." *Sex Roles* 56, no. 5–6 (2007): 309–324.

Marche, Stephen. "The Case for Filth." *The Opinion Pages* (blog), *New York Times*, December 7, 2013. http://www.nytimes.com/2013/12/08/opinion/sunday/the-case-for-filth.html?pagewanted=3&_r=0&hp&rref=opinion.

Marche, Stephen. "Home Economics: The Link between Work-Life Balance and Income Equality." *The Atlantic,* July/August 2013. http://www.theatlantic.com/magazine/archive/2013/07/the-masculine-mystique/309401/2.

Marks, Michelle, and Crystal Harold. "Who Asks and Who Receives in Salary Negotiation." *Journal of Organizational Behavior* 32, no. 3 (2011): 371–394.

Marks, Stephen R. "Multiple Roles and Role Strain: Some Notes on Human Energy, Time and Commitment." *American Sociological Review* 42, no. 6 (1977): 921–936.

Martin, Kelly D., and Ronald Paul Hill. "Life Satisfaction, Self-Determination, and Consumption Adequacy at the Bottom of the Pyramid." *Journal of Consumer Research* 38, no. 6 (2012): 1155–1168.

Martin, Rachel M. "To the Tired Mom." *HuffPost Parents* (blog), *Huffington Post*, October 21, 2013. http://www.huffingtonpost.com/rachel-m-martin/to-the-tired-mom_b_4104515.html.

Martin, Richard M., Rita Patel, Michael S. Kramer, Lauren Guthrie, Konstantin Vilchuck, Natalia Bogdanovich, and Natalia Sergeichick. "Effects of Promoting Longer-term and

Exclusive Breastfeeding on Adiposity and Insulin-Like Growth Factor-I at Age 11.5 Years: A Randomized Trial." *JAMA* 309, no. 10 (2013): 1005–1013.

Mauss, Iris B., Maya Tamir, Craig L. Anderson, and Nicole S. Savino. "Can Seeking Happiness Make People Unhappy? Paradoxical Effects of Valuing Happiness." *Emotion* 11, no. 4 (2011): 807–815.

McBride, Michael. "Relative-Income Effects on Subjective Well-Being in the Cross-Section." *Journal of Economic Behavior & Organization* 45, no. 3 (2001): 251–278.

McCullough, Michael E. "Forgiveness as Human Strength: Theory, Measurement, and Links to Well-Being." *Journal of Social and Clinical Psychology* 19, no. 1 (2000): 43–55.

McCullough, Michael E., and Charlotte Vanoyen Witvliet. "The Psychology of Forgiveness." In *Handbook of Positive Psychology*, vol. 2, edited by C. R. Snyder and Shane J. Lopez, 446–455. New York: Oxford University Press, 2002.

McKenna, James J., and Thomas McDade. "Why Babies Should Never Sleep Alone: A Review of the Co-Sleeping Controversy in Relation to SIDS, Bedsharing and Breast Feeding." *Paediatric Respiratory Reviews* 6, no. 2 (2005): 134–152.

McLanahan, Sara, and Julia Adams. "The Effect of Children on Adults' Psychological Well-Being: 1957–1976." *Social Forces* 68, no. 1 (1989): 124–146.

McMunn, Anne, Yvonne Kelly, Noriko Cable, and Mel Bartley. "Maternal Employment and Child Socio-Emotional Behaviour in the UK: Longitudinal Evidence from the UK Millennium Cohort Study." *Journal of Epidemiology & Community Health* 66, no. 7 (2011).

McNall, Laurel A., Jessica M. Nicklin, and Aline D. Masuda. "A MetaAnalytic Review of the Consequences Associated with Work-Family Enrichment." *Journal of Business and Psychology* 25, no. 3 (2010): 381–396.

Melman, Shari, Steven G. Little, and K. Angeleque Akin-Little. "Adolescent Overscheduling: The Relationship between Levels of Participation in Scheduled Activities and Self-Reported Clinical Symptomology." *High School Journal* 90, no. 3 (2007): 18–30.

Mendes, Elizabeth, Lydia Saad, and Kyley McGeeney. "Stay-at-Home Moms Report More Depression, Sadness, Anger: But Low-Income Stay-at-Home Moms Struggle the Most." *Gallup Wellbeing* (blog), Gallup, May 18, 2012. http://www.gallup.com/poll/154685/Stay-Home-Moms-Report-Depression SadnessAnger.aspx?utm_source=alert&utm_medium= email&utm_campaign=syndication&utm_content_morelink&utm_term= All%20Gallup%20Headlines.

Mercer, Ramona T., and Sandra L. Ferketich. "Experienced and Inexperienced Mothers' Maternal Competence during Infancy." *Research in Nursing and Health* 18, no. 4 (1995): 333–343.

Meyerson, Debra, and Joyce K. Fletcher. "A Modest Manifesto for Shattering the Glass Ceiling." *Harvard Business Review* 78, no. 1 (2000): 127–136.

Mezzacappa, Elizabeth Sibolboro, Robert M. Kelsey, and Edward S. Katkin. "Breast Feeding, Bottle Feeding, and Maternal Autonomic Responses to Stress." *Journal of Psychosomatic Research* 58, no. 4 (2005): 351–365.

Milkie, Melissa A., Suzanne M. Bianchi, Marybeth J. Mattingly, and John P. Robinson. "Gendered Division of Childrearing: Ideals, Realities, and the Relationship to Parental Well-Being." *Sex Roles* 47, no. 1–2 (2002): 21–38.

Miller, Lisa. "The Retro Wife: Feminists Who Say They're Having It All—By Choosing to Stay Home." *New York Magazine*, March 17, 2013. http://nymag.com/news/features/retro-wife-2013-3.

Minkel, Jared D., Siobhan Banks, Oo Htaik, Marisa C. Moreta, Christopher W. Jones, Eleanor L. McGlinchey, Norah S. Simpson et al. "Sleep Deprivation and Stressors: Evidence for Elevated Negative Affect in Response to Mild Stressors When Sleep Deprived." *Emotion* 12, no. 5 (2012): 1015–1020.

Minnesota Management and Budget. Reporting Forms, Instructions, Software, 2005. http://www.mmb.state.mn.us/reporting-forms-instructions-software.

Mirkinson, Jack. "All-Male Fox Panel Freaks Out about Female Breadwinners." Video. *Huff-Post Media* (blog), *Huffington Post*, May 30, 2013. http://www.huffingtonpost.com/2013/05/30/fox-female-breadwinners_n_3358926.html.

Misra, Joya, Michelle Budig, and Irene Boeckmann. "The Motherhood Penalty in Cross-National Perspective: The Importance of Work-Family Policies and Cultural Attitudes." *Social Politics* 19, no. 2 (2012): 163–193.

Moen, Phyllis, and Erin L. Kelly. *Flexible Work and Well-Being Study.* Minneapolis, MN: Flexible Work and Well-Being Center, University of Minnesota, 2007, iv–viii.

Morrongiello, Barbara A., and Kerri Hogg. "Mothers' Reactions to Children Misbehaving in Ways That Can Lead to Injury: Implications for Gender Differences in Children's Risk Taking and Injuries." *Sex Roles* 50, no. 1–2 (2004): 103–118.

Moyer, Anne E., Judith Rodin, Carlos M. Grilo, Nancy Cummings, Lynn M. Larson, and Marielle Rebuffé-Scrive. "Stress-Induced Cortisol Response and Fat Distribution in Women." *Obesity Research* 2, no. 3 (1994): 255–262.

Mrazek, Michael D., Michael S. Franklin, Dawa Tarchin Phillips, Benjamin Baird, and Jonathan W. Schooler. "Mindfulness Training Improves Working Memory Capacity and GRE Performance While Reducing Mind Wandering." *Psychological Science* 24, no. 5 (2013): 776–781.

Murray, Noel, Harish Sujan, Edward R. Hirt, and Mita Sujan. "The Influence of Mood on Categorization: A Cognitive Flexibility Interpretation." *Journal of Personality and Social Psychology* 59, no. 3 (1990): 411–425.

Myers, David G. "The Funds, Friends, and Faith of Happy People." *American Psychologist* 55, no. 1 (2000): 56–67.

Myers, David G., and Ed Diener. "Who Is Happy?" *Psychological Science* 6, no. 1 (1995): 10–19.

Nakamura, Jeanne, and Mihaly Csikszentmihalyi. "Flow Theory and Research." In *Handbook of Positive Psychology*, edited by C. R. Snyder and Shane J. Lopez, 195–206. New York: Oxford University Press, 2009.

Nakamura, Suad, Marilyn Wind, and Mary Ann Danello. "Review of Hazards Associated with Children Placed in Adult Beds." *Archives of Pediatrics & Adolescent Medicine* 153, no. 10 (1999): 1019–1023.

Nakata, Akinori. "Work Hours, Sleep Sufficiency, and Prevalence of Depression among Full-Time Employees: A Community-Based Cross-Sectional Study." *Journal of Clinical Psychiatry* 72, no. 5 (2011): 605–614.

Nakonezny, Paul A., and Wayne H. Denton. "Marital Relationships: A Social Exchange Theory Perspective." *American Journal of Family Therapy* 36, no. 5 (2008): 402–412.

National Association for the Advancement of Colored People. "Misplaced Priorities: Over Incarcerate, Under Educate: Excessive Spending on Incarceration Undermines Educational Opportunity and Public Safety in Communities." National Association for the Advancement of Colored People, 2011.

Neisser, Ulric, Gwyneth Boodoo, Thomas J. Bouchard, Jr., A. Wade Boykin, Nathan Brody, Stephen J. Ceci, Diane F. Halpern et al. "Intelligence: Knowns and Unknowns." *American Psychologist* 51, no. 2 (1996): 77–101.

Nelson, Edmund Anthony Severn, B. J. Taylor, Alejandre Jenik, John Vance, Karen Walmsley, Katie Pollard, Michelle Freemantle et al. "International Child Care Practices Study: Infant Sleeping Environment." *Early Human Development* 62, no. 1 (2001): 43–55.

Nelson, S. Katherine, Kostadin Kushlev, Tammy English, Elizabeth W. Dunn, and Sonja Lyubomirsky. "In Defense of Parenthood: Children Are Associated with More Joy than Misery." *Psychological Science* 24, no. 1 (2013): 1–8.

Nelson, Margaret K. *Parenting out of Control: Anxious Parents in Uncertain Times.* New York: New York University Press, 2010.

Nepomnyaschy, Lenna, and Jane Waldfogel. "Paternity Leave and Fathers' Involvement with Their Young Children: Evidence from the American Ecls–B." *Community, Work & Family* 10, no. 4 (2007): 427–453.

Nes, R. B., E. Røysamb, K. Tambs, J. R. Harris, and T. Reichborn-Kjennerud. "Subjective Well-Being: Genetic and Environmental Contributions to Stability and Change." *Psychological Medicine* 36, no. 7 (2006): 1033–1042.

New Mexico Pay Equity Initiative. New Mexico General Services Department. Executive Order #2009–049. December 18, 2009. http://www.generalservices.state.nm.us/statepurchasing/Pay_Equity.aspx.

Nickerson, Carol, Norbert Schwarz, Ed Diener, and Daniel Kahneman. "Zeroing in on the Dark Side of the American Dream: A Closer Look at the Negative Consequences of the Goal for Financial Success." *Psychological Science* 14, no. 6 (2003): 531–536.

Nomaguchi, Kei M. "Change in Work-Family Conflict among Employed Parents Between 1977 and 1997." *Journal of Marriage and Family* 71, no. 1 (2009): 15–32.

——. "Maternal Employment, Nonparental Care, Mother-Child Interactions, and Child Outcomes during Preschool Years." *Journal of Marriage and Family* 68, no. 5 (2006): 1341–1369.

Nomaguchi, Kei M., and Melissa A. Milkie. "Costs and Rewards of Children: The Effects of Becoming a Parent on Adults' Lives." *Journal of Marriage and Family* 65, no. 2 (2003): 356–374.

Nomaguchi, Kei M., Melissa A. Milkie, and Suzanne M. Bianchi. "Time Strains and Psychological Well Being: Do Dual-Earner Mothers and Fathers Differ?" *Journal of Family Issues* 26, no. 6 (2005): 756–792.

Nordenmark, Mikael, and Charlott Nyman. "Fair or Unfair? Perceived Fairness of Household Division of Labour and Gender Equality among Women and Men: The Swedish Case." *European Journal of Women's Studies* 10, no. 2 (2003): 181–209.

Ochs, Elinor, and Carolina Izquierdo. "Responsibility in Childhood: Three Developmental Trajectories." *Ethos* 37, no. 4 (2009): 391–413.

Ochs, Elinor, and Tamar Kremer-Sadlik, eds. *Fast-Forward Family: Home, Work, and Relationships in Middle-Class America.* Berkeley: University of California Press, 2013.

Offer, Shira, and Barbara Schneider. "Revisiting the Gender Gap in Time-Use Patterns Multitasking and Well-Being among Mothers and Fathers in Dual-Earner Families." *American Sociological Review* 76, no. 6 (2011): 809–833.

Office of Economic Cooperation and Development (OECD). "OECD Better Life Index: Work-Life Balance." http://www.oecdbetterlifeindex.org/topics/work-life-balance.

Olfson, Mark, Steven Shea, Adriana Feder, Milton Fuentes, Yoko Nomura, Marc Gameroff, and Myrna M. Weissman. "Prevalence of Anxiety, Depression, and Substance Use Disorders in an Urban General Medicine Practice." *Archives of Family Medicine* 9, no. 9 (2000): 876–883.

Olsen, Suzanne Frost, Chongming Yang, Craig H. Hart, Clyde C. Robinson, Peixia Wu, David A. Nelson, Larry J. Nelson et al. "Maternal Psychological Control and Preschool Children's Behavioral Outcomes in China, Russia, and the United States." In *Intrusive Parenting: How Psychological Control Affects Children and Adolescents*, edited by Brian K. Barber, 235–262. Washington, DC: American Psychological Association, 2002.

Oransky, Matthew, and Jeanne Maracek. "'I'm Not Going to Be a Girl': Masculinity and Emotions in Boys' Friendships and Peer Groups." *Journal of Adolescent Research* 24, no. 2 (2009): 218–241.

Otero, Hanna. "Resentment: How an Equal Division of Labor Almost Destroyed My Marriage." Babble, January 22, 2009. http://www.babble.com/mom/working-mom-and-stay-at-home-shared-parenting-marriage-trouble.

Otero-López, José Manuel, Estíbaliz Villardefrancos Pol, Cristina Castro Bolaño, and Maria José Santiago Mariño. "Materialism, Life-Satisfaction and Addictive Buying: Examining the Causal Relationships." *Personality and Individual Differences* 50, no. 6 (2011): 772–776.

Padilla-Walker, Laura M., and Larry J. Nelson. "Black Hawk Down? Establishing Helicopter Parenting as a Distinct Construct from Other Forms of Parental Control during Emerging Adulthood." *Journal of Adolescence* 35, no. 5 (2012): 1177–1190.

Parker, Kim, and Wendy Wang. "Modern Parenthood: Roles of Moms and Dads Converge as They Balance Work and Family." Pew Research Social and Demographic Trends, posted March 14, 2013. http://www.pewsocialtrends.org/2013/03/14/modern-parenthood-roles-of-moms-and-dads converge-as-they-balance-work-and-family.

Pehlke, Timothy Allen II, Charles B. Hennon, M. Elise Radina, and Katherine A. Kuvalanka. "Does Father Still Know Best? An Inductive Thematic Analysis of Popular TV Sitcoms." *Fathering: A Journal of Theory, Research, and Practice about Men as Fathers* 7, no. 2 (2009): 114–139.

Peisner-Feinberg, Ellen S., Margaret R. Burchinal, Richard M. Clifford, Mary L. Culkin, Carollee Howes, Sharon Lynn Kagan, and Noreen Yazejian. "The Relation of Preschool Child-Care Quality to Children's Cognitive and Social Developmental Trajectories through Second Grade." *Child Development* 72, no. 5 (2001): 1534–1553.

Penn International Strengths Project. "VIA–Inventory of Strengths." Penn International Strengths Project, 2006. http://www.authentichappiness.sas.upenn.edu/aiesec/content.aspx?id=821.

Percheski, Christine. "Opting Out? Cohort Differences in Professional Women's Employment Rates from 1960 to 2005." *American Sociological Review* 73, no. 3 (2008): 497–517.

Peterson, Christopher, Martin E. Seligman, and George E. Vaillant. "Pessimistic Explanatory Style Is a Risk Factor for Physical Illness: A Thirty-Five-Year Longitudinal Study." *Journal of Personality and Social Psychology* 55, no. 1 (1988): 23–27.

Pickert, Kate. "The Man Who Remade Motherhood." *Time*, May 21, 2012. http://content.time.com/time/magazine/article/0,9171,2114427,00.html.

Piff, Paul K., Michael W. Kraus, Stéphane Côté, Bonnie Hayden Cheng, and Dacher Keltner. "Having Less, Giving More: The Influence of Social Class on Prosocial Behavior." *Journal of Personality and Social Psychology* 99, no. 5 (2010): 771–784.

Piff, Paul K., Daniel M. Stancato, Stéphane Côté, Rodolfo Mendoza-Denton, and Dacher Keltner. "Higher Social Class Predicts Increased Unethical Behavior." *Proceedings of the National Academy of Sciences* 109, no. 11 (2012): 4086–4091.

Pilcher, June J., and Allen J. Huffcutt. "Effects of Sleep Deprivation on Performance: A Meta-Analysis." *Journal of Sleep Research & Sleep Medicine* 19, no. 4 (1996): 318–326.

Pomerantz, Eva M., Elizabeth A. Moorman, and Scott D. Litwack. "The How, Whom, and Why of Parents' Involvement in Children's Academic Lives: More Is Not Always Better." *Review of Educational Research* 77, no. 3 (2007): 373–410.

Poortman, Anne-Rigt, and Tanja Van Der Lippe. "Attitudes toward Housework and Child Care and the Gendered Division of Labor." *Journal of Marriage and Family* 71, no. 3 (2009): 526–541.

Pratt, Laura A., and Debra J. Brody. "Depression and Smoking in the U.S. Household Population Aged 20 and Over, 2005–2008." *NCHS Data Brief* 34 (April 2010): 1–8.

Pratt, Laura A., and Debra J. Brody. "Depression in the United States Household Population, 2005–2006." *NCHS Data Brief* 7 (September 2008): 1–8.

Prentice, Deborah A., and Erica Carranza. "What Women and Men Should Be, Shouldn't Be, Are Allowed to Be, and Don't Have to Be: The Contents of Prescriptive Gender Stereotypes." *Psychology of Women Quarterly* 26, no. 4 (2002): 269–281.

Protzko, John, Joshua Aronson, and Clancy Blair. "How to Make a Young Child Smarter: Evidence from the Database of Raising Intelligence." *Perspectives on Psychological Science* 8, no. 1 (2013): 25–40.

Pruncho, R., L. Litchfield, and M. Fried. *Measuring the Impact of Workplace Flexibility: Findings from the National Work/Life Measurement Project.* Chestnut Hill, MA: Center for Work and Family at Boston College, 2000.

Raimi, Sam, dir. *For the Love of the Game.* 1999; Universal City, CA: Universal Studios, 2000, DVD.

Ramey, Garey, and Valerie A. Ramey. "The Rug Rat Race." Working Paper 15284, National Bureau of Economic Research, Cambridge, MA, 2009.

Ramos, Kathleen Dyer, Davin Youngclarke, and Jane E. Anderson. "Parental Perceptions of Sleep Problems among Co-Sleeping and Solitary Sleeping Children." *Infant and Child Development* 16, no. 4 (2007): 417–431.

Rampell, Catherine. "Working Parents, Wanting Fewer Hours." *Economix* (blog), *New York Times*, July 10, 2013. http://economix.blogs.nytimes.com/2013/07/10/working-parents-wanting-fewer hours/?src=rechp.

Ratelle, Catherine F., Karine Simard, and Frédéric Guay. "University Students' Subjective Well-Being: The Role of Autonomy Support from Parents, Friends, and the Romantic Partner." *Journal of Happiness Studies* 14, no. 3 (2012): 893–910.

Rauscher, Frances H., Gordon L. Shaw, Linda J. Levine, Eric L. Wright, Wendy R. Dennis, and Robert L. Newcomb. "Music Training Causes Long-Term Enhancement of Preschool Children's Spatial-Temporal Reasoning." *Neurological Research* 19, no. 1 (1997): 2–8.

Redshaw, Maggie, and Jane Henderson. "Learning the Hard Way: Expectations and Experiences of Infant Feeding Support." *Birth* 39, no. 1 (2012): 21–29.

Reed, Justy, and Sarah Buck. "The Effect of Regular Aerobic Exercise on Positive-Activated Affect: A Meta-Analysis." *Psychology of Sport and Exercise* 10, no. 6 (2009): 581–594.

Reis, Harry T., Kennon M. Sheldon, Shelly L. Gable, Joseph Roscoe, and Richard M. Ryan. "Daily Well Being: The Role of Autonomy, Competence, and Relatedness." *Personality and Social Psychology Bulletin* 26, no. 4 (2000): 419–435.

Reis, Harry T., Shannon M. Smith, Cheryl L. Carmichael, Peter A. Caprariello, Fen-Fang Tsai, Amy Rodrigues, and Michael R. Maniaci. "Are You Happy for Me? How Sharing Positive Events with Others Provides Personal and Interpersonal Benefits." *Journal of Personality and Social Psychology* 99, no. 2 (2010): 311–329.

Rijavec, Majda, Lana Jurčec, and Ivana Mijočević. "Gender Differences in the Relationship between Forgiveness and Depression/Happiness." *Psihologijske teme* 19, no. 1 (2010): 189–202.

Rik, Pieters. "Bidirectional Dynamics of Materialism and Loneliness: Not Just a Vicious Cycle." *Journal of Consumer Research* 40, no. 4 (2013): 615–631.

Rizzo, Kathryn M., Holly H. Schiffrin, and Miriam Liss. "Insight into the Parenthood Paradox: Mental Health Outcomes of Intensive Mothering." *Journal of Child and Family Studies* 22, no. 5 (2013): 614–620.

Robb, Michael B., Rebekah A. Richert, and Ellen A. Wartella. "Just a Talking Book? Word Learning from Watching Baby Videos." *British Journal of Developmental Psychology* 27, no. 1 (2009): 27–45.

Robins, Richard W., and Jennifer S. Beer. "Positive Illusions about the Self: Short-Term Benefits and Long-Term Costs." *Journal of Personality and Social Psychology* 80, no. 2 (2001): 340–352.

Rochlen, Aaron B., Ryan A. McKelley, and Tiffany A. Whittaker. "Stay-at-Home Fathers' Reasons for Entering the Role and Stigma Experiences: A Preliminary Report." *Psychology of Men & Masculinity* 11, no. 4 (2010): 279–285.

Rochlen, Aaron B., Marie-Anne Suizzo, Ryan A. McKelley, and Vanessa Scaringi. "'I'm Just Providing for my Family,' A Qualitative Study of Stay-at-Home Fathers." *Psychology of Men & Masculinity* 9, no. 4 (2008): 193–206.

Rosenblatt, J. S. "Nonhormonal Basis of Maternal Behavior in the Rat." *Science* 156, no. 3781 (1967): 1512–1513.

Rosenfeld, Alvin, and Nicole Wise. *The Over-Scheduled Child: Avoiding the Hyper-Parenting Trap.* New York: St. Martin's Press, 2000.

Rosenthal, Lisa, Amy Carroll-Scott, Valerie A. Earnshaw, Alycia Santilli, and Jeannette R. Ickovics. "The Importance of Full-Time Work for Urban Adults' Mental and Physical Health." *Social Science and Medicine* 75, no. 9 (2012): 1692–1696.

Rosin, Hanna. "The Case against Breast-Feeding." *The Atlantic,* April 1, 2009. http://www.theatlantic.com/magazine/archive/2009/04/the-case-against-breast-feeding/307311/?single_page=true.

Rossin, Maya. "The Effects of Maternity Leave on Children's Birth and Infant Health Outcomes in the United States." *Journal of Health Economics* 30, no. 2 (2011): 221–239.

Rotkirch, Anna, and Kristiina Janhunen. "Maternal Guilt." *Evolutionary Psychology: An International Journal of Evolutionary Approaches to Psychology and Behavior* 8, no. 1 (2009): 90–106.

Rubin, Stacey E., and H. Ray Wooten. "Highly Educated Stay-at-Home Mothers: A Study of Commitment and Conflict." *Family Journal* 15, no. 4 (2007): 336–345.

Ruderman, Marian N. "Benefits of Multiple Roles for Managerial Women." *Academy of Management Journal* 45, no. 2 (2002): 369–386.

Rudman, Laurie A., and Kris Mescher. "Penalizing Men Who Request a Family Leave: Is Flexibility Stigma a Femininity Stigma?" *Journal of Social Issues* 69, no. 2 (2013): 322–340.

Ryan, Richard M., and Edward L. Deci. "Self-Determination Theory and the Facilitation of Intrinsic Motivation, Social Development, and Well-Being." *American Psychologist* 55, no. 1 (2000): 68–78.

Ryff, Carol D., and Burton H. Singer. "Know Thyself and Become What You Are: A Eudaimonic Approach to Psychological Well-Being." *Journal of Happiness Studies* 9, no. 1 (2008): 13–9.

Sacks, Daniel W., Betsey Stevenson, and Justin Wolfers. "The New Stylized Facts about Income and Subjective Well-Being." *Emotion* 12, no. 6 (2012): 1181–1187.

Sánchez-Villegas, Almudena, Lisa Verberne, Jokin De Irala, Miguel Ruíz-Canela, Estefanía Toledo, Lluis Serra-Majem, and Miguel Angel Martínez-González. "Dietary Fat Intake and the Risk of Depression: The SUN Project." Edited by Lorraine Brennan. *PLoS ONE* 6, no. 1 (2011): e16268.

Sandberg, Sheryl. *Lean In: Women, Work, and the Will to Lead*. New York: Random House, 2013.

Sargent, Paul. "The Gendering of Men in Early Childhood Education." *Sex Roles* 52, no. 3–4 (2005): 251–259.

Sastre, María Teresa Muñoz, Geneviève Vinsonneau, Félix Neto, Michelle Girard, and Etienne Mullet. "Forgivingness and Satisfaction with Life." *Journal of Happiness Studies* 4, no. 3 (2003): 323–335.

Saxbe, Darby E., Rena L. Repetti, and Anthony P. Graesch. "Time Spent in Housework and Leisure: Links with Parents' Physiological Recovery from Work." *Journal of Family Psychology* 25, no. 2 (2011): 271–281.

Saxbe, Darby E., Rena L. Repetti, and Adrienne Nishina. "Marital Satisfaction, Recovery from Work, and Diurnal Cortisol among Men and Women." *Health Psychology* 27, no. 1 (2008): 15–25.

Scheers, N. J., George W. Rutherford, and James S. Kemp. "Where Should Infants Sleep? A Comparison of Risk for Suffocation of Infants Sleeping in Cribs, Adult Beds, and Other Sleeping Locations." *Pediatrics* 112, no. 4 (2003): 883–889.

Schellenberg, Glenn E. "Long-Term Positive Associations between Music Lessons and IQ." *Journal of Educational Psychology* 98, no. 2 (2006): 457–468.

———. "Music and Cognitive Abilities." *Current Directions in Psychological Science* 14, no. 6 (2005): 317–320.

———. "Music Lessons Enhance IQ." *Psychological Science* 15, no. 8 (2004): 511–514.

Schindler, Holly S. "The Importance of Parenting and Financial Contributions in Promoting Fathers' Psychological Health." *Journal of Marriage and Family* 72, no. 2 (2010): 318–332.

Schkade, David A., and Daniel Kahneman. "Does Living in California Make People Happy? A Focusing Illusion in Judgments of Life Satisfaction." *Psychological Science* 9, no. 5 (1998): 340–346.

Schön, Regine A., and Maarit Silvén. "Natural Parenting: Back to Basics in Infant Care." *Evolutionary Psychology* 5, no. 1 (2007): 102–183.

Schulte, Brigid. *Overwhelmed: Work, Love and Play When No One Has the Time*. New York: Sarah Crichton Books / Farrar, Straus & Giroux, 2014.

Schwartz, Barry. *The Paradox of Choice*. New York: HarperCollins, 2004.

———. "Self-Determination: The Tyranny of Freedom." *American Psychologist* 55, no. 1 (2000): 79–88.

Schwartz, Pepper. *Peer Marriage: How Love between Equals Really Works*. New York: Free Press, 1994.

Schweinhart, Lawrence L., David P. Weikart, and Mary B. Larner. "Consequences of Three Preschool Curriculum Models through Age 15." *Early Childhood Research Quarterly* 1, no. 1 (1986): 15–45.

Seagram, Samantha, and Judith C. Daniluk. "'It Goes with the Territory': The Meaning and Experience of Maternal Guilt for Mothers of Preadolescent Children." *Women & Therapy* 25, no. 1 (2002): 61–88.

Sears, William, and Martha Sears. *The Attachment Parenting Book: A Commonsense Guide to Understanding and Nurturing Your Baby.* Boston: Little, Brown, 2001.

Segrin, Chris, Michelle Givertz, Paulina Swaitkowski, and Neil Montgomery. "Overparenting Is Associated with Child Problems and a Critical Family Environment." *Journal of Child and Family Studies* (October 2013): 1–10.

Segrin, Chris, Alesia Woszidlo, Michelle Givertz, and Neil Montgomery. "Parent and Child Traits Associated with Overparenting." *Journal of Social and Clinical Psychology* 32, no. 6 (2013): 569–595.

Seligman, Martin E. *Learned Optimism: How to Change Your Mind and Your Life.* New York: Vintage Books, 2006.

Seligman, Martin E. P., Tayyab Rashid, and Acacia C. Parks. "Positive Psychotherapy." *American Psychologist* 61, no. 8 (2006): 774–788.

Seligman, Martin E. P, Tracy A. Steen, Nansook Park, and Christopher Peterson. "Positive Psychology Progress: Empirical Validation of Interventions." *American Psychologist* 60, no. 5 (2005): 410–421.

Senior, Jennifer. "All Joy and No Fun: Why Parents Hate Parenting." *New York Magazine*, July 4, 2010. http://nymag.com/news/features/67024.

Sephton, Sandra E., Robert M. Sapolsky, Helena C. Kraemer, and David Spiegel. "Diurnal Cortisol Rhythm as a Predictor of Breast Cancer Survival." *Journal of the National Cancer Institute* 92, no. 12 (2000): 994–1000.

Shafer, Emily Fitzgibbons. "Wives' Relative Wages, Husbands' Paid Work Hours, and Wives' Labor-Force Exit." *Journal of Marriage and Family* 73, no. 1 (2011): 250–263.

Shahabi, Shohreh, Shiquan He, Michael Kopf, Marisa Mariani, Joann Petrini, Giovanni Scambia, and Cristiano Ferlini. "Free Testosterone Drives Cancer Aggressiveness: Evidence from US Population Studies." Edited by Lars Berglund. *PLoS ONE* 8, no. 4 (2013): e61955.

Shallcross, Amanda J., Allison S. Troy, Matthew Boland, and Iris B. Mauss. "Let It Be: Accepting Negative Emotional Experiences Predicts Decreased Negative Affect and Depressive Symptoms." *Behaviour Research and Therapy* 48, no. 9 (2010): 921–929.

Sheldon, Kennon M., and Sonja Lyubomirsky. "Achieving Sustainable Gains in Happiness: Change Your Actions, Not Your Circumstances." *Journal of Happiness Studies* 7, no. 1 (2006): 55–86.

——. "Achieving Sustainable New Happiness: Prospects, Practices, and Prescriptions." In *Positive Psychology in Practice*, edited by P. Alex Linley and Stephen Joseph, 127–145. Hoboken, NJ: Wiley, 2004.

——. "The Challenge of Staying Happier: Testing the Hedonic Adaptation Prevention Model." *Personality and Social Psychology Bulletin* 38, no. 5 (2012): 670–680.

——. "How to Increase and Sustain Positive Emotion: The Effects of Expressing Gratitude and Visualizing Best Possible Selves." *Journal of Positive Psychology* 1, no. 2 (2006): 73–82.

Shoup, Rick, Robert M. Gonyea, and George D. Kuh. "Helicopter Parents: Examining the Impact of Highly Involved Parents on Student Engagement and Educational Outcomes." Paper presented at the 49th Annual Forum of the Association for Institutional Research, Atlanta, GA, 2009.

Shpancer, Noam. "The Effects of Daycare: Persistent Questions, Elusive Answers." *Early Childhood Research Quarterly* 21, no. 2 (2006): 227–237.

Shulruf, Boaz. "Do Extra-Curricular Activities in Schools Improve Educational Outcomes? A Critical Review and Meta-Analysis of the Literature." *International Review of Education* 56, no. 5-6 (2010): 591–612.

Sieber, Sam D. "Toward a Theory of Role Accumulation." *American Sociological Review* 39, no. 4 (1974): 567–578.

Sin, Nancy L., and Sonja Lyubomirsky. "Enhancing Well-Being and Alleviating Depressive Symptoms with Positive Psychology Interventions: A Practice-Friendly Meta-Analysis." *Journal of Clinical Psychology* 65, no. 5 (2009): 467–487.

Slaughter, Anne-Marie. "Why Women Still Can't Have It All." *The Atlantic*, July/August 2012. http://www.theatlantic.com/magazine/archive/2012/07/why-women-still-cant-have-it all/ 309020.

Smith, Allen. "Gender Difference in Yahoo Paid Parental-Leave Program is OK Legally." *Society for Human Resource Management*, June 4, 2013. http://www.shrm.org/legalissues/federalresources/pages/yahoo-paid-leave.aspx.

Smith, Jennifer L., and Fred B. Bryant. "Are We Having Fun Yet? Savoring, Type A Behavior, and Vacation Enjoyment." *International Journal of Wellbeing* 3, no. 1 (2013): 1–19.

Smith, Richard H. "Assimilative and Contrastive Emotional Reactions to Upward and Downward Social Comparisons." In *Handbook of Social Comparison: Theory and Research*, edited by Jerry Suls and Ladd Wheeler, 173–200. New York: Kluwer Academic / Plenum, 2000.

Soenens, Bart, and Maarten Vansteenkiste. "Antecedents and Outcomes of Self-Determination in 3 Life Domains: The Role of Parents' and Teachers' Autonomy Support." *Journal of Youth and Adolescence* 34, no. 6 (2005): 589–604.

Soenens, Bart, Maarten Vansteenkiste, Willy Lens, Koen Luyckx, Luc Goossens, Wim Beyers, and Richard M. Ryan. "Conceptualizing Parental Autonomy Support: Adolescent Perceptions of Promotion of Independence versus Promotion of Volitional Functioning." *Developmental Psychology* 43, no. 3 (2007): 633–646.

Solberg, Emily C., Edward Diener, and Michael D. Robinson. "Why Are Materialists Less Satisfied?" In *Psychology and Consumer Culture: The Struggle for a Good life in a Materialistic World,* edited by Tim Kasser and Allen D. Kanner, 29–48. Washington, DC: American Psychological Association, 2004.

Spencer, Steven J., Claude M. Steele, and Diane M. Quinn. "Stereotype Threat and Women's Math Performance." *Journal of Experimental Social Psychology* 35, no. 1 (1999): 4–28.

State of California Employment Development Department. "Paid Family Leave Benefits." State of California Employment Development Department. http://www.edd.ca.gov/disability/PFL_Benefit_Amounts.htm.

Steffel, Mary, and Daniel M. Oppenheimer. "Happy by What Standard? The Role of Interpersonal and Intrapersonal Comparisons in Ratings of Happiness." *Social Indicators Research* 92, no. 1 (2009): 69–79.

Stephens, Nicole M., and Cynthia S. Levine. "Opting Out or Denying Discrimination? How the Framework of Free Choice in American Society Influences Perceptions of Gender Inequality." *Psychological Science* 22, no. 10 (2011): 1231–1236.

Stone, Pamela. *Opting Out? Why Women Really Quit Careers and Head Home.* Berkeley: University of California Press, 2007.

Stone, Pamela, and Lisa Ackerly Hernandez. "The All-or-Nothing Workplace: Flexibility Stigma and "Opting Out" among Professional-Managerial Women." *Journal of Social Issues* 69, no. 2 (2013): 235–256.

Stone, Pamela, and Meg Lovejoy. "Fast-Track Women and the 'Choice' to Stay Home." *Annals of the American Academy of Political and Social Science* 596, no. 1 (2004): 62–83.

Straw, Barry M., Robert I. Sutton, and Lisa H. Pelled. "Employee Positive Emotion and Favorable Outcomes at the Workplace." *Organization Science* 5, no. 1 (1994): 51–71.

Suh, Eunkook, Ed Diener, and Frank Fujita. "Events and Subjective Well-Being: Only Recent Events Matter." *Journal of Personality and Social Psychology* 70, no. 5 (1996): 1091–1102.

Sullivan, Cath, and Suzan Lewis. "Home-Based Telework, Gender, and the Synchronization of Work and Family: Perspectives of Teleworkers and Their Co-Residents." *Gender, Work and Organization* 8, no. 2 (2001): 123–145.

Sullivan, Oriel. "An End to Gender Display through the Performance of Housework? A Review and Reassessment of the Quantitative Literature Using Insights from the Qualitative Literature." *Journal of Family Theory & Review* 3, no. 1 (2011): 1–13.

Sunderland, Jane. "Baby Entertainer, Bumbling Assistant and Line Manager: Discourses of Fatherhood in Parentcraft Texts." *Discourse & Society* 11, no. 2 (2000): 249–274.

———. "'Parenting' or 'Mothering'? The Case of Modern Childcare Magazines." *Discourse & Society* 17, no. 4 (2006): 503–528.

Sutherland, Jean-Anne. "Mothering, Guilt and Shame." *Sociology Compass* 4, no. 5 (2010): 310–321.

Tanaka, Sakiko. "Parental Leave and Child Health across OECD Countries." *Economic Journal* 115, no. 501 (2005): F7–F28.

Taylor, Shelley E., Margaret E. Kemeny, Geoffrey M. Reed, Julienne E. Bower, and Tara L. Gruenewald. "Psychological Resources, Positive Illusions, and Health." *American Psychologist* 55, no. 1 (2000): 99–109.

Taylor, Shelley E., Rena L. Repetti, and Teresa Seeman. "Health Psychology: What Is an Unhealthy Environment and How Does It Get under the Skin?" *Annual Review of Psychology* 48, no. 1 (1997): 411–447.

Teigen, Karl Halvor, and Tine K. Jensen. "Unlucky Victims or Lucky Survivors? Spontaneous Counterfactual Thinking by Families Exposed to the Tsunami Disaster." *European Psychologist* 16, no. 1 (2011): 48–57.

Thoits, Peggy A., and Lyndi N. Hewitt. "Volunteer Work and Well-Being." *Journal of Health and Social Behavior* 42, no. 2 (2001): 115–131.

Thompson, Michael. *The Pressured Child: Freeing Our Kids from Performance Overdrive and Helping Them Find Success in School and Life*. New York: Ballantine, 2004.

Tobak, Steve. "The Gender Pay Gap Is a Myth." FoxBusiness, May 3, 2013. http:// www.foxbusiness.com/business-leaders/2013/05/03/gender-pay-gap-is-myth/ #ixzz2UtaMK5La.

Toepfer, Steven M., Kelly Cichy, and Patti Peters. "Letters of Gratitude: Further Evidence for Author Benefits." *Journal of Happiness Studies* 13, no. 1 (2012): 187–201.

Toussaint, Loren, and Philip Friedman. "Forgiveness, Gratitude, and Well-Being: The Mediating Role of Affect and Beliefs." *Journal of Happiness Studies* 10, no. 6 (2009): 635–654.

Trépanier, Sarah- Geneviève, Claude Fernet, and Stéphanie Austin. "The Moderating Role of Autonomous Motivation in the Job Demands-Strain Relation: A Two Sample Study." *Motivation and Emotion* 37, no. 1 (2013): 93–105.

Tsapelas, Irene, Arthur Aron, and Terri Orbuch. "Marital Boredom Now Predicts Less Satisfaction 9 Years Later." *Psychological Science* 20, no. 5 (2009): 543–545.

Tuttle-Singer, Sarah Emily. "We Need to Quit Telling Lies on Facebook." *Kveller: A Jewish Twist on Parenting* (blog), February 25, 2013. http://www.kveller.com/blog/parenting/we-need-to-quit-telling-lies-on-facebook/?fb_action_ids=10151785558844225& fb_action_types=og.likes&fb_source=other_multiline&ac-tion_object_map=%7B%2210151785558844225%22%3A503877192984086%7D&ac-tion_type_map=%7B%2210151785558844225%22%3A%22og.likes%22%7D&ac-tion_ref_map=%5B%5D.

Twenge, Jean M. "Changes in Masculine and Feminine Traits over Time: A Meta-Analysis." *Sex Roles* 36, no. 5–6 (1997): 305–325.

Twenge, Jean M., W. Keith Campbell, and Craig A. Foster. "Parenthood and Marital Satisfaction: A Meta-Analytic Review." *Journal of Marriage and Family* 65, no. 3 (2003): 574–583.

Umberson, Debra, and Walter R. Gove. "Parenthood and Psychological Well-Being: Theory, Measurement, and Stage in the Family Life Course." *Journal of Family Issues* 10, no. 4 (1989): 440–462.

United Nations. "Convention on the Elimination of All Forms of Discrimination against Women." United Nations Entity for Gender Equality and the Empowerment of Women, 2000–2009. http://www.un.org/womenwatch/daw/cedaw.

U.S. Department of Labor. "Fact Sheet #28F: Qualifying Reasons for Leave under the Family Medical Leave Act." U.S. Department of Labor, Wage and Hour Division, August 2013. http://www.dol.gov/whd/regs/compliance/whdfs28f.pdf.

U.S. Senate Joint Economic Committee. *Invest in Women, Invest in America: A Comprehensive Review of Women in the U.S. Economy*. A report by the Majority Staff of the Joint Economic Committee, Representative Carolyn B. Maloney, Chair. Washington, DC: Joint Economic Committee, 2010, 1–252.Usui, Wayne M., Thomas J. Keil, and K. Robert Durig. "Socioeconomic Comparisons and Life Satisfaction of Elderly Adults." *Journal of Gerontology* 40, no. 1 (1985): 110–114.

Valenti, Jessica. *Why Have Kids?: A New Mom Explores the Truth about Parenting and Happiness*. Seattle: Amazon, 2012.

Vandell, Deborah Lowe. "Do Effects of Early Child Care Extend to Age 15 Years? Results from the NICHD Study of Early Child Care and Youth Development." *Child Development* 81, no. 3 (2010): 737–756.

Vandello, Joseph A., Vanessa E. Hettinger, Jennifer K. Bosson, and Jasmine Siddiqi. "When Equal Isn't Really Equal: The Masculine Dilemma of Seeking Work Flexibility." *Journal of Social Issues* 69, no. 2 (2013): 303–321.

Vansteenkiste, Maarten, Bart Duriez, Joke Simons, and Bart Soenens. "Materialistic Values and Well-Being among Business Students: Further Evidence of Their Detrimental Effect." *Journal of Applied Social Psychology* 36, no. 12 (2006): 2892–2908.

Velasquez-Manoff, Moises. "Status and Stress." *The Opinion Pages* (blog), *New York Times*, July 27, 2013. http://opinionator.blogs.nytimes.com/2013/07/27/status-and-stress/?hpw& _r=0.

Vigeland, Tess, and Jolie Myers. "Tough Choices: How the Poor Spend Money." American Public Media's *Marketplace*, October 5, 2012. http://www.marketplace.org/topics/wealth-poverty/tough-choices-how-poor-spend-money.

Virden, Susan Flagler. "The Relationship between Infant Feeding Method and Maternal Role Adjustment." *Journal of Nurse-Midwifery* 33, no. 1 (1988): 31–35.

Virtanen, Marianna, Katriina Heikkilä, Markus Jokela, Jane E. Ferrie, G. David Batty, Jussi Vahtera, and Mika Kivimäki. "Long Working Hours and Symptoms of Anxiety and Depression: A 5-Year Follow-Up of the Whitehall II Study." *Psychological Medicine* 41, no. 12 (2011): 2485–2494.

Virtanen, Marianna, and Mika Kivimäki. "Saved by the Bell: Does Working Too Much Increase the Likelihood of Depression?" *Expert Review of Neurotherapeutics* 12, no. 5 (2012): 497–499.

Vohs, Kathleen D., Nicole L. Mead, and Miranda R. Goode. "The Psychological Consequences of Money." *Science* 314, no. 5802 (2006): 1154–1156.

Volling, Brenda L, and Lynne V. Feagans. "Infant Day Care and Children's Social Competence." *Infant Behavior and Development* 18, no. 2 (1995): 177–188.

Wade, Mary E. "Women and Salary Negotiation: The Costs of Self-Advocacy." *Psychology of Women Quarterly* 25, no. 1 (2001): 65–76.

Wadsworth, Lori L., and Bradley P. Owens. "The Effects of Social Support on Work-Family Enhancement and Work-Family Conflict in the Public Sector." *Public Administration Review* 67, no. 1 (2007): 75–87.

Waldfogel, Jane. "International Policies toward Parental Leave and Child Care." *Future of Children* 11, no. 1 (2001): 99–111.

Wall, Glenda. "Mothers' Experiences with Intensive Parenting and Brain Development Discourse." *Women's Studies International Forum* 33, no. 3 (2010): 253–263.

Wall, Glenda, and Stephanie Arnold. "How Involved Is Involved Fathering?: An Exploration of the Contemporary Culture of Fatherhood." *Gender & Society* 21, no. 4 (2007): 508–527.

Wallentin, Mikkel. "Putative Sex Differences in Verbal Abilities and Language Cortex: A Critical Review." *Brain and Language* 108, no. 3 (2009): 175–183.

Waller, Willard. *The Family: A Dynamic Interpretation.* New York: Gordon, 1938.

Wallis, Deborah J., and Marion M. Hetherington. "Emotions and Eating. Self-Reported and Experimentally Induced Changes in Food Intake Under Stress." *Appetite* 52, no. 2 (2009): 355–362.

Walsh, Janet, and Human Rights Watch. *Failing Its Families: Lack of Paid Leave and Work-Family Support in the US.* New York: Human Rights Watch, 2011.

Wang, Wendy, Kim Parker, and Paul Taylor. "Breadwinner Moms: Moms Are the Sole or Primary Provider in Four-in-Ten Households with Children; Public Conflicted about Growing Trend." Pew Research Social and Demographic Trends, posted May 29, 2013. http://www.pewsocialtrends.org/2013/05/29/breadwinner-moms.

Warner, Judith. "The Opt-Out Generation Wants Back In." *New York Times Magazine*, August 7, 2013. http://www.nytimes.com/2013/08/11/magazine/the-opt-out-generation-wants-back-in.html?pagewanted=5&adxnnl=1&adxnnlx=1381955314-mp25GLFR4GCaal0MAZktDg.

———. *Perfect Madness: Motherhood in the Age of Anxiety.* New York: Riverhead Books, 2005.

Watad, Mahmoud M., Gregory T. Jenkins, and William Paterson. "The Impact of Telework on Knowledge Creation and Management." *Journal of Knowledge Management Practice* 11, no. 4 (2010).

Watkins, Philip C., Kathrane Woodward, Tamara Stone, and Russell L. Kolts. "Gratitude and Happiness: Development of a Measure of Gratitude, and Relationships with Subjective Well-Being." *Social Behavior and Personality: An International Journal* 31, no. 5 (2003): 431–451.

Wayne, Julie Holliday, and Bryanne L. Cordeiro. "Who Is a Good Organizational Citizen? Social Perception of Male and Female Employees Who Use Family Leave." *Sex Roles* 49, no. 5-6 (2003): 233–246.

Weber, Lauren. "Why Dads Don't Take Paternity Leave: More Companies Offer New Fathers Paid Time Off, but Many Fear Losing Face Back at the Office." *Wall Street Journal*, June 12, 2013. http://online.wsj.com/news/articles/SB10001424127887324049504578541633708283670.

Weiser, Stanley, and Oliver Stone. *Wall Street*. Directed by Oliver Stone. Los Angeles: Twentieth Century Fox Film Corporation, 1987.

Wells, Michael B., and Anna Sarkadi. "Do Father-Friendly Policies Promote Father-Friendly Child-Rearing Practices? A Review of Swedish Parental Leave and Child Health Centers." *Journal of Child and Family Studies* 21, no. 1 (2011): 25–31.

West, Candace, and Don H. Zimmerman. "Doing Gender." *Gender and Society* 1, no. 2 (1987): 125–151.

White, Bonnie A., Caroline C. Horwath, and Tamlin S. Conner. "Many Apples a Day Keep the Blues Away: Daily Experiences of Negative and Positive Affect and Food Consumption in Young Adults." *British Journal of Health Psychology* 18, no. 4 (2013): 782–798.

White, Chris M., and Ulrich Hoffrage. "Testing the Tyranny of Too Much Choice against the Allure of More Choice." *Psychology & Marketing* 26, no. 3 (2009): 280–298.

White House: President Barack Obama. "Education: Knowledge and Skills for the Jobs of the Future." White House: President Barack Obama. http://www.whitehouse.gov/issues/education/early-childhood.

White, Judith B., Ellen J. Langer, Leeat Yariv, and John C. Welch IV. "Frequent Social Comparisons and Destructive Emotions and Behaviors: The Dark Side of Social Comparisons." *Journal of Adult Development* 13, no. 1 (2006): 36–44.

White, Mathew P., and Paul Dolan. "Accounting for the Richness of Daily Activities." *Psychological Science* 20, no. 8 (2009): 1000–1008.

Wiens, Steve. "To Parents of Small Children: Let Me Be the One Who Says It Out Loud." *The Blog* (blog), *Huffington Post*, May 3, 2013. http://www.huffingtonpost.com/steve-wiens/let-me-be-the-one-who says-it-out-loud_b_3209305.html.

Wilkie, Jane Riblett, Myra Marx Ferree, and Kathryn Strother Ratcliff. "Gender and Fairness: Marital Satisfaction in Two-Earner Couples." *Journal of Marriage and the Family* 60, no. 3 (1998): 577–594.

Wilkinson, Richard G., and Kate E. Pickett. "The Problems of Relative Deprivation: Why Some Societies Do Better than Others." *Social Science & Medicine* 65, no. 9 (2007): 1965–1978.

Williams, Joan C., and Heather Boushey. "The Three Faces of Work-Family Conflict: The Poor, the Professionals, and the Missing Middle." *Work Life Law: UC Hastings College of the Law*, Center for American Progress (2010): 1–86.

Williams, Joan C., and Holly Cohen Cooper. "The Public Policy of Motherhood." *Journal of Social Issues* 60, no. 4 (2004): 849–865.

Wills, Thomas Ashby. "Downward Comparison Principles in Social Psychology." *Psychological Bulletin* 90, no. 2 (1981): 245–271.

Wilson, Timothy D., and Daniel T. Gilbert. "Affective Forecasting: Knowing What to Want." *Current Directions in Psychological Science* 14, no. 3 (2005): 131–134.

Winnicott, Donald W. "Transitional Objects and Transitional Phenomena: A Study of the First Not-Me Possession." *International Journal of Psychoanalysis* 34 (1953): 89–97.

Women's Workforce Council. "Boston: Closing the Wage Gap: Becoming the Best City in America for Working Women." Women's Workforce Council, 2013. http://www.cityofboston.gov/images_documents/Boston_Closing%20the%20Wage%20Gap_Interventions%20Report_tcm3–41353.pdf.

Wood, Julia T. "Which Ruler Do We Use? Theorizing the Division of Domestic Labor." *Journal of Family Communication* 11, no. 1 (2011): 39–49.

Workaholics Anonymous World Service Organization. "Storyline: From Workaholics Anonymous." Workaholics Anonymous World Service Organization, Summer 2012. http://www.workaholics-anonymous.org/pdf_files/news_summer2012.pdf.

Worthington, Everett L., Jr., Charlotte Van Oyen Witvliet, Pietro Pietrini, and Andrea J. Miller. "Forgiveness, Health, and Well-Being: A Review of Evidence for Emotional Versus Decisional Forgiveness, Dispositional Forgivingness, and Reduced Unforgiveness." *Journal of Behavioral Medicine* 30, no. 4 (2007): 291–302.

Wrzesniewski, Amy, Clark McCauley, Paul Rozin, and Barry Schwartz. "Jobs, Careers, and Callings: People's Relations to Their Work." *Journal of Research in Personality* 31, no. 1 (1997): 21–33.

Wrzus, Cornelia, Martha Hänel, Jenny Wagner, and Franz J. Neyer. "Social Network Changes and Life Events across the Life Span: A Meta-Analysis." *Psychological Bulletin* 139, no. 1 (2013): 53–80.

Zachrisson, Henrik D., Eric Dearing, Ratib Lekhal, and Claudio O. Toppelberg. "Little Evidence that Time in Child Care Causes Externalizing Problems during Early Childhood in Norway." *Child Development* 84, no. 4 (2013): 1152–1170.

Zero to Three. "Brain Development." Zero to Three: National Center for Infants, Toddlers, and Families. http://www.zerotothree.org/child-development/brain-development.

Zimmerman, Frederick J., Dimitri A. Christakis, and Andrew N. Meltzoff. "Associations between Media Viewing and Language Development in Children Under Age 2 Years." *Journal of Pediatrics* 151, no. 4 (2007): 364–368.

——. "Television and DVD/Video Viewing in Children Younger Than 2 Years." *Archives of Pediatrics & Adolescent Medicine* 161, no. 5 (2007): 473–479.

Zlomek, Erin. "Women and Work: A Harvard Prof's Take." *Bloomberg Business Week*, May 10, 2013. http://www.businessweek.com/articles/2013-05-10/women-and-work-a-harvard-profs-take.

Index

active constructive responding. *See* savoring

adaptation: circumstances, 140–141; experiences, 150; material goods, 75–76, 79; savoring, 152; strengths, 147

affordable childcare, 132–135; Child Care Aware of America data on, 132, 134; Child Care Development Block Grants (CCDBG) and, 132, 135; child outcomes associated with, 134; Comprehensive Childcare Development Act and, 134; decreased crime and, 134; low income families and, 132–133; middle class and, 133; opting out and, 133; other countries' models of, 135; work-family balance, barrier to, 132. *See also* childcare

Alcorn, Katrina, 137

American Academy of Pediatrics, 40, 46, 128

Amish shooting, 155

Aristotle, 2

attachment parenting, 36–43; feminism and, 43; work-family balance and, 36–37. *See also* baby wearing; breastfeeding; co-sleeping; Sears

autonomy, 4, 16, 63; belief in gender differences limit, 96; benefits of, 143; decision to work and, 163; division of labor and, 111; downside of, 144; increasing, 143–144; inverted U-shaped curve and, 143; maximizing benefits of, 144; telecommuting and, 66. *See also* autonomy support

autonomy support, 50–51, 56

baby blues. *See* post-partum depression

Baby Einstein, 44, 46

baby strike, vii

baby wearing, 37–38

basic needs. *See* autonomy; competence; self-determination theory; relatedness

best possible self. *See* strengths

brain: attachment parenting and, 36; gender differences at birth, 85; gender differences in adults, 89–91; intellectual stimulation and, 43–44; music and, 45

breastfeeding, 17, 40–43; benefits, 40; leave policies and, 128; limits to benefits, 41–42; pressure to breastfeed, 40, 162

Campaign for a Commercial-Free Childhood, 46

Campbell, Don, 45

Carli, Linda, 122

Childcare: attachment and, 31; attitudes toward, 28; effects on children's academics, 29; limitations to the research on, 28; negative behavioral effects, 30; quality of childcare, 30; social benefits, 30; stress and, 31. *See*

About the Authors

Miriam Liss grew up in New York City and attended Wesleyan University in Middletown, Connecticut, as an undergraduate majoring in psychology. She went to the University of Connecticut for her PhD in clinical psychology and did her dissertation on autism and sensory processing sensitivity. She is a professor of psychology at the University of Mary Washington and teaches the psychology of women, personality, clinical psychology, general psychology, and a freshman seminar on feminism. She was recently named one of Princeton Review's Best 300 Professors. This is her first book but she has written thirty-five academic journal articles and three book chapters on a variety of topics including autism, feminism, division of labor, parenting, self-injury, and women's body image and objectification. She loves to mentor students and is proud that many of her publications involve undergraduate students as coauthors. She lives in Fredericksburg, Virginia, with her husband, a guidance counselor at a local high school, her 8-year-old son and her 6-year-old daughter. In her spare time she likes to go on family adventures, visit amusement parks and festivals, relax at the pool with her family, sing in choir, and read.

Holly H. Schiffrin, PhD, is an associate professor of psychology at the University of Mary Washington. She received her degree in developmental psychology from the University of Miami in 1998. She teaches courses in child development, exceptional child development, positive psychology, and statistics. She also received a master's-level certificate in parent coaching from the Parent Coaching Institute at Seattle Pacific University. Her research has been published in the *Journal of Child and Family Studies*, *Journal of Positive Psychology*, *Journal of Happiness Studies*, *Cyberpsychology, Behavior, and Social Networking*, *Research in Development Disabilities*, and the *Journal of Development & Behavioral Pediatrics*. She has given numerous presentations at conferences, including the Association for Psychological Science, the Society for Research in Child Development, and the National Institute for the Teaching of Psychology among others. Dr. Schiffrin recently served as president of the Virginia Academic and Applied Psychologist Academy of the Virginia Psychological Association. She has been interviewed about her research on parenting and well-being by radio programs, newspapers, and magazines across the nation. She lives in Virginia with her husband, Jon, and two daughters Lauryn (11) and Jordan (7). They have a one-year-old dog, Tucker, that they rescued from a shelter in Tennessee. She enjoys singing in the choir, relaxing by the pool, and watching her daughters dance.